Redesigning
Social Security

EDITED BY HORST SIEBERT

Institut für Weltwirtschaft
an der Universität Kiel

Mohr Siebeck

Die Deutsche Bibliothek – CIP-Einheitsaufnahme

Redesigning social security / Institut für Weltwirtschaft an der Universität
Kiel. Ed. by Horst Siebert. – Tübingen : Mohr Siebeck, 1998
  ISBN 3–16–146923–2

Printed in Germany

Contents

II. Country Studies: Problems and Responses

III. Reforming Social Security

Preface

Old-age pension systems are increasingly under pressure in many countries. One reason for this is that old-age pensions are a major part of public transfers, which after decades of expansion are increasingly seen as constituting a major drag on the economy and a factor contributing to the high level of unemployment. In addition, demographic trends threaten the viability of existing unfunded public pension systems. As a result, social security reform is on the political agenda in a great number of countries. In industrial nations, the substitution of funded systems for pay-as-you-go systems is being considered. Some smaller newly industrializing countries have done so already.

Against this background, the Kiel Week Conference 1997 addressed the issue of social security reform in depth. The conference analyzed the problems of the prevailing systems and discussed, from different perspectives, ways and means of redesigning old-age pension systems in industrial countries. It offered an opportunity for discussion of viable long-term solutions.

This volume contains the conference papers and the comments thereon. In the introductory article, I provide an overview on the different dimensions of the problem of social security reform, setting out the main elements of the problem, and demonstrate, using the results of OECD projections and calculations based on the method of generational accounts, the unsustainability of prevailing pay-as-you-go systems in major industrial countries. In what follows, I discuss arguments for favoring a capital-funded pension system over the pay-as-you-go system: the capital-funded system has a higher rate of return and pension income can be obtained at lower costs to the individual. Both of these arguments imply efficiency gains in terms of higher savings and reduced distortion in the labor markets. Thereafter, I focus on the problem of transition from one system to the other, and present calculations in order to illustrate how transition could be effected. The concluding section touches upon a number of important aspects of pension reform, including the political dimension of the problem, details of institutional arrangements (for example, for coping with the problems of moral hazard), and alternative reform proposals. The conclusions are: that funded elements should be introduced increasingly into the pension system; that to make reforms politically feasible the intertemporal budget constraint should be explained to the public and future obligations implicit in the existing system should be made clear; and that, ultimately, a reform should give the individual more freedom of choice.

Increased saving and investment is one option for expanding the pool of resources available to meet the consumption needs of both workers and retirees. In their contribution, *Barry Bosworth* and *Gary Burtless* examine the effect of an increase in national savings following a reform of the pension system. As a result of demographic trends, significant and persistent declines in the rate of labor force growth are to be expected that translate into a sharp slowdown of output growth. This will lead to a reduced demand for savings, while, at the same time, the supply of savings will be increased. As a consequence, efforts to expand domestic capital formation will involve large declines in the return to capital, and substantial redistributions of aggregate income between capital and labor income. The authors illustrate the extent of the effect with a simulation exercise that uses a model of the U.S. economy, and they show that investing funds abroad would only provide a partial solution to the problem.

Oliver Lorz deals with the effects of social security on the labor market. He argues that the current unfunded social security pension systems generally provide a rate of return which is less than the interest rate, which results in distortion of the labor supply decision. He shows that the possible solution of introducing additional lump-sum contributions can lead to undesirable distribution effects and that a low average rate of return may induce households to exit from the labor market. Using a model of optimal social security design, he illustrates the consequences of this exit option when information is asymmetric and shows that distortions of the labor-leisure decision might arise endogenously, thus reducing the number of households choosing the exit option. He then discusses transition to a funded pension system from a welfare point of view and concludes that the time path of the labor market distortion and the social discount rate determine whether aggregate welfare declines or rises: the larger distortions in the future are expected to be, the more attractive a transition becomes.

The widespread difficulties being faced by public pay-as-you-go pension systems in the light of an aging population have put an increased emphasis on occupational or corporate pensions as an alternative means of financing and provision. *E. Philip Davis* gives an account of the present state of company pension funds in major industrial countries: its determinants, problems, and prospects. He finds that company pensions can significantly contribute to retirement income provision and may encourage saving and capital market development as well as enhance labor market performance. He also concludes that corporate pension systems are more viable than pay-as-you-go systems, and that external funding is superior to internal. In general, funding regulations need careful design and implementation, particularly because certain regulatory provisions are shown to impact adversely on benefit security in the case of external funding.

A series of three papers provides detailed analyses of pension systems in countries that rely heavily on pay-as-you-go financing and that are trying to find an answer to the challenge posed by adjustments within their respective system. In the first paper, *Axel Börsch-Supan* analyzes the German pay-as-you-go system and concludes that it cannot provide the flexibility that is necessary to cope with the demographic changes to come. To escape the dismal choice between a low pension level and a high contribution rate, the system must switch to funding, at least partially. He proceeds to show that the transition is much less severe than frequently argued when it takes place in an environment where investing funds globally provides a rate of return that generates a macroeconomic per capita consumption path that strongly dominates per capita consumption under the existing system.

In the second paper, *Edward M. Gramlich* discusses the recent report of the U.S. Advisory Council on Social Security. After finding that the actuarial status of the existing system displays a significant amount of uncovered liabilities at given rules, he turns to approaches of reform. One option is to maintain the existing system in principle but allow Social Security funds to be invested in common stock, which would increase the rate of return. A second approach involves a switch of the system from the present defined benefit system to a defined contribution system with funds being privately owned and managed. The third approach is personally favored by the author. It consists of two pillars, one of which is a combination of cuts in benefits and raising of the retirement age to stabilize the share of the nation's output that is devoted to pension spending. The second pillar is an extra pay roll tax introduced to build individual accounts that effectively raise saving and help financing consumption in the future.

In the third paper, which is about Sweden, a country that is pursuing a strategy of gradualism in reforming social security, *Mats Persson* concludes that the main reason for the failure of the old system is its lack of actuarial fairness in the sense that the benefit rules distribute wealth in a rather arbitrary fashion. He also stresses the role of the political process in social security reform. As a result, changes in a system often are resisted even when the old system is obviously hard to justify by any social welfare function. Consequently, he suggests that the political sector is not really suited to be in charge of such an important sector of the economy as the pension system and that privately managed pension schemes due to the forces of competition would ultimately be more robust.

In the following two papers, a more radical approach to reforming social security is examined. As *Richard Disney* and *Paul Johnson* point out in the first of these two papers, the pension system in the United Kingdom is a "halfway" house between traditional comprehensive social security and full-fledged privatization of pensions. It basically consists of largely privately funded pension provision, underpinned by a floor of pay-as-you-go social security. The system is also characterized by the fact that there are no prospective large-scale financial crises looming. It is, however, concluded that the complex incentive structures intrinsic to the United Kingdom pension scheme may work towards further change of the system so that the present coexistence of different supplementary pension arrangements may not represent a steady state.

In the second of these two papers, *Sebastian Edwards* takes stock of Chile's pioneering experience with replacing an existing government-run pension sys-tem with a privately managed system based on individual retirement accounts. He concludes, that, while this system obviously represents a vast improvement over its precedent, some qualifications are warranted. Some shortcomings of the system, which include a limitation for multiple funds, distortionary incentives generated by the government, and the high cost of high administering the sys-tem, will probably induce a continued evolution of the system.

Another approach to reforming traditional social security is changing to a flat-benefit (basic pension) system. *Friedrich Breyer* discusses, in his paper, efficien-cy, equity, and public choice aspects of flat-benefit pension systems. He con-cludes that while securing a minimum-pension level will inevitably distort labor supply decisions, these distortions should be kept to a minimum. From a politi-cal perspective, he notes that the future benefit level can be set at the discretion of future generations, much the same as income-related pensions are, but they have the advantage that the burden placed on future generations is smaller. He argues, in conclusion, that a transition to a basic pension system should begin before demographic change is fully completed, in order to realize a beneficial ef-fect on the intergenerational distribution.

When the superiority of funded pension systems in the case of aging popula-tions is accepted, the problem of transition instantly arises. In his paper, *Martin Feldstein* elaborates on this matter. He focuses on a gradual transition strategy that during the transition period retains pension benefits on a pay-as-you-go ba-sis, although in diminishing magnitude. He finds that for the first 18 years of transition there is an extra cost for contributors to the system which, however, is reasonably small and declining. From the 19th year onwards the present benefit level (in real terms) can be maintained at contribution rates which are below to-day's rates and rapidly declining to a low of roughly one-fifth of the present con-tribution rate. In what follows, he discusses some possible objections to his cal-culations. He finds that neither a reasonable discount on the assumed rates of re-turn on capital nor the consideration of risk or distributional aspects can qualita-tively affect the attractiveness of changing to a funded system.

In the following paper, *Laurence J. Kotlikoff*, *Kent Smetters*, and *Jan Walliser* study the economic impact of pension reform in a series of simulations using a stylized model representing the U.S. economy. They analyze various forms of fi-nancing the pension claims already accrued and find that Social Security's pri-vatization has significant and beneficial long-run effects in any case. They also find that although long-run gains are substantial, a major part of welfare gains enjoyed by future generations comes at the cost of welfare losses suffered by initial generations. With respect to the mode of financing of the transition, their results suggest that using a consumption tax produces much more rapid economic gains than does either wage or income tax finance.

In the last paper, *Harrie A.A. Verbon*, *Theo Leers*, and *Lex Meijdam* focus on the issue of the political feasibility of converting pay-as-you-go systems into funded pension systems. They find that in the context of a direct democracy the prospects for such a conversion are rather bleak. This is because the median voter, who in this model is decisive, also tends to get older as society ages. However, under some form of representative democracy where all living generations have some influence, their analysis suggests that conversion is more likely to occur. They come up with the seemingly paradoxical result that the chances for a switch to a funded system rise with the influence of the old generations. The reason is that if old generations are highly influential and have made politicians opt for a relatively large pay-as-you-go system, the damages of such a system to the economy tend to dominate the political resistance to pension reform.

The Kiel Institute is indebted to all participants in the 1997 Kiel Week Conference for having presented interesting and challenging papers and for having conducted stimulating discussions. Financial support provided by Allianz Versicherung is gratefully acknowledged. We owe thanks to the Deutsche Bank, the Dresdner Bank, and the Landesbank Schleswig-Holstein for their hospitality. Klaus-Jürgen Gern, Margitta Führmann, and Almut Hahn-Mieth helped to prepare and organize the conference, and Paul Kramer prepared the conference volume for publication.

Kiel, April 1998   Horst Siebert

I.

The Challenges for the Existing System

Horst Siebert

Pay-as-You-Go versus Capital-Funded Pension Systems: The Issues

1. Social Security in Crisis

1. Social security is in crisis in many countries with an old-age pension system financed predominantly on a pay-as-you-go basis. The single most important factor behind this is a demographic development that will lead to a progressive aging of societies the coming decades as a result of declining fertility and increasing longevity. In the OECD area as a whole, the elderly dependency ratio, i.e., the number of people aged 65 or over per 100 people of working age (15 to 64), is expected to double between 1990 and 2030 (Table 1). While the projections for demographic developments vary according to assumptions about net migration and fertility,[1] the fact that societies are progressively graying is not really in dispute. The aging of societies is most pronounced in Germany and Italy, which have extremely high elderly dependency ratios of 49.2 and 48.3 percent, respectively, and is particularly fast in Japan, which enjoyed a relatively low ratio of 17.1 percent in 1990 and will be facing a ratio well above the OECD average in the year 2030.

2. One approach with which to identify the need to reform the prevailing public pension systems is to compare the present value of current and future entitlements with the present value of future contributions implied in current rates of contribution. Table 2 presents OECD estimates on this for the seven major countries. Gross liabilities add up from entitlements already accrued by today's pensioners or contributors still working, and liabilities expected to be incurred in the future. The volume of these liabilities, expressed in relation to 1990 GDP, varies across countries according to the generosity of the system and assumptions about the development of a number of determinants, including the old-age dependency ratio, average retirement age, and employment ratio. They also de-

Remark: I appreciate critical comments by Friedrich Breyer, Klaus-Jürgen Gern, and especially Jens Oliver Lorz, to whom I am indebted for the preparation of Tables 6 and 7.

[1] For details of a recent projection of demographic developments in Germany using alternative scenarios on fertility, see the Appendix.

pend crucially on assumed discount rates and real growth. Estimated gross liabilities range from a low of 309 percent of 1990's GDP in the United States to a high of 742 percent of GDP in Italy.

Table 1 —   Elderly Dependency Ratios[a] in Industrial Countries

	1990	2000	2010	2020	2030	Change from 1990 to 2030 in percent
United States	19.1	19.0	20.4	27.6	36.8	92.7
Japan	17.1	24.3	33.0	43.0	44.5	160.2
Germany	21.7	23.8	30.3	35.4	49.2	126.7
France	20.8	23.6	24.6	32.3	31.1	88.0
Italy	21.6	26.5	31.2	37.5	48.3	123.6
United Kingdom	24.0	24.4	25.8	31.2	38.7	61.3
Canada	16.7	18.2	20.4	28.4	39.1	134.1
Total OECD	19.3	20.9	23.5	29.8	37.7	95.3
OECD Europe	20.6	22.1	24.7	30.8	39.2	90.3

[a]Population aged 65 and over as a percent of working-age population.

Source: World Bank (1994), own calculations.

Table 2 —   Estimates of Net Pension Liabilities[a]—Present Value of Current and Future Rights and Future Contributions (percent of 1990 GDP)

	United States	Japan	Germany	France	Italy	United Kingdom	Canada
Gross liabilities	309	496	467	729	742	537	482
Accrued rights	113	162	157	216	259	156	121
New rights	196	334	310	513	483	381	361
Assets	265	296	306	513	508	350	231
Existing assets	23	18	–	–	–	–	–
Future contributions	242	278	306	513	508	350	231
Net liabilities	43	200	160	216	233	186	250
Memorandum item: Gross public sector debt as of 1995	64.3	80.7	61.6	60.0	122.0	60.0	99.6

[a]On the basis of a representative set of assumptions about the details of the system.

Source: Van den Noord and Herd (1993: Table 7), OECD (1996).

To arrive at net liabilities, assets of the system have to be deducted. They consist of the present value of future contributions and assets accumulated in the past. The resulting net liabilities represent the part of public pension systems that has yet to be financed under prevailing arrangements. In most countries, the net liabilities of the public pension system exceed the stock of official gross public sector debt, which is a popular indicator of the public sector financial position, to a significant degree. It is evident that current benefit levels cannot be financed in the future with rates of contribution that are anywhere near current rates.

In Germany, given the prevailing level of benefits, public pension outlays are expected to rise to 17 percent of GDP in the year 2035, from currently 10 percent (OECD 1995), which will result in a deficit of the public pension system amounting to 9 percent of GDP at current rates of contribution to the system. To close this gap, contributions to the public pension system (Gesetzliche Rentenversicherung), which have risen in the past, will have to be raised from 18.6 percent of wages and salaries in 1995 to between 26.3 and 28.5 percent in the year 2030, depending on the scenario (Prognos 1995). Under these circumstances, it is doubtful whether the current system of old-age insurance in Germany is sustainable.

3. Another way of illustrating the fact that prevailing public pension arrangements are not sustainable in many countries is to devise generational accounts. Generational accounts have been developed as a more meaningful alternative to traditional deficit accounting (Auerbach et al. 1991, 1994). They explicitly take into account the need to satisfy an intertemporal budget restriction in which the present value of all future tax payments has to equal the present value of all future government consumption plus the initial stock of debt. It allows the present value of the lifetime net tax payments (tax payments minus transfer receipts) of a newborn in the base year to be compared to the present value of the lifetime net tax payments of a representative member of unborn generations, indicating the extent of intergenerational redistribution implied in current policies.[2] Underlying these calculations is the assumption that today's policies remain unchanged throughout the lifetime of all existing generations (including the newborn), while policy changes necessary to eventually satisfy the intertemporal budget constraint will affect only future generations.

Generational accounting models are available for only a small set of countries on a comparable basis. While the calculations have to be viewed with caution for a variety of reasons (Haveman 1994; Diamond 1996), it seems fair to state that

---

[2]   For existing generations, only the net taxes over the remaining lifespan are considered in the analysis. Without extensive retrospective calculations necessary to arrive at estimates of full lifetime net taxes for existing generations, a meaningful comparison of net tax burdens can only be made between the newborn generation and unborn generations that will ultimately have to restore fiscal balance.

there is clear evidence of generational imbalance of current policies in favor of living generations. Future generations will have to bear tax burdens that will exceed the tax burden of newborns in the base year (1993) to a significant degree, ranging from roughly 30 percent in Germany and Sweden to 450 percent in Italy. (Table 3). The single most important factor behind this is the effect of demographic developments, most prominently through their effect on public pension systems, thus indicating the unsustainable character of current public pension arrangements.

Table 3 — Generational Imbalance Implied in Current Fiscal Policies—Present Value of Net Tax Payments per Capita (males) of Future Generations Discounted at a Rate of 5 Percent (newborn generation = 100)

	Productivity growth rate		
	1	1.5	2
United States	215	200	189
Germany	126	127	127
Italy	633	546	485
Norway	134	153	168
Sweden	136	131	126

Source: Leibfritz et al. (1995: Table 1).

4. One possible way of dealing with the obvious problems is to adjust the prevailing systems in order to secure their solvency in the future. Corresponding strategies include increasing retirement ages, lowering benefit levels, or correcting benefits for changes in the demography. However, there seems to be mounting skepticism with respect to the chances of being able to stabilize public pension systems by making such limited adjustments. It is becoming increasingly clear that more fundamental changes in old-age insurance are inevitable.

5. Some countries, like Chile, Argentina, Colombia, and Singapore, have switched to a funded pension system or plan to do so. In the United Kingdom, the public pension system is primarily restricted to a tax-financed uniform basic pension.[3] In other countries, such as Switzerland or the United States, the focus has traditionally been more on individual savings accounts or financial assets to provide for retirement. In the transformation countries, where, such as in China,

---

[3] The second pillar of the public pension system, the State Earnings Related Pension System (SERPS), while on a pay-as-you-go basis, allows for contracting out to funded private sector pension schemes.

pensions used to be paid by state firms, old-age insurance will have to be uncoupled from the firms and will have to rely more on private savings.

6. Besides the different ways of financing social security, a main point of interest is the effect on the labor market that results from rising labor costs due to increasing social security contributions (for Germany, see Table 4). In a pension system that is tied to employment, social security contributions can work as a tax on labor (Siebert 1997). While increased social security contributions add to the cost of labor, they reduce the net wage and widen the tax wedge. In effect, the probability that workers will accept only moderate (gross) wage increases in wage negotiations is lowered. Insofar as the total of wage increases and increases in social security contributions—i.e., the rise in labor cost in total—exceeds the growth in labor productivity, labor demand is weakened. Thus, the secular rise in contribution rates of pay-as-you-go public pension systems contributes to the problem of unemployment.

Table 4 — Contribution Rates[a] of the Pay-as-You-Go System in Germany

1950	1960	1970	1980	1990	1995	1996	1997
10.0	14.0	17.0	18.0	18.7	18.6	19.2	20.3

[a]In percent of gross wages.

Last but not least, deadweight losses engendered by reduced capital accumulation and, as a consequence, lower growth in a pay-as-you-go system have to be taken into consideration when a comparison of different pension systems is made.

7. As a yardstick for the evaluation of social security reform alternatives, the following desiderations should be considered:

— A pension system has to satisfy an intertemporal budget restriction in the sense that contributions today and payments tomorrow must relate to each other.
— A pension system should be "efficient," i.e., associated with minimal cost (burden). A system that provides a given level of retirement benefits with lower contributions should be preferred. In this context, effects on important goals of economic policy, including capital accumulation, growth, and employment, should be taken into account.
— The system should realize a maximum of equivalence between the present value of contributions and benefits for the individual.

— The goal of a pension system is to provide income after retirement (and insure against invalidity). This goal has to be separated from redistributional ambitions.

2. Comparing Pay-as-You-Go and Capital-Funded Pension Systems

8. The ultimate yardstick for evaluating the alternatives from an economic point of view is efficiency. The system that delivers more benefits from a given amount of contributions, i.e., that has the higher rate of return, is superior in terms of efficiency.

In a pay-as-you-go system, contributions of one period are directly transferred to the recipients of benefits in the same period. While members acquire claims against the system by virtue of their making contributions in the present, no actual capital is accumulated. Contrary to this, in a funded system claims to benefits are covered by a capital stock built up by contributions in the past. After retirement, benefits are paid from interest on the capital stock and successive capital consumption.

9. In a pay-as-you-go system, the rate of return, ρ_{UV}, on contributions for individuals of a given generation is zero in a stationary economy.[4] The total of contributions of the active generation equals the sum of benefits to the retired generation. Under stationary conditions, a pure pay-as-you-go system without interpersonal redistribution produces benefits that correspond to contributions for every individual. The rate of return is zero.

In a growing economy, the contributions of active generations (used to finance the pensions of the retired) realize a return in the sense that contributors can expect a higher level of pensions in the future because contributions will be higher then. The growth of income results in a pension level that exceeds the contributions of the past. The increase of pension benefits relative to the contributions of the past can be interpreted as the (implicit) rate of return from the individual's perspective.

When contributions are a constant share of labor income (constant rate of contribution), the system's rate of return is given by the real rate of growth of wages and salaries. The change in real wages and salaries adds up from the rate of population growth, n, (Samuelson's [1958] "natural rate of interest") and labor productivity growth, g. Thus it is

---

[4]   The first generation of recipients in the start-up phase of a pay-as-you-go system receives pensions without having made contributions. I deal with this issue when analyzing the transition to a funded system.

[1] $1 + \rho_{UV} = (1+n)(1+g)$,   or $\rho_{UV} \approx n + g$.

A change in the rate of contribution would have to be considered additionally.

10. In the case of a funded pension system, the internal rate of return, ρ_{KV}, corresponds to the real rate of interest, r, i.e.,

[2] $1 + \rho_{KV} = 1 + r$,   or $\rho_{KV} = r$.

According to this analysis, a funded pension system is better than a pay-as-you-go system when the real rate of interest exceeds the real rate of growth of wages and salaries:

[3] $r > n + g$.

11. The rates of return of both types of social security system depend on a number of factors. In a fast-growing economy, both real interest rates and wage growth are usually high due to abundant investment opportunities and high growth of labor productivity. But while the profit from high returns primarily goes to savers in a funded system, it is the pensioners who benefit from high productivity growth in a pay-as-you-go system. Thus, in Germany the pay-as-you-go system was very attractive for pensioners when the annual growth rate of labor productivity was high, as in the 1960s (5.4 percent) and in the 1970s (4.1 percent). With lower productivity increases of only 2.4 percent since 1980, the system has become less attractive.

In a situation, where a significant decrease in the population is to be expected (the projected annual rate of population growth, n, is –0.4 percent over the next 40 to 50 years), the rate of return in the pay-as-you-go system is additionally suppressed. With zero productivity growth, the rate of return would be negative. The pay-as-you-go system is much more sensitive to demographic developments than a funded pension system.[5]

12. According to classical growth theory,[6] the market interest rate is higher than the real growth rate of wages and salaries. This is true even with a rate of time preference of zero, i.e., when there is no preference for consumption today versus consumption tomorrow. This can be shown most easily in a model with capital accumulation only, i.e., for $n + g = 0$. If the time preference were zero, capital would be accumulated until the marginal product of capital fell to zero (Point S'' in Figure 1, which is approached asymptotically on the capital-intensity

---

5   A funded pension system is not totally immune to declining populations because the capital stock has to adjust when optimal capital intensity has already been realized.

6   Overlapping-generation models yield different results than classical growth models of the Ramsey type (Samuelson 1975). Note that Ricardian equivalence is not assumed to hold.

axis, $k = K/L$). In this stationary situation, real growth of wages and salaries is also zero. In the periods before the steady state is reached, less than the optimal capital stock is accumulated and marginal productivity of capital is higher than the growth rate of the labor force.[7] With people having a positive time prefer-. ence, however (depicted here by the discount rate, δ), the market interest rate exceeds real growth of wages and salaries during the adjustment to the long-term equilibrium as well as in the long-term equilibrium itself.

Figure 1—Rates of Return in the Pay-as-You-Go and the Funded System

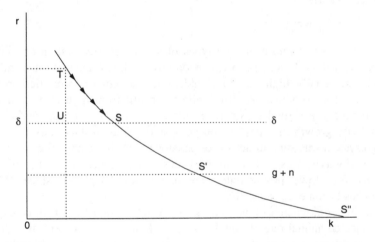

Allowing for positive population growth, $n > 0$, capital is accumulated to the extent that is necessary to equip additional workers with capital goods. In the extreme case of a rate of time preference of zero, the market interest rate approaches n in the long term. But with a positive time preference, it seems realistic to assume that the rate of time preference exceeds the population growth rate.[8] In this case, the rate of return of a funded pension system exceeds the rate of return in a pay-as-you-go system.

---

7   Assuming a Cobb–Douglas production function $Q = A^\alpha K^{1-\alpha}$, with $g = 0$, the condition $r = F_K > (\hat{wL})$ translates into $(1-\alpha)Q/K > [(1-\alpha)][(1-\alpha)\dot{K}/K] + \alpha n$, or $(1-\alpha)C/K > \alpha n$, which clearly must be satisfied for $n = 0$, since consumption (C) must be positive. ($\wedge$ denotes the rate of change.)

8   In the industrial countries, population growth has been an annual 0.9 percent in the period 1950–1992, the real interest rate has been higher.

The rate of return on capital increases when technological progress is introduced. Thus, together with the rate of population growth, n, the rate of technological progress, g, constitutes a lower bound for the market interest rate.

But there is a lower bound that is still higher: the rate of time preference, δ, which stops capital accumulation before the equality of the interest rate, r, and the rate of growth, $g + n$, is satisfied. While a situation in which $n + g > \delta$ is theoretically possible, it is not a realistic scenario because it would mean being in an economic Cockaigne, where supply would grow more rapidly than necessary to compensate for the time preference.

Taxation is one reason to presume that the market interest rate exceeds the discount rate because it establishes a wedge between the marginal productivity of capital and the discount rate. Take, for example, a situation when a unit of capital is taxed at rate τ. Considering the simple case of an economy without technological progress, the optimality condition[9] states that the market interest rate has to exceed $\delta + n$ by τ. From this follows that the market interest rate is higher than the discount rate for an economy with a stationary population in long-term equilibrium.

[4] $f'(k) - \tau = \delta + n$

Two further modifications strengthen the argument that the rate of return of a funded pension system is higher than the rate of return of a pay-as-you-go system. When technological knowledge is incorporated in investment—in younger cohorts of the capital stock—it is not possible anymore to discriminate between steady-state equilibrium and the growth path to this equilibrium. Every capital accumulation results in an upward shift of the steady-state equilibrium. In addition, in the context of an open economy, it has to be considered that in a funded system, capital can be invested in the world market, thus realizing high rates of return even when domestic investment opportunities are limited. Summing up, there are a variety of reasons to expect on theoretical grounds the rate of return in a funded pension system to exceed the rate of return in a pay-as-you-go system.

13. Empirical investigations for Germany confirm that the rate of return for capital funds is higher than the implicit rate of return of the public pension system working on a pay-as-you-go basis. Estimates on nominal rates in the business sector (enterprise sector) are well above 10 percent. The Sachverständigen-

---

[9]   Maximizing the function $\int_0^\infty u(c)e^{-\delta t}\,dt$ subject to $\dot{k} = f(k) - c - nk - \tau k$ yields $H = u(c) + \lambda[f(k) - c - nk - \tau k]$, $\partial H / \partial c = u'(c) - \lambda = 0$, and $\dot{\lambda} = \lambda - [f'(k) - n - \tau]$, with $\dot{\lambda} = 0$ in the long-term equilibrium. c is per capita consumption.

rat (1996: Section 406) finds that the real rate of return on capital in western Germany, at an average rate of 4.7 percent per year, exceeded the average annual real growth rate of gross wages and salaries by 2.3 percentage points (Table 5). Note that the rate of return is relatively low, since it includes the rate of return in the housing sector in terms of national accounting, where capital gains and taxation aspects are not included. Nominal rates without the housing sector are way above 10 percent.[10] The standard pension during the same period showed real growth of only 1.9 percent per year; during the period between 1980 and 1995 the increase in the standard pension slowed down to a mere 0.5 percent per year.[11] Note that these rates are overstated because of increasing unemployment; the full employment rates would be lower.

Table 5 — Return on Capital, Real Interest Rate, and Real Wage Growth in Western Germany, 1970–1995

| | Nominal rate of return on capital in the business sector[a] | Nominal rate of return on capital[b] | Return on real assets[c] | Real interest rate Return on securities[c] deflated by | | Growth rate of real gross compensation of employees[c] | Growth rate of real "standard" pension[c] |
				domestic producer price index	consumer price index of all households		
1970–1994[d]	11.7	14.7	4.7	4.6	4.1	2.4	1.9
1970–1979[d]	11.8	14.7	4.9	3.3	3.2	3.9	3.7
1980–1989[d]	11.2	13.9	4.3	5.0	4.7	1.3	0.9
1990–1994[d]	12.6	16.4	5.1	6.3	3.9	1.8	0.2
1990–1995[d]	12.8	–	–	6.3	4.5	1.6	–0.1

[a]OECD (1996: Table 25). — [b]Sachverständigenrat (1994: Table B1). — [c]For details of the definitions, see Table 1 in the Appendix. — [d]Arithmetic average; real gross compensation and "standard" pension: geometric average.

---

10   On rates of return, see also Döpke (1994).

11   For the United States, Feldstein (1996) calculates an implicit rate of return for participants in the Social Security system (OASDI) of 2.6 percent per year since 1960 using the average annual rate of growth of real wages as a proxy. He points out, however, that in reality the effective rate of return has been substantially higher because the rates of contribution have increased rapidly, with the consequence that pensioners who have contributed at low rates now enjoy high level benefits (intergenerational redistribution). According to Feldstein's calculations, the real rate of return on capital in the business sector since 1960 amounted to an average of 9.3 percent per year. From this follows that interest forgone in the pay-as-you-go system was a substantial 6.7 percent per year.

14. One could object that a proper comparison of the rates of return of both systems should consider risk and should be made from an ex ante point of view. This opens the field for a debate on which kind of risks should be taken into account. It cannot be denied that investment risk (including the portfolio investment risk), inflation risk, exchange rate risk and country risk exist (Sachverständigenrat 1996: Sections 410 ff.), but these risks can be partly hedged, or they can be avoided. In addition, some regulation is needed to reduce these risks and protect those who save for their old age. The capital-funded system loses its advantage in the case of major political upheavals in which the capital stock is destroyed (war) or property rights are not respected (revolutions). Institutional arrangements of a society, such as old-age systems, should, however, not be based on such extreme situations. It must be the aim of policy and constitutions to provide an umbrella of stability under which economic decisions can be taken.

15. The superior rate of return of a funded system means that a given pension level can be financed with lower contributions. The possibility of buying the same product at a lower price represents a welfare gain for individuals. Putting it the other way around, by forcing people into a pay-as-you-go system, the cost of old-age insurance is driven up, resulting in a loss of welfare.

From a macroeconomic point of view, the pay-as-you-go system has a zero rate of return because forced savings of contributors are instantly consumed by pensioners. In contrast, in the funded pension system the average insured individual owns a capital stock. This very capital produces the macroeconomic rate of return of a funded system.[12]

The macroeconomic rate of return can be interpreted as the "productivity" of an institutional arrangement. This argument draws on a macroeconomic production function that includes the institutional arrangement of the pension system as an additional factor of production. With respect to a national product, net of the cost for old-age insurance over the life cycle of a generation, the productive capacity of an economy using a funded pension system is higher compared to an economy using a pay-as-you-go system.

16. When comparing pay-as-you-go and funded pension systems, it also has to be considered that in the former the equivalence of contributions and benefits is usually not possible. According to Aaron's (1966) theorem, equivalence is secured by a constant rate of contribution when the growth rate of wages and salaries in each period is as high as the market rate of interest. In the more realistic case that the market interest rate exceeds the growth rate of wages and salaries, equivalence of contributions and benefits requires the rate of contribution to be raised every period—a situation that is obviously not sustainable. It is true that

---

12   Welfare gains engendered by the reduction of inefficiencies on the labor market have to be included.

the insured acquire higher claims with higher contributions. But even when borrowing against these claims on the capital market is allowed for, contributory equivalence is unsustainable (Breyer 1990:134) when borrowing is limited (in relation to wages and salaries). It is interesting to note that the German constitutional court has reduced the meaning of contributory equivalence to an equivalence of rank.

3.   Efficiency Gains for the Economy

17. Using a funded pension system results in welfare gains on the level of the individual that transform into increased efficiency for the total economy. Economic efficiency is enhanced when allocative distortions are reduced (in other words, when wedges between price signals are smaller). Two different sources of increased efficiency can be isolated: (1) more capital is accumulated in an economy with a funded pension system, and (2) distortions on the labor market are reduced. In the following section, the efficiency aspects of both systems are discussed; in the section thereafter the problems of transition to a funded system are discussed.

a.   Enhanced Capital Accumulation

18. In contrast to a pay-as-you-go system, the contributions to a funded system represent savings that are invested in the capital market. Capital accumulation is enhanced.

In order to investigate the influence of the type of pension system on savings, a situation with no public pension system is taken as a point of reference (Figure 2). The active generation saves to provide for consumption after retirement,[13] C_{t+1}, realizing a return that corresponds to the market interest rate, r; the slope of the resulting budget line IH is $1 + r$. The point of optimal consumption (savings) is C. Such a situation corresponds to a funded system on a voluntary basis.

The introduction of a pay-as-you-go system requires the active generation to pay contributions of bw, shifting the budget line to the left by amount IP. Individuals expect a pension, R, that shifts the budget line outside again (but to a smaller extent than bw because of incomplete equivalence).[14] For all other in-

---

[13]   The formal problem is one of maximization over two periods under an intertemporal budget restriction. Using more complex general equilibrium models with overlapping generations yields similar results (Blanchard and Fischer 1989:112).

[14]   The slope of the line IC' (not drawn) indicates the "interest rate" of the pay-as-you-go system. Note that this rate may be zero (45° line).

tertemporal decisions, the relevant interest rate remains r. The individual chooses point C' (with the present value of consumption reduced by NM). Comparing the points C' (pay-as-you-go system) and C (funded system) reveals that a funded system produces a higher level of consumption in the present period, namely ON instead of OM, and higher savings for the second period, namely $CN > DM$. The funded system is associated both with higher savings and higher consumption.[15]

Figure 2 — Pension Systems and Saving

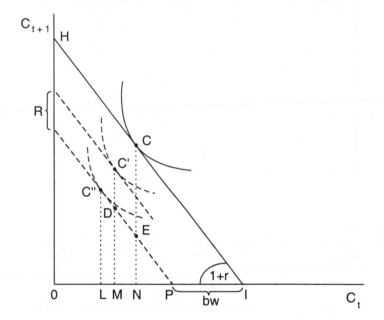

19. Figure 3 illustrates the effect of a pay-as-you-go scheme on the capital market. Point G depicts the capital market equilibrium with voluntary savings for retirement (corresponding to Point C in Figure 2). Assuming contributions to the pay-as-you-go system of AB and assuming that the savings supply curve indicates the intertemporal decisions of households at varying interest rates (it con-

---

[15] Assume the rate of return of the pay-as-you-go system were equal to the market rate, then the intertemporal equilibrium would be given by C. Savings, however, would decline even further to EN.

sists of households with differing time preferences), the introduction of a pay-as-you-go system in a closed economy leads to a shift of the equilibrium point from G to G'.[16] The pay-as-you-go system implies reduced savings, driving up the market interest rate. In turn, a change from pay-as-you-go financing to capital funding in the pension system would result in a movement from G' to G. Savings would rise, and the market rate of interest would fall. From all this follows that, both systems compared, the equilibrium real rate of interest tends to be lower in the funded pension system.

Figure 3 — Effect of Pay-as-You-Go Financing on the Capital Market

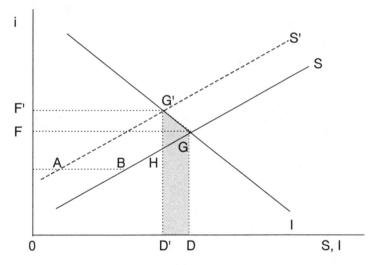

The shaded area, $DGG'D'$, in Figure 3 depicts the forgone future income due to lower savings that is the result of entertaining a pay-as-you-go system.[17] As a result of lower savings and a lower capital stock, the level of GDP per head and the growth rate are both lower compared to an economy with a funded system. The income loss in the future is accentuated when the fact is taken into account

---

16   Note that the distance AB is estimated to be as high as 10 percent of GDP, which is in the magnitude of the savings ratio of private households. In Figure 3, the rate of return of the pay-as-you-go system is set equal to the interest rate.

17   Note that the lower capital stock, OD', is associated with a higher interest rate. The overall effect on capital income depends on the elasticity of investment with respect to the interest rate. Feldstein (1996) calculates a deadweight loss of 2 percent of GDP for the United States.

that technological knowledge is incorporated in new capital. To sum up, pay-as-you-go financing leads to losses in output and growth.

20. In the case of a (small) open economy, these results do not change fundamentally when a significant segmentation of national capital markets is assumed. With perfect international capital mobility, the world market interest rate would continue to be relevant after introducing a pay-as-you-go system into the *Gedankenexperiment* presented here; there would be no change in interest rates. Because of the decline in domestic savings, however, capital must increasingly be imported and, at given rates, interest payments to foreigners do rise.

b.   Increased Efficiency of the Labor Market

21. A funded pension system removes distortions on the labor market that result from the extra cost of old-age insurance inherent in a pay-as-you-go system. The extra cost works like a tax on labor, driving a wedge between gross and net wages and distorting the decision between work and leisure. The tax effects a rotation of the budget line downwards at point H (Figure 4, where h denotes hours), the optimal point changes from A to B (associated with a lower level of utility). The incentive to work is reduced in the course of a lower (net) wage (resulting in the substitution effect AD towards leisure), while the associated reduction of income that results for a given amount of working hours works in favor of an increased labor supply (income effect DB). The total effect on labor supply is negative when the substitution effect dominates the income effect.

22. In the case of contributions being partially paid by employers, two effects of a pay-as-you-go system on the labor market can be distinguished (Figure 5):

1. As a reaction to the extra cost of old-age insurance that is working as an extra tax on labor income, workers will reduce their labor supply (assuming a dominating substitution effect). The labor supply curve shifts to the left; equilibrium moves from G to G', corresponding to the movement AB in Figure 4. The quadrangle $RMGG'$ depicts the associated income loss, the vertical distance between the labor supply curves being the relevant tax wedge from the worker's point of view. In addition, workers will consume less and save more (not shown in the figure).
2. The part of the contributions paid by the employer effects a downward shift in the labor demand curve due to increasing labor costs. The resulting new equilibrium lies at G''.

Combining both effects yields a reduction of labor input to the point Q. The shaded area, $GKLM$, depicts the efficiency loss for the economy.[18]

Figure 4 — Pension Systems and Labor Supply

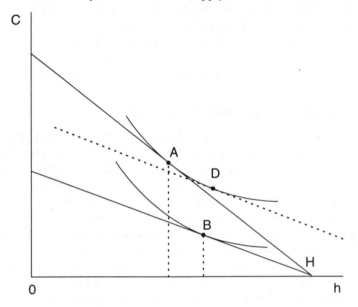

23. The above effects on capital accumulation and the labor market have been investigated using partial analytics. It is, however, to be considered that repercussions in a general equilibrium framework have to be taken into account. For example, with the introduction of a pay-as-you-go system, labor income declines to the area $OLQB$, as illustrated in Figure 5. The elasticity of wages and salaries, which are the basis of contributions to social security, with respect to the type of system is an important variable in order to estimate the effects of a transition from one system to another. In the case of a significant elasticity in a general equilibrium framework, the introduction of a pay-as-you-go system would substantially undermine the capacity to finance the system, with the result that rates of contribution would have to be raised. Furthermore, there are incentives to reduce the base for contributions by substituting income that is tax-exempt (e.g., labor income of "nondependents," fringe benefits) or other kinds of noncash earnings (Feldstein 1996) for income that is subject to the social security tax.

---

[18]   For the United States, this deadweight loss has been estimated to be 1 percent of GDP (Feldstein 1996).

Another important aspect is the effect of capital accumulation on labor productivity and vice versa. Because $F_A(A,K) > 0$ and $F_{AK} > 0$, lower investment results in lower labor productivity and in further suppressed labor demand.

Figure 5 — Effect of Pay-as-You-Go Financing on the Labor Market

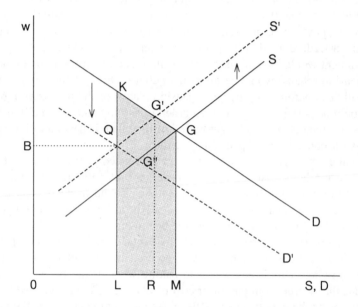

4.   The Transition towards a Funded System

24. Recognizing the superiority of a funded pension system to a pay-as-you-go system in terms of economic efficiency does not necessarily mean that a transition to a funded system should be recommended, because transition is associated with an additional burden.[19] The problem is that the claims of the generations that have contributed to the pay-as-you-go system still have to be financed. While the claims in a pay-as-you-go system are not funded on real assets because the contributions of the active generations are instantly consumed by retired generations, pensioners are certainly justified in expecting that, because they have paid contributions, they should rightfully receive a pension.

---

[19] This corresponds to the phenomenon that in the start-up period of the pay-as-you-go system, the first generation receives a pension without having made contributions. With a finite planning horizon, the last generation of pensioners receives nothing.

These existing claims have to be financed from taxes that ultimately have to be borne by the active generations. Therefore, active generations have to bear an additional burden: in addition to forgoing consumption (savings) to provide for their own retirement under the new funded system they need to make tax payments to finance the claims inherited from the pay-as-you-go system.[20]

25. The transition could be designed in a way that from a fixed date contributions would have to be made to a funded system. Claims stemming from contributions to the pay-as-you-go system in the past would be retained in a certified form. This procedure would effectively make an implicit public debt explicit;[21] the government would have to serve the resultant debt. Contributions to the new funded pension scheme would be lower than contributions to the pay-as-you-go system had been before. By certifying pension claims of the pay-as-you-go system, it would be possible to spread the burden of serving and eventually redeeming the associated debt over a longer period of time than is needed to fully phase in a newly introduced funded pension system.

26. An alternative proposal would restrict the funded pension scheme to new entrants into the labor market. This, however, would only shift the burden of transition further into the future. Against the background of decreasing populations, the burden per head would tend to rise. Accordingly, the funded pension scheme should include all workers from the beginning.

27. The question is whether a transition to a funded pension system that fully assumes the obligations of the pay-as-you-go system accumulated in the past is welfare-improving. This is equivalent to asking whether the benefits of future generations that accrue from the lower cost of old-age insurance exceed the burden from serving the debt that results from exchanging the claims to the pay-as-you-go system for government bonds. Formally, the necessary condition for the present value of the net gain of transformation to be positive[22] (Feldstein 1995:14) is

---

[20]   If these taxes are raised as taxes on labor income, they will also cause distortions on the labor market.

[21]   Making public debt explicit is not associated with additional absorption in the capital market.

[22]   It is assumed that during the transition, savings would be unchanged from the pay-as-you-go system. The inherited debt is made explicit by issuing government bonds with interest rate r. Then (assuming $n = 0$) the net gain in individual periods is

$$\left[(1+g)^0(r-g)-r\right]T_0, \left[(1+g)^1(r-g)-r\right]T_0, \left[(1+g)^2(r-g)-r\right]T_0, \ldots,$$

$$\left[(1+g)^{t-1}(r-g)-r\right]T_0.$$ The present value of the gains from transition is

$$\Sigma_t(r-g)T_0(1+g)^{t-1}(1+\delta)^{-t} \Sigma_t \, rT_0(1+\delta)^{-t}.$$

(1) $$T_0 \left[\frac{r-n-g}{\delta-n-g} - \frac{r}{\delta} \right] > 0, \text{ or}$$

(1') $$T_0 \left[\frac{(r-\delta)(n+g)}{(\delta-n-g)\delta} \right] > 0,$$

where δ is the marginal rate of time preference and T_0 the amount of government bonds compensating for the claims against the old system.

As can be seen from condition (1) the sufficient condition for the net gain of the transition to be positive is that $r > \delta > g + n > 0$ is satisfied. The condition $\delta > g + n$ is necessary for convergence that allows condition (1) to be interpreted as the present value of the net utility and can be expected to hold because, otherwise, the discounted stream of all future income would be infinite (see Section 2).

For the condition $r > n + g$ to hold, marginal productivity of capital has to exceed the real rate of wage growth. This condition is satisfied during adjustment to the steady state; it also holds in the steady state if the marginal rate of time preference exceeds the real economic growth rate, and if capital is taxed, driving the market interest rate higher still.

In addition, $r > \delta$ has to be satisfied. This condition says that the market interest rate, i.e., the marginal productivity of capital, has to exceed the marginal rate of time preference. In other words, the marginal rate of transformation between consumption today and tomorrow has to exceed the marginal rate of substitution over time. Note that this condition for a transition to a funded system to be welfare-improving is not required when the rates of return of both systems are compared. The condition may considered to be problematic in the sense that the market interest rate equals the marginal rate of time preference in the steady state. According to condition (1'), no Pareto-improving transition would then be possible. During adjustment towards the steady state, the marginal rate of time preference, while depending on the level of consumption, equals the market interest in every period (in a transitory equilibrium). However, a capital tax is sufficient to establish a wedge between the marginal productivity of capital and the marginal rate of time preference (see Section 2).[23] Then, $r > \delta$ is satisfied. In addition, positive real growth ($n + g > 0$) is assumed for the analysis below.

28. The development of net gains per period over time is depicted in Figure 6. In time $\tilde{t}$, gains and burdens per period cancel out. In later periods, net gains result; with an infinite horizon, the area of net benefits is open to ∞ while the

---

[23]   In an intuitive interpretation, the pay-as-you-go system itself introduces a distortion in the interest rate relative to a capital-funded system. See Section 3a.

area of net losses is limited. As has been shown before, gains and losses per period have to be discounted to calculate the present value of net gains of transforming the system. In other words, to decide upon a change of systems, a social welfare function would be needed. Discounting gains and losses over time using a constant discount rate, δ, corresponds to applying a simple social welfare function.

Figure 6 — Time Profile of Net Burden and Net Benefit per Period

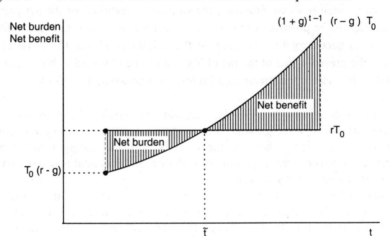

29. Estimating the point in time at which net losses are turned into net gains is a difficult task. The estimate depends on various factors, including the difference in the rates of return, assumed demographic developments, details of the pay-as-you-go system started from, and how the inherited claims are handled. In a quantitative assessment under the assumption that the rate of return in a funded system exceeds the implicit rate of return in the pay-as-you-go system by 2 percentage points, the Sachverständigenrat estimated the transition to be profitable within 40 to 50 years.

30. The assessment of the period $\tilde{t}$ for Germany may go as follows. From a fixed date new claims arise exclusively within a funded system. Existing claims for pensions are respected. A person retiring in the period in which the change of the system takes place will receive his/her pension according to the pay-as-you-go system. The implicit rate of return of the pay-as-you-go system is assumed at 2 percent in real terms; the pension, accordingly, is raised by 2 percent annually. Workers who retire in later periods realize a part of their pensions from the pay-as-you-go system (according to the number of years of contribution), while the

other part comes from the funds accumulated in the years after the system's change. Assuming 45 years of work, a worker who retires 10 years after the change of the system has claims against the pay-as-you-go system for 35 years. The corresponding pension is raised by 2 percent per year. As time goes by, the share of pensions stemming from the pay-as-you-go system successively decreases because newly retired cohorts have increasingly fewer years of contribution to the pay-as-you-go system. It, however, takes as much as 59 years to fully phase out the old system when 15 years of retirement is assumed.

Table 6 — Pension Claims from the Pay-as-You-Go System during Transition

t	Pension claim of newly retired ($t_0 = 1$)	Pension claim of average retired ($t_0 = 1$)	Pension outlays in time t (billion DM)	Present value of pension outlays (billion DM)
0	1.00	1.00	314.30	314.30
10	0.78	0.92	351.91	237.74
20	0.56	0.71	332.11	151.57
30	0.33	0.49	278.33	85.81
40	0.11	0.27	185.06	38.55
45	0.00	0.16	119.19	20.41
50	0.00	0.07	56.40	7.94
55	0.00	0.01	13.84	1.60
59	0.00	0.00	0.00	0.00

Note: Assumed is a pension growth of 2 percent per year and a discount rate of 4 percent per year.

31. The present value of pensions due in the years 0 to 59 is calculated using a discount rate of 4 percent. The present value of all pension claims from the pay-as-you-go system is DM 6,890 billion. The present value of pensions is decreasing over time, the present value of the annual burden shrinks from DM 314 billion to DM 86 billion in 30 years (Table 6). Using a credit to be redeemed within 45 years to finance the present value of these pension obligations, according to these back-of-the-envelope calculations, yields a gross burden of 14.5 percent of wages and salaries. The gross gain of the newly established funded pension system increases over time. In the transition period, therefore, the economy is confronted with an additional burden that decreases over time.

32. It has to be borne in mind, however, that in a funded system a given level of pension benefits can be financed with lower contributions. Assuming a level of benefits of 60 percent of wages and a ratio of three contributors per pensioner, the pay-as-you-go system produces a rate of contribution of 20 percent of wage

income.[24] Because of the higher rate of return in the funded system, a lower rate of contribution yields the same level of benefits. As time goes by, the funded system will increasingly displace and eventually drive out the pay-as-you-go system. Consequently, the average rate of contribution to the funded system successively decreases (Table 7). Eventually, the contribution rate in percent of gross wages is reduced from 20 percent of gross wages to 11 percent, implying a gain of 9 percentage points.

Table 7 — Contribution Rates in Percent of Gross Wages

t	Contribution rate in the pay-as-you-go system	Contribution rate in the capital-funded system	Reduction in contribution rate (percentage point)
0	20	13.9	6.1
10	20	12.6	7.4
20	20	11.7	8.3
30	20	11.2	8.8
40	20	10.9	9.1
45	20	10.9	9.1
50	20	10.9	9.1

33. When the cost of transition to a funded system is calculated, the tax burden of 14.5 percent of wages and salaries in the transition period of 45 years has to be taken into account. The net benefit from transition is the difference between the gross benefit, i.e., the difference between the rates of contribution to the alternative systems, and the tax burden. Net benefits are negative at first, and increase successively. After 45 years, the net benefit for every following period amounts to some 9 percent of wages and salaries (Figure 7).

When the government bonds issued to compensate for pension claims against the pay-as-you-go system are redeemed over a longer period of 90 years, the tax burden would be reduced to 10.2 percent of wages and salaries during transition (Figure 8). In the extreme case of infinite maturity, the corresponding tax burden would be 8.4 percent. Accepting the pension claims only at a discount in order to let older generations bear some of the burden of the transition, could also reduce the tax rate needed to finance redemption in the transition period.

---

[24]   In order to simplify the analysis, I do not distinguish between gross and net wages.

Figure 7 —   Gross Benefit and Net Benefit per Period in Percent of Gross Wage
Income during Transition Using 45-year Bonds

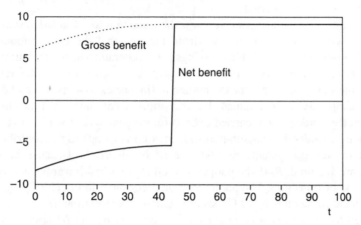

Figure 8 —   Gross Benefit and Net Benefit per Period in Percent of Gross Wage
Income during Transition Using Bonds with Longer Maturity

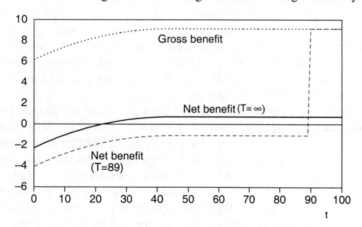

34. The underlying assumption of an annual rise in pensions of 2 percent per
year over the next 30 years is not particularly realistic. In Germany, the real
standard pension increased by only 0.9 percent from 1980 to 1995, and by a
mere 0.1 percent from 1990 to 1995. The revision of the pension law in 1992 has
slowed down pension growth further (Glismann and Horn 1995). Contributing to
the low rate of return in the pay-as-you-go system is the decrease in population
(by an average 0.4 percent per year). Calculating the transition with an implicit

real rate of return in the pay-as-you-go system of zero reduces the present value of pension claims to DM 5,300 billion. As a result, the long-run gains of a transition increase to 14.5 percent.

35. Turning to the effect on savings, the transition to a funded system results in increased savings. This follows from the fact that the contributions to the funded system lead to additional savings. The generation of the transition period has to build up the pension funds to finance their consumption after retirement and, at the same time, bear the tax burden to finance existing pension claims.

For simplicity, it is assumed that transition is completed within one period and that the burden is not carried over to future generations via issuing of long-term bonds. Under these assumptions, the tax corresponds to the contributions in the pay-as-you-go system, bw (distance IP in Figure 2). Because no pension claims are acquired, $R=0$, the budget restriction is shifted inwards once again for the period of transition. The point of optimal consumption is C''. The individual has to increase savings by LM to secure income after retirement.

When the transition is completed, the budget restriction IH applies, with optimal consumption in C. Savings increase once again because the present value of income increases by IP. Note that reduced expected pension income induces individuals to increase savings as well as disposable income in their active years.

36. During the transition towards a funded system, the economy displays a higher savings ratio. Higher savings tend to promote growth. In addition, employment rises as a result of enhanced efficiency in the labor market. The additional tax revenue associated with higher growth and employment helps to finance the transition. Such general equilibrium repercussions have not been taken into account in the above calculations.

37. Often it is argued that the capital stock necessary to fund the prevailing level of benefits in a funded pension system is unrealistically high. The capital stock necessary to cover the present value of existing pension claims amounts to DM 6,900 billion at a discount rate of 4 percent and an average real annual pension growth of 2 percent (DM 5,300 billion at constant real pensions). The replaceable gross stock of fixed assets in the economy amounts to a much higher figure in Western Germany, DM 14,400 billion (in 1991 prices). Furthermore, it has to be considered that total savings and the real capital stock in relation to GDP can be expected to rise with the introduction of a funded system.

38. The problem to be decided upon by economic policy can be clearly seen from Figures 6, 7, and 8. From time $\tilde{t}$, significant gains from the reduced cost of old-age insurance can be realized in every following period. During a transition period a substantial additional burden has to be shouldered. The transition to a funded system can thus be interpreted as an investment that requires forgoing consumption today to yield profits in the future. It seems evident that such an investment by a society needs a long-term policy orientation.

Societal developments are path-dependent. The introduction of a funded system is complicated by the fact that a pay-as-you-go system has already been established. Societies should, however, be able to overcome their path dependency. Societies should be able to transform their institutional arrangements in order to improve efficiency in the long term even when a limited number of generations is required to give up some consumption and when the utility of a limited number of generations is reduced. For important historical changes, the Pareto criterion or the Kaldor–Pareto criterion of compensation may not be a sufficient guideline. These criteria prevent economic change.[25]

5.   Some Practical Aspects of Introducing a Funded System

39. It is evident that the level of pensions in the public old-age pension system (in Germany, 70 percent of net wages in the standard case) will have to be lowered in the future. A lower expected level of benefits can be expected to induce the active generation to increase individual provisions for retirement. Consequently, individual accounts for the purpose of providing income after retirement will play an increasingly important role in financing the consumption of retired generations in the future. This is in the self-interest of young generations even if the relative burden in their active years increases compared to that experienced by older generations.

40. Economic policy would be wise to accept this tendency towards a funded system. Keeping in mind the superior efficiency of a funded system, economic policy should support this kind of process by adjusting the institutional framework. What is required most is a clear long-term perspective for old-age pension systems that reduces uncertainty and helps individuals to plan their consumption pattern over their life cycle. Within this framework, an option for a funded pension system should be explicitly introduced, or at least be left open. Since a transition to a funded system involves two generations (of 30 years each), a long-term commitment of policy is required. One instrument of policy to commit itself to stick to a transformation of the system could be a constitutional amendment fixing certain principles of the pension system that could only be changed by a broad majority in parliament. In the following, some practical aspects of a transformation of the pension system will be considered.

41. When evaluating the state of the prevalent pay-as-you-go system, it is not sufficient that the budget restriction is satisfied at a given point in time. Instead,

---

[25]   A criterion may have to disregard sunk costs and sunk positions of individuals. In deciding on future development, a society could abstract from its path dependency and mimic the decision of a country that is in a different initial position.

the accrual of future obligations has to be taken into account. The present value of future obligations has to equal the present value of future contributions. This requirement cannot be attained through adjustment of the pension benefit formula alone. It is important to explain the intertemporal budget constraint to the public. Future obligations should be made clear.

One option of a public pension system facing financial disequilibrium in the future is to build a capital stock in due course in order to finance excess expenditures in later periods. In such a way, a funded system could be introduced over several generations.

42. Individual pension claims should be published regularly (e.g., on a yearly basis) in order to reduce uncertainty and, at the same time, to open the possibility of certifying claims.

43. While a funded pension system, in principle, can be part of a public old-age insurance, the transformation of the system usually is associated with privatization. Individuals should be free to choose between suppliers of old-age insurance; private companies could compete with public agencies. An important additional aspect is that with a private sector system the danger of politicians abusing the funds is reduced.

The additional savings associated with a funded system must not be used to fund additional public expenditures (Sachverständigenrat 1988: Section 373). Therefore, limits to public deficits should be respected.

44. To exclude problems of adverse selection, private insurers must not be allowed to discriminate when contracting. For the individual, the change of insurers should be possible at low cost. The risks associated with individually different longevity are borne by the insurer when the contract provides for paying monthly pension benefits.

45. The institutional framework should contain an obligation to insure for old-age at a minimum level, i.e., to contribute to a pension scheme in order to reduce moral hazard. The proposal of a tax-financed basic pension that provides a—unconditional—minimum income after retirement does not solve this problem. The problem with this proposal is that the principle of equivalence of benefits and contributions, which is still prevalent in the pay-as-you-go system in a rudimentary form, is totally abandoned in a basic pension system. Such a system would have detrimental incentives and cannot be recommended on similar grounds as various negative income tax proposals (Siebert 1995).

46. Introducing a minimal old-age insurance that is obligatory and financed with contributions could help to avoid this kind of adverse incentives. Contributions for pensions that exceed the minimum pension level would be on a voluntary basis. To prevent old-age poverty, retirement income would be provided by social assistance to persons whose income in active years did not allow them to contribute to the minimum pension scheme. In order to provide incentives to

contribute, the minimum pension must exceed the level of social assistance sufficiently. This is a specific problem in Europe, where social welfare provides a lower income floor.

47. The share of voluntary savings in providing retirement income would also be increased if the maximum income subject to contribution to the public pension system is frozen at its current level for a substantial period of time, say two generations, or if the maximum income is lifted by less than the rate of growth of net wages and salaries. In such an approach, the equivalence of contributions and pension claims could prevail. Proceeding in such a way, would leave more and more income (in relation to national income) outside the public pension system, effectively altering the overall pension system through the back door. At the same time, however, the public pension system would increasingly get into financial disequilibrium; in the transition phase, pension outlays would more and more have to be financed through external sources, or pension levels would have to be cut.

48. A basic principle for the reform of old-age insurance should be that contributions are to be separated from employment contracts. The fact that employers pay part of the contributions does not mean that they actually bear the associated burden. Effectively, workers have to pay for old-age insurance in full: in the long run, to keep the real gross compensation of employees within the limits given by productivity, wages have to adjust, or, otherwise, unemployment will increase. To make the system more transparent, the full share of contributions should be paid from workers' income.

49. One precondition for such a reform would be to create equivalence of pension claims and contributions by eliminating interpersonal distribution from the old-age insurance scheme. Retirement incomes of contributors whose resulting pension claims would be below the (social) subsistence level because they had low incomes in their active years would have to be supplemented by social assistance.

50. Separating the obligation to contribute to the public pension system from whether an individual is actually employed eliminates incentives to manipulate one's labor status in order to be exempt from membership in the system. Decisions about whether to be employed or self-employed, how many hours to work, or occupation to choose would not be influenced by rules in the public pension system.

51. To sum up, a strengthening of funded elements can contribute to overcoming the problems the public pension system is currently facing. A major goal of reform should, from an economic perspective, always be to increase the individual's freedom to choose.

Appendix

Table A1 —Demographic Development and Old-Age Dependency Ratios for Germany, 1995–2040, Using Various Assumptions on Fertility[a]

		1995	2000	2010	2020	2030	2040
Constant fertility	Population	81,539	82,182	81,036	78,445	74,347	68,800
	Aged 20 – 59[b]	47,113	45,967	45,629	42,709	36,011	33,118
	60 years and over[b]	16,874	18,758	20,447	22,695	26,376	25,308
	Old-age dependency ratio[c]	35.8	40.8	44.8	53.1	73.2	76.4
	Aged 20 – 65[b]	51,445	51,493	49,966	48,414	42,512	37,406
	65 years and over[b]	12,542	13,232	16,110	16,990	19,875	21,020
	Old-age dependency ratio[d]	24.4	25.7	32.2	35.1	46.8	56.2
Declining fertility	Population	81,539	82,034	80,117	76,667	71,685	65,043
	Aged 20–59[b]	47,113	45,967	45,629	42,562	35,098	31,255
	60 years and over[b]	16,874	18,758	20,447	22,695	26,376	25,308
	Old-age dependency ratio[c]	35.8	40.8	44.8	53.3	75.1	81.0
	Aged 20–65[b]	51,445	51,493	49,967	48,266	41,600	35,642
	65 years and over[b]	12,542	13,232	16,110	16,990	19,875	21,020
	Old-age dependency ratio[d]	35.8	25.7	32.2	35.2	47.8	59.0
Increasing fertility	Population	81,539	82,399	82,379	81,049	78,347	74,523
	Aged 20–59[b]	47,113	45,967	45,629	42,924	37,345	35,702
	60 years and over[b]	16,874	18,758	20,447	22,695	26,376	25,308
	Old-age dependency ratio[c]	35.8	40.8	44.8	52.9	70.6	70.9
	Aged 20–65[b]	51,445	51,493	49,967	48,629	43,847	39,989
	65 years and over[b]	12,542	13,222	16,110	16,990	19,875	21,020
	Old-age dependency ratio[d]	35.8	25.7	32.2	34.9	45.3	52.6

[a]For net migration, a medium scenario (A) has been assumed. — [b]Thousand persons. — [c]Number of persons aged 60 and over in percent of persons aged 20–59. — [d]Number of persons aged 65 and over in percent of persons aged 20–64.

Source: Bundesministerium des Innern (1996), own calculations.

Table A2 — On the Rates of Return of Pension Systems in Western Germany

Year	Nominal rate of return on capital in the business sector[a]	Nominal rate of return on capital[b]	Return on real assets[c]	Real interest rate Return on securities[c] deflated by		Growth rate of real gross compensation of employees[c]	Growth rate of real "standard" pension[d]
				domestic producer price index	consumer price index of all households		
1970	12.8	16.6	5.9	3.3	4.7	14.0	2.9
1971	12.3	15.8	5.5	3.5	2.6	4.8	0.9
1972	12.4	15.3	5.2	5.2	2.4	3.9	10.2
1973	12.3	15,0	4.8	2.5	2.2	5.0	3.9
1974	11.1	13.5	4.0	−2.5	3.4	1.6	4.3
1975	10.7	12.4	3.8	4.1	2.9	−2.7	4.2
1976	11.5	14.2	4.7	4.5	4.0	3.3	5.7
1977	11.5	14.2	4.7	3.9	3.0	2.8	6.2
1978	11.7	15.1	5.1	5.2	3.6	3.4	−2.0
1979	11.8	15.4	4.9	2.9	3.5	3.4	0.9
1980	10.6	13.0	3.6	0.9	3.0	3.0	−1.3
1981	10.0	11.9	2.9	2.3	3.7	−2.0	−1.9
1982	9.9	11.3	2.8	3.0	3.5	−2.2	0.2
1983	10.7	13.3	3.9	6.6	4.7	−1.5	2.0
1984	11.1	13.9	4.2	4.9	5.6	1.6	0.9
1985	11.3	14.3	4.4	4.6	4.9	1.4	0.9
1986	11.8	15.2	5.0	9.2	6.6	5.2	2.7
1987	11.6	14.9	4.9	9.0	6.0	3.5	4.0
1988	12.2	15.7	5.5	5.3	5.2	2.8	2.0
1989	12.5	15.9	5.6	3.7	4.1	1.9	0.0
1990	13.2	17.5	5.9	7.0	6.0	5.4	0.2
1991	12.5	17.8	5.6	5.9	4.7	4.9	1.0
1992	12.3	16.8	5.1	6.5	3.8	2.6	−1.2
1993	12.0	14.4	4.5	6.6	2.9	−2.9	0.5
1994	12.9	15.7	5.0	6.4	4.2	−0.8	0.3
1995	13.7	–	–	5.2	5.1	0.7	−1.7

[a]OECD (1996: Table 25). — [b]Sachverständigenrat (1994: Table B1). — [c]For details of the definitions, see Sachverständigenrat (1996: Table 53). — [d] Calculations of Sachverständigenrat.

Bibliography

Aaron, H. (1966). The Social Insurance Paradox. *Canadian Journal of Economics and Science* 32(3):371–374.

Auerbach, A.J., J. Gokhale, and L.J. Kotlikoff (1991). Generational Accounts: A Meaningful Alternative to Deficit Accounting. *Tax Policy and the Economy* 5:55–110.

—— (1994). Generational Accounting: A Meaningful Way to Evaluate Fiscal Policy. *Journal of Economic Perspectives* 8(1):73–94.

Blanchard, O.J., and S. Fischer (1989). *Lectures on Macroeconomics*. Cambridge, Mass.: MIT Press.

Breyer, F. (1990). *Ökonomische Theorie der Alterssicherung*. Munich: Verlag Vahlen.

Bundesministerium des Innern (1996). Modellrechnungen zur Bevölkerungsentwicklung in der Bundesrepublik Deutschland bis zum Jahr 2000. Mimeo.

Diamond, P. (1996). Generational Accounts and Generational Balance: An Assessment. *National Tax Journal* 49(4):597–607.

Döpke, J. (1994). Sachkapitalrendite und Investitionstätigkeit in Westdeutschland. *Die Weltwirtschaft* (3):334–348.

Feldstein, M. (1974). Social Security, Induced Retirement, and Aggregate Capital Accumulation. *Journal of Political Economy* 82(5):905–926.

—— (1995). Would Privatizing Social Security Raise Economic Welfare? NBER Working Paper 5281. Cambridge, Mass.

—— (1996). The Missing Piece in Policy Analysis: Social Security Reform. *American Economic Review, Papers and Proceedings* 86(2):1–14.

Glismann, H.H., and E.-J. Horn (1995). Die Krise des deutschen Systems der staatlichen Alterssicherung. *ORDO, Jahrbuch für die Ordnung von Wirtschaft und Gesellschaft* 46:309–344.

Gischer, H. (1996). Die Höhe der Rentenversicherungsbeiträge im Kapitaldeckungsverfahren. Einige einfache Zusammenhänge und Beispielrechnungen. *Wirtschaftswissenschaftliches Studium* 25(6):274–279.

Haveman, R. (1994). Should Generational Accounts Replace Public Budgets and Deficits? *Journal of Economic Perspectives* 8(1):95–111.

Homburg, S. (1988a). *Theorie der Alterssicherung*. Berlin: Springer-Verlag.

—— (1988b). Umlage- versus Kapitaldeckungsverfahren. *Wirtschaftswissenschaftliches Studium* 17(12):605–609.

Kotlikoff, L.J. (1996). Privatization of Social Security: How It Works and Why It Matters. *Tax Policy and the Economy* 10:1–32.

Leibfritz, W., D. Roseveare, D. Fore, and E. Wurzel (1995). Ageing Populations, Pension Systems and Government Budgets: How Do They Affect Saving? OECD Economics Department Working Paper 156. OECD, Paris.

Mitchell, O.S., and S.P. Zeldes (1996). Social Security Privatization: A Structure for Analysis. *American Economic Review* 86(25):363–367.

Neumann, M. (1986). *Möglichkeiten zur Entlastung der gesetzlichen Rentenversicherung durch kapitalbildende Vorsorgemaßnahmen*. Tübingen: Mohr Siebeck.

—— (1998). Vom Umlageverfahren zum Kapitaldeckungsverfahren: Optionen zur Reform der Alterssicherung. Stellungnahme für das Frankfurter Institut—Stiftung Marktwirtschaft und Politik. Mimeo.

Noord, P. van den, and R. Herd (1993). Pension Liabilities in the Seven Major Economies. OECD Working Paper 15. Paris.

OECD (1995). *OECD Economic Outlook*. 57 (June). Paris: OECD.

—— (1996). *OECD Economic Outlook*. 60 (December). Paris: OECD.

Prognos (1995). Perspektiven der gesetzlichen Rentenversicherung für Gesamtdeutschland vor dem Hintergrund veränderter politischer und ökonomischer Rahmenbedingungen. DRV-Schriften, Band 4. Frankfurt am Main.

Sachverständigenrat zur Begutachtung der gesamtwirtschaftlichen Entwicklung (1988). *Arbeitsplätze im Wettbewerb*. Jahresgutachten 1988/89. Stuttgart: Kohlhammer.

—— (1996). *Reformen voranbringen*. Jahresgutachten 1996/97. Stuttgart: Metzler-Poeschel.

Samuelson, P.A. (1958). An Exact Consumption Loan Model of Interest with or without the Social Contrivance of Money. *Journal of Political Economy* 66(6):467–482.

—— (1975). Optimum Social Security in a Life-Cycle Growth Model. *International Economic Review* 16(3):539–544.

Siebert, H. (1995). *Geht den Deutschen die Arbeit aus? Wege zu mehr Beschäftigung*. Munich: Goldmann.

—— (1997). Die Einschränkung des Lohnbildungsspielraums durch die Kosten der Sozialversicherung. *Die Weltwirtschaft* (1):2–8.

Weizsäcker, R.K. von (1990). Population Aging and Social Security: A Political-Economic Model of State Pension Financing. *Public Finance* 45(3):491–509.

World Bank (1994). *World Population Projections 1994/95*. Baltimore: Johns Hopkins University Press.

Barry Bosworth and Gary Burtless

Social Security Reform and Capital Formation

1. Introduction

In the 1990s, all of the major industrial countries are struggling with significant public sector budget deficits. Yet, as we look ahead, the current problems seem minor compared to those that will be raised by an aging of the population. The demands on public sector programs will be growing at a time when limited growth in the labor force implies little or no expansion of national income and the tax revenues needed to support the programs. It is increasingly evident that many countries will be forced to revamp those programs that provide health and income support for the elderly. To date, much of this discussion is highly divisive in that it has focused on who should pay: the elderly through a lower standard of living in retirement, or the future workers in the form of higher taxes. However, if nations plan ahead, it is possible to meet a portion of the future costs through added saving today. Increased saving and investment provides a means of expanding the pool of future resources available to meet the consumption needs of both workers and retirees.

2. The Magnitude of the Problem

Over the next few decades the populations of the industrial countries will grow considerably grayer. By 2030, when the baby-boom generation will have moved into retirement, the dependency rate (the ratio of people past age 64 to those aged 15–64) will be about 30 percent in the United States, close to 40 percent in France and Britain, and nearly 50 percent in Germany and Japan (Table 1). While all the industrial countries share the prospect of an aging population, variations in the size and timing of the demographic change, as well as important differences in public programs for the elderly, mean that population aging has different implications in each country.

Remark: Thanks are due James J. Prescott for outstanding research assistance. We would also like to thank Charles Schultze for helpful comments.

Table 1 —   Population Structure in the G-5 Countries, 1960–2050

Country	1960	1990	2000	2010	2020	2030	2050
	Dependency rate (percent)[a]						
France	18.8	20.8	23.6	24.6	32.3	39.1	43.5
Germany	15.9	21.4	24.3	30.1	35.0	47.1	51.3
Japan	8.9	17.3	25.1	34.1	43.2	43.5	50.2
United Kingdom	17.9	24.2	24.2	25.5	30.5	38.3	40.9
United States	15.2	18.7	18.7	19.1	24.8	31.9	33.5
High-income	14.0	19.3	21.5	24.6	31.5	39.8	n.a.
Other	7.9	8.3	9.1	8.7	11.4	14.6	n.a.
	Elderly population, 65+ (1990=100)						
France	69	100	118	127	161	187	198
Germany	51	100	115	139	153	180	164
Japan	36	100	146	186	220	215	211
United Kingdom	67	100	103	112	132	157	161
United States	54	100	111	124	165	213	233
High-income	55	100	117	138	172	206	n.a.
Other	47	100	132	164	228	324	n.a.
	Working-age population, 15–64 (1990=100)						
France	76	100	104	107	104	99	95
Germany	68	100	101	99	94	82	68
Japan	70	100	101	95	88	86	73
United Kingdom	91	100	103	106	105	99	96
United States	66	100	110	121	125	125	130
High-income	75	100	105	108	105	100	n.a.
Other	49	100	121	157	167	184	n.a.

[a]The dependency rate is the ratio of the number of persons over age 64 to the number of persons aged 15–64.

Source: National sources. The data for France and the global aggregates are from
      Bos et al. (1994).

   The dependency rate will rise most steeply in Germany and Japan, where the economic problems of population aging will be compounded by large declines in the population of working age. Thus, what is often described as population aging might more accurately be characterized as population decline. Fertility rates are far below the "replacement rate" needed to maintain a constant population, now about 2.1 children per woman. Official Japanese projections assume the fertility rate will average about 1.5 in the future; German projections assume it will remain close to the current level, 1.4. Forecasts of the German population also incorporate substantial (but declining) immigration—an annual net flow of about 2 immigrants per 1,000 residents, compared with 5.6 earlier this decade. Immigration is assumed to be negligible for Japan.

France and the United Kingdom face less dramatic population change. Fertility rates in both have declined (to 1.8), but less than in Germany or Japan. Over the next quarter century the total populations of France and Britain are expected to grow, while the working-age populations will remain roughly unchanged. Dependency rates will rise because of the growing number of old.

Though the elderly population is projected to grow fastest in the United States, the American aged dependency rate will grow the least. The U.S. fertility rate is now above 2.0, and immigration remains strong (4.4 net immigrants per thousand residents), so the working-age population will continue to expand, albeit much more slowly than it has in the past.

Official forecasts in all five countries suggest only modest gains in life expectancy. In Japan, for example, life expectancy is predicted to improve over the next 30 years at one-sixth the rate of the past 30 years. In the United States, life expectancy is predicted to rise at just one-half the rate of the recent past. Many demographers believe these projections understate likely improvements in longevity, implying that the future rise in the aged dependency rate may be greater than the official forecasts.

From an economic growth perspective, the most striking feature of Table 1 is the pervasive deceleration of labor force growth, and the outright declines in Germany and Japan. Few countries have had experience with the economic consequences of a shrinking workforce. Combined with a continuation of the post-1973 slowdown in total factor productivity gains, one implication is much reduced rates of aggregate income growth—and, thus, low investment requirements.

The differences between the countries in projected pension costs are even greater than implied by the disparate demographic trends because of variations in the generosity of the basic pension schemes. As shown in Table 2, Germany and France have the highest pension costs as a percent of GDP because they provide a very generous public pension; they allow retirement at an early age (63/60); and, at least in the case of Germany, they have used the pension system to finance even earlier retirement of the long-term unemployed. The United States and the United Kingdom have the smallest current pension burden, and their costs will rise the least in the future. In fact, in the U.K.'s case pension costs will decline as a share of GDP because it is in the process of scaling back its public pension system and encouraging individuals to opt out into private systems. In essence, assuming that the cutbacks are sustainable, the United Kingdom has no fiscal crisis of aging.

Table 2 — Public Sector Financing of Programs for the Aged in the G-5
Countries, 1995 (percentage of GDP)

		France	Germany	Japan	United Kingdom	United States
1.	Public pension costs	10.6	11.1	8.6	6.5	5.1
2.	Net replacement rate[a]	78.0	63.0	55.0	50.0	50.0
3.	Pension cost, 1995–2040					
	1995	10.6	11.1	8.6	6.5	5.1
	2000	11.5	11.4	10.5	6.3	5.1
	2010	12.6	12.0	14.0	6.2	5.3
	2020	14.8	13.3	14.8	6.0	6.1
	2030	17.2	14.1	15.5	6.2	6.8
	2040	20.4	14.2	n.a.	5.7	6.8
4.	Present value of net pension liabilities	115.0	110.0	105.0	5.0	25.0
5.	Health care spending					
	Total (public plus private)	9.1	8.5	6.6	6.6	13.7
	Public spending	6.1	6.1	4.8	5.5	6.1

[a]After-tax value of public pension as a percent of after-tax wage while at work for average-wage worker.

Sources: 1. Roseveare et al. (1996) for France and Germany; Takayama (1996)
for Japan; Franco and Munzi (1994) for United Kingdom; and the
Social Security Administration (1997) for the United States.

2. and 3. Bosworth and Burtless (1998).

4. Chand and Jaeger (1997).

5. OECD Health Datafile.

Another summary perspective is available from a recent IMF study that estimated the future costs of each country's public pension system up to 2050 and
provided a measure of the present discounted cost of the net liabilities. Those liabilities are shown in line 4 of Table 2 as a percent of GDP. Again, it is France,
Germany, and Japan with the largest future problems—net liabilities in excess of
current GDP—whereas the net liabilities are only 5 percent of GDP for the
United Kingdom and 25 percent for the United States.

Aging raises significant fiscal concerns for the United States; but the problem
arises later than that of other countries and it is more a problem of health care,
not social security. Recently, the Congressional Budget Office (CBO) compiled
estimates of the long-term cost of maintaining the existing structure of federal

programs.[1] Those projections are summarized in Table 3. If policies are unchanged, outlays on programs directed toward the elderly are projected to rise
from 8 percent of GDP in 1995 to 15 percent in 2025 and 17 percent in 2050. In
part, these costs can be met by reduced spending in other areas, but the net increase in program outlays is about 5 percent of GDP by 2025. On the other hand,
under existing tax laws, revenues rise only in proportion to GDP. The budget
deficit, fed by the added program outlays and by rapidly increasing debt costs,
could reach 9 percent of GDP by 2025, a level likely to exceed private saving.
Those policies are unsustainable because with no net investment, the economy
would begin to shrink and standards of living decline.

Table 3 —   Projected Federal Budget Outlays and Revenues, 1960–2050
(percent of GDP)

	1960	1980	1995	2010	2025	2050
Program outlays	15.7	20.5	19.5	20.0	24.0	26.0
Social security (OASDI)	2.2	4.3	4.5	5.0	6.0	6.0
Medicare	0.0	1.3	2.5	4.0	7.0	8.0
Medicaid	0.0	0.5	1.3	2.0	2.0	3.0
Consumption programs	9.7	7.7	6.3	5.0	5.0	5.0
Other programs	3.8	6.6	4.9	4.0	4.0	4.0
Interest	1.3	1.9	3.2	3.0	5.0	12.0
Total outlays	17.0	22.4	22.6	23.0	29.0	38.0
Receipts	18.4	20.2	20.4	20.0	20.0	20.0
Budget balance	1.4	-2.2	-2.2	-3.0	-9.0	-18.0

Source: *Survey of Current Business*, various issues, and CBO (1997b).

Public pensions are, however, only a small part of the problem. In the CBO
projections, benefit payments will rise by about one percent of GDP over the
next quarter century, and by two percentage points over the next 75 years.[2] On
the other hand, Medicare outlays for the aged will surpass those of Social Security by 2020, and the financing deficit will be three times that of Social Security
in both 2025 and 2050 (Social Security Administration 1997). Social Security

---

[1]   The latest analysis is provided in CBO (1997b).

[2]   There is a larger financial deficit in the trust fund because of an erosion of the tax
base—a decline in the ratio of taxable wages to GDP due to continued growth in the
nontaxed portions of labor compensation, contributions to private pension and health
insurance plans.

and Medicare have very similar beneficiary populations. But, whereas the annual benefit of Social Security will be cut back relative to the average wage by about 10 percent by 2025, Medicare costs per beneficiary are projected to exceed the rate of wage growth by 2020 and parallel it thereafter.[3] One of the peculiarities of the U.S. policy debate is that most of the discussion of reform focuses on the retirement income programs, whereas most of the added fiscal burden is associated with providing medical care for the aged.

Finally, we should note that, while the aging high-income economies account for three-quarters of the world's income, they represent only 15 percent of the world's population. The rest of the world will have quite different demographic trends. As shown in Table 1, the population of working age will continue to grow rapidly in the rest of the world; and, given the very low initial levels of capital per worker, there is a very large potential demand for capital in that region. Even though the developing portions of the world will also be faced with a rising aged dependency rate, it lags behind that of the high-income countries by more than half a century.

a.   The Option of Advanced Funding

To restore long-term solvency to public programs for the aged, policy-makers confront a choice between four basic reform alternatives. Three—cutting benefits, increasing contributions, or lifting the age of retirement—can be implemented within the present pay-as-you-go framework. Proposals to address the financing problem through benefit cuts and tax increases are inherently divisive, however, because they force generations and income classes to vie over who will have to make the larger sacrifice. At the same time, they do little to change the fundamental problem, since the number of elderly and their needs remain the same.

It is possible to mitigate these divisions by increasing the emphasis on a fourth alternative that moves away from pay-as-you-go financing toward advance funding of retirement obligations. This move can occur either within the current public system or in privately owned and managed pension funds. In effect, the current generation is asked to increase its saving to finance more of its own retirement. Larger accumulations in retirement systems over the coming decades would raise the nation's capital stock and national output. In the next century, the nation would be spending more on pension programs, but paying for it

---

[3]   The decline in the Old-Age and Survivors Disability Insurance (OASDI) benefit rate is largely due to the scheduled increase in the normal retirement age from 65 to 67. In contrast, the projected slowing of medical care costs is only an assumption.

out of a larger economic pie, leaving more for the consumption of future workers.

The current pay-as-you-go system of financing public pensions does not increase national saving. In all the national systems under discussion here, payroll taxes from today's workers go almost entirely to pay for pensions for today's retirees. During the 1950s and 1960s, pay-as-you-go financing looked like a good idea. The labor force was growing briskly, and real wages were climbing 2–5 percent a year. The return on contributions once the system was mature was expected to be 4–7 percent a year, far more than ordinary workers could earn on their own savings.

Declining labor force growth and the dramatic slowdown in labor productivity growth have eliminated those advantages of a pay-as-you-go system. The rate of return has fallen below 2 percent a year in most countries and may soon become negative. Private investment alternatives offer workers and pension fund managers real returns exceeding 3 percent a year. In view of the difference in expected rates of return, many of today's workers and young voters would choose prefunded retirement accounts over a pay-as-you-go system.

Unfortunately, the pay-as-you-go system has inescapable consequences. Governments have accumulated huge pension liabilities to retirees and older workers. Democracies are unlikely to default on these obligations. Over the next several decades, current and future workers will pay for the promised pensions, regardless of whether governments adopt new advance-funded systems. The double burden of paying off those obligations *and* saving in advance for their own retirement makes it costly for younger workers to move cleanly from pay-as-you-go financing to advance funding.

Nonetheless, it is reasonable to evaluate variations in the mix of financing at the margin without going so far as to eliminate the existing pay-as-you-go system. Today's workers could increase the portion of retirement income they expect to derive from capital income and reduce the portion coming from payroll contributions of future workers. Governments could move toward partial funding of future retirement obligations either by modifying current public systems or by converting them fully or partially to private systems. In either case the central question is whether the increment to funding would really add to national saving and capital formation and boost future national income or whether it would be offset by reduced public or private saving elsewhere.

Advanced funding is simplest to accomplish within existing public programs because it would leave accrued benefit claims intact. Increased contribution rates or reduced benefits (or both) would create a reserve, which should be strictly separated from other government accounts. The reserve would then be invested in either public or private securities. From the point of view of economy-wide gains, it matters little whether public or private securities are chosen. If the public pension fund purchased government debt, more private saving would go to finance private investment; if the public fund invested in private debt or equities, private savers would be forced to purchase more government debt.

Public management of a huge retirement fund, however, raises thorny political issues. Politics might skew investment decisions. Even worse, public officials might use reserve accumulations to offset deficits in other government accounts.

Private retirement accounts can reduce these political risks. In addition, they offer workers flexibility in managing their own retirement savings. Partial privatization, as in the two-tier system adopted by Chile in the early 1980s, is a possibility. A first-tier public program could provide a flat benefit or one related to the number of years of participation; the second-tier program could support a private defined contribution pension program, with individual accounts invested in a range of capital market assets by the individual contributors.

But privatization, too, carries risks. Explicitly separating out the redistributional component could create strong pressure to reduce or eliminate it. A two-tier partially privatized system may not provide adequate income security for retirees with low lifetime earnings. Workers may make bad investment decisions. Converting individual accounts into annuities when workers retire or become disabled presents a huge challenge. Solving this and other problems entails high administrative costs that may eat into the returns of small accounts.

Furthermore, just as saving within a public fund may be offset by increased spending on other programs, the buildup of savings within mandatory individual private accounts might be offset by reduced saving in other forms. Employers in particular, may find it attractive to phase out their own retirement plans. The extent to which households offset pension wealth with reductions in other wealth has been a frequent subject of past research. In simple theories of saving, the offset should be complete except for those who face binding borrowing constraints. A recent study reviewed the past research and, employing an improved estimation technique, provided a new set of estimates for the United States (see Gale 1997). The author concluded that the offset was generally quite large, but marked by wide variation between different socioeconomic groups.

The effect of privatization on saving is highly dependent on workers' valuation of the existing public benefit. If they are fully aware of the magnitude of the future benefit, and incorporate it into their retirement plans, the transfer from an unfunded public plan to a funded private plan should represent a net addition to national saving. On the other hand, if, as is sometimes argued, they have already discounted the likelihood of receiving the future benefit, the switch to a funded private plan is more likely to lead offsetting reductions in other private saving.[4]

---

4   For some proposals, the situation is even worse, as the proponents suggest a simple diversion of payroll taxes into private funds. The result is a possible increase in private saving at the cost of a certain increase in public dissaving. Workers earn a better

b.   Saving and Growth

At the level of the aggregate economy, the question of how societies ought to respond to an aging of their populations is a surprisingly controversial issue. In part, that is because there is no consensus about the future trend of saving in the absence of any policy action. The life-cycle model postulates a hump-shaped profile of saving over the life cycle in which workers save during their work life and dissave during their retirement. Several studies have used that framework to conclude that an increase in the proportion of aged dissavers in the population of the industrial countries will reduce the aggregate future saving rate.[5]

There is, however, a substantial body of evidence suggesting that the life-cycle model is an inadequate and partial representation of the influence of demographics on saving. First, the model does not accord well with past trends in aggregate saving where survey data suggest that most of the change in saving has been the result of changes within age cohorts rather than reflective of the changed proportions of workers and retirees.[6] In addition, a large number of American workers enter retirement without any significant savings, and many of those who do accumulate assets continue to add to them in retirement. For the United States, the movement of the baby-boom generation into the age brackets with high saving should have had a substantial positive effect on private saving over the past decade that is not evident in the published data. Nor has the saving of workers gone up in step with the dramatic lengthening of planned retirement periods.

Moreover, as emphasized by Tobin (1967), the life-cycle model with forward-looking expectations would lead to an inverse correlation between rates of saving and rates of income growth as individuals postpone the sacrifice of reduced consumption to a future period of higher income. Yet, we observe a persistent positive association between rates of saving and long-term rates of income growth, and the slowing of aggregate income growth in the OECD economies over the past quarter century has been associated with a significant decline in rates of private saving.

Furthermore, it is important to view the issue within a general equilibrium context that takes account of the demand for saving as well as its supply. Within all of the major industrial economies, the future will be marked by large and per-

---

return only because it is assumed that they can borrow at the low government rate and invest in higher yielding equity instruments.

5   Examples are provided in Auerbach et al. (1989, 1990) and Heller (1989).

6   Bosworth et al. (1991), Bosworth (1993), and Attanasio (1994). Horioka (1992) does find a strong time-series correlation between the decline in the Japanese saving rate and population aging, but the microeconomic survey data suggest it is not due to a shift in the proportion of workers versus retirees.

sistent declines in the rate of labor force growth. That slowdown, unless it is off-set by an increase in the rate of labor-augmenting technical change, will translate into a sharply reduced rate of output growth and thus the demand for new capital. For example, in the long-term projections of the CBO, discussed above, the annual growth of the U.S. labor force slows by a full percentage point by 2025. Under conditions of balanced growth, the warranted investment rate would drop by an amount equal to the slowing of output growth times the capital-output ratio. The ratio of reproducible business capital to GDP is about unity, and with the inclusion of residential investments the capital-output ratio to about 2. Thus, we might anticipate that as much as 40 percent (2 percent of GDP) of the increased U.S. budget costs could be met out of reduced domestic investment requirements.

To a large extent, these forces are already evident in the saving-investment balance for the OECD countries. As shown in Figure 1, saving and investment averaged a relatively steady 15 percent of domestic output during the 1960s; there is even some evidence of an upward trend until 1973, the year of the first oil crisis and a subsequent worldwide recession. Both saving and investment fell precipitously in the 1974/75 recession; but even more notable is the lack of a complete recovery in the expansion that followed. Rates of saving and investment declined again in the 1980s; and both have been below 10 percent of income in recent years. The declines in saving and investment are widespread across all of the OECD countries, and for saving at the level of the nation, the private sector, and households.

Relative to theory, it is the falloff in saving, not investment, that is the surprise. The decline in investment rates is very much in line with the general slowing of economic growth since 1973 and a roughly unchanged capital-output ratio. It can be related to slower rates of growth in the labor force and total factor productivity. It is more difficult to account for the decline in saving, since modern forward-looking variants of the life-cycle model would anticipate a rise in response to what must by now be an expected fall in the rate of income growth. That is, a negative productivity shock should lower the investment rate, but raise the saving rate.[7]

It might be possible to argue that international capital mobility is limited and that saving has been forced down by the need to maintain a balance with domestic investment requirements. However, it is difficult to reconcile that argument with the general increase in real rates of interest since the 1970s. If the problem

---

[7]   Various growth accounting studies have decomposed the growth in output into the contributions of capital and labor and improvements in total factor productivity. From those studies it is evident that the largest portion of the decline in output can be attributed to a slower rate of gain in total factor productivity. See OECD (1997:A68).

were a surplus of saving, rates of interest should have fallen and the OECD region as a whole should have moved toward current account surplus, rather than the observed deficit.

Figure 1 —   Savings and Investment in the OECD, 1960–1995 (percentage of net domestic product)

Source: OECD, *National Accounts*.

Despite the difficulties of explaining past patterns of saving, it is useful to examine the question of what would be desirable for the future. From one perspective, it seems reasonable to argue that a cohort of individuals who expect to live longer in retirement should increase their saving during their work life in anticipation of the greater retirement needs, avoiding an increase in the burden on future generations of workers. That is the view adopted in an earlier study in which we focused on the consequence of accumulating a substantial reserve within the Social Security fund (Aaron et al. 1989).

On the other hand, the sharp slowing of future growth in the workforce implies a reduced demand for capital in the future, and a decline in the rate of investment required to achieve any given capital-output ratio. As long as saving and investment are linked, the projected aging of the population gives society a near-term consumption dividend. That is the perspective adopted by Cutler et al.

in their analysis of the relationship between increased dependency and the optimal rate of saving (Cutler et al. 1990). Efforts to accumulate capital at a rate greater than that dictated by growth in the labor force and labor-augmenting technical change must translate into a continually falling rate of return to capital. Furthermore, with positive gains in total factor productivity, future workers will have much higher levels of income. In models in which the utilities of different generations are linked and the consumption needs of future generations are discounted, it is rational to tax the higher-income future generations more than the current generation. Hence the optimal rate of saving should decline in response to an aging of the population.

It can be argued that the effects of a slowing of labor force growth could be counterbalanced by some offsetting improvements in total factor productivity (TFP)—a workforce with fewer new entrants is a more experienced workforce. Cutler et al. report some evidence in support of that view, and it is incorporated in the CBO projections discussed in the prior section (Cutler et al. 1990:39–45).

Alternatively, some of the models developed as part of the new endogenous growth theory literature suggest that increases in capital formation can induce a more rapid rate of technological innovation. The empirical evidence in support of such models is very limited, however. In fact, in a recent growth accounting study for 88 developed and developing countries over the period of 1960 to 1994, changes in TFP and capital accumulation were found to be largely orthogonal (Collins and Bosworth 1996). It seems reasonable to believe that those projects with large advances in technology have very high returns and are among the first to be undertaken. Thus, TFP growth would not be associated with variations in investment at the margin.

On the other side, recent technological innovations—particularly in the area of electronics—have led to a dramatic decline in the relative price of capital goods. In the United States the price of capital goods has fallen at an annual rate of 1.5 percent relative to that of consumption over the past decade. A continuation of that trend would dramatically reduce future investment needs measured in terms of foregone consumption.

The general equilibrium perspective of Cutler et al. is most useful in pointing out that a policy of increased saving may not be an effective response to population aging because it is occurring against a backdrop of declining investment opportunities. However, their model makes use of a social planner who treats the utility of different generations as fungible in a fashion that is similar to that of an infinitely lived consumer. The notion that the consumption of differing generations is fully interchangeable may not be the most appropriate for public policy. An alternative model would adopt more of a perspective of self-sufficiency in which individuals are motivated not to increase the burden on future generations, either because they fear that younger generations will not pay or because of a genuine concern for the welfare of those future generations. Thus, reduced labor force growth may drive down the return to capital without implying a decline in the saving of the current generation.

3. Simulation Analysis

We can illustrate some of these issues with a small simulation growth model of the U.S. economy that we constructed to explore some of the options for reform of the U.S. public pension and health care systems. The model is calibrated to match the economic and demographic assumptions that underlie the government's long-run projections for Social Security and Medicare.[8] It incorporates a Cobb–Douglas production function for the nonfarm business sector of the economy with a capital income share of about 28 percent. Rates of net saving in the public and private sectors can be controlled exogenously, and investment is disaggregated between housing, inventories, short-lived computer equipment, and other fixed business capital. We have assumed a baseline case in which the growth of the business capital stock parallels that of output, maintaining a constant rate of return to capital. That results in a domestic rate of net investment that declines slightly in real terms as labor force growth slows.[9] The net national saving rate is 5 percent of net national product (NNP) in 1995 and it drifts down in the baseline to about 3 percent in 2020 and thereafter.

4. Higher Saving, Invested Domestically

In the simulation summarized in Table 4, net saving is raised by one percent of NNP in the year 2000 and held at that rate for 50 years.[10] At the margin, most of the added saving flows into the business sector, where the supply of capital services expands by nearly one percent per year. We assumed that the relative price of capital goods would continue to decline in the future, but at a diminish-

---

8   The structure of the model is very similar to the version discussed in Aaron et al. (1989).

9   The gross investment rate is affected by additional factors, rising in real terms as the mix of investment shifts toward shorter-lived assets, and falling in nominal terms as the relative price of investment goods continues to decline.

10   The effects of an increase in the net saving rate need to be sharply distinguished from those associated with an increase in the gross saving rate. In the latter case, the increment to the capital stock is gradually replaced by an increase in depreciation allowances, and the impact on the capital stock and output recedes toward zero.

ing rate.[11] As a result, saving, measured in foregone consumption, yields a bonus in increased real capital. Thus, by 2025, capital services are 25 percent higher than in the baseline. The gain to NNP is 2.9 percent after 25 years and 5.2 percent after 50. Consumption is reduced for the first 10 years by the need to finance the increased investment, but it is raised by 1.5 percent in 2025. The implication is that the national saving rate would have to be raised today and each year in the future by 2–3 percentage points to raise the resources available for consumption by an amount equal to the added fiscal costs imposed by the aging population by 2025.

Table 4 — Economic Effects of a Permanent Rise in the U.S. Saving Rate, Invested Domestically (percent change from baseline)

Year	Wealth	Capital services	GDP	NNP	Consumption	Rate of return	Wage rate
2000	1.0	0.9	-0.1	-0.1	-1.3	-0.4	0.0
2010	9.8	10.9	1.9	1.1	-0.2	-8.5	2.7
2020	18.2	20.6	3.8	2.4	1.0	-15.7	5.1
2025	22.5	25.5	4.8	2.9	1.5	-19.1	6.3
2030	26.8	30.2	5.7	3.5	2.0	-22.3	7.4
2040	34.9	39.2	7.4	4.4	2.8	-28.3	9.4
2050	43.1	48.1	9.0	5.2	3.5	-34.0	11.3

Note: Net saving rate raised by one percent of NNP beginning in 2000. All values are measured in constant prices.

The more striking feature is the sharp fall in the rate of return to capital, one-fifth after 25 years and one-third after 50 years. That decline follows directly from the large rise in the capital-output ratio, since the return to capital is equal to capital's share in income times the capital-output ratio. It implies a very large redistribution of income from old capital to labor: the real wage rate is increased by 6 percent in 2025 and 11 percent in 2050. Thus, in addition to the gains in aggregate output, a policy of raising national saving and domestic investment would be good for future workers.

Very little is known about how much such a decline would be reflected in the returns to different types of financial assets. It is surprisingly difficult to observe a correlation between the returns on real and financial assets, despite the fact that

---

11   The relative prices of individual components are constant after 2020, but the overall price of capital continues to fall at about 0.1 percent per year because of a shift toward lower-cost capital, computers.

they are opposite sides of the same coin.[12] Over long periods of time, the return on physical capital should be highly correlated with the returns to bonds and equities, but a substantial portion of the return to physical capital is retained and reinvested and the market returns on financial assets are dominated by fluctuations in their capital values. We have simply assumed that financial market rates move proportionately with a smoothed measure of the return on real assets.

5.   The External Investment Option

Concern with the consequences of diminishing returns to capital has led to the suggestion that in an increasingly open global economy some of the increased saving would flow abroad, moderating the decline in the rate of return. In fact, Cutler et al. (1990) explored some of these issues by incorporating the rest of the OECD into a two-country model. Since the falloff in future labor force growth and capital needs are even more pronounced in the other countries, the extension reinforced the arguments in favor of reduced U.S. saving. In the near term, consumption rises in the United States as the rest of the OECD takes advantage of the investment opportunities in the United States as an offset to the greater fall in their own.

That analysis did leave out a major portion of the world economy. As shown in Table 1, the labor force in the remaining portions of the global economy accounts for 80 percent of the total and will continue to grow rapidly for several more decades. Using purchasing power parity exchange rates, they represent 40 percent of global output. With their low capital-labor ratios, these economies also have a latent capacity to absorb large volumes of capital. Furthermore, they have been growing at an average rate twice that of the industrial countries. Thus, the considerations that limit the attractiveness of large net capital flows within the OECD may not apply.[13]

Aggregate resource flows to developing countries have nearly tripled in the last 6 years (Table 5). While official assistance has leveled off and even declined, private capital flows have grown from $45 billion in 1990 to $245 in 1996. Most of that increase has been in direct investment and purchases of marketable financial instruments: commercial bank lending, which was so dominant

---

[12]   One example of the effort to discern such a relationship is give by Howe and Pigott (1992).

[13]   However, in a commercial context these countries are still small. They represent only about 20 percent of global production using commercial exchange rates, and an even smaller portion of world financial markets. Thus, there are significant limits on their ability to absorb large amounts of capital in the near term without encountering the same sharp decline in the rate of return.

prior to the 1981 debt crisis, has played a much smaller role. In addition, the re-
payments, interest and profit repatriation, have grown more slowly, leaving an
even faster growth of the net resource transfer.

Table 5 —   Net Resource Flows to Developing Countries, 1980–1996 (billions
of dollars)

	1980	1990	1991	1992	1993	1994	1995	1996
Total resource flow	86.1	100.6	122.5	146.0	212.0	207.0	237.2	284.6
Official development finance	34.3	56.3	65.6	55.4	55.0	45.7	53.0	40.9
Total private flows	51.7	44.4	56.9	90.6	157.1	161.3	184.2	243.8
Foreign direct investment	5.1	24.5	33.5	43.6	67.2	83.7	95.5	109.5
Portfolio equity flows	0	3.2	7.2	11.0	45.0	32.7	32.1	45.7
Debt flows	46.6	16.6	16.2	35.9	44.9	44.9	56.6	88.6
Commercial banks	30.8	3.0	2.8	12.5	-0.3	11.0	26.5	34.2
Bonds	2.6	2.3	10.1	9.9	35.9	29.3	28.5	46.1
Others	13.2	11.3	3.3	13.5	9.2	4.6	1.7	8.3
Interest and profits	56.7	73.4	74.1	75.6	75.6	84.3	100.9	109.0
Net resource transfer	29.4	27.2	48.4	70.4	136.4	122.7	136.3	175.6

Source: World Bank (1997a).

At present, American investments in the rest of the world total about $2 tril-
lion at current, or replacement, cost, compared with foreign investments in the
United States of about $4 trillion. Rates of return on those investments, com-
pared with the rate of return in the nonfinancial corporate sector, are shown in
Figure 2. Over the 1991–1995 period, U.S. investors earned an average of 10
percent on overseas assets compared with a 7 percent return on domestic corporate capital. Foreign investors earned 6 percent in the United States. Those
measures of the return on foreign assets may represent an overstatement because
there is a large statistical discrepancy between the flow and stock data. It appears
that U.S. investors have suffered significant capital losses on their investments,
due to exchange rates and other factors, that would not be recorded in the national accounts' concept of income earned from production.[14]

---

[14]   This is evident if we deflate the annual flows to adjust for general inflation and cu-
mulate the resulting flows. The estimate of the stock obtained on that basis is significantly larger than the real value of the reported stocks.

Figure 2 — Rates of Return on Domestic and Foreign Investments, 1961–1995

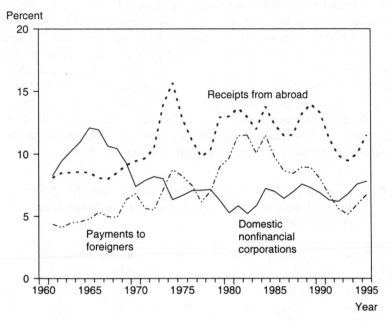

Note: Assets are measured at current replacement cost. Income is before payment of U.S. taxes.

Source: Board of Governors (1995).

We can use the model to provide a very simple and extreme example of the implications of investing the additional national saving abroad. The before-tax return on foreign investments is assumed equal to that in the baseline for domestic nonfarm business: the foreign investment is not subject to diminishing returns. But, the foreign tax on capital income, which is assumed equal to 25 percent, reduces the return that flows back to the United States. In addition, when the financial capital initially moves out of the United States, it will need to be financed by increased net exports of goods and services, something that would normally be expected to require some reduction in the relative price of American products. In subsequent periods, the exchange rate would appreciate as the capital inflow of earnings on the investments comes to equal and then exceed the capital outflow. We simulate this process in a simple way by assuming that a change in the trade balance equal to one percent of GDP would require a 5 percent appreciation of the currency, and allow the real exchange rate to change in line with net capital flows (investment minus earnings).[15]

The basic results are reported in Table 6. The overall gain in national wealth is very similar to that reported for the case of domestic investment.[16] There is, however, essentially no increase in GDP as the gains accrue in the form of capital income earned from the rest of the world. The resulting increases in NNP and consumption are slightly smaller, but with a similar pattern over time. The largest difference is in the distribution of the income gains. Since there in no increase in the domestic capital stock, wage rates change only as a result of terms-of-trade gains and losses associated with exchange rate changes. All of the income gains are received in the form of capital income from abroad.

Table 6 — Economic Effects of a Permanent Rise in the U.S. Saving Rate, Invested Abroad, Assuming a Variable Exchange Rate (percent change from baseline)

Year	Wealth	Capital services	GDP	NNP	Consump-tion	Rate of return	Wage rate
2000	0.8	–0.0	–0.1	–0.1	–1.7	–4.5	–0.5
2010	8.8	0.0	–0.0	0.8	–0.4	–1.0	–0.1
2020	16.4	–0.0	0.2	1.7	0.7	1.8	0.2
2025	20.3	–0.0	0.2	2.1	1.3	3.2	0.3
2030	24.0	–0.0	0.3	2.5	1.8	4.4	0.4
2040	31.3	–0.0	0.5	3.4	2.9	6.8	0.7
2050	38.7	–0.0	0.7	4.2	3.9	9.1	0.9

Note: Net saving rate raised by one percent of NNP beginning in 2000. All values are measured in constant prices.

Exchange rate variability has only a modest effect on aggregate output because, although the change in the exchange rate alters the value of the investment funds when they go out, the effect is reversed when they return. Investors lose in this simple model only to the extent that the exchange rate appreciates

---

[15] This implies a slightly higher degree of substitution between U.S. and foreign goods than was evident in the experience with large exchange rate swings in the 1980s.

[16] The two simulations are not precisely equivalent because, while we have equated the return on foreign investment with that of the nonfarm business sector, the domestic simulation has a more complex pattern of allocating capital among different assets, and the output of other sectors is related to changes in GDP, not GNP.

over time, which it does.[17] However, there are more significant implications for consumers. As the United States becomes a creditor nation, the surplus on capital account is offset by a growing net trade inflow. Since the United States is exporting less and less, its products become relatively scarce on world markets, driving up their price. That is, the appreciation of the real exchange rate, which totals about 3 percent in 2025 and 9 percent in 2025, implies a significant terms-of-trade gain for American consumers. Using current proportions of imports in consumption, consumption prices might decline by about one-tenth of the relative reduction in import prices. Thus, American consumers experience a gain from the change in the terms of trade of about 0.3 percent in 2025. This suggests that changes in exchange rates and the terms of trade are likely to be a significant element in any evaluation of the net benefits of an increase in national saving.

6.   Conclusion

An increase in national saving is an effective option for reducing the burden of population aging on future generations of workers. For the United States, increases in the net national saving rate in the order of two percent of national income, would provide additional resources that would finance most of the net public sector costs of an aging population. Much of the debate over this issue takes place within the context of proposals to privatize the public pension system. However, from an economic perspective, the crucial issue is the extent to which societies increase saving today—a partial funding of future retirement costs. That goal could be achieved with either public or privately managed funds.

Efforts to expand domestic capital formation in the face of a falling rate of growth in the labor force will, however, involve large declines in the return to capital and substantial redistributions of aggregate income between capital and labor income. The projected slowing of future labor force growth in the high-income economies is a significantly limiting factor in calculating the gains of increased saving in a closed economy.

Investing in a broader global economy provides a partial solution to the problem of falling rates of return; but our results probably overstate the gains. It is likely that returns of such investments would be subject to the same diminishing returns that plagued the effort to raise domestic saving. To the extent that is true, the induced redistribution is between capital and foreign workers. Thus,

---

[17]   In this simple illustrative model, there is no anticipation of future price changes by rational investors, or smoothing of the exchange rate movements.

Americans would lose as capitalists without the offsetting gains as workers. This is a particularly severe problem if other aging economies are trying to follow the same strategy.

Bibliography

Aaron, H.J., B. Bosworth, and G. Burtless (1989). *Can Americans Afford to Grow Old?* Washington, D.C.: Brookings Institution.

Attanasio, O.P. (1994). Personal Saving in the United States. In J. Poterba (ed.), *International Comparisons of Household Saving*. Chicago: University of Chicago Press.

Auerbach, A.J., L.J. Kotlikoff, R.P. Hagemann, and G. Nicaletti (1989). The Economic Dynamics of an Aging Population: The Case of Four OECD Countries. *OECD Economic Studies* 12:97–130.

Auerbach, A.J., J. Cai, and L.J. Kotlikoff (1990). U.S. Demographics and Saving: Predictions of Three Models. NBER Working Paper 3404. Cambridge, Mass.

The Board of Governors of The Federal Reserve System (1995). *Balance Sheets for the U.S. Economy, 1948–94.* C.9 release (June). Washington, D.C.: Board of Governors.

Börsch-Supan, A. (1997). The Impact of Population Aging on Saving, Investment, and Growth in the OECD Area. In OECD (ed.), *Future Global Capital Shortages: Real Threat or Pure Fiction.* Paris: OECD.

Bos, E., et al. (1994). *World Population Projections 1994–1995* Washington, D.C.: World Bank.

Bosworth, B. (1993). *Saving and Investment in a Global Economy.* Washington, D.C.: Brookings Institution.

Bosworth, B., and G. Burtless (eds.) (1998). *Aging Societies: The Global Dimension.* Washington, D.C.: Brookings Institution.

Bosworth, B., G. Burtless, and J. Sabelhaus (1991). The Decline in Saving: Evidence From Household Surveys. *Brookings Papers on Economic Activity* (1):183–241.

CBO (Congressional Budget Office) (1997a). *The Economic and Budget Outlook: Fiscal Years 1998–2007.* Washington, D.C.: Superintendent of Documents.

—— (1997b). *Long-term Budgetary Pressures and Policy Options.* Washington, D.C.: Superintendent of Documents.

Chand, S., and A. Jaeger (1997). Aging Populations and Public Pension Schemes. Occasional Paper 147. Washington, D.C.: International Monetary Fund.

Collins, S.M., and B. Bosworth (1996). Economic Growth in East Asia: Accumulation Versus Assimilation. *Brookings Papers on Economic Activity* (2):135–191.

Cutler, D.M., J.M. Poterba, L.M. Sheiner, and L. Summers (1990). An Aging Society: Opportunity or Challenge. *Brookings Papers on Economic Activity* (1):1–73.

Feldstein, M. (1976). The Social Security Fund and National Capital Accumulation. In *Funding Pensions: Issues and Implications for Financial Markets*. Conference Series 16. Boston: Federal Reserve Bank of Boston.

Feldstein, M., and C. Horioka (1980). Domestic Saving and International Capital Flows. *Economic Journal* 90:314–329.

Franco, D., and T. Munzi (1996). Public Pension Expenditure Prospects in European Union: A Survey of National Projections. In European Commission (ed.), *European Economy: Ageing and Pension Expenditures Prospects in the Western World*. Reports and Studies 3/1996. Luxembourg: Office for Official Publications of the European Communities.

Frankel, J. (1992). Measuring International Capital Mobility: A Review. *American Economic Review, Papers and Proceedings* 82(2):197–202.

Gale, W. (1997). The Effects of Pensions on Household Wealth: A Re-Evaluation of Theory and Evidence. Discussion Paper. Washington, D.C.: Brookings Institution.

Heller, P. (1989). *Aging, Saving and the Sustainability of the Fiscal Burden in the G-7 Countries: 1980–2025*. Washington, D.C.: International Monetary Fund.

Horioka, C. (1992). Future Trends in Japan's Saving Rate and the Implications Thereof for Japan's External Balance. *Japan and the World Economy* 3:307–330.

Howe, H., and C. Pigott (1992). Determinants of Long-Term Interest Rates: An Empirical Study of Several Industrial Countries. *Federal Reserve Bank of New York Quarterly Review* 16(4):12–28.

International Monetary Fund (1997). *World Economic Outlook*. May 1997. Washington, D.C.: International Monetary Fund.

Leibfritz, W., D. Roseveare, D. Fore, and E. Wurzel (1996). Ageing Populations, Pension Systems and Government Budgets—How Do They Affect Saving? In OECD (ed.), *Future Global Capital Shortages: Real Threat or Pure Fiction?* Paris: OECD.

OECD (Organization for Economic Cooperation and Development) (1988). *Aging Populations: The Social Policy Implications*. Paris: OECD.

—— (1996). *OECD Economic Outlook*. June. Paris: OECD.

—— (1997). *Future Global Capital Shortages: Real Threat or Pure Fiction*. Paris: OECD.

Roseveare, D., W. Leibfritz, D. Fore, and E. Wurzel (1996). Ageing Populations, Pension Systems and Government Budgets: Simulations for 20 OECD Countries. Economics Department Working Paper 168. OECD, Paris.

Social Security Administration (1997). *The 1996 Annual Report of The Board of Trustees, Federal Old-Age and Survivors Insurance and Disability Insurance Trust Fund*. Washington, D.C.: Government Printing Office.

Takayama, N. (1996). Possible Effects of Ageing on the Equilibrium of the Public Pension System in Japan. In European Commission (ed.), *European Economy: Ageing and Pension Expenditures Prospects in the Western World.* Reports and Studies 3/1996. Luxembourg: Office for Official Publications of the European Communities.

Tobin, J. (1967). Life Cycle Saving and Balanced Growth. In *Ten Economic Studies in the Tradition of Irving Fisher.* New York: John Wiley and Sons.

United Nations (1994). *The Sex and Age Distribution of the World Populations.* New York: United Nations.

World Bank (1997a). *Global Development Finance.* Washington, D.C.: World Bank.

—— (1997b). *Private Capital Flows to Developing Countries: The Road to Financial Integration.* Oxford: Oxford University Press.

Comment on Barry Bosworth and Gary Burtless

Manfred Neumann

A change from pay-as-you-go financing of social security to a funded system may yield an increase in capital formation. If it does, it is a welcome option to reduce the burden entailed by the aging of population. That is the first proposition of the paper by Barry Bosworth and Gary Burtless. As demonstrated by a simulation analysis, they continue to show that an increase in capital formation in the face of a falling rate of growth of the labor force will involve a large decline in the return to capital and a substantial redistribution of income between capital and labor. These conclusions depend crucially on the role attributed to the variables involved. In the simulation analysis the authors assume the savings ratio to be exogenous. The same apparently applies to technical change.

In contrast, for me the appropriate strategy to elucidate the consequences of both a slowing down of population growth (or even a decline in population) and financing social security seems to be assuming these two factors to be exogenous, whereas all the rest, in particular saving, technical change, and income distribution, come about endogenously. I thus prefer to use a model in which both savings and technical change are endogenous, i.e., are determined by the maximizing behavior of households and firms. The exogenous variables to be specifically considered are population growth and the method of financing old-age pensions. Using such a model with endogenous technical change yields much more favorable prospects. However, before embarking on such an exercise, I would like to offer two preliminary observations which appeal to economic common sense.

First, for the sake of the argument, let us take it for granted that a change to a funded system will yield an increase in savings. Contrary to the assumption of Bosworth and Burtless, the additional savings will not only be devoted to raising the level of physical capital per head. They will also be used to increase expenditures for R&D and education such that the rate of technical change goes up. Insofar as technical change is labor-augmenting, it will offset the law of diminishing returns to physical capital. Hence the dismal prospects concerning the returns to capital calculated by Bosworth and Burtless appear far too pessimistic.

Second, it may be argued that a change to a funded system does not yield a net increase in savings, since additional savings arising within such a system just offset private savings which would come about anyway. In contrast to this line of reasoning, I would prefer to join Bosworth and Burtless in assuming that total savings increase. In fact, savings of private households in Germany, which at the present time are about 11 percent of disposable income, account for no more than about a third of gross investment, the rest being financed by internal savings of firms. Moreover, the distribution of ownership in business firms is highly skewed in favor of wealthy persons and the bulk of private saving is done by high-income earners. Employees, on average, are likely to save considerably less than 11 percent of their disposable income. It is thus hardly conceivable that an increase in savings of employees which might follow upon a transition to a funded system would completely be offset by a decline in savings of more wealthy individuals. Hence a change to a funded system is in fact likely to give rise to a net increase in national savings.

To be more precise let us consider a model in which both savings and technical change are endogenous. We shall proceed stepwise and at first disregard technical change.

We may start from the obvious fact that mandatory contributions of employees and firms to a pay-as-you-go system are, at least to some extent, taxes on income regardless of whether people consider them as such or not. In fact, many people entertain the notion that they have been paying during their working life to build up wealth which in the future will be available to cover old-age pensions. Under a pay-as-you-go system, however, they have only acquired claims to be honored by the government by levying taxes on future generations. Political advocates of the present system of pay-as-you-go financing in Germany usually refer to the system as embodying a contract between generations. This should be taken as a piece of political salesmanship. Stripped down to the economic facts, it remains true that within a certain period of time the proceeds from taxing active people are used to pay for retirees' consumption. Actually, the pay-as-you-go system, as practiced in Germany, involves some redistribution, in particular insofar as it provides pensions for widows and orphans and favors early retirement. Moreover, at the present time and in the near future, working generations, because of the prospective aging of the population, are likely to receive pensions which fall short of those which are presently paid to retirees. For these reasons the system is not actuarially fair. In this respect, contributions are in fact taxes the proceeds of which are used to cover transfer payments. Moreover, since social security taxes are levied on labor income, they will distort the choice between work and leisure. Thus the outcome falls short of a Pareto optimum.[1]

---

[1]   It might be argued that, following a change to a funded system, once-acquired entitlements to pensions under the old system would have to be honored such that distortions inherent in the pay-as-you-go system were carried over into the future. This is certainly true until the pay-as-you-go system has been completely replaced by the funded system. Moreover, the excess burden entailed by distortions inherent in the old pay-as-you-go system, which is going to be replaced, would fall short of the burden to be borne if the old system were perpetuated into the indefinite future.

With regard to modeling the impact of taxes on capital formation, I prefer the framework of an eternal family, since it, more easily than a life-cycle model, accounts for covering the transfer of wealth from one generation to the next one. In this framework, a representative member of the work force is assumed to maximize utility from the present to an indefinite future, i.e.,

[1] $$\int_0^\infty Lu(c)e^{-\rho t}dt,$$

where L denotes the size of the work force, c is consumption per head, ρ is the rate of pure time preference, and $u(c) = c^{1-\varepsilon} / (1 - \varepsilon)$ is utility of consumption per head subject to diminishing marginal utility, ε being a constant elasticity. As a matter of simplification, only working people are assumed to save, whereas the income of retirees is completely spent for consumption.

To cover the expenditures for supporting the retirees, the government may either levy a tax on total income or on labor income. In the first case, tax proceeds per employee are $\tau f(k)$, which gives rise to capital accumulation following the equation

[2] $$\dot{k} = (1 - \tau)f(k) - c - nk,$$

where k is capital per head and c is consumption per head of members of the work force, n being the constant growth rate of the labor force.

Insofar as the so-called *Bundeszuschuß* is concerned, which is a subsidy of the federal government to the social security system, social security in fact gives rise to some taxation of income. In addition, as far as inefficiency arises because of distortions concerning the choice between labor and leisure, the shortfall of actual income from its potential level which would be achieved at a Pareto optimum has the same effect as a tax levied on income.

Alternatively, if taxes are levied only on labor income, capital accumulation occurs according to

[3] $$\dot{k} = kf'(k) + (1 - b)\left[f(k) - kf'(k)\right] - c - nk,$$

where all individuals are assumed to be alike and to receive both labor income $f(k) - kf'(k)$ and capital income $kf'(k)$ per head.

Still some of the contribution of workers may be considered by them as savings which do not distort the choice between labor and leisure, nor need they have a detrimental effect on total savings. However, distortionary effects on business investments do obtain as far as the pay-as-you-go system is not actuarially fair and the share of contributions to social security borne by employers are visualized by them as supplementary labor costs.

The objective function [1] is then to be maximized subject to either [2] or [3].

Solving the problem gives rise to a steady state where alternatively

$$(1-\tau)f'(k) = \rho$$

or

$$f'(k) + bkf''(k) = \rho$$

applies, the latter one being equivalent to

$$f'(k)[1 - b(1-\alpha)/\sigma] = \rho,$$

where α is the share of profits in total income and σ is the elasticity of substitution between labor and capital.

In the first case an increase in the rate of taxation obviously causes capital per head to decrease. In the second case the elasticity of substitution not exceeding unity is sufficient for an increase in the tax rate to lower capital per head. The same effect arises if σ does not exceed unity too much. These conditions are likely to be satisfied.

Thus, as a matter of simplification, we may focus on the case of a social security tax on total income. If it is abolished by introducing a funded system, capital per head increases, and the savings ratio goes up. This result may come about by either one of two alternative institutional arrangements. It may either be left to each individual to provide for his/her own time of retirement by means of private savings or such savings may be made mandatory under a system of social security run by the government. Thus, there is an offsetting relationship between private saving and mandatory saving within the system of social security.

Technical change will then be assumed to be endogenously determined. I assume the rate of purely labor-augmenting technical progress to depend on expenditures for research and development. This relationship is subject to diminishing returns. Hence, utility, as depicted by [1], has to be maximized subject to capital accumulation,

$$\dot{x} = (1-\tau)f(x) - r(a) - \tilde{c} - (n+a)x,$$

where capital $x := K / AL$, expenditures for research and development $r := R/AL$, and consumption $\tilde{c} := C / AL$ are expressed in efficiency units of labor, and a is the rate of labor-augmenting technical change,

$$\dot{A} = aA.$$

A steady-state solution of this problem is given by the set of equations

[4] $$(1-\tau)f(x) - r(a) - \tilde{c} - (n+a)x = 0$$

[5] $(1-\tau)f'(x)-\varepsilon a = \rho$

[6] $[(1-\tau)f'(x)-n-a]r'(a)+r(a)-(1-\tau)[f(x)-xf'(x)]=0.$

Equations [5] and [6] can be used to determine x^* and a^*, as graphically shown in Figure 1. Hence, both the rate of technical change and the ratio of capital per efficiency unit of labor are endogenously determined. The same applies to consumption per head and savings. Exogenous variables are the rate of taxation, τ, the growth rate of the labor force, n, and the rate of time preference.[2]

A change from pay-as-you-go financing of social security to a funded system implies a reduction of taxation. If, upon replacing the pay-as-you-go system partially or completely by a funded system, the rate of taxation is reduced, both curves shift, as shown in Figure 1. The XX' schedule depicting [5] moves to the right, and the AA' schedule depicting [6] moves down.

Figure 1 — Endogenous Technical Change Depending on Taxation

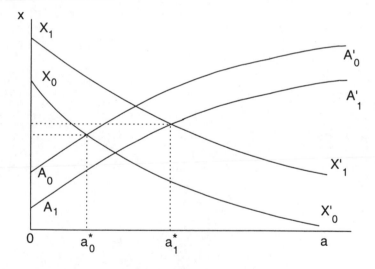

The result is an increase in the rate of technical change and consequently a higher rate of growth of income per head. This effect is unequivocal. On the other hand, the impact on capital per efficiency unit of labor, and for that matter

---

2   For the details of the model and its solution, see Neumann (1997).

on the rate of return on capital, is indeterminate. The same applies to the savings ratio (Neumann 1997:144).

In the framework of the model, as given above, the rate of technical change can be shown to decline upon a reduction in the rate of population growth. Thus, if, in the face of an expected decline in population growth, a funded system of old-age support is introduced, there are two opposing effects on technical progress. It decreases in consequence of the decline in population growth, and it is enhanced following the reduction in taxation. Likewise, the effect on the rate of return to capital and income distribution is indeterminate. Thus the dismal predictions of Bosworth and Burtless appear to be exaggerated.

Bibliography

Neumann, M. (1997). *The Rise and Fall of the Wealth of Nations*. Cheltenham: Edward Elgar.

Oliver Lorz

Social Security and Employment

1. Introduction

This paper deals with the effects of social security on the labor market. It focuses on three central issues: First, because social security contributions are usually raised as taxes on labor income, they may distort the individual substitution between labor and leisure. Social security then prevents a Pareto-optimal allocation of the factor labor. How does a social security system have to be designed to avoid these distortions? Can a nondistortionary form of financing social security also be implemented in an unfunded system? Is intragenerational redistribution still possible in a nondistortionary social security system? What are the effects of social security with respect to other dimensions of labor supply such as the retirement decision or human capital accumulation?

As the second issue, unemployment has become one of the most striking social problems in many countries. Social security may lower the incentives for an individual to participate in the labor market. This effect aggravates the unemployment problem. Can this negative employment effect of social security be avoided? What are the characteristics of an optimal social security system if both the participation decision and labor-leisure substitution are considered simultaneously?

The third issue arises from the current discussion on social security reform. Negative employment effects may increase the economic costs of the social security system. These employment effects then might be a reason for downsizing existing social security systems and for a transition to alternative forms of pension provision. What is the optimal size of social security given these economic

Remark: I am grateful to my discussant D. Peter Broer and other conference participants for their constructive comments. I have also benefited from discussions with my colleague Frank Stähler.

costs? What are the welfare effects of a transition away from unfunded social security? Under which conditions is such a transition beneficial?

This paper provides some guidance in answering these questions. In Section 2, it recapitulates the basic microeconomics of individual labor supply with social security. In a simple 2-period partial equilibrium framework, the properties of a nondistortionary social security system are derived and interpreted. Section 3 extends the basic model, introducing unemployment as an outside option for the working individual. It illustrates fundamental characteristics of an optimally designed unfunded social security system, given the constraint that no individual is unemployed. Section 4 treats the welfare effects of a transition from unfunded social security to an alternative system. Section 5 discusses some implications of social security on those dimensions of labor supply which cannot be treated adequately in the basic model. These extensions are the effects of social security on retirement, on human capital accumulation, and on unionized labor supply.

2.   Social Security and Individual Labor Supply

In a labor market equilibrium, social security can affect employment only if the supplied quantity of labor is somehow variable. The standard textbook model of individual labor supply thus seems to be a good starting point to analyze the basic relations between social security and employment.[1] According to this model, an individual can freely divide his labor endowment, L_E, between work, L, and leisure $l \equiv L_E - L$.[2] To capture the intertemporal dimension of social security, the individual is assumed to live for two periods: a working period and a retirement period. In addition to labor supply, he then also decides about savings, s. There is no uncertainty and the individual faces a constant wage and interest rate and fixed product prices. In the working period he has to pay a social security

---

[1]   Sandmo (1985) treats the effects of income taxes in this model.

[2]   Labor is modeled here as a one-dimensional variable. In the most straightforward interpretation of this variable, the individual can be thought of as deciding about total hours of work in the working period. The model, however, may also serve as an stylized characterization of other dimensions of individual labor supply, such as work effort (the wage rate then denotes the wage per efficiency unit of labor) or the choice of occupation (with a negative relationship between salary, w, and nonpecuniary benefits, l, of the respective occupation). See also Atkinson and Stiglitz (1980: 44–46).

contribution, τ, which is assumed to be a differentiable function of L. During retirement, he receives a social security benefit, b. The size of this benefit depends on the individual's social security contribution. The individual maximizes a strictly quasi-concave utility function with working period consumption, c_w, retirement consumption, c_r, and leisure, l, as arguments, subject to his budget constraint:[3]

[1] $$\max_{c_w, c_r, l} U(c_w, c_r, l), \text{ s.t. } c_w + \frac{pc_r}{1+r} = w[L_E - l] - \tau(L_E - l) + \frac{b(\tau(L_E - l))}{1+r}.$$

The first-order conditions can be written as follows:[4]

[2] $$\frac{U_2}{U_1} = \frac{p}{1+r},$$

[3] $$\frac{U_3}{U_1} = w - \tau'(L) + b'(\tau) \, \tau'(L)[1+r]^{-1}.$$

According to [3] the individual works up to the point where the marginal rate of substitution between leisure and working period consumption equals his opportunity costs of leisure, i.e., the present value of additional net labor income foregone. With a competitive labor and product market, the wage rate denotes the social opportunity costs of leisure, because it is then equal to the marginal product of labor. The private opportunity cost of leisure equals the social opportunity cost for $\lambda_m \tau'(L) = 0$, with λ_m defined as $\lambda_m \equiv 1 - b'(\tau)[1+r]^{-1}$. A social security system satisfying this property for all individuals causes no distortions on the labor market. For a given level of contributions and benefits, it ensures a Pareto-optimal quantity of labor supply (see also Breyer and Straub 1993). For $\lambda_m \tau'(L) \neq 0$, social security drives a wedge between the wage rate and the private opportunity costs of leisure. In this case, social security contributions cause an excess burden with respect to labor supply.

An excess burden of social security contributions does not necessarily imply a negative impact on labor supply. Comparable to the case of income taxation, the

---

3   The price level in the working period is set to one, so that p denotes the relative price level in the period of retirement. The terms w and r denote the nominal wage and interest rate. The function $b(\tau)$ relating benefits to contributions is also assumed to be differentiable.

4   The second-order condition is assumed to be satisfied. If the marginal burden of social security decreases with the supplied quantity of labor, a strictly quasi-concave utility function will not be sufficient for this condition (see Hausmann 1985).

uncompensated labor supply effects of social security are instead ambiguous.[5] On the one hand, a decreasing net marginal labor income causes a substitution effect which decreases the supplied quantity of labor; on the other hand, social security may cause an income effect. With contributions exceeding discounted benefits, this (normal) income effect implies lower consumption of leisure and therefore a higher supplied quantity of labor. Only the substitution effect is relevant for the excess burden, so a social security system which leaves aggregate labor supply unaffected might nonetheless be distortionary (see Fullerton 1989).

The no-distortion condition, $\lambda_m \tau'(L) = 0$, is satisfied for lump-sum contributions, since then the term $\tau'(L)$ equals zero.[6] The other term of the no-distortion condition, λ_m, denotes the discounted net effect of the marginal social security contribution on individual income. To illustrate the main determinants of λ_m, the linkage between contribution and benefit is rewritten as follows:

[4] $b(\tau) \equiv [1 + \rho] / \beta(\tau)$.

The term ρ denotes the nominal rate of return of the implicit social security asset. The function β denotes the implicit relative price of this asset. If contributions to a certain pension system were not mandatory, then β would have to adjust accordingly to equate supply of a certain social security asset with demand for this asset in equilibrium. In such an equilibrium, the effective rate of return would be equal to the market interest rate for all values of ρ and social security would be nondistortionary. With mandatory social security contributions, the function β is determined exogenously. The labor market distortion of social security then depends on both, the marginal price, $\beta'(\tau)$, of the implicit social security asset and its rate of return, ρ. The rate of return of aggregate social security contributions equals the interest rate, r, in a social security system (i) which is fully funded, (ii) where contributions are entirely used for pension provision, and (iii) which has the same access to the capital market and the same costs of allocating its capital as the individual. A system that meets conditions (i)–(iii) will not distort individual labor supply, if $\beta'(\tau) = 1$ for all individuals. Intragenerational redistribution may still be possible in such a system. For exam-

---

5   See Hausmann (1985) for a general treatment of the effects of taxes on labor supply.

6   Whereas lump-sum contributions are sufficient for a nondistortionary form of financing social security, they are not necessary—even without equivalence between the contribution and the discounted benefit at the margin. Instead, the condition $\tau'(L) = 0$ needs to hold only in the neighborhood of the undistorted L.

ple, a part of the benefits may be distributed lump-sum according to individual characteristics—such as age or gender.[7]

In contrast to a funded system, the rate of return of an unfunded system is given by the growth rate of aggregate social security contributions. This growth rate equals the growth rate of aggregate labor income as long as the relation between aggregate contributions and aggregate labor income remains constant. If the interest rate exceeds the growth rate of aggregate labor income, a social security asset will offer a lower rate of return than a private capital asset. With $\beta'(\tau) = 1$, such a social security system will decrease the relative price of leisure and thus distort individual labor supply. However, $\beta'(\tau)$ need not be set equal to one in general. In fact, as Auerbach and Kotlikoff (1987) have pointed out, for all implicit rates of return, there exists a $\beta'(\tau)$ keeping the social security system nondistortionary at the margin.[8] A simple example may help to illustrate this point.[9] In this example, social security is completely unfunded and the contribution and the benefit of individual, i $(i=1,...,N)$, are calculated according to the following linear formulae:

[5] $\quad \tau_t^i = \tilde{\tau} \ [wL]_t^i + T_t,$

[6] $\quad b_{t+1}^i = \tilde{b}\,\tilde{\tau} \ [wL]_t^i.$

In an unfunded social security system, aggregate contributions have to equal aggregate benefits:

[7] $\quad \sum_{i=1}^{N_t} \tilde{\tau}[wL]_t^i + N_t T_t = \sum_{i=1}^{N_{t-1}} \tilde{b}\,\tilde{\tau}[wL]_{t-1}^i.$

Such a system both ensures equivalence between contribution and discounted benefit at the margin and satisfies the budget constraint as long as it meets the following conditions, with g as the growth rate of average labor income, $[wL]^{av}$, and n as the rate of employment growth:

---

[7]   Naquib (1985) assumes a constant implicit price of the social security asset. In such a restricted social security system, intragenerational redistribution distorts the individual labor supply decision.

[8]   According to Feldstein and Samwick (1992), the marginal net burden of social security in the United States varies significantly for different groups of households. This result indicates that the marginal price of the implicit social security asset differs between different groups of households and is not generally equal to one.

[9]   See Auerbach and Kotlikoff (1987:156–161) for a more detailed example for marginal contribution-benefit linkage.

[8] $\tilde{b} = 1 + r,$

[9] $T_t = \dfrac{1 + r - [1+g][1+n]}{[1+g][1+n]} \tilde{\tau} \left[\overline{wL}\right]_t^{av}.$

The lump-sum contributions finance the difference between individual benefit claims and the part of the contributions which depends on labor income. The practical feasibility of this kind of social security financing depends on the size of the necessary lump-sum contributions.[10] To obtain a rough image of their magnitude, the simple 2-period model has been extended to include 55 periods, where the individual pays contributions for 45 periods and obtains benefits for 10 periods (see the Appendix, Part a). In this setting, the contribution rates, $\tilde{\tau}$ and T, can be calculated for alternative interest and growth scenarios. Assume for example a nominal interest rate of 5 percent and a growth rate of average wages of 3 percent.[11] To ensure a benefit level of 60 percent of average labor income, a contribution rate, $\tilde{\tau}$, of 7.6 percent and a lump-sum contribution, T, of 5.7 percent of average labor income are necessary.[12] With a higher interest rate of 7 percent, the contribution rate, $\tilde{\tau}$, declines to 4.2 percent, whereas the lump-sum contribution, T, rises to 9.2 percent of average labor income. Lump-sum contributions of these dimensions are far from being negligibly small. Because of their regressive characteristics, they could lead to considerable undesired redistributional effects (see also Kotlikoff 1996b). The practical feasibility of a nondistortionary unfunded social security system therefore seems to be limited.

The results in this section have been derived using some quite restrictive assumptions, so they should be interpreted with caution. The perfect capital market appears to be the most crucial of these assumptions. In contrast to a perfect capital market, in the real world households usually face higher interest rates for borrowing than for saving and also some kinds of credit rationing. Social security may then distort the optimal intertemporal allocation of consumption and

---

10   See also Feldstein and Samwick (1996), or Feldstein (1996: footnote 19), on this point.

11   The term n is set to zero in this example.

12   This result is quite insensitive with respect to the absolute value of the interest rate and the growth rate as long as the difference between both variables remains constant. The interest growth differential of 2 percentage points roughly equals the 2.3 percentage point difference between the real return of investment and the real growth rate of labor income in Germany between 1970 and 1994 (SVR 1996).

this in turn also affects labor supply. Suppose, for example, that social security contributions exceed the individually desired level of savings and that the individual cannot neutralize this effect because of a credit limit. The marginal utility of present consumption then exceeds the discounted marginal utility of future consumption. An increasing discounted benefit is then valued less than an increasing present contribution, and a system providing equivalence between the contribution and the discounted benefit at the margin still distorts individual labor supply.

3.   Unemployment as an Outside Option

The analysis so far has neglected the individual's alternatives to social-security-covered employment. These outside options, however, exist in reality. On the one hand, the individual may choose a form of employment with no social security obligation, as for example self-employment in Germany. On the other hand, he may also choose to be unemployed and live from public transfers, such as social assistance. This latter option is of particular relevance with respect to the employment effects of social security and is therefore considered in more detail in this section.[13]

The choice between being employed or unemployed and living from public transfers can be characterized as a binary decision: either the individual chooses to work with an optimal labor supply and to receive an indirect utility $V(\tau, b(\tau))$, or he chooses to be unemployed with a utility of M from the public transfer and leisure time $l = L_E$. For a comparison of both alternatives, not only the marginal effects of social security are important but also its total impact on individual utility. Even a social security system satisfying $\lambda_m \tau'(L) = 0$ may cause negative employment effects as long as it places a net burden on the individual. However, a system with $\lambda_m \tau'(L) = 0$ minimizes the incentives to choose the outside option, because it provides the highest possible indirect utility for a given contribution and benefit level. Figure 1 illustrates this. For this graphical representation, the direct utility function is assumed to be linear with respect to present and

---

[13]   Calculations of the difference between labor income and social security transfers for Germany indicate that for certain groups of households voluntary unemployment is already a financially attractive outside option (see Boss 1993).

future consumption and the rate of time preference is assumed to be equal to the market interest rate. In this case, the level of savings does not affect the individual's welfare, so that the savings decision can be neglected. The individual labor supply decision then can be represented as a substitution between the present value of labor income, y, and the relative utility of leisure.[14] The respective contribution and benefit formulae are assumed to be linear as represented in [5] and [6].

Figure 1 — Social Security, Labor Supply, and Outside Options

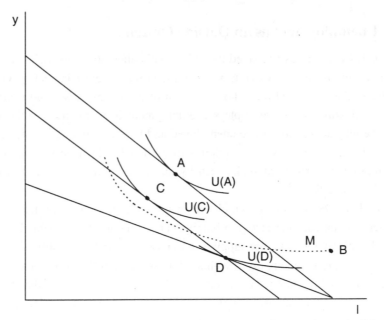

Without social security, the individual chooses point A on the budget constraint and receives utility U(A). The outside option is depicted by the point B with utility M. Now the nondistortionary social security system [8] and [9] is introduced. If the interest rate exceeds the growth rate of labor income, the budget line will be shifted inwards, leading to a new equilibrium at C. Such a social se-

---

[14]   Figure 1 then closely resembles the graphical representation of the 1-period model of labor supply.

curity system may already induce unemployment, since $U(C)$ may be lower than M. With $T=0$, utility will further decrease to $U(D)$ and the outside option will become even more attractive.

As mentioned in Section 2, redistributionary goals of the government might be a reason for *distortionary financing of social* security. To avoid the regressive effects of lump-sum contributions, governments may try to place a higher burden on individuals with a higher wage rate and in turn to lower the burden for individuals receiving a comparatively low wage rate. Governments, however, cannot observe the individual wage rate directly but only the individual labor income, wL. In this situation, social security financing becomes a problem comparable to the optimal taxation of income, where it is optimal to give up some incentive compatibility of the system because of redistributional concerns (see Atkinson and Stiglitz 1980).

The outside option of the individuals leads to an analogous situation for the government: With an equal burden of social security financing, individuals receiving a low wage rate are more likely to choose the unemployment option than individuals receiving a high wage rate. To keep the low-wage individuals in work, the government then eventually has to reduce the burden for this group. This unequal treatment may induce high-wage individuals to imitate the low-wage individuals by offering less labor and earning the same labor income as the low-wage individuals. The government can prevent this situation by reducing the incentive compatibility for the low-wage individuals. Then imitation of low-wage individuals is no longer attractive for high-wage individuals. The combination of outside options with asymmetric information can thus be responsible for an endogenous deviation from equivalence between the contribution and the discounted benefit at the margin.

A simple model may help to illustrate this point.[15] Suppose, in every period, t, the economy consists of two individuals at the working age, one receiving a wage rate $\underline{w}$, the other $\overline{w}$, with $\overline{w} > \underline{w}$. Each individual lives for two periods, a working period and a retirement period. At the beginning of the working period, the individual decides whether to participate in the labor market and, when participating, how much labor to offer. Both individuals are assumed to possess pri-

---

[15] This model is closely related to the 2-type optimal regulation model of Laffont and Tirole (1993: Chapter 1.3) and to the model of Pareto-efficient labor income taxation of Stiglitz (1982).

vate information concerning their type $\underline{w}$ or $\overline{w}$. The government does not possess this information. The government also cannot observe the wage rate ex post. All it can observe is the labor income, wL, of each individual. Social security consists of a contribution-benefit combination, $(\underline{\tau}_t, \underline{b}_{t+1})$ for the low-wage and $(\overline{\tau}_t, \overline{b}_{t+1})$ for the high-wage individual, and is assumed to be unfunded.

The self-selection constraint requires that the social security system does not offer an incentive for the individuals to choose another labor supply than the one revealing their respective type correctly. Formally, this condition can be written as follows:[16]

[10] $V(\overline{w}, \overline{w}) \geq V(\overline{w}, \underline{w})$,

[11] $V(\underline{w}, \underline{w}) \geq V(\underline{w}, \overline{w})$.

As labor income is observable ex post, an incorrect revelation of an individual's type needs a pooling of labor income of both types. This gives the following condition for the labor supply of the high-wage individual:

[12] $L(\overline{w}, \underline{w}) = [\underline{w}/\overline{w}] L(\underline{w}, \underline{w})$.

As in Figure 1, the direct utility of both individuals is assumed to be linear with respect to present and future consumption, so that the savings decision of the individual can be neglected. It is given by the following function:

[13] $U = wL - \tau + b[1 + r]^{-1} - \frac{1}{2} L^2$.

Without the existence of a social security system, the individual supplies labor up to the point where the following first-order condition holds:

[14] $w = L$.

The assumed utility function thus implies a positive uncompensated wage effect on labor supply.[17] The optimal form of social security financing can now be

---

16   The function V measures the indirect utility of the individual. The first term in parentheses in this function denotes the true type of the individual, and the second term denotes the type revealed by his action.

17   With the utility function [13], no income effect influences the consumption of leisure. Point C then lies exactly below point A in Figure 1.

derived, given the restriction that no individual should choose the outside option of being unemployed. The social welfare function is specified as follows:

[15] $\quad W = \varphi(\underline{b}_0 + \overline{b}_0) + \sum_{t=0}^{T} \{V(\underline{w}_t, \underline{w}_t) + V(\overline{w}_t, \overline{w}_t)\}[1+\delta]^{-t}.$

The function φ denotes the social valuation of the income of retirees in the initial period, and the term δ gives the social discount rate of future generations' lifetime utility.[18] The optimization problem is to find a vector of social security contributions, $(\underline{\tau}_0, \overline{\tau}_0, ..., \underline{\tau}_T, \overline{\tau}_T)$, and of labor quantities, $(\underline{L}_0, \overline{L}_0, ..., \underline{L}_T, \overline{L}_T)$, maximizing the social welfare function subject to (i) the budget constraints of the unfunded social security system, $\underline{\tau}_t + \overline{\tau}_t \geq \underline{b}_t + \overline{b}_t$, (ii) the participation constraints, $V(\underline{w}_t, \underline{w}_t) \geq M_t$,[19] and (iii) the self-selection constraints for the high-wage individuals:[20]

(iii) $\quad \overline{w}_t \overline{L}_t - \overline{\tau}_t + \overline{b}_{t+1}[1+r]^{-1} - \frac{1}{2}[\overline{L}_t]^2 \geq \underline{w}_t \underline{L}_t - \underline{\tau}_t + \underline{b}_{t+1}[1+r]^{-1}$
$$- \frac{1}{2}\{[\underline{w}_t/\overline{w}_t]\underline{L}_t\}^2.$$

This leads to the following first-order conditions for the optimal values of the instrument variables τ and L, with λ, μ, and σ as shadow prices of restrictions (i), (ii), and (iii), respectively (see the Appendix, Part b):

[16] $\quad \Omega_{\underline{L}_t} = [\underline{w}_t - \underline{L}_t]\{[1+\delta]^{-t} + \mu_t\} - \sigma_t\{\underline{w}_t - [\underline{w}_t^2/\overline{w}_t^2]\underline{L}_t\} = 0,$

[17] $\quad \Omega_{\overline{L}_t} = [\overline{w}_t - \overline{L}_t]\{[1+\delta]^{-t} + \sigma_t\} = 0,$

[18] $\quad \Omega_{\underline{\tau}_t} = -[1+\delta]^{-t} + \lambda_t - \mu_t + \sigma_t = 0,$

[19] $\quad \Omega_{\overline{\tau}_t} = -[1+\delta]^{-t} + \lambda_t - \sigma_t = 0.$

According to [17], the supplied quantity of labor of the high-wage type is in optimum at its undistorted level. This is the "no distortion at the top" condition

---

18   The social welfare function abstracts from social motives for redistribution between the two household types in each generation.

19   The indirect utility of the high-wage type always exceeds the indirect utility of the low-wage type, so that only the participation constraint of the low-wage type has to be considered explicitly (see Appendix, Part a).

20   The Appendix, Part b, shows that the self-selection constraint for the low-wage type can be neglected.

of optimal income taxation (see Seade 1977) which also has to be satisfied by an optimal social security system in this model. If the participation constraint is not binding at t, then $\mu_t = \sigma_t = 0$, and labor supply of the low-wage individual is also undistorted. More interesting, however, is the case $\mu_t > 0$. In this case, the participation constraint of the low-wage individual is binding, and this individual is indifferent between participating in the labor market or being unemployed. According to [18] and [19], $\mu_t = 2\sigma_t$, and, according to [16], the optimal form of financing social security decreases the quantity of labor supply of the low-wage individual compared to the undistorted level.

4.   Welfare Gains from a Transition?

As the previous section has shown, an unfunded social security system may distort individual labor supply if the government, compared to individuals, has an information disadvantage. A transition from unfunded social security to an alternative system, therefore, seems to be an appropriate reform to reduce this distortion and thus to increase aggregate welfare. The results of several papers on the possibility of a Pareto-superior transition seem to confirm this prediction.[21] Along a Pareto-superior transition path, the generations losing welfare in the course of the transition can be fully compensated by debt-financed transfers. This debt can be repaid in finite time by raising taxes from other generations, who gain from the transition, still leaving the gaining generations no worse off than before the transition (see Homburg 1990).

There exists, however, one fundamental difference between the models predicting the possibility of a Pareto-superior transition and the model set up in the previous section. The papers on a Pareto-superior transition all assume an exogenously given form of distortionary financing of social security. In these papers, contributions are raised from labor income with less than marginal equivalence between contributions and discounted benefits. The transition then allows switching from a distortionary to a less distortionary form of intergenerational

---

21   See Homburg (1990, 1997) and Breyer and Straub (1993), who prove the existence of a Pareto-superior transition path in their respective models, or Kotlikoff (1996a, 1996b), who employs a simulation model to show what such a Pareto-improving path and alternative transition paths may look like.

redistribution.[22] In the model of the previous section, the design of the unfunded social security system is not exogenously given, but arises endogenously. This section investigates whether in this setting a transition is also beneficial.[23] In contrast to the Pareto criterion, the social welfare function [15] is employed as a reference for a welfare improvement.

Possible alternatives to an unfunded social security system reach from funded social security organized by the public sector to more or less regulated privatized pension systems. In the model employed here, it does not matter which of these alternatives is chosen—as long as the capital market is perfect and as long as a minimum mandatory pension system is kept.[24] None of the funded forms of social security then affects individual utility and the welfare effects of a transition entirely come from reducing the benefit level of the unfunded system. The partial derivatives of the Lagrange function [*5 in the Appendix] with respect to the benefit levels give the welfare effects of changing the size of the unfunded pension system. With the first-order conditions [18] and [19], these derivatives can be written as follows: [25]

[20] $\Omega_{\underline{b}_0} = \Omega_{\bar{b}_0} = \varphi'(.) - \lambda_0,$

[21] $\Omega_{\underline{b}_{t+1}} = \Omega_{\bar{b}_{t+1}} = \lambda_t [1+r]^{-1} - \lambda_{t+1},$ $t = 0,...,T-1.$ [26]

---

22 Fenge (1995) considers a transition where a social security system as in [5] and [6] with $T=0$ is abolished and where the debt raised to finance compensating payments is repaid by a reduction of future pensions. In such a setting, the labor market distortion is not reduced by the transition, and no Pareto improvements can be achieved.

23 Brunner (1994) also considers different labor incomes of households. In his paper, a social security system with proportional contributions and equal benefits for all households redistributes intragenerationally between households with different labor incomes. In this setting, a Pareto-superior transition is generally not possible as long as governments cannot observe labor income.

24 The minimum pension prevents the moral hazard problem of individuals not saving enough to keep a subsistence level of income during retirement (see the contribution by Breyer in this volume).

25 According to [20] and [21], the marginal social welfare effects of increasing benefits is the same for both individuals. Thus, in this model, the welfare effects of a transition only depend on the aggregate benefit level in each period and not on its distribution between both individuals.

26 The benefit level in the final period, T, has to be zero to keep the budget constraint (i) satisfied.

Equation [20] gives the welfare effects of changing the benefit level for the retirees in the initial period. Whether a reduction of b_0 decreases or increases social welfare depends on the size of the marginal redistributional motive measured by $\varphi'(.)$ compared to the shadow price λ_0 of the social security budget constraint. The term λ_0 will exceed the value of one if social security distorts labor supply in this period. For $\varphi'(.) = 1$, the income of retirees has the same social value as the lifetime income of the working generation and a reduction of a distortionary transfer from the working generation to the retirees then improves welfare. In a matured social security system, however, reducing b_0 is a problematic kind of reform, since the benefits are reduced *ex post* for those individuals who have already contributed to social security in the past and therefore have acquired an explicit or implicit claim for social security benefits. A reduction of b_0 might therefore not be politically feasible. In this case, only a reduction of benefits in future periods remains as social security reform. The effects of changing the future benefit level are given by [21]. According to [21], a reduction of future benefits causes two opposing effects on social welfare. On the one hand, reducing benefit payments in $t+1$ has a positive effect on the social security budget in $t+1$, so that contributions can be reduced in this period. This effect leads to an increasing welfare, measured by the shadow price λ_{t+1} of the budget constraint. On the other hand, the benefit reduction decreases the present value of lifetime income of the working generation in t. The welfare effect of this income reduction is measured by the shadow price λ_t. Using [19] to determine λ, [21] can be written as follows:

$$[22] \quad \Omega_{\underline{b}_{t+1}} = \frac{\delta - r}{[1+\delta]^{t+1}[1+r]} + \sigma_t [1+r]^{-1} - \sigma_{t+1}.$$

The first term influencing $\Omega_{\underline{b}_{t+1}}$ is the difference between the social discount rate and the market interest rate. This difference measures the motive for redistribution between working generations in different time periods. It disappears for $\delta = r$; in this case the economy is on its modified golden rule path (see Feldstein 1995). Then only the self-selection shadow prices in t and $t+1$ affect $\Omega_{\underline{b}_{t+1}}$.[27] To get an impression of their influence, suppose, for example, the self-selection and the participation constraints were not binding in t but in the subse-

---

[27]   These shadow prices are in turn influenced by the values of the exogenous benefit levels, the wage rates for both types of individuals, and the outside utility, M.

quent period $t+1$. In other words, financing social security benefits distorts labor supply in $t+1$ but not in t. A reduction of benefits in $t+1$ then increases aggregate welfare. With such a reduction, a nondistortionary burden is imposed for the generation working in t to reduce the distortionary burden for the subsequent generation.[28]

Equation [22] not only denotes the impact of a marginal social security reform, it also gives the necessary conditions for the optimal level of benefits in all periods. With optimal social security benefits, [22] equals zero. For $\delta = r$, this implies declining shadow prices of the self-selection and participation constraints; the shadow prices have to decrease with a rate equal to the interest rate, r. With the possibility of granting social security benefits, a distortion caused by contributions in a certain period can be transferred to the subsequent period. It is therefore not optimal to eliminate a distortionary social security system completely. Instead, if financing current benefits today implies a labor market distortion today, then it will be optimal to spread this distortion over all planning periods. For a further interpretation of this result, [16] is rewritten as follows:

$$[23] \quad \alpha_t = \frac{\sigma_t}{[1+\delta]^{-t} + 2\sigma_t}, \qquad \text{with } \alpha_t \equiv \frac{w_t - L_t}{\underline{w}_t - \left[w_t^2 / \overline{w}_t^2\right] \underline{L}_t}.$$

Then $\sigma_{t+1} = \sigma_t [1+r]^{-1}$ implies $\alpha_t = \alpha_{t+1}$. Interpreting α as a measure of the current distortion caused by the social security system, this distortion has to be of equal size in each period. This result gives a simple guideline for the optimal time path of unfunded social security with labor market distortions: The optimal time path of social security benefits leads to an equal labor market distortion in all periods for $\delta = r$.

So far, the analysis has neglected the possibility that the government can raise debt or invest on a perfect capital market in the same way as the private households can. To include this possibility, assume that each individual gets a positive or negative public transfer $\underline{d}$ or $\overline{d}$ in the working period. These transfers are financed on the capital market. The government has to obey the intertemporal

---

28 However, it also may be possible that the participation and the self-selection constraints do not bind in $t+1$ and instead are binding in t. A reason for this could be an increasing wage for the low-wage individual, so that the outside option becomes less attractive in the future. In this case, a transition reduces social welfare.

budget constraint $\Sigma_t[\underline{d}_t + \overline{d}_t][1+r]^{-t} \leq 0.$ An optimal transfer policy of the government satisfies the following first-order conditions, with ε as the shadow price of the intertemporal budget constraint:

[24] $\quad \Omega_{\underline{d}_t} = [1+\delta]^{-t} + \mu_t - \sigma_t - \varepsilon[1+r]^{-t} = 0,$

[25] $\quad \Omega_{\overline{d}_t} = [1+\delta]^{-t} + \sigma_t - \varepsilon[1+r]^{-t} = 0.$

Inserting these equations in [18] and [19] then gives the following condition for the intertemporal evolution of λ:

[26] $\quad -\lambda_t[1+r]^{-1} + \lambda_{t+1} = 0.$

Access to the capital market can be used to achieve an optimal intertemporal time path of the shadow price of the social security budget constraint. According to [26], this shadow price optimally decreases at a rate equal to the market interest rate. Then [21] becomes zero and a changing benefit level has no impact at all on aggregate welfare. This result holds for all values of the social discount parameter, δ, and thus does not depend on the degree of the intergenerational redistribution motive. Optimal debt or investment policy leads to the same first-order conditions as optimal social security policy. Thus, both kinds of policy can be used interchangeably to achieve an optimal intertemporal allocation of the labor market distortion. Consequently, the same welfare effects as engendered by reforming social security can be achieved by reforming public debt policy.

5.   Other Dimensions of the Labor Supply

As already noted in Section 2, the term "labor supply" covers several dimensions (see footnote 2). Some kinds of labor supply cannot be treated adequately—even in a stylized way—in the basic 2-period model of individual labor supply (see also Rosen 1980). This section mentions three important extensions of the basic model and interprets the general properties of a nondistortionary social security system with respect to these extensions.

a.   Retirement Decision

Social security not only affects individual labor supply for a given time period of the working life but also the length of this working life. In the basic model, this decision is neglected, since the length of the working life is restricted exogenously to only one period. There exist several alternative approaches in the literature, where the date of retirement, and thus the length of the working life, appears as an endogenous decision variable.[29] This section does not attempt to restate these approaches; it restricts itself to a nonformal description of sufficient conditions for a nondistortionary social security system. With a perfect capital market, social security does not affect the retirement decision as long as it leaves the discounted additional income of prolonging or decreasing the length of the working life unaffected. This condition is the intertemporal equivalent to $\lambda_m \tau'(L) = 0$. For all contributions which increase with the length of the working life, the condition of equivalence between contribution and discounted benefit has to be satisfied at the margin to keep social security nondistortionary with respect to the retirement age.[30]

The benefit formula of the linear social security system [5] and [6] has to be modified slightly to satisfy the condition of marginal equivalence with more than one working period. With $\hat{t}$ as the date of (hypothetically) distributing all individual benefits, the following formula ensures marginal equivalence for contributions made at t:

$$[27] \quad b_t = [1 + r]^{\hat{t}-t} \, \tilde{\tau} \, [wL]_t.$$

In this formula, benefits are assumed to be paid out at one point in time. For benefits paid out as annuities, the length of the working life affects the length of retirement and of receiving benefits inversely. The annuities thus have to increase for two reasons with an additional period of staying in work: First, the discounted benefit has to be raised according to [28]. Second, the annuities have to increase because the time period of receiving benefits becomes smaller with an additional working period.

---

[29] See, for example, Sheshinski (1978), Burbridge and Robb (1980), and Crawford and Lilien (1981).

[30] The marginal contribution is now defined with respect to the length of the working life and not, as in Section 3, with respect to the level of individual labor supply in a certain time period.

For an implicit rate of return of aggregate contributions below the interest rate, a fixed contribution, T, has to be raised in addition to τ. Two forms of raising this fixed contribution ensure that it is nondistortionary with variable retirement: It can either be raised for a certain fixed time period, whether the individual works the whole period or retires in this period. Or the fixed contribution can be raised only in early periods of working life where retirement is not attractive. The fixed contribution then has to be higher to satisfy the budget constraint of social security. Both forms of raising the fixed contribution have their specific disadvantages. In the first case, people who involuntarily have to retire early still have to continue to pay social security contributions. In the second case, a high-fixed contribution is raised in early periods of working life, where income is usually lower than in later periods. This form of raising the fixed contribution then increases the relative attractiveness of voluntary unemployment as an outside option for young individuals.

b.   Human Capital Formation

A social security system that places a net burden on the individual's lifetime income may distort the incentives to invest in human capital formation. The fundamental relationships in this respect can be characterized as follows:[31] The individual invests in human capital formation up to the point where marginal benefits equate with marginal costs. The effects of a better human capital endowment on the individual's labor productivity determine the marginal benefits of a human capital investment. The marginal costs are given, on the one hand, by the direct monetary and nonmonetary costs of schooling—such as the fees and the foregone leisure time for attending courses—and, on the other hand, by the opportunity costs in terms of foregone earnings (Boskin 1975)—since years at university or in school are years reducing working life.

Social security will affect the benefit of a marginal human capital investment, if the contribution rises with the wage of the household. It will reduce this benefit, if $\tau'(w)\lambda_m > 0$. However, social security may affect not only the future benefits but also the foregone earnings costs of a marginal schooling period, so that the total effects on human capital formation income are in general ambiguous. For example, a social security system with contributions raised propor-

---

[31]   See also Rosen (1980) for the effects of labor taxes in this respect.

tionally to labor income will be neutral with respect to human capital formation if direct costs of schooling are neglected. A system of type [8] and [9] which ensures $\tau'(w)\lambda_m = 0$ even works as a subsidy to human capital formation as long as the lump-sum contribution, T, is raised only from employed households. Such a system does not reduce the benefits of a marginal human capital investment, but it decreases the foregone earnings costs, as the individual can escape from social security contributions by prolonging the time of schooling.[32] For the social security system [8] and [9] to be neutral with respect to human capital formation, the fixed contribution has to be raised from working as well as from schooling individuals.

c.   Unionized Labor Supply

Trade unions can be seen as labor supply cartels founded to achieve wages above the competitive level for their members. In such a setting, social security may influence the equilibrium in the labor market through its effects on the unions' wage demands. The basic monopoly model of wage determination in a unionized labor market illustrates some important relationships in this respect.[33] According to this model, a single union has the power to set the wage level in its respective labor market. Given this wage rate, the firms then subsequently decide on the level of employment. With profit-maximizing firms, the aggregate employment level, N, decreases with the wage rate demanded: $N = N(w)$ with $N'(w) < 0$.

The union is assumed to maximize the expected income of its representative member.[34] This expected income is given by the respective probability of being employed or unemployed and by the income level in both situations. If all individuals have an equal chance of being employed, the unemployment probability is equal to the rate of unemployment in the respective labor market. For simplic-

---

[32]   In this case, the incentive effects of social security with respect to schooling time are just the mirror image of the incentive effects concerning early retirement.

[33]   For a description of the monopoly model and an overview of alternative trade union models, see, for example, Oswald (1985). Holmlund (1989) discusses the effects of taxes in this model.

[34]   This is a simplifying assumption compared to the standard monopoly union model where unions are assumed not to maximize the expected income but the expected utility of the representative worker with a strictly concave utility function.

ity, individual labor supply is assumed to be constant and set equal to one. This gives the following objective function of the union, with $\overline{N}$ as the number of individuals supplying labor in this respective labor market and w_0 as the lifetime income of an unemployed individual:

[28] $G = \dfrac{N(w)}{\overline{N}} \left[w - \tau + b[1+r]^{-1} \right] + \dfrac{\overline{N} - N(w)}{\overline{N}} w_0.$

The equilibrium wage level maximizes [28] given that the employment level and social security contributions depend on the wage rate.[35] This leads to the following first-order condition:[36]

[29] $\dfrac{N(w)}{\overline{N}} \left[1 - \lambda_m \tau_w \right] + \dfrac{N'(w)}{\overline{N}} \left[w - \tau + b[1+r]^{-1} - w_0 \right] = 0.$

According to [29], an increasing wage rate has two opposing effects on the expected income of the union's members: on the one hand, it raises the income of the employed, and, on the other hand, it lowers the probability of employment. In the optimum, both effects are equalized. Concerning the potential impact of social security on the wage demands, the total burden of social security and the marginal burden work in opposite directions. To isolate the first effect, assume $-\tau + b[1+r]^{-1} < 0$ and $\lambda_m \tau'(w) = 0$. In this case social security increases the wage demands of the union, as it lowers the income of the employed.[37] For the second effect, assume $-\tau + b[1+r]^{-1} = 0$ and $\lambda_m \tau'(w) > 0$. In this case, social security decreases the net profitability of a marginal wage increase and thus lowers the wage demands of the union.[38] The combination of

---

[35]   The unions are implicitly assumed here to be the Stackelberg followers of the government. In the opposite situation, where the gross wage is set before the government moves, social security contributions raised from the employees have no effects on the labor market.

[36]   Given $N=N(w)$, the objective function of the union is assumed to be strictly concave, so that the second-order condition is satisfied.

[37]   Social security contributions and benefits may also influence the income of an unemployed individual if this individual supplies labor in an alternative labor market instead of receiving public transfers. The net income burden of social security then has no impact on wage demands by unions, as it decreases both the income of the employed and the alternative income.

[38]   Gelauff (1992) derives the effects of an increasing average and marginal social security contribution rate and obtains a similar result, showing that an increasing marginal contribution rate lowers the union's wage demands, whereas an increasing average contribution rate increases them. He obtains this result for a social security system where $\lambda_m = 0$.

both effects implies that $\lambda_m \tau'(w)$ will have to exceed zero to keep social security neutral in a unionized labor market if its implicit rate of return is lower than the interest rate.

6.   Summary and Conclusions

According to the basic model of labor supply, a nondistortionary social security system can be implemented quite easily—even if this system is unfunded. All that is needed is equivalence between the marginal contribution based on labor income and the discounted benefit granted for this contribution. A fixed contribution may then be raised to finance the difference between the aggregate return of social security and the interest rate. If this fixed contribution is paid irrespective of the length of individual working life, it will also leave human capital investments and individual retirement decisions undistorted.

This paper has emphasized two reasons why the applicability of such a system may be limited in reality: First, the necessary lump-sum contribution has to be of a significant magnitude even for moderate differences between the interest rate and the growth rate of labor income. This may lead to undesired redistributional effects. Second, marginal equivalence does not totally eliminate social security distortions arising with respect to the number of employed individuals: On the one hand, a social security burden on labor income may increase the wage demands of trade unions, maximizing the expected income of their members. On the other hand, it may induce low-wage households to choose the outside option of unemployment instead of working in a social-security-covered labor market. An illustrative model of optimal social security design has shown that this outside option can lead to an endogenous deviation of marginal equivalence.

Given the distortions of the existing unfunded social security system, the question arises whether a transition to another system can improve welfare. This transition has been shown to cause two opposing welfare effects, so that the result in general is indeterminate: On the one hand, lowering future benefits lowers the burden for contributing households in the future. On the other hand, such a reform decreases the welfare of present contributors. This generation has to pay the same contributions as before the transition but will get less in return. The sign of the total social welfare effect depends on the shadow price of social security benefits in both periods. If the social discount rate is equal to the market interest rate, the optimal time path of social security benefits leads to an equalization of labor market distortion in all periods.

The treatment of such a broad issue as the employment effects of social security in a paper like this necessarily has to be incomplete. Several important topics have been touched upon only rudimentarily. Most notably, these are the effects of social security on the various dimensions of labor supply, such as retirement, human capital formation, and work effort. Other issues—including the effects of social security on involuntary unemployment—have been neglected completely. A detailed analysis of these issues would certainly provide deeper insights into the effects of social security on the labor market.

Appendix

a.   Necessary Fixed Contributions

Assume all individuals receive the same labor income. An individual who saves a constant proportion $\tilde{\tau}$ of his labor income from period t_l to period t_h, will accumulate the following wealth in t_h:

$$[*1] \quad \tilde{W}_{t_h} = \sum_{t=t_l}^{t_h} \tilde{\tau}[wL]_{t_l} [1+g]^{t-t_l} [1+r]^{t_h-t}.$$

If the discounted sum of all benefit payments $\tilde{b}$ at t_h equals $\tilde{W}_{t_h}$, then equivalence between $\tilde{\tau}$ and $\tilde{b}$ will be satisfied. Benefits are assumed to be paid from t_{h+1} on for 10 periods and to grow with the rate g. The benefit payment in t_{h+1} then has to be of the following size:

$$[*2] \quad \tilde{b}_{t_h+1} = \tilde{W}_{t_h} [1+g] \Big/ \sum_{\theta=1}^{10} \left[\frac{1+g}{1+r} \right]^{\theta}.$$

All 10 generations of retirees in period t_h+1 expect the same benefit level $\tilde{b}_{t_h+1}$. With a constant relation of 4.5 contributors per retiree, this gives the following budget constraint:

$$[*3] \quad \tilde{b}_{t_h+1} = 4.5 \left\{ \tilde{\tau}[wL]_{t_h+1} + T_{t_h+1} \right\}.$$

Inserting from [*1] and [*2] gives the following equation:

$$[*4] \quad T_{t_h+1} = \tilde{b}_{t_h+1} \left\{ \frac{2}{9} - \frac{[1+g]^{t_h-t_t} \sum_\theta [1+g]^\theta [1+r]^{-\theta}}{\sum_t [1+g]^{t-t_t} [1+r]^{t_h-t}} \right\}.$$

Inserting $\tilde{b}_{t_h+1} = 0.6$, $1+g = 1.03$ and $1+r = 1.05$ then gives a lump-sum contribution of 5.7 percent of labor income.

b.   Optimal Social Security Contributions

The Lagrange function of the optimal social security model in Section 3 reads as follows:

$$[*5] \quad \Omega = \varphi\left(\underline{b}_0 + \overline{b}_0\right)$$

$$+ \sum_t \left\{ \underline{w}_t \underline{L}_t - \underline{\tau}_t + \underline{b}_{t+1}[1+r]^{-1} - \tfrac{1}{2}[\underline{L}_t]^2 \right\}[1+\delta]^{-t}$$

$$+ \sum_t \left\{ \overline{w}_t \overline{L}_t - \overline{\tau}_t + \overline{b}_{t+1}[1+r]^{-1} - \tfrac{1}{2}[\overline{L}_t]^2 \right\}[1+\delta]^{-t}$$

$$+ \sum_t \lambda_t \left[\underline{\tau}_t + \overline{\tau}_t - \underline{b}_t - \overline{b}_t \right]$$

$$+ \sum_t \mu_t \left\{ \underline{w}_t \underline{L}_t - \underline{\tau}_t + \underline{b}_{t+1}[1+r]^{-1} - \tfrac{1}{2}[\underline{L}_t]^2 - M_t \right\}$$

$$+ \sum_t \sigma_t \left\{ \overline{w}_t \overline{L}_t - \overline{\tau}_t + \overline{b}_{t+1}[1+r]^{-1} - \tfrac{1}{2}[\overline{L}_t]^2 \right\}$$

$$- \sum_t \sigma_t \left\{ \underline{w}_t \underline{L}_t - \underline{\tau}_t + \underline{b}_{t+1}[1+r]^{-1} - \tfrac{1}{2}[[\underline{w}_t/\overline{w}_t] \, \underline{L}_t]^2 \right\}.$$

This Lagrange function neglects the participation constraints of the high-wage individuals and the self-selection constraints of the low-wage individuals. It has to be shown that these simplifications are correct. According to [10], $V(\overline{w},\overline{w}) \geq V(\overline{w},\underline{w})$. Inserting [12] in [13] implies $V(\overline{w},\underline{w}) - V(\underline{w},\underline{w}) = \underline{L}^2/2[1 - \underline{w}^2/\overline{w}^2] > 0$. Thus, $V(\overline{w},\overline{w}) > V(\underline{w},\underline{w})$ and the participation constraints for the high-wage individuals are not binding. The self-selection constraints of the low-wage individuals are not binding for $V(\underline{w},\underline{w}) \geq V(\underline{w},\overline{w})$. Suppose, the opposite were true, then the following inequality would have to be satisfied at t:

[*6] $-\overline{\tau}_t + \overline{b}_{t+1}[1+r]^{-1} + \underline{\tau}_t - \underline{b}_{t+1}[1+r]^{-1} >\ \underline{w}_t \underline{L}_t - \frac{1}{2}[\underline{L}_t]^2 - \overline{w}_t \overline{L}_t$
$$+ \frac{1}{2}\{[\overline{w}_t/\underline{w}_t]\,\overline{L}_t\}^2.$$

This inequality cannot be satisfied for a binding self-selection constraint of the high-wage individual, since the latter implies the following:

[*7] $-\overline{\tau}_t + \overline{b}_{t+1}[1+r]^{-1} + \underline{\tau}_t - \underline{b}_{t+1}[1+r]^{-1} =\ \underline{w}_t \underline{L}_t - \frac{1}{2}\{[\underline{w}_t/\overline{w}_t]\,\underline{L}_t\}^2$
$$- \overline{w}_t \overline{L}_t + \frac{1}{2}[\overline{L}_t]^2.$$

Both self-selection constraints cannot be satisfied together. The case where only the self-selection constraint of the low-wage individual is binding is not relevant for optimal policy, because in this case the constraint can be made non-binding for a given labor quantity by lowering the contribution of the low-wage individual and increasing the contribution of the high-wage individual.

Bibliography

Atkinson, A.B., and J.E. Stiglitz (1980). *Lectures on Public Economics*. London: McGraw-Hill.

Auerbach, A.J., and L. Kotlikoff (1987). *Dynamic Fiscal Policy*. Cambridge: Cambridge University Press.

Boskin, M.J. (1975). Notes on the Tax Treatment of Human Capital. NBER Working Paper 116. Stanford.

Boss, A. (1993). Zur Entwicklung der Arbeitseinkommen und der Transfereinkommen in der Bundesrepublik Deutschland. *Die Weltwirtschaft* (3):311–330.

Breyer, F., and M. Straub (1993). Welfare Effects of Unfunded Pension Schemes when Labour Supply Is Endogenous. *Journal of Public Economics* 50:77–91.

Brunner, J.K. (1994). Redistribution and the Efficiency of the Pay-as-You-Go Pension System. *Journal of Institutional and Theoretical Economics* 150:511–523.

Burbridge, J.B., and A.L. Robb (1980). Pensions and Retirement Behaviour. *Canadian Journal of Economics* 13:421–437.

Crawford, V.P., and D.M. Lilien (1981). Social Security and the Retirement Decision. *Quarterly Journal of Economics* 96:505–529.

Feldstein, M. (1995). Would Privatizing Social Security Raise Economic Welfare? NBER Working Paper 5281. Cambridge, Mass.

Feldstein, M. (1996). The Missing Piece in Policy Analysis: Social Security Reform. *American Economic Review* 86:1–14.

Feldstein, M., and A. Samwick (1992). Social Security Rules and Marginal Tax Rates. *National Tax Journal* 45:1–22.

—— (1996). The Transition Path in Privatizing Social Security. NBER Working Paper 5761. Cambridge, Mass.

Fenge, R. (1995). Pareto-Efficiency of the Pay-as-you-go Pension System with Intragenerational Fairness. *Finanzarchiv* 53:357–363.

Fullerton, D. (1989). If Labor Is Inelastic, Are Taxes Still Distorting? NBER Working Paper 2810. Cambridge, Mass.

Gelauff, G.M.M. (1992). Taxation, Social Security and the Labour Market: An Applied General Equilibrium Model for the Netherlands. Tilburg. Dissertation.

Hausmann, J.A. (1985). Taxes and Labor Supply. In A.J. Auerbach and M. Feldstein (eds.), *Handbook of Public Economics*. Vol. 1. Amsterdam: Elsevier Science B.V.

Holmlund, B. (1989). Wages and Employment in Unionized Economies: Theory and Evidence. In B. Holmlund, K.-G. Löfgren, and L. Engström (eds.), *Trade Unions, Employment and Unemployment Duration*. Oxford: Clarendon Press.

Homburg, S. (1990). The Efficiency of Unfunded Pension Schemes. *Journal of Institutional and Theoretical Economics* 146:640–647.

—— (1997). Old Age Pension Systems: A Theoretical Evaluation. In H. Giersch (ed.), *Reforming the Welfare State*. Berlin: Springer.

Kotlikoff, L. (1996a). Privatization of Social Security: How It Works and Why It Matters. *Tax Policy and the Economy* 10:1–32.

—— (1996b). Simulating the Privatization of Social Security in General Equilibrium. NBER Working Paper 5776. Cambridge, Mass.

Laffont, J.-J., and J. Tirole (1993). *A Theory of Incentives in Procurement and Regulation*. Cambridge, Mass.: MIT Press.

Naquib, F.M. (1985). Some Redistributive Aspects of Social Security and Their Impact on the Supply of Labor. *Public Finance/Finances Publiques* 40:230–246.

Oswald, A.J. (1985). The Economic Theory of Trade Unions: An Introductory Survey. *Scandinavian Journal of Economics* 87:160–193.

Rosen, H.S. (1980). What Is Labor Supply and Do Taxes Affect It? *American Economic Review* 70:171–176.

Sandmo, A. (1985). The Effects of Taxation on Savings and Risk Taking. In A.J. Auerbach and M. Feldstein (eds.), *Handbook of Public Economics*. Vol. 1. Amsterdam: Elsevier Science B.V.

Seade, J.K. (1977). On the Shape of Optimal Tax Schedules. *Journal of Public Economics* 7:203–235.

Sheshinski, E. (1978). A Model of Social Security and Retirement Decisions. *Journal of Public Economics* 10:337–360.

Stiglitz, J.E. (1982). Self-Selection and Pareto Efficient Taxation. *Journal of Public Economics* 17:213–240.

SVR (Sachverständigenrat zur Begutachtung der gesamtwirtschaftlichen Entwicklung) (1996). Reformen voranbringen—Jahresgutachten 1996/97. Stuttgart: Metzler Poeschel.

Comment on Oliver Lorz

D. Peter Broer

Oliver Lorz's paper is an interesting account of a number of issues in social security reform. It provides a clear discussion of the basic distortions in social security and the efficiency conditions that need to be imposed for the system to operate in a nondistortionary fashion. More importantly, it considers the effects of household heterogeneity on the optimal social security system. Much work on social security deals with an environment in which the only source of heterogeneity is the difference in age between households. In that case, the role of social security as an insurance device is much reduced, as aging is not an unpredictable event that a risk-averse household would want to buy insurance against.[1] In fact, as Lorz shows, in this case the optimal scheme is actuarially fair, and could be implemented also as a private saving scheme.

The main case in Lorz's paper distinguishes households also by human capital level. This provides an extra reason for a social security system, to insure people against the risk of being born with low ability. This kind of insurance is ex ante, of course, before a person's ability is revealed. In fact, it fits in nicely with the specification of the welfare function, since, if we are willing to assume that the probabilities between being born with high or low ability are equally distributed, the term in braces in equation [15] can be given an expected value interpretation. The specification of the social welfare function nevertheless raises a few issues:

— The use of a social welfare function that is not derived from individual preferences is always somewhat problematical, as it is not clear whose decisions are represented by the social welfare function. In particular, the use of a social discount rate suggests that some sort of intergenerational altruism is in operation. In that case, this altruism factor might also affect other household decisions and should be incorporated in the individual utility function.
— The inclusion of the function φ in the social welfare function is not without problems. It represents the social valuation of the income of retirees in the initial period. This creates an asymmetry between the specification

---

[1] Of course, there may exist *macroeconomic* uncertainty that households would want to insure against, as it affects different generations differently. See, e.g., Gordon and Varian (1988).

of the welfare of the elderly and that of new generations, that may give rise to time-consistency problems. Calvo and Obstfeld (1988) show that in general it is necessary to include the full lifetime utility of existing generations to avoid this problem.

The issue of a time-consistent treatment of the elderly is particularly relevant in the discussion of the transition problem in Section 3. Lorz assumes that it is possible to adjust the transfers to the retirees in the initial period ($\underline{b}_0$ and $\bar{b}_0$). However, these transfers are part of the social contract of the previous period. If it is possible to renege on these contracts in the first planning period, it is presumably possible to do this again in subsequent periods. That is, the optimal reform path is not credible, because the government cannot commit itself to this path. In the absence of commitment, a subgame-perfect noncooperative Nash equilibrium may be a more appropriate solution concept than the one used by Lorz. In that case, the recursive structure of the welfare effects of the benefit levels, λ_t in [20] and [21], disappears, which may affect the conclusions on the welfare gains from a social security reform.

In Section 4, Lorz discusses a number of possible extensions of the setup in Section 3. I should like to add a few suggestions to that list.

— *Physical Capital*: Dynamic efficiency issues aside, unfunded social security will typically crowd out saving. In the present model this has no permanent effects. However, with physical capital, this will negatively affect future generations.
— *Human Capital*: In addition to the comments made by Lorz, it may be observed that a lump-sum tax on high-wage earners, as emerges from his optimal social security system, is equivalent to a progressive tax on human capital.
— *Active Labor Market Policy*: In Lorz's model, a fundamental characteristic is the existence of an outside option for the household, i.e., leisure paid for by social security. A straightforward attempt to deal with this would be the introduction of active labor market programs, if only to appropriate the time of the unemployed otherwise spent on leisure. On this point, see, for example, Hansen and Trenæs (1997).

Bibliography

Calvo, G.A., and M. Obstfeld (1988). Optimal Time-consistent Fiscal Policy with Finite Lifetimes. *Econometrica* 56:411–432.

Gordon, R.H., and H.R. Varian (1988). Intergenerational Risk Sharing. *Journal of Public Economics* 37:185–202.

Hansen, C.T., and T. Tranæs (1997). Effort Commitment in Active Labour Market Programmes: Consequences for Participation Incentives and Wage Formation. Paper presented at the conference Macroeconomic Perspectives on the Danish Economy, Hornbæk, Denmark. June 19–20.

E. Philip Davis

Pensions in the Corporate Sector

1. Introduction

The widespread difficulties being faced by pay-as-you-go social security pension schemes in the light of the aging of the population[1] put an increased emphasis on funding of pensions as an alternative means of financing and provision. In this context, this article analyzes issues raised by occupational or corporate pensions. The article is structured as follows: In the first section, I consider the determinants of the size of company pension sectors. In the second, I note some broad issues relating to the impact of company pensions on the wider economy. In the third, I assess the main regulatory issues arising with company pensions. In the fourth section, I assess the possible strains that company pensions could face in the future. The analysis focuses on the United States, Germany, the United Kingdom, and Japan.

2. The Size of Company Pension Sectors

There are major differences between the countries studied in the degree to which funding, largely via company pensions, has developed. In particular, as shown in Table 1, the assets of company pension sectors in the United Kingdom and United States far outstrip those in Germany and Japan, especially when one considers externally funded schemes. Coverage is more comparable, but this reflects the differing scope of benefit promises.

Various influences can be traced that could account for the differences in the importance of funded sectors in the provision of pensions across the four countries. Not surprisingly, the growth of private plans can be related to the scale of social security pension provision, particularly if there is generous provision for

Remark: The author thanks Chris Daykin, Richard Disney, and Bill Gale for advice. Views expressed are those of the author and not necessarily those of the institutions to which he is affiliated. The article draws on Davis (1995a).

[1] See World Bank (1994) and Davis (1997b, 1997c).

individuals at higher income levels or if contributions for low-income individuals are too high to allow further saving. There is a close relation between indicators of the generosity of social security (especially the shape of the replacement ratio/final earnings relation) and the development of private pensions (see Table 2).

Table 1 — Externally Funded Company Pension Financing, End-1994

	Billions of dollars	Percent of GDP	Memo: coverage of funded schemes (in percent)
United Kingdom	706	68	50 (voluntary)
Germany	111	6	46 (voluntary)
United States	4,527	67	42 (voluntary)
Japan (March 1994)	260	6	50 (voluntary)

Note: Excludes funds managed by life insurers (who in the United Kingdom manage personal pensions for 25 percent of the workforce). In 1994, German book-reserve pensions are estimated to be equivalent to 9 percent of GDP, and 4 percent of GDP in Japan.

Source: EFRP (1996), national flow-of-funds data.

Second, where provision is voluntary, taxation provisions make it more or less attractive for the firm to offer a pension fund (Table 2). Exemption of contributions and asset returns from taxation (as in the United Kingdom and United States) will increase funds' attractiveness, while tax disadvantages (as in Germany and Japan) may hinder growth of an occupational pension sector. Regulatory features may also encourage or discourage growth of company pensions. Preconditions for voluntary adoption of pension funds would seem to require a balance between cost to the sponsor, economic efficiency, equity, and benefit security. As shown in Section 3, such a balance is not always attained. Notably, external funding would appear to be discouraged in Germany, while defined benefit funds in the United Kingdom and United States are being replaced by defined contribution, owing largely to costs of regulation.

Detailed study of national funded sectors (Davis 1995a) suggests that other important factors in the development of occupational pension funds are the ability of employees to opt out of earnings-related social security for an equivalent private pension (as in the United Kingdom[2] and Japan), and encouragement of

---

[2]   In the United Kingdom, individuals may opt out of their corporate pension into a personal pension. The scale of this is not apparently such as to threaten the viability of

supplementary defined contribution plans to which employees may contribute, as in the case of 401(k) plans in the United States.[3] (Indeed, recent experience in the United Kingdom and United States suggests defined contribution funds may "crowd out" defined benefit plans where the latter are not customary or compulsory.)

Table 2 — Determinants of the Size of Funded Sectors

	Social security replacement rate (1992), based on final salary of $20,000 and $50,000[a] (in percent)	Form of taxation[b]
United States	65–40	EET—Contributions and asset returns tax-free. Benefits taxed.
United Kingdom	50–26[c]	EET—Contributions and asset returns tax-free. Benefits taxed, except for tax-free lump sum.
Germany	70–59	TET—Employers' contributions taxed as wages; employees' contributions and asset returns tax-free. Benefits taxed at low rate. (For booked benefits, employers contributions tax-free, benefits taxed at normal rate.)
Japan	54[d]	ETT—Contributions tax-free. Tax on asset returns. Benefits taxed, except for tax-free lump sum. (Partial tax exemption of contributions to booked benefits.)

[a]For married men. — [b]The abbreviations refer to taxation of contributions, returns and benefits, hence EET means contributions and returns are exempt and benefits are taxed. — [c]Includes state earnings-related pension scheme (SERPS). For those contracted out, the ratios are 35 percent and 14 percent . — [d]Ratio to average earnings in 1986.

Source: Davis (1995a), Wyatt Data Services (1993) for married men.

---

corporate pension funds, not least because companies tend not to contribute to personal pensions of those who opt out (Davis 1997a).

[3] Elsewhere there is compulsion to have private pensions (Australia, Switzerland) and funding of civil service pensions (the Netherlands).

3.   Effects on the Broad Economy

In selectively addressing effects of company pensions on financial markets and labor markets, one may include, first, the distinctive effects of company pensions, second, the effects of an increase in funding per se, and, third, the effect of a relative shift from pay-as-you-go to funding.

To commence with financial issues, there are a number of mechanisms whereby company pensions may change *savings behavior*: imperfect substitution arising, for example, from illiquidity of pension assets may mean that other saving is not reduced one-to-one for an increase in pension wealth; liquidity constraints may imply that any forced saving (such as pension contributions) cannot be offset either by borrowing or reducing discretionary saving (Hubbard 1986); the interaction between pensions and retirement behavior may increase saving in a growing economy, as workers increase saving in order to provide for an earlier planned retirement (Feldstein 1974); tax incentives which raise the rate of return on saving via pension funds may encourage higher aggregate saving; and finally, as social security is typically seen to reduce saving, a switch towards funding via company funds should increase it (World Bank 1994).

On the other hand, one should note that taxation provisions boosting rates of return will only influence saving at the margin for those whose desired saving is below that provided by social security and private pensions; for those whose desired saving exceeds this level, there will be an income effect but no offsetting substitution effect, and saving will tend to decline; also, even if tax provisions and the other mechanisms outlined above increase private sector saving, this could be more than offset at a macroeconomic level by the government's revenue loss due to tax concessions.

Growth in company pension schemes does appear to boost saving,[4] subject to a partial offset via declines in discretionary personal saving. Much of the literature,[5] which is focused on U.S. defined benefit funds, suggests that an increase in personal saving of around 0.35 results from every unit increase in pension fund assets, though the cost to the public sector of the tax incentives to pension funds reduces the overall benefit to around 0.2. Hubbard (1986) suggests a

---

[4]   Direct international comparisons of personal saving ratios are, however, not supportive of a simple relationship between pension funding and saving at a macro level. Countries with high levels of pension funding such as the United States and the United Kingdom have comparatively low saving, while countries dependent on pay-as-you-go, such as France and Germany, have high saving ratios. These data show that saving depends on a large number of factors, such as the demographic structure of the population, income per capita, income growth, and the nature of credit markets as well as pension systems (Masson et al. 1995).

[5]   See Feldstein (1978), Avery et al. (1985), Munnell and Yohn (1992) and Pesando (1992).

larger effect of 0.84, Gale (1997), rather less. Estimation for subgroups suggests extra saving is generated notably for lower-income households with less education who are often subject to liquidity constraints, who have no assets to pledge, have less secure employment, and may save less than they would require for retirement purposes (Bernheim and Scholz 1992). For all types of fund, one may otherwise suggest that liquidity effects on saving may weaken where credit markets are liberalized and thus access to credit is less restricted, or participation in pension funds is optional. They would also be less marked for defined contribution funds, where the worker is more likely to be able to borrow against pension wealth and participation is indeed generally optional. On the other hand, there is some contested[6] evidence for the United States (Poterba et al. 1996) that individual, albeit company-provided, 401(k) defined contribution accounts have strongly added to aggregate saving, with tax incentives being the main reason. Finally, regarding social security, Feldstein (1995) suggests that saving falls 0.5 for every unit increase in social security wealth. Neumann (1986) gives similar estimates for Germany.

The impact of development of pension funds on capital markets, abstracting from potential increases in saving and wealth, arises from differences in behavior from the personal sector. Pension funds in most cases hold a greater proportion of capital-uncertain, long-term assets than households (Table 3).

Table 3 — Portfolios of Pension Funds 1994 (percent of assets)

	Equities	Bonds and loans	Property	Liquidity and deposits	Of which: foreign assets	*Memo:* households' equity holdings (in percent)
United Kingdom	80	11	6	3	30	12
Germany	11	75	11	3	6	6
United States	48	38	0	7	10	19
Japan (March 1994)	27	61	2	3	7	7

Source: EFRP (1996), national data.

These differences can be explained partly by time horizons, which for households are relatively short, whereas given the long-term nature of liabilities, pension funds may concentrate portfolios on long-term assets yielding the highest returns. But pension funds also have a comparative advantage in compensating

---

6   For a countervailing view, see Engen et al. (1994) and Thomas and Towe (1996).

for the increased risk by pooling across assets whose returns are imperfectly correlated. The implication is that a switch to funding via company pensions would increase the supply of long-term funds to capital markets, notably in the form of equities, and reduce bank deposits, even if saving and wealth did not increase, so long as persons do not adjust their portfolios to offset growth of pension funds.[7] Funding would also increase international portfolio investment. These overall shifts to long-term assets should in turn reduce the cost of capital[8] to companies, and hence productive capital formation. Economically efficient capital formation should in turn raise output and, "endogenously," growth itself (Holzmann 1997). Interestingly, a shift to defined contribution plans where individuals determine their own asset allocations may reduce or eliminate these shifts to longer-term assets, if households are rather risk-averse (Friedman 1996).

The development of pension funds is also often held to be directly responsible for a number of the key qualitative developments in financial markets in recent years. For example, Bodie (1990) suggests that their need for hedging against shortfalls of assets against liabilities has led to the development of a number of recent financial innovations such as zero coupon bonds and index futures. Similarly, the development of indexation strategies by and for pension funds has increased demand for futures and options. In countries where reversion of surplus assets to the sponsor is permitted, corporate takeovers may be motivated by desire to release such assets (Mitchell and Mulherin 1989).

Other key issues for capital markets raised by pension funds are better seen as implications of the broader process of institutionalization of saving. They may, for example, affect the structure of capital markets, in terms of market infrastructure and regulation (Steil 1996); they encourage securitization of loans and securities market financing generally (Davis 1993, 1996).

One of the key topics is institutions' effect on liquidity and price formation. Do pension funds increase or dampen volatility? In normal times, institutions, having good information and low transactions costs, are likely to speed the adjustment of prices to fundamentals. It need hardly be added that such market sensitivity generates an efficient allocation of funds and acts as a useful discipline on lax macroeconomic policies. Again, the liquidity that institutional activity generates may dampen volatility, as is suggested by lower share price volatility in countries with large institutional sectors. And evidence on average day-to-day asset price fluctuations shows no tendency for such volatility to in-

---

7   King and Dicks-Mireaux (1988) found no such offset for Canada. See also Davis (1988).

8   Evidence from studies such as Blanchard (1993), which show a decline in the premium of equity over bond yields corresponding to the growth of pension funds, tend to confirm this.

crease. On the other hand, some medium-term deviations of asset prices from levels consistent with fundamentals—at times affecting global capital markets—may link to institutionalization. Examples (see Davis 1994, 1995b) are the stock market crash of 1987, the ERM crises of 1992/93, the bond markets in 1993/94, and the Mexican crisis of 1994/95. Such events were characterized by features such as heavy involvement of institutional investors in both buying and selling waves; international investment; signs of overreaction to the fundamentals and excessive optimism prior to the crisis; at times, inappropriate monetary policies; a shock to confidence which precipitated the crisis, albeit not necessarily sufficient in itself to explain the scale of the reaction; and rapid and wholesale shifts between markets, often facilitated by financial innovations. Underlying factors are, crucially, influences on fund managers which induce herding behavior (notably the prevalence of performance measurement, due in turn to principal-agent problems between the sponsor and the fund manager). Such pressures may be greater for defined benefit funds, where companies have a direct interest in funds' performance.

As is the case for excess volatility as outlined above, regular performance evaluation of pension fund managers by trustees is said to underpin the short-termist hypothesis (entailing undervaluation of firms with good earnings prospects and willingness of funds to sell shares in takeover battles). This in turn is held to discourage long-term investment or R&D as opposed to distribution of dividends. Some recent research seems to confirm the existence of short-termist effects in the United Kingdom, with overvaluation of profits in the short term (Miles 1993). Evidence from a survey of U.S. CEOs goes in the same direction (Poterba and Summers 1992). Against this, Marsh (1990) notes that in the absence of information relevant to valuations, excessive turnover will hurt performance of asset managers, and reaction to relevant information on firms' long-term prospects, which itself generates turnover, is a key function of markets. High stock-market ratings of drug companies, with large research expenditures and long product lead times, would seem to tell against the short-termist hypothesis.[9] The "corporate governance movement" reflects dissatisfaction among pension funds with costs of the takeover mechanism, and preference for direct influence as equity holders on incumbent management (Davis 1995a).

A further point is that pension funds and other institutional investors may be reticent in investing in small firms, which are often seen as crucial for economic growth.[10] For example, Revell (1994) shows that in 1989 U.K. pension funds

---

[9]   Indeed markets seem to favor capital gains over dividends (Levis 1989), and some research suggests announcement of capital expenditure or R&D boosts share prices (McConnell and Muscarella 1985).

[10]   This tendency may link to illiquidity or lack of marketability of shares, levels of risk which may be difficult to diversify away, difficulty and costs of researching firms

held 32 percent of large firms and only 26 percent of smaller ones. There are sharp cross-country differences: U.K. funds reportedly invest at most only 1–2 percent in venture capital compared with 5–10 percent in the United States. The consequence of neglect of small firms (assuming individual investors do not fill the gap) may be biases in the economy towards sectors with larger firms, which may be contrary to the comparative advantage of the economy as a whole. Of course, such problems are much more severe with internal funding as in Germany, which tends to preserve the existing industrial structure and not aid financing of new firms (Nürk and Schrader 1996).

Turning to *effects on labor markets*,[11] since contributions are likely to be seen as saving and not taxes, funded pensions are less likely than social security to hinder work incentives. Funding may also increase overall economic efficiency and flexibility by reducing the conflict between labor and capital, helping wage moderation and reducing demand for job security provisions, as these would be seen as benefiting future incomes from capital in retirement (Holzmann 1997). Arguably, these incentives should be particularly strong for defined contribution funds.

On the other hand, defined benefit funds may reduce labor mobility, if the employer is allowed to institute imperfect vesting (so that employees only accrue pension rights after several years of contributions made on their behalf), or early-leavers' pensions are not inflation-indexed. In such cases, early-leavers do not gain a proportionate share of benefits in relation to contributions and effectively subsidize long-stayers. Again, nonindexation of frozen benefits of a job-changer may make the pension virtually worthless, thus discouraging job-switching. Even with perfect vesting and inflation-indexing, workers tend to lose out by changing between defined benefit funds when they move jobs, because average earnings tend to rise faster than prices, and also because of promotion. In effect, pension accruals in final-salary defined benefit funds tend to increase with the time that the worker remains with the same firm—a phenomenon known as "backloading."[12] Either career-average calculations or "transfer cir-

---

without track records, and limits on the proportion of a firm's equity that may be held. The development and improvement of stock markets for small company shares is one initiative that may make such holdings more attractive to pension funds.

11 For an overview of U.S. evidence, see Gustman and Mitchell (1992).

12 Backloading is of course partly an "arithmetic" consequence of the shorter time to fund benefits when one is close to retirement. It may be exacerbated for some high-income individuals by sharp salary rises prior to retirement. Backloading may also be a feature of career average and defined contribution funds, but usually to a lesser extent. As an indication of effects of job changes on pensions, the U.S. GAO (1989) simulated equal cost defined benefit and defined contribution plans with identical earnings and work histories, and found that five jobs with companies with identical de-

cuits" which allow shifts between similar defined benefit funds on an agreed basis can reduce these problems of labor mobility. Defined contribution schemes tend to avoid these problems although they raise the difficulty that assets may be disbursed and dissipated during job changes (Turner 1993).

Although they are an attraction to a firm, these effects of labor mobility may of course be a disadvantage to the economy as a whole, as they imply that defined benefit funds can be a source of labor market inflexibility, and defined contribution funds superior (McCormick and Hughes 1984; World Bank 1994).[13] This is of particular importance if the industrial structure is in a state of flux and labor needs to be redeployed to more productive uses. Counterarguments may, nonetheless, be mentioned, if, for example, ability of employers to use pension plans to manage their workforces leads them to invest more in training.

The structure of funded pension provision also has an important role to play in retirement. The element of backloading in defined benefit funds gives firms an incentive to lay off workers in middle age to save on later pension accruals. For workers, funds often offer increasing pension wealth only up to the first optional retirement date, after which it turns down, offering a powerful inducement to retire. The incentive should not be present in the case of defined contribution funds.[14] U.S. research also shows that workers with generous private pensions tend to retire earlier than those with less generous ones.[15] Meanwhile, workers may defer retirement if offered sufficient pension rewards for doing so, while, conversely, funds which do not offer further benefit accruals may offer a strong disincentive to retiring late (Pesando 1992).

---

fined benefits plans gave a pension of $9,800, and with defined contribution plans $12,100, while one job covered by the defined benefit plan would give $19,100.

[13] Consistent with these arguments, studies find that workers with defined benefit pension coverage are less mobile than those without.

[14] In this context, Stock and Wise (1988) show that an increase from 55 to 60 in the early retirement age in a company defined benefit fund in the United States will cause the percentage of workers aged 50 staying until 60 to rise from 35 to 58 percent, and the number aged 55 leaving before 59 to fall from 45 to 13 percent, although more leave between 50 and 54, since the early retirement age recedes.

[15] This pattern may be linked to liquidity constraints; if workers are unable to borrow against future labor income and pension assets to boost consumption, there may be an incentive to retire early in order to redistribute consumption across the life cycle.

4.   Regulatory and Fiscal Issues

It was noted that taxation is a key element in development of funded pensions. Meanwhile, regulations[16] of company pension schemes, key elements of which are reviewed below, may be divided into those of pension fund assets (funding, portfolio distributions and surpluses), liabilities (social security integration, benefit insurance, indexation, portability, defined benefit/defined contribution) and broader structural regulations (trustees, fraud protection, information, regulatory structures, compulsion). It is noted that many of the issues which arise for defined benefit funds are absent or arise differently for defined contribution funds. Also, the distinction between reserve-funded and externally funded schemes makes a major difference to regulatory provisions.

The basic choice in *taxation of savings* such as pensions, assuming there is not to be double taxation of contributions and pensions, is between a regime where asset returns are tax-free (expenditure tax treatment) and where they are taxed (comprehensive income tax treatment). Expenditure taxes are optimal for all saving (as they do not distort the choice between current and future consumption), but even if only pensions are so privileged, there may be a case for special treatment if the contractual annuities as offered by pension funds have unique features in retirement income provision, absent from other forms of saving (inability to dissipate pension funds prior to, and in most cases after, retirement). Measures to minimize abuse of tax privileges by high earners are nonetheless clearly justified, as are limitations to the degree to which benefits may be taken as lump sums.[17]

Thus, in the United States, which basically follows an expenditure tax approach, employers'[18] contributions and asset returns are tax-free, while pensions are taxed. Funding is essential in order to obtain tax exemption. There are also limits to contributions; notably, employer contributions that would drive the funding level above 150 percent of the wind-up liabilities or accumulated benefit obligation (ABO)[19] are not tax-exempt. The United Kingdom has similar provi-

---

16   For a more detailed overview of regulatory issues, see Davis (1995a) and Turner and Watanabe (1996).

17   For a comprehensive analysis of the economics of pension fund taxation, see Dilnot (1992) and Dilnot and Johnson (1993).

18   The exception is 401(k) plans, where employees may also make contributions tax free.

19   As noted by Bodie (1991), the "wind-up" definition of liabilities, the "solvency" level at which the firm can meet all its current obligations, is known as the accumulated benefit obligation (ABO). Allowance in advance for the fact that rights will be indexed to earnings rises up to retirement, as is normal in a final-salary scheme, gives the projected benefit obligation (PBO). The indexed benefit obligation (IBO) also assumes indexation after retirement.

sions,[20] except that employee contributions are also tax-exempt and maximum funding is based on the indexed benefit obligation (IBO). The IBO/PBO may be better for the long-term solvency of pension funds, as it allows advance provision for the burden of aging; U.S. companies may face severe burdens in maintaining funding levels in future (Schieber and Shoven 1994). An anomaly in the United Kingdom is a tax-free lump sum at retirement. In the United States, assets may be withdrawn from defined contribution funds, particularly when changing jobs, subject to taxation (Turner 1993), threatening retirement income security.

In Germany and Japan, relative or absolute fiscal privileges for pension funds are less, which has contributed to lesser growth. In Japan (Clark 1991), pension funds' asset returns are subject to a special 1 percent corporate tax, any contributions which would raise funding levels above the regulatory minimum (ABO) are taxed and book reserve liabilities are 40 percent tax-deductible. In Germany, employer contributions to pension funds (*Pensionskassen*) and direct insurance are treated as current income of employees and are subject to wage tax[21]—hence deferred taxation is absent—although pensions and lump sums are taxed lightly compared with earned income, partly to compensate. In addition, part of fund returns are also taxed, as pension funds may not reclaim withholding tax on dividends; this discourages equity holding. Meanwhile, tax-deductible contributions to support funds are severely limited. Pension liabilities held on the books of the sponsor (*Direktzusagen*) are, in contrast, fully tax-deductible[22] against the firm's corporation tax obligation.[23] Premiums for insurance of such obligations are also tax-deductible. No doubt partly as a consequence (albeit also reflecting benefits to company liquidity), booked benefits are the dominant form of private pension obligation, accounting for 60 percent of pension liabilities, compared with 40 percent for externally funded pensions.

Regulation of the funding of benefits is a key aspect of the regulatory framework for defined benefit pension funds. Note that by definition, a defined contribution plan, whether occupational or personal, is by definition always fully funded, as assets equal liabilities, whereas with defined benefit plans there is a distinction between the pension plan (setting out contractual rights) and the fund

---

20 For details see Davis (1997a). In the United Kingdom, other forms of saving such as equities and deposits have been accorded (limited) expenditure tax treatment, reducing the relative advantage of pensions.

21 However, the employer can assume the employee's tax liability up to DM 3,400 at a special flat rate tax of 20 percent.

22 Book-reserve-funded pensions are taxed as income to compensate, although 40 percent is tax-free up to a low minimum.

23 As noted by Hannah (1992), the reasons for this are partly historical, to encourage reinvestment of funds in firms facing very high tax rates after the war.

(a pool of assets to collateralize the promised benefits). One may distinguish between external and internal funding. The latter implies that pension contributions are accumulated in firms' balance sheets, and the claim of pensioners is against firms' future income. The benefit claims are hence closely tied to the fortunes of the sponsoring company. External funding offers a diversified and hence less risky alternative backup for the benefit promise. In this context, minimum funding limits (notably for externally funded schemes) seek to protect security of benefits against default risk by the company, given unfunded benefits are liabilities on the books of the firm. As noted, there are usually also upper limits on funding, to prevent abuse of tax privileges (overfunding).

In terms of internal versus external funding, there is a distinction between the United Kingdom and United States, on the one hand, and Germany and Japan, on the other, in that, as noted, reserve funding is strongly discouraged in the first two countries (it would not benefit from tax advantages[24]), while in the latter countries reserve funding is encouraged, although incentives have been reduced in recent years in Japan. There are also contrasts in the regime for externally funded pensions, which link also to accounting rules.

In the United States, the ABO must be funded. This has an important influence on portfolio distributions, since underfunding on this basis ("shortfall risk") can be avoided, and tax benefits to the firm maximized, by holding bonds; equities are only suitable for overfunded schemes. Under the U.S. accounting standard FASB 87, if pension assets fall below this level for a period, the unfunded liability must be reported in the firm's balance sheet as senior debt, which hinders the firm in raising funds; there are higher benefit-insurance premia if the pension scheme is underfunded. In the United Kingdom, there was historically no minimum funding requirement except to cover the proportion which replaced social security. As noted, typically funds aim for covering the IBO. Another crucial difference from other countries is that adequacy of funding was judged (by actuaries) by current and projected cash flows from assets and not current market values; this allows volatile assets such as equities to be heavily used.[25] However, the 1995 Pensions Act introduced a minimum funding requirement (based on the ABO, albeit with allowance for future inflation—a "revalued" or "indexed" ABO) for the first time; which may make portfolio selection more cautious.

---

[24] On the other hand, there is evidence that around 25 percent of assets in U.S. 401(k) plans is invested in the sponsor's equity (Poterba and Wise 1996).

[25] Historically, this has not conflicted with the need to cover obligations if the fund were wound up, since the PBO has tended to exceed the ABO. But compulsory indexation will increase the ABO and could put the system under threat (Riley 1992).

In Japan, externally funded company pensions[26] must be funded only up to the ABO, and there is reportedly very little overfunding, partly because contributions which would raise funding levels above the ABO are taxed. In Japan (Clark 1994) book-value accounting[27] is held to obscure poor performance of pension funds and prevent a clear assessment of funding. It may also prevent funds from selling poorly performing shares and prevent switching of asset managers (as both would entail realization of losses). In Germany, various laws or court decisions have enforced minimum standards of funding for externally funded schemes and what amounts to inflation indexing of pensions. However, although this implies funding the IBO, it appears that provisions for indexation are taxed—only the PBO is tax-free. These provisions are felt to be particularly burdensome, despite the relatively low level of German inflation, and, together with other taxation and regulatory provisions, have helped blunt the growth rate of externally funded private pension schemes.[28] In Germany, accounting conventions have an impact on funding decisions, as shortfalls (defined at the lower of cost and market value of assets at a given point in time) are penalized quite heavily (Hepp 1992). It is suggested that this helps to account for conservative investment strategies, independently of portfolio regulations.

Quantitative regulation of portfolio distributions may entail limits on holdings of assets with relatively volatile returns, such as equities and property, as well as foreign assets. There are also often limits on self-investment, to protect against the associated concentration of risk regarding insolvency of the sponsor. Apart from the control of self-investment, the degree to which such regulations actually contribute to benefit security is open to doubt, since pension funds, unlike insurance companies, face the risk of increasing liabilities as well as the risk of holding assets, and hence need to trade volatility with return. Moreover, appropriate diversification of assets can eliminate idiosyncratic risk, and international investment will actually reduce otherwise undiversifiable or "systematic" risk.

Such limits may be particularly inappropriate for defined benefit pensions, given the addition "buffer" of the guarantee on the part of the company to the worker. Clearly, in such cases, portfolio regulations may affect the attractiveness to companies of funding pensions—and the generosity of provision—if they constrain managers in their choice of risk and return, forcing them to hold low-yielding assets and increasing their risks by limiting their possibilities of diversification. They will also restrict the benefits to the capital markets from the de-

---

[26] These are tax-qualified pension funds (TQPFs) and employee pension funds (EPFs).

[27] A reform is currently shifting funds to market-value accounting (*Pensions and Investments* 1997).

[28] Deutsche Bundesbank (1984), Ahrend (1996), Nürk and Schrader (1996).

velopment of pension funds. In particular, in the case of restrictions which explicitly or implicitly[29] oblige pension funds to invest in government bonds, which must themselves be repaid from taxation, there may be no benefit to capital formation and the "funded" schemes may, at a macroeconomic level, be equivalent to pay-as-you-go.

Pension funds in the United States are subject to a "prudent man rule" which requires managers to carry out sensible portfolio diversification; there are no limits to portfolio distributions other than a 10 percent limit on self-investment for defined benefit funds. U.K. pension funds are generally subject to trust law and implicitly[30] follow the "prudent man" concept; there are limits on self-investment (5 percent) and concentration.

Japanese funds face ceilings on holdings of certain assets[31] (such as 30 percent for foreign assets and 50 percent for equities), which Tamura (1992) suggests "(inappropriately) imitate regulations devised for trust banking and life insurers."[32] There are also limits on foreign management of pension fund assets, which may weaken overall performance by limiting competitive pressure on fund managers (Clark 1994). German pension funds, besides a 10 percent self-investment limit, remain subject to the same panoply of regulation as life insurers (including a 20 percent limit on foreign assets). It is arguable that these are particularly inappropriate for pension funds given the indexed nature of their liabilities.[33] Both U.S. and U.K. funds hold 50 percent or more of their portfolios in equities, while proportions are much lower for Germany and Japan (Table 3). Note that by offering tax privileges to "booking," Germany and Japan effectively impose no limits on self-investment of book reserves—and pressures from the capital market to maximize returns on these investments are weak (Nürk and Schrader 1996).

Insurance of defined benefit pension rights against default risk for the sponsoring firm is a common feature of the countries studied. Note that insurance of benefits of defined contribution plans is not needed to protect rights, as there is

---

29 For example, by closing down all alternative investment strategies, such as international diversification.

30 There is no explicit prudent man rule, but the duty of prudence to trustees can be interpreted as requiring diversification.

31 These are currently being abolished (*Pensions and Investments* 1997).

32 The similarities to life insurance extend also to asset return strategies, where pension funds, rather than investing for the long term, seek to obtain a yearly minimum rate of return. Combined with book-value accounting and portfolio restrictions, this causes particular difficulties in bear market conditions and may lead to severe underfunding on a market-value basis.

33 One way to avoid the regulations on equities and foreign investment is reportedly to invest via special security funds, whose investments are not subject to restriction.

no fixed pension right to guarantee, but it may be justified to protect against insolvency of the provider, or insolvency of the sponsor if there is self-investment. Any system of guarantees faces the difficulty of moral hazard, i.e., that it may create incentive structures leading recipients to undertake excessively risky investments, which in turn give the risk of large shortfall losses to the insurer. In other words, in the absence of appropriate controls, losses may not arise merely from fraud or incompetence but the incentive structure itself (Bodie and Merton 1992).

In the United States the Pension Benefit Guarantee Corporation (PBGC), which guarantees basic retirement benefits for defined benefit funds, shows the difficulties that arise when controls are not properly applied.[34] PBGC premia have traditionally been non-risk-related, thus encouraging risk-taking, and even when attempts have been made to relate premia to risk, these have focused on underfunding per se and not the risk of assets, which may also be an important determinant of potential liabilities to the PBGC. As a result of these and other difficulties, plans that are terminated are often vastly underfunded (typically by as much as 60 percent). Sponsoring firms either minimize pension contributions directly or encourage early retirement of workers whose pensions are not funded. The PBGC itself suggested in late 1993 that the pensions shortfall in the worst 50 companies was $38 billion at the end of 1992 and around $50 billion in 1993. Germany has a mutual insurance scheme for benefits covered by book reserves in respect of vested rights (PSV) (Ahrend 1996), which could in principle face the same moral hazard risks as those in the United States, especially as there are no controls over investment of reserves (although formation of provisions has been compulsory since 1987) and premia are not related to risk. Also, "good risks" could switch to external funding to avoid PSV obligations. Germany avoids insurance for *Pensionskassen,* but as a trade-off has tended to impose extremely severe asset restrictions.

In Japan, there is a pension guarantee program for EPFs, albeit only covering 130 percent of the portion "contracted out" of social security. Booked benefits are generally not insured, although there are provisions to do so voluntarily in the 1976 wage payment law. In the United Kingdom, absence of a guarantee scheme for defined benefit company plans (except for the Guaranteed Minimum Pension which replaced social security for opted-out funds) has historically obviated the need for portfolio regulations, while imposing greater risk on the beneficiaries in cases of fraud such as Maxwell. However, under the 1995 Pension Act, a guarantee scheme has been set up to cover up to 90 percent of losses from fraud and misappropriation only, which should minimize moral hazard problems. In addition, defined contribution schemes run by insurance companies

---

[34] Ippolito (1989), Bodie (1992), Bodie and Merton (1992), Smalhout (1996).

are covered against bankruptcy by (mutual) insurance compensation arrangements, covering 90 percent of the investment.

Vesting, treatment of transfers between schemes, and treatment of prior service credits for defined benefit plans may, as noted, limit labor mobility.[35] Solutions include shorter vesting periods, which ensure that benefits are nonforfeitable on retirement; transfers permitted with full allowance for benefits accrued; or service credits (in the case of final-salary based schemes) indexed till retirement. Note that such problems do not arise with defined contribution funds, nor do problems arising from "backloading" arise for career-average-based defined benefit plans. Also transfer of assets is inherently more straightforward for external than for internal funding.

In the United States there is vesting in 5 years, although there is no indexation of accrued benefits of defined benefit funds. Lump-sum distributions are permitted on transfer in defined contribution funds, thus allowing pension assets to be dissipated. This is also the case in Japan. In the United Kingdom there is vesting in 2 years, and accrued benefits are indexed. Transfers must be made to other pension funds. In Germany, there is vesting in 10 years of service and age 35. There is no possibility of transfer of assets to another fund in the case of book reserves. Accrued benefits are indexed and plans tend to be career-average-based. In Japan, there are no vesting regulations; whereas the contracted out element of social security vests immediately (and may be transferred without loss to another company), vesting for other benefits is typically graded between 3 and 20 years (Clark 1991). There is a low transfer value for voluntary leavers, usually paid as a lump sum. Hence, labor mobility is sharply restricted by company pensions in Germany and Japan, while pension obligations are limited (thus "incidentally" protecting the mutual insurance of booked benefits in Germany).

Statutory inflation indexation[36] *of defined benefit pensions after retirement* improves the protection of beneficiaries while entailing major burdens on sponsors. Thus policy-makers have tended historically to avoid legal provisions enforcing indexation. This is still the case in the United States and Japan, where postretirement benefits are rarely fully indexed. However, in the United King-

---

[35] Indeed, Lazear and Moore (1988) estimate that labor turnover in the United States would be twice as high in the absence of pension funds, because of the losses in pension benefits that may be incurred by early-leavers compared with those staying in one job.

[36] The move from career-average to final-salary defined benefit pension plans in the United Kingdom and the United States in the 1970s can be seen as an attempt to correct for effects of inflation prior to retirement. However, in Japan the dependence of pensions on basic salary and not full remuneration may mean that preretirement indexation is imperfect.

dom laws now enforce indexation for up to 5 percent inflation (they already insist on preretirement indexation of accrued benefits), and indexation is mandatory in Germany.[37] In the United Kingdom, defined contribution pensioners must also buy an indexed annuity to cover the element of their pension equal to social security.

It was noted in Section 1 that the size and nature of company pensions links strongly to regulation. Notably, the regulations outlined above are making firms increasingly unwilling to offer defined benefit funds, notably in the United Kingdom and United States. Clearly, there are also important links from the choices on the regulatory side to the potential effects of funds on the wider economy enumerated in Section 2. Beneficial effects on capital markets may be underpinned by certain regulations such as those encouraging or enforcing external funding but also blunted by factors such as portfolio regulations, risk aversion of fund boards, and the structure and behavior of the fund management sector. The benefits to the capital market would be absent in the case of book reserves, and hence external funding is seen as more desirable. Equally, funds' effect on labor mobility is determined by regulatory choices. For defined benefit funds, rapid vesting and career-average-based benefit calculations or "transfer circuits" are needed to minimize barriers to mobility.

5. Determinants of the Long-Term Viability of Company Pensions

An important question that must be answered by those favoring funding is whether it is any more viable than pay-as-you-go, faced with coming demographic difficulties. This question can be addressed at a micro and macro level. One objection to all types of funding, taking a "closed economy" view, is that it is actually equivalent to pay-as-you-go in that pensions must be paid from domestic production (Samuelson 1958). In this context, pension funds are likely to become sellers of assets as the population ages, which could depress asset prices (Schieber and Shoven 1994).

However, funding may raise growth potential by reducing distortions to labor and financial markets relative to pay-as-you-go, shifting the structure of saving towards longer-term instruments such as equities and possibly raising saving per se (Holzmann 1997). Hence the future state of the economy may differ between the cases of funding and pay-as-you-go. Moreover, the possibility of interna-

---

[37] Employers must adjust pensions for inflation every three years, up to the lower of prices and net earnings inflation, having taken into account the position of the pensioners and their own economic situation.

tional investment leaves pensions less dependent on the performance of the domestic economy. Indeed, there are strong arguments that investment from funding should flow to countries with younger populations, whose investment needs exceed national saving. Conceptually, this allows a form of burden-sharing at a global level. Moreover, when these countries age in the next century, they may be willing buyers for assets sold by pension funds from OECD countries.

At a micro level, aspects of pension fund regulation may have an important role to play in ensuring funds remain viable. Adequacy of funding is essential; underfunding, as was rife in the United States in the 1980s and in Japan now, may put benefits under threat (Smalhout 1996). External as opposed to internal funding spreads the risks to an individual firm of the aging and diminution of its workforce. Internal funding is also subject to liquidity risks when pensions are paid, which are absent for external funding. Adequate provision of internally funded pensions, as in Germany, is likely to be particularly difficult for declining industries, as the worker/pensioner ratio falls (Frijns and Petersen 1992).[38]

As regards regulations for external funding, defined contribution funds impose less of a burden on firms than defined benefit and are in that sense more sustainable—the risk to the worker is that aging may reduce returns in the capital markets, and/or this may make inadequate contributions (Samwick and Skinner 1993). For defined benefit funds, an important argument in favor of funding the PBO/IBO over the ABO is that it ensures advance provision for the burden of maturity of the plan, when there are many pensioners and fewer workers, by spreading costs over the life of the plan[39] (Frijns and Petersen 1992). Such burdens would otherwise be severe owing to "backloading." More generally, taking account of future obligations instead of purely focusing on current liabilities is likely to permit smoother levels of contributions as the fund matures, which may be better for the financial stability of the sponsor. As noted, funding and taxation provisions in the United States and Japan encourage firms to delay funding; the risk to future pensioners is that firms will in due course find the burden too great, leading to curtailment of benefit promises (Schieber and Shoven 1994).

Again, portfolio regulations, if they make benefit provision expensive, may make the burden of providing company pensions much greater than would otherwise be the case. Typically, estimates suggest that a 1 percent higher rate of return can reduce contributions by 2.5–3 percent of labor costs (EFRP 1996). In Japan, effects of portfolio restrictions on rates of return may be aggravated by

---

[38] Andrews (1993) points to the U.S. railroad fund as an example of the plight a reserve-funded scheme gets into in a declining industry.

[39] The facility with which funds of declining industries in the United Kingdom funded on a PBO/IBO basis (such as coal mining and railways) coped with maturity are a case in point.

effects of accounting conventions and limits on foreign management of pension funds. Some U.S. commentators suggest that the strict minima and maxima to funding in that country force firms to advert a risk-averse investment strategy and short time horizon.

The overall success of a system of corporate pensions may also be measured by the degree to which it can provide comprehensive cover. Experience typically shows that voluntary coverage leads to a focus on subgroups of the population (men, white collar, large companies, unionized, etc.). Compulsory provision as in Australia, Switzerland, and Denmark can avoid this. It would facilitate job mobility by standardizing terms and conditions. Notably for personal pensions, compulsory participation should help to avoid adverse selection problems which typify free markets in annuities. It could be argued that if funds are compulsory, then relative tax advantages are not needed. On the other hand, compulsion could also have an adverse effect on the corporate sector, since it would impose an unavoidable burden on companies, which in turn could affect international competitiveness of the economy. These effects would make measures to minimize costs, such as a prudent man rule and competitive fund management, all the more urgent. Also, such schemes tend to be defined contribution, thus imposing greater risk on workers than would a combination of (voluntary) defined benefit schemes and social security.

6. Conclusion

The role of company pension funds varies sharply between major OECD countries. The level of state benefits and fiscal and regulatory features have a crucial role to play in making the setting up of funds attractive to firms (assuming their establishment remains voluntary). In this context, it has been shown that company pensions can play an important role in overall economic performance as well as in retirement income provision per se. They may encourage saving and capital market development as well as have a pervasive influence on labor markets. Company pension funds raise important regulatory issues. Funding regulations need particularly careful design and implementation, while portfolio regulations are best set in the form of a "prudent man rule" enjoining portfolio diversification; lacking controls, benefit insurance may lead to underfunding and heightened risk-taking. Finally, whereas funded pensions are considered more viable than pay-as-you-go, and external funding superior to internal, certain regulatory provisions have been shown to impact adversely on benefit security in the case of external funding.

Bibliography

Ahrend, P.R. (1996). Pension Financial Security in Germany. In Z. Bodie, O.S. Mitchell, and J.A. Turner (eds.), *Securing Employer-Based Pensions: An International Perspective*. Philadelphia: Pension Research Council and University of Pennsylvania Press.

Andrews, E.S. (1993). *Private Pensions in the United States*. OECD Series on Private Pensions and Public Policy. Paris: OECD.

Avery, R.B., G.E. Elliehausen, and T.A. Gustafson (1985). Pension and Social Security in Household Portfolios: Evidence from the 1983 Survey of Consumer Finances. Research Papers in Banking and Financial Economics. Board of Governors of the Federal Reserve System, Washington, D.C.

Bernheim, B.D., and J.K. Scholz (1992). Private Saving and Public Policy. NBER Working Paper 4213. Cambridge, Mass.

Blanchard, O.J. (1993). The Vanishing Equity Premium. In R. O'Brien (ed.), *Finance and the International Economy 7*. Oxford: Oxford University Press.

Bodie, Z. (1990). Pension Funds and Financial Innovation. *Financial Management* (Autumn):11–21.

—— (1991). Shortfall Risk and Pension Fund Asset Management. *Financial Analysts Journal* May/June:57–61.

—— (1992). Federal Pension Insurance: Is It the S and L Crisis of the 1990s? Paper presented at the Industrial Relations Research Meeting, New Orleans, January.

Bodie, Z., and R.C. Merton (1992). Pension Benefit Guarantees in the United States: A Functional Analysis. In R. Schmitt (ed.), *The Future of Pensions in the United States*. Philadelphia: University of Pennsylvania Press.

Clark, R.L. (1991). *Retirement Systems in Japan*. Homewood, Illinois: Irwin.

—— (1994). *The Impact of Market Access and Investment Restrictions on Japanese Pension Funds*. Washington, D.C.: Employee Benefit Research Institute.

Davis, E.P. (1988). Financial Market Activity of Life Insurance Companies and Pension Funds. Economic Paper 21. Basle: Bank for International Settlements.

—— (1993). The Development of Pension Funds: An Approaching Financial Revolution for Continental Europe. In R. O'Brien (ed.), *Finance and the International Economy 7*. Oxford: Oxford University Press.

—— (1994). Market Liquidity Risk. In D. Fair and R. Raymond (eds.), *The Competitiveness of Financial Institutions and Centres in Europe*. Dordrecht: Kluwer Academic Publishers.

—— (1995a). *Pension Funds, Retirement-Income Security and Capital Markets: An International Perspective*. Oxford: Oxford University Press.

Davis, E.P. (1995b). Institutional Investors, Unstable Financial Markets and Monetary Policy. In F. Bruni, D. Fair, and R. O'Brien (eds.), *Risk Management in Volatile Financial Markets*. Amsterdam: Kluwer. (Also Special Paper 75, LSE Financial Markets Group.)

—— (1996). The Role of Institutional Investors in the Evolution of Financial Structure and Behaviour. In M. Edey (ed.), *The Future of the Financial System. Proceedings of a conference*. Sydney: Reserve Bank of Australia.

—— (1997a). *Private Pensions in OECD Countries: The United Kingdom*. Paris: Organization for Economic Cooperation and Development.

—— (1997b). Population Ageing and Retirement Income Provision in the European Union. Special Paper. Royal Institute of International Affairs, London.

—— (1997c). Public Pensions, Pension Reform and Fiscal Policy. EMI Staff Paper 5. European Monetary Insitute, Frankfurt/Main.

Deutsche Bundesbank (1984). Company Pension Schemes in the Federal Republic of Germany. *Monthly Report* (August):30–37.

Dilnot, A. (1992). *Taxation and Private Pensions: Costs and Consequences in Private Pensions and Public Policy*. Paris: Organization for Economic Cooperation and Development.

Dilnot, A., and P. Johnson (1993). *The Taxation of Private Pensions*. London: Institute for Fiscal Studies.

EFRP (1996). *European Pension Funds: Their Impact on Capital Markets and Competitiveness*. Brussels: European Federation for Retirement Provision.

Engen, E.M., W.G. Gale, and J.K. Scholz (1994). Do Saving Incentives Work? *Brookings Papers on Economic Activity* 1:85–151.

Feldstein, M. (1974). Social Security, Induced Retirement and Aggregate Capital Accumulation. *Journal of Political Economy* 82:902–956.

—— (1978). Do Private Pensions Increase National Savings? *Journal of Public Economics* 10:277–293.

—— (1995). Social Security and Saving. New Time Series Evidence. NBER Working Paper 5054. Cambridge, Mass.

Friedman, B.M. (1996). Economic Implications of Changing Share Ownership. *Journal of Portfolio Management* 22:59–70.

Frijns, J., and C. Petersen (1992). Financing, Administration and Portfolio Management; How Secure Is the Pension Promise? In *Private Pensions and Public Policy*. Paris: Organization for Economic Cooperation and Development.

Gale, W. (1997). The Effects of Pensions on Household Wealth: A Re-Evaluation of Theory and Evidence. Mimeo. Brookings Institute.

GAO (1989). *Private Pensions: Portability and Preservation of Vested Pension Benefits*. Washington, D.C.: U.S. General Accounting Office.

Gustman, A., and O.S. Mitchell (1992). Pensions and the US Labor Market. In Z. Bodie and A. Munnell (eds.), *Pensions and the US Economy. Pensions Research Council.* Philadelphia: University of Pennsylvania Press.

Hannah, L. (1992). *Similarities and Differences in the Growth and Structure of Private Pensions in OECD Countries: Private Pensions and Public Policy.* Paris: Organization for Economic Cooperation and Development.

Hepp, S. (1992). Comparison of Investment Behaviour of Pension Plans in Europe— Implications for Europe's Capital Markets. In J. Mortensen (ed.), *The Future of Pensions in the European Community.* London: Brassey's.

Holzmann, R. (1997). On Economic Benefits and Fiscal Requirements of Moving from Unfunded to Funded Pensions. Forschungsbericht 9702. University of Saarland, Saarbrücken.

Hubbard, R.G. (1986). Pension Wealth and Individual Saving: Some New Evidence. *Journal of Money, Credit and Banking* 18:167–178.

Ippolito, R.A. (1989). *The Economics of Pension Insurance.* Homewood, Illinois: Pension Research Council, Dow Jones Irwin.

King, M.A., and L. Dicks-Mireaux (1988). Portfolio Composition and Pension Wealth: An Econometric Study. In Z. Bodie, J.B. Shoven, and D.A. Wise (eds.), *Pensions in the US Economy.* Chicago: University of Chicago Press.

Lazear, E.P., and R.L. Moore (1988). Pensions and Turnover. In Z. Bodie, J.B. Shoven, and D.A. Wise (eds.), *Pensions in the US Economy.* Chicago: University of Chicago Press.

Levis, M. (1989). Stock Market Anomalies: A Reassessment Based on UK Data. *Journal of Banking and Finance* 13:675–696.

Marsh, P. (1990). *Short-Termism on Trial.* London: Institutional Fund Managers Association.

Masson, P.R., T.A. Bayoumi, and H. Samiei (1995). International Evidence on the Determinants of Private Saving. IMF Working Paper WP/95/51. Washington, D.C.

McConnell, J.J., and C.J. Muscarella (1985). Corporate Capital Expenditure Decisions and the Market Value of the Firm. *Journal of Financial Economics* 14:399–422.

McCormick, B., and G. Hughes (1984). The Influence of Pensions on Job Mobility. *Journal of Public Economics* 23(1/2):183–206.

Miles, D.K. (1993). Testing for Short Termism in the UK Stock Market. Bank of England Working Paper 4. London.

Mitchell, M.L., and J.H. Mulherin (1989). Pensions and Mergers. In J. Turner and D.J. Beller (eds.), *Trends in Pensions.* Washington, D.C.: U.S. Department of Labor.

Munnell, A.H., and F.O. Yohn (1992). What Is the Impact of Pensions on Saving? In Z. Bodie and A.H. Munnell (eds.), *Pensions and the Economy.* Philadelphia: Pensions Research Council and University of Pennsylvania Press.

Neumann, M. (1986). Möglichkeiten zur Entlastung der gesetzlichen Rentenversicherung durch kapitalbildende Vorsorgemaßnahmen. Universität Tübingen.

Nürk, B., and A. Schrader (1996). From Pension Reserves to Pension Funds: An Opportunity for the German Financial Market. Deutsche Bank Research. Frankfurt/Main.

Papke, L.E. (1996). Are 401(K) Plans Replacing Other Employer-Provided Pensions? Evidence from Panel Data. NBER Working Paper 5736. Cambridge, Mass.

Pensions and Investments (1997). Japan Dumps Fund Investment Restrictions. April 14.

Pesando, J.E. (1992). The Economic Effects of Private Pensions. In *Private Pensions and Public Policy*. Paris: Organization for Economic Cooperation and Development.

Poterba, J.M., and L.H. Summers (1992). *Time Horizons of American Firms: New Evidence from a Survey of CEOs*. Cambridge, Mass.: Harvard Business School.

Poterba, J.M., and D.A. Wise (1996). Individual Financial Decisions in Retirement Savings Plans and the Provision of Resources For Retirement. NBER Working Paper 5762. Cambridge, Mass.

Poterba, J.M., S.F. Venti, and D.A. Wise (1996). Personal Retirement Saving Programs and Asset Accumulation: Reconciling the Evidence. NBER Working Paper 5599. Cambridge, Mass.

Revell, J. (1994). Institutional Investors and Fund Managers. *Revue de la Banque* 2:55–68.

Riley, B. (1992). The Cost of Safer Pensions. *Financial Times* 13/7/92.

Samuelson, P.A. (1958). An Exact Consumption-Loan Model of Interest with or without the Social Contrivance of Money. *Journal of Political Economy* 66:467–482.

Samwick, A.A., and J. Skinner (1993). How Will Defined Contribution Pension Plans Affect Retirement Income? Mimeo. Stanford University.

Schieber, S.J., and J. Shoven (1994). The Consequences of Population Aging on Private Pension Fund Saving and Asset Markets. NBER Working Paper 4665. Cambridge, Mass.

Smalhout, J. (1996). *The Uncertain Retirement*. Burr Ridge, Illinois: Irwin.

Steil, B. (ed.) (1996). *The European Equity Markets: The State of the Union and an Agenda for the Millennium*. London: Royal Institute of International Affairs.

Stock, J.H., and D.A. Wise (1988). The Pension Inducement to Retire: An Option Value Analysis. NBER Working Paper 2660. Cambridge, Mass.

Tamura, M. (1992). Improving Japan's Employee Pension Fund System. *Nomura Research Institute Quarterly* (Summer):66–83.

Thomas, A., and C. Towe (1996). US Private Saving and the Tax Treatment of IRAs/401(k)s: A Re-Examination Using Household Survey Data. IMF Working Paper WP/96/87. Washington, D.C.

Turner, J. (1993). *Pension Policy for a Mobile Labor Force*. Kalamazoo, Michigan: W.E. Upjohn Institute for Employment Research.

Turner, J., and N. Watanabe (1996). *Private Pension Policies in Industrialized Countries*. Kalamazoo, Michigan: W.E. Upjohn Institute for Employment Research.

World Bank (1994). *Averting the Old Age Crisis. Policies to Protect the Old and Promote Growth*. Washington, D.C.: World Bank.

Wyatt Data Services (1993). *1993 Benefits Report Europe USA*. Brussels: Wyatt Company.

Comment on E. Philip Davis

Ketil Hviding

1. Introduction

Philip Davis's paper provides a good review of corporate pension regimes in various countries. He seems to favor funded corporate pensions with an element of mandatory provisions, claiming, inter alia, that the viability of the pensions system may be increased by larger reliance on funded corporate pensions. Compared to a pay-as-you-go system, funded corporate pensions would increase long-term national savings, vitalize capital markets, and should have a positive influence on labor markets. He also favors "external funding"—common in most English-speaking countries and the Netherlands—as it would isolate the companies from risks associated with a reduction in the workforce. Portfolio regulations should be flexible along the lines of the "prudent man" principle, allowing a substantial share to be invested in equities. Such a system contrasts with book-reserve funding, which is the norm in Germany and Japan.

I consider the paper to be useful in the context of a discussion on pension reform, since it deals with the major challenge of a move to privately funded and managed old-age pensions: the regulation of private pensions. In my view the macro effects of pension reform are secondary to the issue of who manages the capital stock, and how it is regulated/governed. The positive savings effects could be generated by traditional fiscal consolidation—which in macroeconomic terms is equivalent to increased funding—and the labor market distortions could be removed by establishing a legal link between contributions to the actuarially fair value of benefits, irrespective of the degree of funding.

The switch to privately funded pensions is—if not accompanied by some sort of fiscal consolidation—a poor instrument to use against a rapidly aging population or a chronically low level of savings. Pension fund "privatization" might, however, make a lot of sense, even if it consists of a pure assets swap from the public sector to the private sector, such as using the proceeds from privatized industries to build up a private pension funds as suggested in several transition economies. The gains from such an assets swap might be very large, as the shrinking of the government might make everybody better off. The build-up of a private pension industry should also improve the functioning of financial mar-

Remark: The opinions expressed in these comments are those of the author and do not represent the views of the OECD or its member governments.

kets, strengthen corporate governance, and ensure a better allocation of resources.

These benefits will, however, only materialize if financial markets are appropriately regulated and supervised. Privatization involves a complicated transition
from direct government control to a system of limited private ownership, constrained by new regulations and public institutions playing the role of arbiters.
The success or failure of such a transition is fully dependent on the success of
the regulatory system that is put in place.

2.   How to Regulate Private Pension Funds

The overall objectives of regulating pension funds are very similar to those of
other types of financial market regulations. The performance of both pension
fund regulation and regulation of other financial industries depends on how well
it deals with market failures and maintains political support. This entails walking
on a thin line between too much regulation and too little regulation. Too much
regulation would lock out many of the potential benefits from privatization in
terms of improved resource allocation and financial innovation. Too little regulation would leave the system open to large disruptions and could result in large
clean-up costs.

The rationale for financial regulation varies from country to country, but most
economists would agree on the following threefold purpose:

— protecting small investors/contributors from fraud,
— avoiding large-scale failures with important spillover effects (systemic
   risk),
— correcting other market failures in financial markets, such as agency
   problems and "adverse selection" in credit and annuities markets.

In addition to these objectives, it is often argued that the government should
ensure adequate income for the elderly, and that this purpose should be reflected
in the regulation of private pensions. In fact, this constitutes a minimum income
guarantee, and poses "moral hazard" problems that are very similar to those that
are posed by deposit guarantees in the banking industry. Thus, given the government's ultimate liability for this guarantee, it seems appropriate to create a special institution dedicated to providing such income guarantees, both as concerns
old-age and the more general type of poverty alleviation. Such an institution
could be backed by financial assets and should have access to information that
would help to reduce the moral hazards inherent in such programs. Minimum

contributions to private pensions could also help to reduce the exposure of the programs to the opportunistic behavior of individuals.

Because of the very complex nature of pension contracts, the objective of investor protection is particularly important. Typically, pensions and life-insurance products are not very easy to understand for the average individual and their "true" value is only revealed far in the future. Large-scale fraudulent sale of pension funds, such as recently experienced in the United Kingdom, highlights the importance of dealing efficiently with this issue. It can also be argued that investor protection is more important in the pension fund and life-insurance industry than in the banking sector, while, on the other hand, prudential issues are more important in banking, owing to its key role in the payment system.

The best way to achieve a reasonable degree of protection for small investors and retirees is to impose strict standards on disclosure, such as methods of calculating present values of pension benefits.[1] "Health warnings," certification, and a public or quasi-private system of ratings can also be helpful in sending the right signals to investors about the solidity and investment strategies of the funds. Legal responsibility of pension funds that could make the management personally liable in case of serious fraud is probably important and may require enlarging the scope for engaging in class action suits, especially in Europe and Japan. Indeed, the increased transparency of private pension markets—often far ahead of the public sector—might be one of the major benefits of the transfer of the pension liabilities from the public sector to the private sector.

A useful lesson from the regulation of other financial services is the danger of relying a lot on direct quantity restrictions on the portfolio allocation of financial institutions (see for example, Edey and Hviding 1995). First, the real risk of pension funds is not reflected in the volatility of the returns in their portfolio. Rather, guarantees such as those implicit in "defined benefit plans" or other return guarantees are generally much more important sources of risks, as Japanese pension funds have recently learned. Second, limiting the portfolio only to a restricted class of assets precludes pension funds from taking advantage of gains from increased diversification, in particular if it excludes foreign investment. Third, putting an upper bound on equity investment might expose "defined benefit" funds to substantial inflation/earnings risk, since, in most countries, liquid markets in indexed-linked bonds are unavailable.

Experience in banking regulation suggests that it is better to manage systemic risk by requiring a minimum level of capital than by restricting investment opportunities. This does not eliminate the need to monitor risk; on the contrary, the

---

[1]   In defined benefit plans, this would probably entail separating out the net present value of accrued benefits from the net worth of corporate pension under given assumptions about the future growth of contributions and benefits.

required level of capital could be made dependent on the risk-taking of the fund.[2] Again, improved levels of disclosure, standardization of methods used to calculate net present values, and risk-levels, as well as legal recourse, should be helpful in limiting the number of "scandals" and large-scale disruptions. In addition, regulators should allow in-house risk management systems, in particular when assessing the riskiness of complex derivative instruments.

Public pensions or group plans as offered in corporate pension plans are often considered as superior to individual pensions in dealing with adverse selection problems in annuities markets. Putting the standard "lemon argument" on its head, an increase in the sale price of annuities tends to attract people with longer life expectancies, thus reducing the net return to the insurance industry.[3] In such a situation, the market for individual annuities would break down or only involve a substantial premium to the actuarially fair price. A collective pensions plan reduces this problem by pooling the risk of people with a given average life expectancy. While there is clear empirical evidence on the existence of an "adverse selection premium" on individual annuities, it is less certain whether this premium is significantly larger than can be found on "other familiar (and almost universally purchased) insurance products."[4] According to Friedman and Warshawsky (1988), the premium ("load factor") paid on property and casualty insurance has been reported to be nearly as large as for annuities.[5]

It is also important to note that any problems of adverse selection can be dealt with independently of the management of the assets (public pensions) or the employment contract (corporate pensions). The adverse selection premium could be reduced by imposing a low price on the annuities in order to render the scheme attractive even to people expecting to live a relatively short time, and finance the potential loss of the institution out of a general tax on the pension funds, paid by everyone whether or not they participate in the annuity scheme. A potentially cheaper way of dealing with the adverse selection problem would be to make participation in the annuity schemes obligatory.

Several proposals for "social security" privatization involve mandatory contribution to private pensions (e.g., Feldstein 1996). This, it is argued, would increase national savings more than voluntary contributions, since it involves

---

2   Funding rules amount to a kind of minimum capital requirement on defined benefit plans. For a more detailed discussion about funding rules in the U.K. context, see Exley et al. (1997).

3   For the "lemon argument," see Akerlof (1970).

4   Friedman and Warshawsky (1988:73). For more recent evidence on the "adverse selection premium," see Mitchell et al. (1997) and Walliser (1997).

5   The premium (the "load factor" less 1) on property and casualty insurance was 37 percent compared to 48 percent on annuities. The potential exclusion from the annuity and insurance markets is not included in these calculations, however.

"forced savings," reflecting credit restrictions—arising, e.g., from problems linked to the use of "human wealth" as collateral—and prevents young workers from offsetting these savings by increased borrowing.[6] But the mandatory nature of contributions pose additional problems for the regulation of the funds. It can be argued that in this case, the government's responsibility for the value of the funds is larger than in the case of voluntary contributions. Such a responsibility is acknowledged in, for example, Chile, where a minimum return benchmark is imposed on certified funds.

The development that large pension funds invest in equity poses important challenges in terms of balancing gains from corporate control and liquidity. On the one hand, active involvement ("voice") in corporate management may reduce the "agency problems" present in most publicly held companies. There is some evidence that pension funds can play an important role in improving the performance of managers through targeted shareholder activism.[7] On the other hand, pension funds holdings are generally small minority holdings and the fund may need to retain the option to sell shares in order to avoid big losses ("exit"). Thus, there is a need to find a system that allows funds to benefit from privileged information in exchange for a temporary restriction on liquidity, allowing the funds to switch from "voice mood" to "exit mood" and vice versa.

3.   Are Corporate Pensions Special?

In general, corporate pensions constitute an integral element of the employment contract, making them fundamentally different from other private pensions. As a consequence of this, it is very difficult to make general statements about the desirability of a particular type of regulatory regime without, at the same time, assessing other important aspects of labor relations. The significance of corporate pensions is bound to be very different in countries were labor unions are very strong, such as Germany, Scandinavia, and the Netherlands, compared to countries were unions are weaker, such as the United States and the United Kingdom.

Historically, corporate pensions developed either as a means to attract and maintain a stable workforce or as a result of paternalistic motivations. It is, however, impossible to understand the development of corporate pensions without considering the labor union movement's role in providing social institutions that

---

6   There would, however, be a "forced saving effect" over and above the effects discussed in the beginning of the comments only if contributions to the mandatory private pensions exceeded the contributions to the public pension system.

7   The most well-known example is the monitoring performed by CalPERS, often in companies where it has only small minority shareholdings.

protect workers' old-age pensions. In most countries with strong labor unions, corporate pensions are either very insignificant (Norway and Germany), are controlled by the unions in cooperation with the employers (the Netherlands and Finland), or are mainly union-controlled, with heavy government involvement (France and Sweden). By contrast, strong firm-specific and independently managed pension schemes are mainly found in countries with weaker unions.

In the same context, vesting periods are generally shorter in countries where labor turnover is high as in the United States and the United Kingdom than in countries with a lower degree of turnover, such as Japan and Germany. In most countries, but in particular in Japan and Germany, the value of a pension is significantly reduced if one leaves the company before normal retirement. Is this a consequence of different pension fund regulations or is it just that common practice is reflected in statutory rules? What explains the apparent discrepancy between the value of a pension at normal retirement and earlier retirement, even in countries where the pension system is voluntarily contracted between the employer and the workers without significant involvement from the labor unions? Is there a tendency of unions to join forces with management in cementing the ties between the company/unions and workers?

This is a small number of the many unanswered questions on the relationship between unions, corporate pensions, and management. Most of these questions are left relatively unexplored in Philip Davis's paper and most other papers on private pensions. The answers to these questions are, however, essential to understanding the economic effects of corporate pensions. Hopefully, future policy research will throw some light on the rather unexplored area of the interactions between labor relations and different corporate and quasi-corporate pension arrangements.

4.   Concluding Remarks

Let me conclude with some remarks on the issue of book-reserve funding or "internal funding," which is commonly used in Germany and Japan. As mentioned in Philip Davis's article, the risks attached to this type of funding are linked to the relative illiquidity of the assets; accrued pension liabilities might therefore block rational downsizing of the labor force without a temporary disruption in the on-going activities of the company. Furthermore, book-reserve funding might be particularly risky if corporate accounts are not transparent, a problem which is likely to be even larger in the case of the evaluation of the company's pension liabilities.

Reflecting the growing need for private pension investment and a need to increase labor market flexibility, the demand for externally funded corporate pensions is likely to increase in Germany. Book-reserve funding might work when the size of the funds is very small, but more sizable funds will probably need to consist of assets invested in other companies' equity, bonds, or indexed securities. The development of strong pension funds with increased equity investment may accelerate a transformation of German financial markets towards a more market-based system, gradually eroding the traditional role of banks and insider control.

Bibliography

Akerlof, G. (1970). The Market for Lemons: Quality Uncertainty and the Market. *Quarterly Journal of Economics* 84:488–500.

Edey, M., and K. Hviding (1995). An Assessment of Financial Reform in OECD Countries. *OECD Economic Studies* 25:7–36.

Exley, C.J., S.J.B. Mehta, and A.D. Smith (1997). The Financial Theory of Defined Benefits Schemes. Mimeo. Institute of Actuaries, London.

Feldstein, M. (1996). The Missing Piece in Policy Analysis: Social Security Reform. *American Economic Review* 86(2):1–14.

Friedman, B.M., and M. Warshawsky (1988). Annuity Prices and Saving Behavior in the United States. In Z. Bodie, J.B. Shoven, and D. Wise (eds.), *Pensions in the U.S. Economy*. Chicago: University of Chicago Press.

Mitchell, O.S., J. Porteba, and M. Warshawsky (1997). New Evidence on the Money's Worth of Individual Annuities. NBER Working Paper 6002. Cambridge, Mass.

Walliser, J. (1997). Understanding Adverse Selection in the Annuities Market and the Impact of Privatizing Social Security. Mimeo. Congressional Budget Office. Washington, D.C.

II.

Country Studies:
Problems and Responses

Adjustments within the System:

Germany, the United States and

Sweden

Axel Börsch-Supan

Germany: A Social Security System on the Verge of Collapse

1. Introduction

Germany relies heavily on pay-as-you-go (PAYG) financing for old-age social security. PAYG pensions constitute more than 80 percent of the income of households headed by persons aged 65 and older, while funded retirement income, such as asset income or firm pensions, plays a much smaller role than in the Netherlands or the Anglo-Saxon countries. At the same time, Germany, together with Austria and Switzerland, is the OECD country with the most pronounced population aging process.

This paper argues that the PAYG system of social security in Germany cannot provide the flexibility that is necessary to master the demographic changes to come. The German PAYG pension system is locked between the Scylla of a low pension level and the Charybdis of a high contribution rate. Even after several reforms and modifications, the German PAYG system has strong incentive effects towards early retirement and escape into disability insurance that are detrimental to the finances of the system.

Additional flexibility can be achieved by funding the pension systems at least partially. This works mainly through two mechanisms. First, intertemporal substitution—possible only in a funded system—permits a smoothing of the demographic burden across a much longer period than the contemporary budget constraint of a PAYG system. Second, international diversification on global capital markets enables the likely decline of domestic rates of return in an aging economy to be escaped.

The paper synthesizes simulations of the German PAYG system with projections of a gradual transition to a (partially) funded system. The paper has three main parts. The first part briefly describes the German public pension system and its main incentive effects. In the second part, I present the demographics of population aging and its implications for the PAYG pension system. I then collect projections of the PAYG contribution rate under alternative labor force scenarios, most notably a change in the retirement age and in female labor force participation, and show that the PAYG system has insufficient flexibility under realistic assumptions. In particular, the German PAYG system yields implicit rates of return that are much lower than in a funded pension scheme. The third part of the paper is therefore concerned with the transition to a (partially) funded system. It shows that the transition problem is much less severe than frequently argued, and that financial risks can be minimized by international diversification. Indeed, a funded system that invests globally can provide a rate of return that generates a macroeconomic per capita consumption path through the entire 2000–2050 period that strongly dominates per capita consumption under PAYG.

2.   The German Public Pension System and Its Incentive Effects

The German public pay-as-you-go pension system (the *Gesetzliche Rentenversicherung* and its equivalents)[1] is by far the largest pillar of retirement income, much more so than in many other countries (Figure 1).[2] It is mandatory for every worker except for the self-employed and those with very small incomes. In addition, the German social security system is very generous. The system has a very high replacement rate, generating net retirement incomes that are currently about 72 percent of preretirement net earnings for a worker with a 45-year earnings history and average lifetime earnings (Figure 2).[3] This is substantially higher than, e.g., the corresponding U.S. net replacement rate of about 53 percent.[4] In addition, it provides relatively generous survivor benefits that constitute a substantial proportion of total unfunded pension wealth.

A detailed description of the German public pension system and how it compares to other public pension systems can be found in Börsch-Supan and Schnabel (1997). In this section, I focus on the incentive effects which make coping with the future demographic challenges particularly difficult.

The German public pension system (or, as it is referred to in Germany, "retirement insurance" system) provides *old-age pensions* for workers aged 60 and

---

1   For example, the retirement system of civil servants. The system was founded in 1889 by Bismarck as a funded system. After WW II, the 1957 pension reform introduced PAYG financing, which was fully phased in by 1967.

2   See the international comparisons in Gruber and Wise (1997).

3   This replacement rate is defined as the current pension of a retiree with a 45-year average earnings history divided by the current average earnings of all dependently employed workers. This is different from the replacement rate relative to the most recent earnings of a retiring worker, which are usually higher than the lifetime average.

4   Using the same replacement rate concept as in footnote 3.

older, *disability benefits* for workers below age 60 that are converted to old-age pensions latest at age 65, and *survivor benefits* for spouses and children. In addition, preretirement (i.e., retirement before age 60) is possible through several mechanisms using the public transfer system, mainly unemployment compensation.

Figure 1 — Sources of Household Income (male heads of household only)

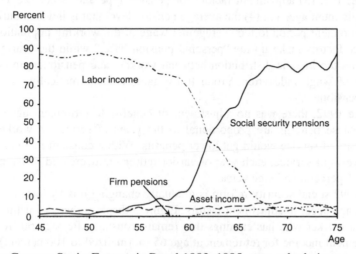

Source: German Socio-Economic Panel 1993–1995, own calculations.

Figure 2 — Replacement Rate of the German Pension System, 1960–1995

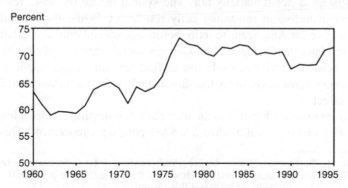

Note: Average pension divided by average wage. Based on 45 years of service. After 1989, West *and* East Germany.

Source: Bundesministerium für Arbeit und Sozialordnung (1977).

A main feature of the German old-age pensions is "flexible retirement" after age 63 for workers with a long service history. In addition, retirement at age 60 is possible for women, unemployed, and workers who cannot be appropriately employed for health or labor market reasons. Benefits are computed on a life-. time contribution basis and adjusted according to the type of pension and retirement age. They are the product of four elements: (1) the employee's relative wage position, averaged over the entire earnings history, (2) the number of years of service life, (3) adjustment factors for pension type and (since the 1992 reform) retirement age, and (4) the average pension level that is indexed during the entire retirement period to the average net wage of the working population. The first three factors make up the "personal pension base," while the fourth factor determines the income distribution between workers and pensioners in general. Because of wage indexation, productivity gains are automatically transferred also to pensioners.

Before 1992, there was no adjustment of benefits to retirement age.[5] However, because benefits are proportional to the years of service, a worker with fewer years of service would get lower benefits. With a constant income profile and 40 years of service, each year of earlier retirement decreased pension benefits by 2.5 percent, and vice versa.

The 1992 social security reform is gradually changing this by introducing retirement age-specific adjustment factors. Figure 3 displays these adjustment factors for a worker who has earnings that remain constant after age 60. It relates the retirement income for retirement at age 65 (normalized to 100 percent) to the retirement income for retirement at earlier or later ages. As references, the figure also displays the corresponding adjustments in the United States and actuarially fair adjustments at a 3 percent discount rate.[6] As can be seen, the German public pension system is not actuarially fair. The system before the 1992 reform was particularly distortive in rewarding early retirement. While there is little economic incentive for Americans to retire before age 65 and only a small disincentive to retire later than at age 65, the German social security system tilts the retirement decision heavily towards the earliest retirement age applicable. The 1992 pension reform in Germany has diminished but by no means abolished this incentive effect.

The failure to adjust benefits in an actuarially fair manner creates a loss in unfunded social security wealth when a worker postpones retirement. This loss is

---

5   Curiously, the German system before 1992 provided a large increase in retirement benefits for work at ages 66 and 67. However, it was ineffective because the inducements to early retirement by far offset this incentive.

6   See Börsch-Supan (1992). The actuarially fair adjustments equalize the expected social security wealth defined there in Appendix 2 for a worker with an earnings history starting at age S=20. A higher discount rate yields steeper adjustments.

large relative to the labor income that could be earned when working longer. Figure 4 shows these losses in percent of potential earnings. They can be interpreted as implicit taxes on the wages earned when postponing retirement. The implicit taxes exceeded 50 percent before the 1992 pension reform but will still be in excess of 20 percent when the 1992 reform has been fully phased in.

Figure 3 — Adjustments of Pension Benefits to Retirement Age

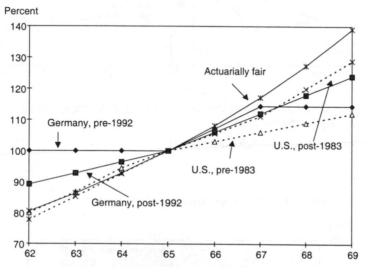

Note: Benefits when retiring at ages 62–69 in percent of benefits when retiring at age 65, assuming the same earnings history.

Source: Own calculations.

The incentive effects are even stronger if one manages to claim disability status. In this case, also after the 1992 reform no adjustments apply. Thus, implicit tax rates are similar to the pre-1992 regime in excess of 60 percent for workers retiring before age 60. Disability is an important pathway to retirement, as Figure 5 shows. Even after tightening disability eligibility from the early 1980s on, still more workers enter retirement through the disability insurance than through old-age pensions. In addition, "preretirement" schemes in combination with early retirement due to unemployment account for another 20 percent of those entering retirement.

The incentive effects are reflected in a mean retirement age below age 60, with a dramatic plunge after the "flexible retirement" option was introduced in 1972 (Figure 6), and a retirement age distribution marked by distinct "spikes" at

Figure 4 — Implicit Tax Rates of Postponing Retirement

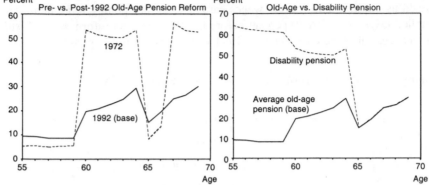

Note: Loss in accrual of unfunded public pension wealth relative to hypothetical wage if retirement postponed by one year.

Source: Börsch-Supan and Schnabel (1997).

Figure 5 — Pathways to Retirement (males), 1958–1995

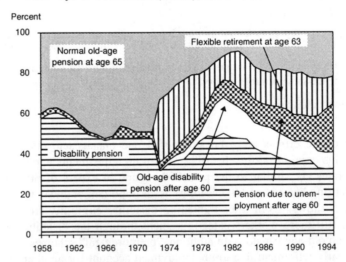

Note: Percentages for entries into retirement by pension type.

Source: Verband Deutscher Rentenversicherungsträger (1997).

Figure 6 — Average Retirement Age, 1960–1995

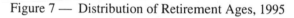

Note: Average age of all new entries into public pension system.

Source: Verband Deutscher Rentenversicherungsträger (1997).

Figure 7 — Distribution of Retirement Ages, 1995

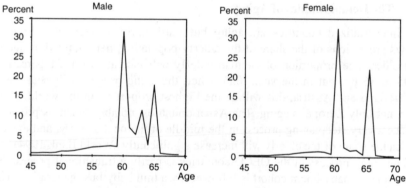

Source: Verband Deutscher Rentenversicherungsträger (1995).

ages 60, 63 and 65 (Figure 7). Age 65 applies mostly to women with a very short earnings history, while the most popular retirement age among men is age 60.

More formal econometric analyses were carried out by Börsch-Supan (1992), Schmidt (1995), and Börsch-Supan and Schmidt (1996). These studies used microeconometric option value analyses to compute the incentive effects of the nonactuarial adjustment of benefits in the German social security system on early retirement. They show that the 1992 reform will increase the average retirement age only by about half a year, and reduce retirement before age 60 from 32.2 percent to 28.2 percent, while a switch to a system with actuarially fair adjustment factors would shift the retirement age by more than two years. The effects of a nondistorting system are most powerful in the reduction of early retirement, i.e., retirement before the official window period. Retirement at ages 59 and below would drop from currently 32.2 percent to 17.8 percent.

3.   Structural Limitations of the German PAYG System

The incentives towards early retirement aggravate an anyway strained situation of the German public pension system. After the PAYG system was introduced in 1957, the system has now matured. High unemployment together with low old-age labor force participation generates a high dependency burden and a contribution rate that is currently in excess of 20 percent of gross income. To all of this, the change in the age composition of the German population is slowly but steadily accelerating.

a.   The Demographics of Aging

All industrialized countries are aging but particularly so Germany. Figure 8 shows projections of the share of the elderly population, here defined as age 60 and older. The proportion of German elderly will increase from 21 percent in 1995 to 36 percent in the year 2035, when the aging process will peak. With Switzerland and Austria, this will be the highest proportion in the world. However, not only Europe is aging. The Asian countries, notably Japan, is projected to face a very steep aging process in the middle of the next century, and even in Africa the share of the elderly will increase significantly (World Bank 1994).

The aging process in the OECD countries is partly a transitional process because a large baby boom cohort is followed by a thin baby bust generation. This transitional process is superimposed by the worldwide secular process of a steadily increasing life expectancy. The increase in life expectancy—about 1.5 years every 10 years in Germany—is not likely to end soon. On the contrary and to the surprise of many demographers, it even has accelerated between the most recent computations of German mortality tables. The combination of both processes will dramatically change the structure of the German age pyramid. As Figure 9 shows, there will be more elderly and fewer working age persons in absolute terms.

Consequently, the ratio of elderly to working age persons—the old-age dependency ratio—will increase steeply in the industrialized countries and particularly so in Germany. The OECD projects an increase from 20.6 percent in 1990 to 39.2 percent in 2030 for its European member countries.[7] In Germany, the old-age dependency ratio will far more than double from 21.7 percent in 1990 to 49.2 percent in 2030.[8]

Figure 8 — Percentage of Persons Aged 60 and Older in Various Countries, 1990–2040

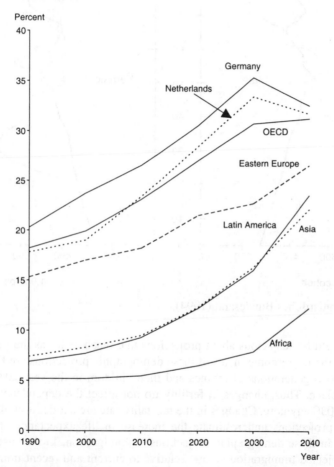

Source: World Bank (1994).

---

[7]   Number of persons aged 65 and older divided by number of persons aged 15–64.

[8]   OECD, based on World Bank projection by Bos et al. (1994). The OECD dependency ratio relates persons aged 65 and older to persons between ages 15 and 64.

Figure 9 — Age Structure of Germany, 1995 and 2040

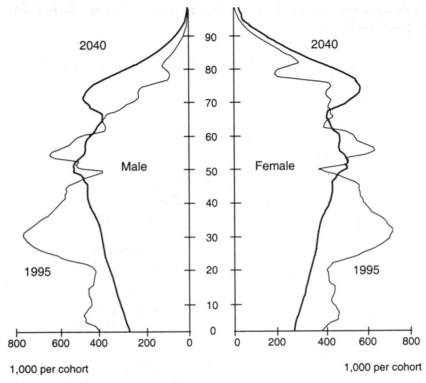

Source: Statistisches Bundesamt (1994).

One might be suspicious about projections that reach as far as the year 2030. However, the major components of these demographic projections are fairly certain. The two generations of retirees and their children in the year 2030 are already in place. Thus, changes in fertility do not affect the dependency ratio in the year 2030 anymore. Changes in the mortality rate are subtle; if at all, current mortality projections underestimate the increase in life expectancy. The main wild card in these demographic projections is immigration. In the case of Germany, projected immigration is low relative to current and recent immigration, characterized by the opening of the iron curtain and its aftermath. I will show further below that immigration has to be huge over more than two decades in order to reverse the demographic trends depicted in Figures 8 and 9.

b.   The Social Insurance Burden

The increase in the dependency ratio has immediate consequences for the pay-as-you-go social insurance system because fewer workers have to finance the benefits of more recipients. This affects not only the PAYG pension system, but also health and long-term care insurance and other social programs financed by general taxes that are geared to the elderly.[9]

Again, Germany faces the strongest challenge. The German social security contribution rate, now at about 20 percent of gross income,[10] will exceed 30 percent of gross income at the peak of population aging if the current replacement rate and the current labor force participation remain as they are now (Figure 10).

Figure 10 — Projected Contribution Rates for Three German PAYG Systems

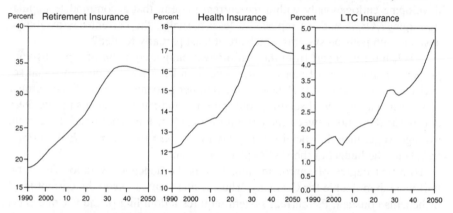

Note: Projections under constant benefit levels and unchanged labor force participation patterns (including retirement age). LTC = Long-Term Care.

Source: Börsch-Supan (1995).

Official estimates range between 26 and 29 percent, assuming some adaptation of the retirement age, the replacement rate, and female labor force participation (Prognos 1995). Because the main share of health care services is consumed by the elderly, health insurance contributions will also increase. Currently at 12.5 percent on average, the contribution rate is projected to increase by almost 50

---

9   About 20 percent of the German old-age social security budget is financed by general taxes.

10   Currently, the total contribution rate is 20.3 percent. Of this, 10.15 percent is deducted from employees' gross pay, and another 10.15 percent is paid by the employer.

percent to 17.5 percent of gross income. The most dramatic increase is in the new long-term care (LTC) insurance because the share of the very old is rising particularly quickly. If current benefit levels are maintained, the contribution rate will double from 1.7 percent now to almost 3.5 percent in 2035. Unlike to the pension and health insurance systems, the contribution rate to the LTC insurance will continue to increase after the peak of population aging in the year 2035 because of the projected increase in life expectancy.

c.   Reforming the PAYG Pension System

Is the current German pay-as-you-go pension system sufficiently flexible to bear the large and increasing retirement burden? What are the policy instruments that can realistically be employed? What are the built-in labor market mechanisms, developing endogenously within the current system, that accommodate population aging? Or should we replace, at least partially, the current pay-as-you-go systems with pension systems which are at least partially funded?

It is helpful to depart from the well-known budget equation of a pay-as-you-go pension system that finances current pension benefits with current social security tax contributions. If P denotes the number of beneficiaries, W the number of workers paying social security contributions, and r the replacement rate, here defined as the ratio between the current average pension benefit and the current average wage, then the social security tax rate, c, *has* to be $c = r \cdot P/W$ in order to balance the budget of the PAYG pension system.

To a first degree of approximation, P/W is the dependency ratio. This ratio will more than double for Germany. Thus, if one wants to keep the current level of benefits constant, the current system requires a doubling of the tax rate. This is the Scylla mentioned in the introduction: already the current social security contribution rate of 20.3 percent in Germany is considered an obstacle to international competitiveness and an incentive to escape taxation, so that the government has pledged to keep the rate at "around 20 percent."

If this were the case, benefits will have to decrease to half of their current levels to keep the PAYG budget balanced. This is Charybdis: it would drive a considerable percentage of retirees below the poverty line,[11] even a less dramatic benefit reduction had severe consequences. For instance, current government proposals recommend that the replacement rate for a worker with a 40-year ser-

---

11   The poverty line for a retired couple was a monthly income of DM 1,298 in 1989 (Bäcker et al. 1989:135). In this year, 38.4 percent of blue-collar and 20.1 percent of white-collar retirees received an old-age pension below DM 1,300 per month (Bundesministerium für Arbeit und Sozialordnung 1990:200–207). Most of these households have some supplemental income, increasing their income by 15–20 percent (Börsch-Supan and Schnabel 1997).

vice history should drop from 64 to 57 percent. This replacement rate implies that a worker with 79 percent of average earnings has a pension just at the poverty line. The PAYG pension system is in a serious dilemma, if not at the verge of collapse.

The only way to escape this dilemma is to change the ratio of beneficiaries to contributors, *P/W*. The most powerful route to achieve this is to change the retirement age, as this increases the number of contributors and at the same time decreases the number of beneficiaries. As pointed out in the first part of this paper, retirement age is rather low in Germany, slightly below age 60 in 1996, mainly because of a generous early retirement policy once designed to reduce the unemployment rate. Thus, increasing the retirement age appears to be a rather natural option. As a first step, removing the actuarial unfairness will increase retirement by about two years (see Section 1). However, this will not suffice. Figure 11 depicts simulations with a detailed demographic and employment

Figure 11 —   Projected Contribution Rates to Public Pension System: Alternative Retirement Ages

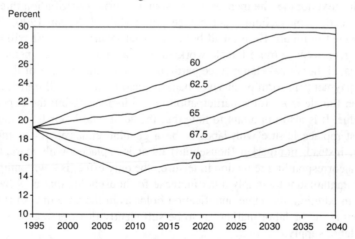

Note: Contribution rates to public pension system (employer and employee) in percent of gross earnings.

Source: Börsch-Supan (1996).

projection model developed elsewhere.[12] It shows that in order to fully compensate for the effects of population aging, the average retirement age has to increase by 9.5 years, to about age 69 (Börsch-Supan 1996). It is unlikely that the labor market is sufficiently flexible to permit this to happen.

A similar argument applies to another instrument of labor market flexibility that has recently gained popularity, namely part-time retirement. Part-time retirees receive only part of their pension benefits, and they pay social security contributions from their part-time labor income. The above-mentioned simulation shows that this will not be an effective mechanism to alleviate the pension crisis. Even if all pensioners began as part-time retirees, 18 years of half-time work would be required to offset the aging effect in Germany—too long in view of a life expectancy at age 60 that is about 17 years for German males.

Increasing the number of workers without a corresponding decrease in the number of retirees is less effective but still helpful. In this sense, an increase in female labor force participation is another mechanism which also helps reduce the retirement burden. However, the effect is small for Germany. Even if female labor force participation were to reach the level of male labor force participation within the next decade, the increase in the social security contribution rate would be dampened by only about 6 percentage points (Börsch-Supan 1996). The effect, depicted in Figure 12, is small because social security benefits will eventually also rise because more female workers will be enrolled in the pension system. Thus, higher female labor force participation eliminates some of the current transfer payments in form of survivor benefits, and it has a small transitional effect when female labor force participation is still increasing but the benefits are not yet due. It is also important to note that the additional labor force participation must replace leisure with labor to be a genuine enlargement of the labor force. If, instead, nonmarket (household) labor is replaced with market labor, without a corresponding reduction in leisure, the only effect is a widening of the tax base, tantamount to simply a tax increase for households that now have two earners. In addition, the same qualification holds as in the case of a shift to later retirement ages: the labor market has to be sufficiently flexible to absorb the additional labor supply.

Migration is another potentially powerful mechanism to alleviate the effects of population aging. Quite clearly, the influx of young immigrants can in theory fully compensate for population aging. In practice, one faces two problems. First and again, the domestic labor market has to be sufficiently flexible to absorb immigrant workers and provide the necessary training. Given high European unemployment rates, there is certainly at least a serious short-run limitation. Second,

---

[12]   In Börsch-Supan (1997a) the demographic scenario "MOSTLIK" with constant age-specific and gender-specific labor force participation rates.

the numbers have to work out. To fully compensate for population aging in Germany at the given typical age structure of immigrants—immigrants into Germany are on average about ten years younger than the resident population—about 800,000 persons (workers and family) have to immigrate annually into Germany from now on through the year 2035 (see the simulation results depicted in Figure 13). These are very large numbers.[13] They are not without a historical precedent but only during a few exceptional years, e.g., after the opening of the iron curtain, and they are unlikely to persist. Felderer (1992) correctly argues that a full compensation of the aging process through migration is impossible. Nevertheless, the simulation results depicted in Figure 13 also show that a steady immigration of 300,000 immigrants will reduce the increase of the social security contribution rate by about a third, provided that labor force participation of these immigrants is equal to current German labor force participation (Börsch-Supan 1994).

Figure 12 — Projected Contribution Rates to Public Pension System: Alternative Female Labor Force Participation Rates

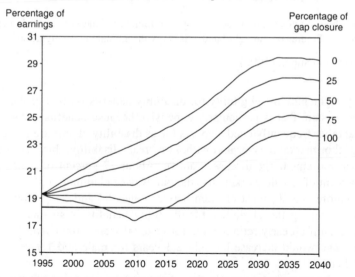

Note: Contribution rates to public pension system (employer and employee) in percent of gross earnings. Percentages on the right-hand axis denote closure of the gap between age-specific female and male labor force participation rates.

Source: Börsch-Supan (1996).

---

[13] The projections in Section 2 assume an annual immigration of some 80,000 persons annually. Note that all numbers refer to net immigration.

Figure 13 —   Projected Contribution Rates to Public Pension System: Alternative Net Migration

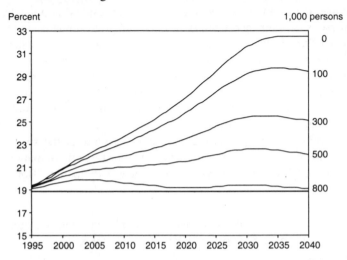

Note: Contribution rates to public pension system (employer and employee) in percent of gross earnings. Figures on the right-hand axis show the annual net immigration.

Source: Börsch-Supan (1996).

Finally, tightening the eligibility for disability benefits—a part of the German retirement system that is particularly expensive because benefits occur early in life—is another frequently cited step. As far as disability claims are made essentially for labor market reasons and without a "real" disability, this amounts to an increase in retirement age discussed above. About 27 percent of male workers and 20 percent of female workers use the pathway of claiming disability in order to retire before age 60, most of them between ages 54 and 59.[14] However, the effect of tightening the eligibility for disability benefits is smaller than often claimed. Even if all early retirement before age 60 were eliminated, the average retirement age would increase by only 2.3 years for male and 1.9 years for female workers.

It should be clear that no single one of these steps can solve the dilemma of the German PAYG pension system.[15] Of course, this does not imply that a com-

---

[14]   Verband Deutscher Rentenversicherungsträger (1995). In addition to this *general* disability pension for workers aged less than 60 years, an almost equal share of workers claim the *old-age* disability pension between ages 60 and 65.

[15]   See Blanchet (1988) who provides similar projections for France.

bination of several steps will inevitably fail to solve the pension crisis within the PAYG system. Such a piecemeal approach could consist of an increase in retirement age (by three steps: two years by making the benefit calculation actuarially fair, another year or two by shifting the pivotal age of the benefit calculation ["normal retirement age"], and another year by tightening disability rules)[16] and by hoping for higher female labor force participation and a steady influx of immigrants below a level that causes concern among residents.

The main problem with this piecemeal approach is that it is far from clear that the labor market is sufficiently flexible and will absorb this additional labor supply during the next two decades. One can only hope that population aging, after all a decrease of the working age population as a share of the total population, will resolve the unemployment problem automatically. To the extent that this will not happen smoothly, the PAYG system must increase contributions and/or decrease benefits rather dramatically in order to remain in balance, as was shown above. Current government proposals tend to be in this direction and include the above-mentioned reduction in replacement rates. In the sequel of this paper, I will argue that this policy is unwise because it forfeits the long-run opportunities provided by a gradual transition to a funded pension system.

d.   Implicit Rates of Return of the German PAYG System

The problem can be cast in terms of a lack of a reasonable rate of return implicit in the PAYG system. In macroeconomic terms, the rate of return of a PAYG system is the sum of the growth rates of the work force and of labor productivity. In microeconomic terms, one relates the flow of lifetime contributions of a specific worker to the flow of expected pension and computes the rate of return that equalizes the present values of both flows (see Schnabel 1997a). Figure 14 shows the average PAYG rates of return under two extreme policy assumptions: maintaining the current replacement rate (and thus increasing the contribution rate as described above) and maintaining the current contribution rate (and thus lowering the pension level). Freezing the contribution rate generates negative rates of return for all cohorts after 1965 because they will receive a low pension after having fully contributed during already half of their working lives. Freezing the replacement rate is more advantageous for them, but does not help for later cohorts. Cohorts born after 1980 will also in this case have negative rates of return because they have to bear the steeply rising contributions that were shown in Figure 10.

Due to the survivor benefits, the rates of return are higher for couples than for males (Figure 15), while they are virtually identical for the average retiree (retir-

---

[16]   These changes are interdependent and are not necessarily additive.

ing at age 60 after 35 years of service) and the reference retiree of German government publications (the *Eckrentner*, retiring at age 65 after 45 years of service).

Figure 14 — Implicit Rates of Return of the German PAYG System for Two Scenarios

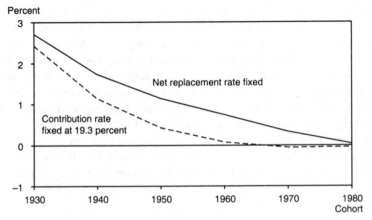

Source: Schnabel (1997a).

Figure 15 — Implicit Rates of Return of the German PAYG System for Various Groups

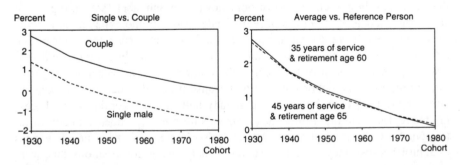

Source: Schnabel (1997a).

4.   Transition to Funding

These very low rates of return contrast with the rates of return in a funded system. The long-run real rate of return of investments funneled into the German business sector was 7.4 percent during the 20 years from 1975 through 1994. This rate is based on a portfolio that includes all equity and debt that was invested from 1975 through 1994 in all corporations in Germany (including foreign-owned corporations), counting interest, dividends, and capital gains from 1975 until 1994 after business and before personal taxes.[17,18] Households would not receive this full rate of return because of financial transaction costs and profits of the pension funds, so a reasonably realistic rate of return of a funded pension would be around 5.9 percent.[19] Even the long-run interest rate on government bonds, about 4 percent, beats the rate of return implicit in the German PAYG system.

Another metric to show the difference between the PAYG and a funded system is the annual payment into the respective system. Assume a worker with average earnings who starts a worklife of 40 years at age 20, retires at age 60, and dies at age 80. This worker has 40 years to save for 20 years of retirement. To fully fund the retirement income at the current replacement rate, which is about DM 22,400 annually (Bundesministerium für Arbeit und Sozialordnung 1997: 108), annual savings of about DM 1,100 are required if a household earned the full 7.4 percent average rate of return of the German corporate sector. This is only 10 percent of the current average annual contribution to the German PAYG pension system, DM 11,500 in 1995.[20] The huge difference is due to the force of compounding a large rate-of-return differential over a long time period. If, more realistically, the household did not receive the full rate of return of the corporate sector but 1.5 percent less for financial transaction costs and profits of the pension fund, the required annual savings would be about DM 1,800. Even at the interest rate on government bonds, the required annual savings of DM 3,300 are

---

[17]   Initial stock in 1975 is counted as inflow, final stock in 1994 as outflow. For a fair comparison to the tax-free pay-as-you-go pension, income from a funded system is assumed to be also free from personal taxation. In any case, note that the interest income of an average earner's pension fund is below the current exemption limit for capital income taxation.

[18]   McKinsey Global Institute (1996) also computed U.S. and Japanese real rates of return (9.1 and 7.1 percent, respectively). The U.S. rate closely corresponds to the rate computed by and used in Feldstein and Samwick (1996).

[19]   Administration costs of Dutch pension funds are about 0.5 percent; they are considerably higher in Chile.

[20]   In 1995, the average household paid DM 11,976 for social insurances (Statistisches Bundesamt 1996: 547). Of these, 48 percent went to the pension system. The same amount was paid by the employer on the employees' behalf.

less than a third of the current contributions. If this worker had a choice *de novo* between the PAYG and the funded system, he quite clearly would "opt out" into a funded system.

Figure 16 — Voluntary Contributions to the German PAYG System, 1984–1996

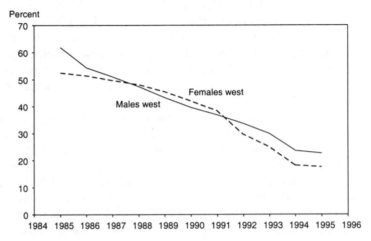

Note: Percentage of voluntarily insured who contribute more than the minimum amount.

Source: Schnabel (1997a), based on Verband Deutscher Rentenversicherungsträger (1997).

And indeed, that is what one can observe in the small part of the German pension system in which workers can actually opt out, namely among the self-employed. As Figure 16 shows, the percentage of self-employed who contributed more than the minimum amount dropped dramatically between 1985 and now from about 60 percent to about 20 percent.

It is important to realize that this rate-of-return difference has changed since the 1957 pension reform. In the early years of the German Federal Republic, the rate of return of the PAYG system was reasonably high—some 3 to 4 percent in real terms from 1950 through 1980—because Germany had a rather steep labor productivity increase in addition to mild labor force growth.[21] At the same time, rates of return in the capital market were much lower than today. For workers re-

---

[21] This is in line with a recent estimate by Eitenmüller (1996) who reports 6.5 percent in nominal terms (the rate of inflation during the 1950–1980 period was 3.1 percent, and 3.0 for the 1980–1993 period).

tiring now, the PAYG system was clearly more advantageous than a fully funded system in which the savings had been invested in the German business sector during the time between 1950 and 1980.

However, this has changed. While the rate of return of savings funneled into the German business sector has increased to 7–8 percent in real terms, labor force growth is now slightly negative and will decline even more. In addition, labor productivity is increasing only at the long-run historical average of about 1.5 percent rather than at the speed during the German economic miracle (Buchheim 1994:15). This has shifted the balance towards a funded system.

a.   Two Transition Models

However, today's workers simply do not have the choice of leaving the PAYG system because they have to finance the pensions of the current retirees. This transition problem requires one generation to pay twice—once for their parents and once for themselves. In a sense, this transition generation has to pay off the debt resulting from the very first generation when the PAYG system was started because the initial generation received pensions without contributions. Obviously, the severity of the transition problem depends on the size of this additional burden for the transition generation. As it will turn out, it is not at all a "double" burden.

There is a wide array of literature on how to solve the transition problem. The theoretical literature has focused on the question whether an intergenerational redistribution scheme exists that permits compensation of the transition generation by those future generations that will profit from the funded system. These schemes require taking up debt during the transition period. However, this demands resources and creates distortions because the debt has to be paid back through taxes. Economic theory shows that if the transition burden is sufficiently smoothened to avoid labor disincentive problems, a transition to a funded system is advantageous for all generations, including the transition generation. A crucial parameter is therefore the elasticity of the labor supply with respect to increases in the contribution and general tax rates. Unfortunately, there is little reliable empirical evidence on this parameter. One can only tentatively conclude from the current electorates' pressure on governments to reduce taxes, and from the fast increase in labor escaping taxation,[22] that this elasticity must be fairly large. Raffelhüschen (1993) and Buslei and Kraus (1996) provide simulations for Germany. Feldstein and Samwick (1996) and Kotlikoff (1996) have computed simulations for the United States. These simulations show that under realistic parameter choices one can indeed design feasible transition schemes that are advanta-

---

[22]   Increases in self-employment and black-market transactions.

geous for all generations. In turn, Fenge (1995) assumes that the actuarially fair part of the German PAYG system does not create any kind of labor supply disincentive. He concludes that a Pareto-improving transition from the PAYG to a funded system is not possible. A problem with Fenge's analysis is that he fixes wages and the rate of return such that potential efficiency gains through the funding mechanism over and above removing the small tax distortion of the actuarially unfair part of social security contributions have no impact on national income. In fact, all of the contributions may be regarded as distortionary taxes if the expected rate of return is negative, and funding may have beneficial effects on capital market efficiency (Börsch-Supan 1997b).

Yet another problem in the literature on Pareto-improving transitions is that it may ask for too much. A welfare gain that includes at least some weight to our children's utility may suffice to convince the electorate to vote for a transition. Because the payment difference between PAYG and fully funded is so large, as shown above, very small "altruism" weights will already offset the disutility of the transition burden. There are also more philosophical arguments which put considerable doubt on whether the concepts of intergenerational Pareto efficiency, intergenerational equity, or even justice across generations are meaningful.[23] In addition to the discounting problem, so many other elements of the historical environment change across generations that it may be rather academic to be "just" in this one aspect of history.

To put the additional burden in its proper perspective, it is helpful to look at the orders of magnitude involved if one generation must indeed carry the full transition burden. In order to do this, I consider two transition scenarios. Both are based on a demographic and labor force projection model described in Börsch-Supan (1997a).[24] Both transition schemes are compared to a continuation of the PAYG system under current benefit levels. Note that in all three scenarios retirement income and retirement age are the same, namely at the current level. Thus, I compare situations with the same utility during the retirement years.

In the first scenario, I assume that the contribution rate to the PAYG system will be frozen from the year 2000 on at the projected rate of then 21.1 percent of gross income. In this case, the annual social security benefits of an average retiree in 2035 will be about DM 8,500 lower than if the current net replacement rate of 72 percent were maintained by increasing the contribution rate as depicted in Figure 10. Figure 17 shows how much an average worker has to save to make up for this "pension gap." This computation assumes the worst case: a

---

23   See the interdisciplinary discussion in Johnson et al. (1989).

24   Demographic scenario "MOSTLIK" with constant age-specific and gender-specific labor force participation rates.

worker born in 1960, who started working in 1980, starts saving in the year 2000, retires in the year 2020, and lives until the year 2040. This worker will have very little time to save and faces the peak of population aging just during the retirement years. This worker faces a pension gap of about DM 7,600 on average between the years 2020 and 2040, reaching a peak of DM 8,500 in the year 2035, and totaling to a present discounted value of almost DM 90,000. In order to accumulate this level of pension wealth from the year 2000 until retirement in 2020, the worker needs to save DM 2,300 annually at a 5.9 percent interest rate. At an average net household income of about DM 51,000,[25] this appears to be quite feasible. The increase of the household saving rate from currently 11.6 percent[26] to 15.1 percent implied by this calculation is large, although not unprecedented.[27]

Figure 17 —   Maintaining PAYG (scenario 1) vs. Transition to Partially Funded System (scenario 2)

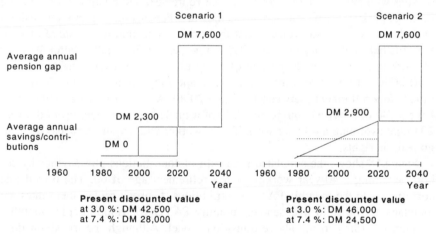

Note: Savings necessary to fill "pension gap" when freezing the contribution rate of public pension system at the projected level at year 2000, versus average rise in contributions if replacement rate is fixed.

Source: Own calculations.

---

[25] Statistisches Bundesamt (1996), inflated to 1996.

[26] Household saving rate in Deutsche Bundesbank (1996).

[27] The household saving rate in 1975 was about this level.

The DM 2,300 annual savings should be compared with the increase in the PAYG contributions that are required to keep the same level of benefits. Current retirement age maintained, PAYG contribution rates will gradually rise to almost 28 percent in the year 2020, when our worker will retire (see Figure 10). The annual contribution increase is on average DM 2,900.[28] Thus, the transition requires on average less resources than maintaining the PAYG system. However, because the contribution increase is back-loaded while savings occur every year at a fixed amount, it depends on the time preference of the household whether the household prefers the transition to a partially funded system or maintaining the PAYG system. Figure 17 shows that even under the high time preference rate, the difference is small.

Figure 18 presents the results of a different transition model that honors all claims to the pay-as-you-go system that are acquired before the transition but will result in a fully funded system after the transition: in 1997, it is announced that the transition to a fully funded system will begin in the year 2005. For all persons who have retired by 2005 (i.e., for retirement age 60 all cohorts that are born before 1945), pensions remain as they are. Persons retiring in the transition period will get a pay-as-you-go contribution in proportion to the share of their worklife before the transition year. Thus, a worker retiring in 2006 after 40 years of work will receive 39/40 percent of a pay-as-you-go pension. The remainder, 1/40 of the retirement income, has to be financed by private savings during the time before retirement (between 1997 and 2006). A worker retiring in 2007 will have 38/40 of a pay-as-you-go and 2/40 of a funded pension, etc. From the year 2045 on, assuming a 40-year worklife, no worker will acquire new pay-as-you-go pension rights.[29]

Figure 18 shows the simulated time path of contributions plus savings by cohort, assuming a 40-year worklife and a retirement age of 60. The dotted line corresponds to the monthly PAYG contributions if current replacement rates are maintained. The solid line denotes monthly PAYG contributions plus monthly savings according to the above transition model. Although the transition does not give any relief to the generation that has to finance the transition burden, this burden turns out to be anything but "double"—in fact, it just smoothens the increase in contributions that are unavoidable under the current German pay-as-you-go system. The maximum transition burden occurs about 2012 to the cohort born in 1952 which has relatively little time to save but already has to finance a substantial part of retirement income by saving. However, the added burden is relatively small and anything but a "double burden." It is less than DM 190 per

---

[28] Total increase between years 2000 and 2020 divided by 20 years.

[29] The transition lasts even longer until all persons with some pay-as-you-go pension share have died.

month for the average earner of this cohort, about the same order of magnitude as in the first scenario. This added burden should be compared to the DM 975 that the average earner currently pays as monthly contributions to the PAYG system. Note that the transition will be advantageous for all cohorts born after 1963.

Figure 18 —   Transition to Fully Funded System vs. Maintaining PAYG

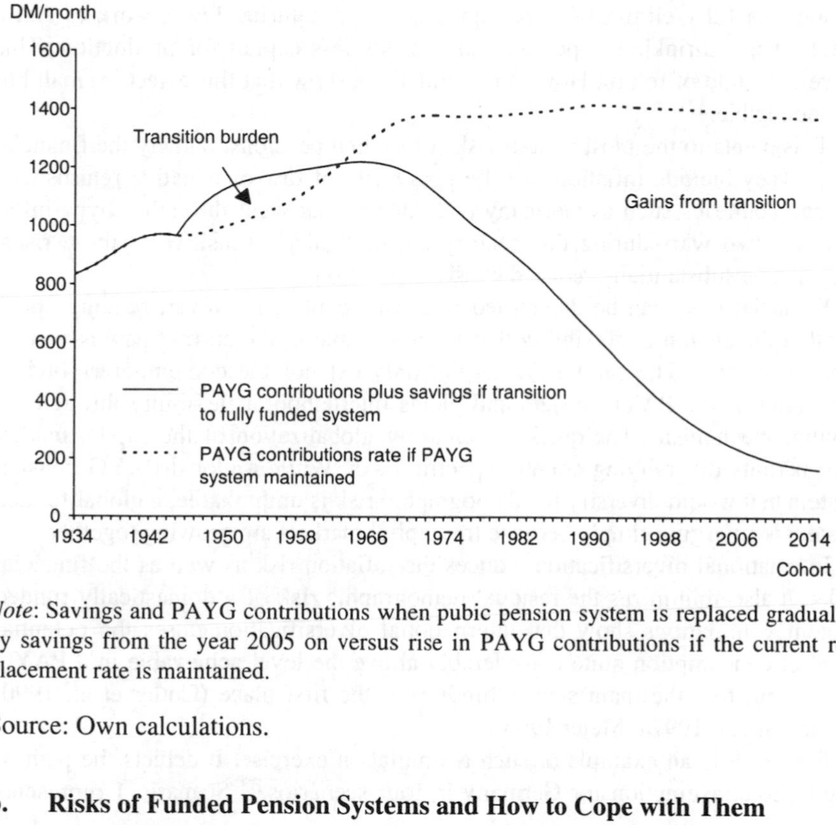

Note: Savings and PAYG contributions when pubic pension system is replaced gradually by savings from the year 2005 on versus rise in PAYG contributions if the current re-placement rate is maintained.

Source: Own calculations.

b.   Risks of Funded Pension Systems and How to Cope with Them

While the PAYG system is not without its own risks—most notably the demo-graphic risk that was in the center of the discussion in Section 3, but also the po-litical instability of a public transfer system that has been modified almost con-tinuously during the last 10 years—the public discussion tends to focus on the risks associated with funded pension systems. A funded system that requires put-ting the accumulated savings into government bonds creates an enormous temptation for government to use these funds to finance current consumption.[30] This generates low returns and submits the funds to a substantial political risk. Similar considerations hold for private firm pensions that are as book reserves invested as equity in the own firm.[31] Both of these risks can be avoided by keeping savings private and under the control of the investors in a competitive capital market. This is why the term "privatization" is frequently used for proposals that recommend transitions from PAYG to partially or fully funded pension systems.

While funding reduces the demographic risk that plagues the PAYG system, it does not fully eliminate it. An aging society, featuring fewer workers and a stable if not shrinking population, also needs less capital for production. This lowers the rate of return. However, simulations show that this effect is small but not negligible.[32]

This points to the most serious risks of funded pensions, namely the financial risks. They include inflation and the possibility of low or negative returns. Although countries such as Germany and Austria that went through a hyperinflation and two wars during this century are particularly sensitive to these risks, they can be substantially reduced by diversification.

Financial risks can be diversified within a country. However, funding opens another dimension of flexibility that is unavailable in the current pay-as-you-go pension system. The capital market not only extends the contemporary budget constraint of the PAYG system and yields intertemporal flexibility through the savings mechanism. The quickly increasing globalization of the capital market also permits diversifying country-specific risks. While a global PAYG pension system that would diversify the demographic risk is unthinkable, a global funded system is emerging simply because the capital markets are growing together.

International diversification reduces the inflation risk as well as the financial risks. It also minimizes the residual demographic risk of a domestically funded system. Simulations show that international diversification raises the potential level of consumption quite considerably above the level achievable in a PAYG system but that the main step is funding in the first place (Cutler et al. 1990; Börsch-Supan 1997a; Meier 1996).

Figure 19 is an example of such a simulation exercise. It depicts the path of aggregate consumption for Germany in four scenarios.[33] Scenario 1 represents

---

[30]   The Social Security Trust Fund in the U.S. is used to reduce the large U.S. government debt.

[31]   This is frequently the case in Germany and in the Netherlands.

[32]   Börsch-Supan (1997a) estimates a range between 30 and 120 basis points. See also Cutler et al. (1990).

[33]   Figure 10 refers to consumption in each year, aggregated across cohorts. It therefore does not permit a welfare comparison across cohorts.

maintaining the current PAYG system, while the other scenarios represent funded systems based on private savings. In Scenario 2, these savings are invested domestically. Scenario 3 depicts a two-region world consisting of Germany and the newly industrialized countries in Southeast Asia.[34] These countries are growing quickly, they still require large sums of capital, and they have a much younger population. I assume perfect capital mobility between the two regions. Scenario 4 includes all OECD countries and models the potential crowding-out effects caused by competition on the capital market—not only Germany but all other aging countries will try to invest in growing economies. The figure shows that while declining consumption appears unavoidable, the decline is small under funding but substantial when the current pay-as-you-go system is maintained. The increase in consumption is due to the fact that capital is now employed where it is scarce and where labor is abundant. This creates higher rates of return than domestically possible. It is important to note that this mechanism improves per capita GDP and aggregate consumption not only in the capital-exporting country but also in the capital-receiving country.

Figure 19 — Projected Consumption Paths under Four Different Pension Systems, 1990–2040

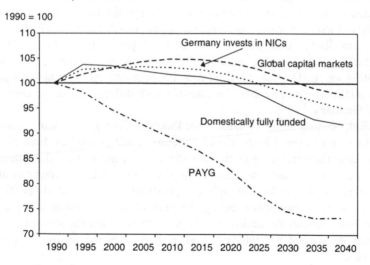

Source: Börsch-Supan (1996).

---

34 Hong Kong, Indonesia, South Korea, Malaysia, the Philippines, Singapore, and Taiwan.

A final point for a country that went through hyperinflation and two wars during this century: while a transition from a pay-as-you-go system to a fully funded system requires time and hurts the transition generation unless an intertemporal redistribution scheme is put in place, the reverse transition can always be made at an instant and without any further losses. If the capital stock is destroyed in a catastrophe, one can restart a pay-as-you-go system from current income, such as was done after World War II in Germany.

5.   Conclusions

The current debate about the implications of population aging on our pay-as-you-go pension systems focuses on patching up the current system. These fixes include downsizing the system by decreasing benefits, increasing the retirement age, and hoping for an increase in female labor force participation and some help from immigrants. These fixes require considerable additional flexibility of the labor market but stay within the realm of the inflexible pay-as-you-go budget constraint. They do not change the very low implicit rate of return of the PAYG system, which becomes negative for cohorts born after 1967.

A gradual transition to funding opens two important dimensions of additional flexibility. First, it permits more intertemporal flexibility through the savings mechanism. Rather than experiencing a 10–20 year squeeze around the year 2030, funding can smoothen the aging burden from now on through the peak of population aging. The additional burden that is levied on the transition generation is relatively small because the rate-of-return differences are so large in the case of Germany.

Second, funding permits international flexibility. An aging country can profit from the lack of capital in developing countries, just as well as these countries can increase their rate of growth with the added capital. The globalization of capital markets decreases the country-specific risks—inflation, financial and residual demographic risks—through the possibility of a broad diversification. While declining consumption during the peak of the population aging process appears unavoidable, the decline can be very small when the savings are internationally diversified, but substantial when the current pay-as-you-go system is maintained.

Of course, it is imperative that the funding mechanisms work decentralized through the capital market. This is different from book reserves (like many German firm pensions) and different from a state-managed fund (such as the U.S. Social Security Trust Fund or as recently proposed for German civil servants). In addition to the financial risk reduction via diversification, decentralization minimizes the political risks of fund appropriation.

Finally, one should keep in mind that changing the retirement system later will become more complicated. First, saving needs time, and it is already fairly late to start saving for the generation that will retire around the peak of population aging. Second, the politics of the social security system will change soon. The political power is quickly shifting from the working population to the retired population—to an electorate which is unlikely to substantially change the balance between per capita benefits and contributions.

Bibliography

Bäcker, G., R. Bispinck, K. Hofemann, and G. Naegele (1989). *Sozialpolitik und soziale Lage in der Bundesrepublik Deutschland*. Köln: Bund.

Blanchet, D. (1988). Immigration et Régularisation de la Structure par Âge d'une Population. *Population* 43(2): 293–309.

Bos, E., M.T. Vu, E. Massiah, and R. Bulatao (1994). *World Population Projections, 1994–95*. Washington, D.C.: The International Bank for Reconstruction and Development/The World Bank.

Börsch-Supan, A. (1992). Population Aging, Social Security Design, and Early Retirement. *Journal of Institutional and Theoretical Economics* (Zeitschrift für die gesamte Staatswissenschaft) 148:(3):533–557.

—— (1994). Migration, Social Security Systems, and Public Finance. In H. Siebert (ed.), *Migration: A Challenge for Europe*. Tübingen: Mohr Siebeck.

—— (1996). Demographie, Arbeitsangebot und die Systeme der sozialen Sicherung (Demography, Labor Supply, and Social Security). In H. Siebert (ed.), *Sozialpolitik auf dem Prüfstand: Leitlinien für Reformen*. Tübingen: Mohr Siebeck.

—— (1997a). The Consequences of Population Aging for Growth and Savings. Forthcoming in L. Bovenberg and C. van Ewijk (eds.), *Lecture Notes on Pensions and Aging*. Oxford: Oxford University Press.

—— (1997b). Sozialpolitik. In J. von Hagen, A. Börsch-Supan, and P. Welfens (eds.), *Springer's Handbuch der Volkswirtschaftslehre*. Heidelberg: Springer.

Börsch-Supan, A., and P. Schmidt (1996). Early Retirement in East and West Germany. In R. Riphahn, D. Snower, and K. Zimmermann (eds.), *Employment Policy in the Transition to Free Enterprise: German Integration and Its Lessons for Europe*. Forthcoming in 1998 at Springer Verlag, Berlin.

Börsch-Supan, A., and R. Schnabel (1997). Social Security and Retirement in Germany. NBER Working Paper 6153. Forthcoming in J. Gruber and D. Wise (eds.), *International Comparison of Social Security Systems*. Chicago: University of Chicago Press.

Buchheim, C. (1994). *Industrielle Revolutionen*. München: dtv.

Bundesministerium für Arbeit und Sozialordnung (1990). *Rentenreform '92*. Ausgabe Januar 1990. Bonn: Bundespresseamt.

—— (1997). *Die Rente*. Ausgabe Januar 1997. Bonn: Bundespresseamt.

Buslei, H, and F. Kraus (1996). Wohlfahrtseffekte eines graduellen Übergangs auf ein niedrigeres Rentenniveau. In V. Steiner and K.F. Zimmermann (eds.), *Soziale Sicherung und Arbeitsmarkt—Empirische Analyse und Reformansätze*. Baden-Baden: Nomos.

Cutler, D., J.M. Poterba, L.M. Sheiner, and L.H. Summers (1990). An Ageing Society: Opportunity or Challenge. *Brookings Papers on Economic Activity* (1):1–73.

Deutsche Bundesbank (1996). *Monatsbericht Dezember*. Frankfurt am Main: Deutsche Bundesbank.

Eitenmüller, S. (1996). Die Rentabilität der deutschen Rentenversicherung — Kapitalmarktanaloge Renditeberechnung für die nahe und die ferne Zukunft. *Deutsche Rentenversicherung* 12/96:784–798.

Felderer, B. (1992). Can Immigration Policy Help to Stabilize Social Security Systems? Discussion Paper. Institute for Advanced Studies, Vienna.

Feldstein, M., and A. Samwick (1996). The Transition Path to Privatizing Social Security. NBER Working Paper 3962. Cambridge, Mass.

Fenge, R. (1995). Pareto-Efficiency of the Pay-As-You-Go Pension System with Intergenerational Fairness. *Finanzarchiv* 52:357–363.

Gruber, J., and D. Wise (1997). *International Comparison of Social Security Systems*. NBER Working Paper. Forthcoming in 1998 at The University of Chicago Press.

Johnson, P., C. Conrad, and D. Thomson (1989). *Workers versus Pensioners*. Manchester: Manchester University Press.

Kotlikoff, L.J. (1996). Simulating the Privatization of Social Security in General Equilibrium. In M. Feldstein (ed.), Privatizing Social Security. NBER Working Paper 5776. Cambridge, Mass.

Meier, M. (1996). Gesamtwirtschaftliche Auswirkungen des demographischen Wandels. Unpublished Doctoral Dissertation. University of Mannheim.

McKinsey Global Institute (1996). *Capital Productivity*. Washington, D.C.: McKinsey Global Institute.

Prognos (1995). *Perspektiven der gesetzlichen Rentenversicherung für Gesamtdeutschland vor dem Hintergrund politischer und ökonomischer Rahmenbedingungen*. Basel: Prognos.

Raffelhüschen, B. (1993). Funding Social Security Through Pareto-Optimal Conversion Policies. *Journal of Economics* 7:105–131.

Schmidt, P. (1995). *Die Wahl des Rentenalters—Theoretische und empirische Analyse des Rentenzugangsverhaltens in West- und Ostdeutschland.* Frankfurt: Lang.

Schnabel, R. (1997a). Internal Rates of Return of the German Pay-As-You-Go Social Security System. Working paper. University of Mannheim.

—— (1997b). Intergenerational Distribution and Pension Reform in Germany. Working paper. University of Mannheim.

Statistisches Bundesamt (1994). Achte koordinierte Bevölkerungsvorausberechnung. Wiesbaden.

—— (1996). *Statistisches Jahrbuch für die Bundesrepublik Deutschland 1996.* Stuttgart: Metzler-Poeschel.

Verband Deutscher Rentenversicherungsträger (1995). *VDR-Statistik Rentenzugang.* Frankfurt am Main: Verband Deutscher Rentenversicherungsträger.

—— (1997). *Rentenversicherung in Zeitreihen.* Vierte vollständig überarbeitete Auflage. Frankfurt am Main: Verband Deutscher Rentenversicherungsträger.

World Bank (1994). *Averting the Old Age Crisis: Policies to Protect the Old and Promote Growth.* Oxford: Oxford University Press.

Edward M. Gramlich

The United States: How to Deal with Uncovered Future Social Security Liabilities

The U.S. Social Security system, first formed back in the 1930s, is a government defined benefit pension program financed by worker payroll taxes. As workers pay in their payroll taxes, they accumulate benefit credits. At any point in time, one can make some economic and demographic assumptions, project forward tax inflows and benefit outflows, and determine the long-run actuarial soundness of the system, or really the long-term consistency of the present set of tax and benefit schedules.

Every year, such forecasts are made by the Social Security and Medicare trustees—three cabinet officers, the commissioner of Social Security, and two outside members. Although earlier Social Security legislation mandated that quadrennial outside advisory councils be appointed to review these forecasts and to comment on relevant policy issues, the last such council to examine the retirement system was the Greenspan Commission in 1983. But a new advisory council was formed in 1994 and I was asked to chair it. It included three members from business, three from unions, and various others from the private pension industry, the self-employment sector, independent representatives, and so forth, making thirteen members in all. We met monthly from mid-1994 to mid-1996, commissioned a number of special studies, appointed two technical panels that made reports, and in January 1997 issued our own report (Advisory Council 1997). In this paper I discuss this report, particularly trying to promote the proposal I put forward for dealing with the uncovered future liabilities of Social Security.

1. Uncovered Liabilities

The council's main point of departure was the annual reports of the Trustees of Social Security (see, for example, Trustees' Report 1997). As has been widely reported in the U.S. press, the intermediate assumptions of this report had the combined assets of the Old-Age, Survivors, and Disability Insurance (OASDI) trust funds going below the safety level, a year's worth of benefits, in 2029. The assets of the Medicare Hospitalization Insurance (HI) Trust Fund, a separate entity that we did not examine, were projected to go below the safety level in 2001, a far more urgent situation. But since the past convention was that these trust funds should be actuarially sound for 75 years, the fact that the OASDI trust fund assets were projected to go below the safety level as soon as 2029 was alarming enough. The sum total of future Social Security liabilities stands now at $2.5 trillion, 34 percent of current GDP, and it would take an immediate 18 percent increase in the OASDI payroll tax to eliminate this long-term actuarial imbalance.

With both the OASDI and HI trust funds, the underlying demographics of the country are such that projected benefits are rising rapidly compared to payroll tax inflows, so that once the fund assets first go below the safety level at some future date, say 2029, the funds will be increasingly far out of actuarial balance after that date. In that sense, $2.5 trillion is an underestimate of future uncovered liabilities, as is the 18 percent payroll tax deficiency.

These numbers reflect two deeper pension-saving issues for the United States. One involves actuarial balance. In a stable defined benefit social security system with pay-as-you-go (PAYG) financing, the underlying accounting identity can be written as:

[1] $t = (B/W) \cdot (S/N) = r \cdot d,$

where t is the OASDI tax rate on taxable wages, B is average social security benefits, W is average taxable wages, S is the number of social security recipients, and N is the number of workers. The overall numerator, $(B \cdot S)$, is aggregate social security benefits. The overall denominator, $(W \cdot N)$, is aggregate taxable wages, with the overall right-hand side equaling the payroll tax rate because of the PAYG identity. This identity can also be written as the product of the aggregate replacement rate, $(r = B/W)$, and the dependency ratio, $(d = S/N)$.

The United States now has an aging population, with people living longer and not having enough babies to stabilize the population share of young people. This means that the dependency ratio, d, is steadily rising, from about 0.29 today to about 0.56 by the end of the 75-year forecast period. According to the PAYG identity, if nothing is done to aggregate replacement rates, the payroll tax rate must rise steadily to pay for the existing defined benefit Social Security plan.

Figure 1, which compares OASDI payroll tax inflows with projected future benefit outflows, all as a percent of taxable payrolls, gives the income flow statement for the OASDI trust funds. These same numbers converted to asset stock form, and shown as the ratio of the asset stocks as a percent of annual outflows—the so-called trust fund ratio—are shown in Figure 2.

Figure 1 — OASI Income Rates and Cost Rates (as a percentage of taxable payroll)[a]

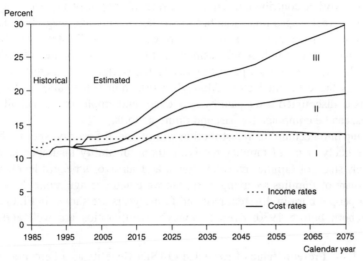

Source: Trustees of Social Security (1997).

Figure 2 — Trust Fund Ratios for OASI and DI Trust Funds, Combined (assets as a percentage of annual expenditures)[a]

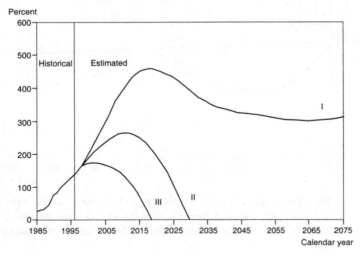

[a] For legend and source see Figure 1.

The second issue involves the rate of return. Another property of a PAYG system, first pointed out by Paul Samuelson, is that the equilibrium real rate of return on worker contributions equals the rate of growth of the economy's real wage base (real wages times number of workers). This real wage base is slated to grow about 1 percent in the long-term forecasts of the Trustees, which means that younger cohorts will be increasingly getting fewer discounted benefits relative to their discounted tax payments (using the overall real interest rate of 2.3 percent as the discount factor). Money's worth ratios, the ratio of discounted benefits to discounted taxes paid by employees and employers on behalf of employees, can be computed for past and future cohorts.

Taking into account the redistribution within Social Security, spousal benefits and the likely share of families receiving them, disability insurance levels and the likely share of families receiving them, and survivor's benefit levels and the likely share of families receiving them, the weighted average money's worth ratios for people born in different past and future years are shown in Figure 3. For people born before 1930, overall money's worth ratios are well above 1.0,

Figure 3 — Present Value of Expected OASDI Benefits as a Percentage of the Present Value of Expected Contributions of Alternative Social Security Systems, by Year of Birth for Grand Composite Workers[a]

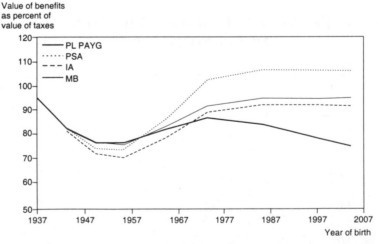

[a] The figure refers to the Pay-As-You-Go system under Present Law (PL PAYG), the Personal Security Accounts (PSA) plan, the Individual Accounts (IA) plan, and the Maintain Benefit (MB) plan. See text for further details.

Source: Advisory Council (1997).

meaning that on average Social Security was a much better investment than government bonds. For people born in the early 1930s and retiring now, overall money's worth ratios are about 1.0—meaning that Social Security has been approximately as good a financial investment as government bonds. For all of these age cohorts, Social Security should be a very attractive proposition—it gives social protection for low-wage and disabled workers and survivor's insurance, and still a decent financial return. Typically, Social Security is indeed very popular with these age groups.

But the story is very different for younger workers. While the overall money's worth ratio cycles a bit because of past movements in real interest rates, over the long run the aggregate money's worth ratio is slated to fall for younger workers, even before any policy changes in OASDI replacement or tax rates are made. With the necessary policy changes to bring the system into actuarial balance, these money's worth ratios would become lower yet. One reflection of this fact is shown in Figure 3. The line labeled "PL (present law) PAYG" assumes that Social Security is operated in the future as it has been for the most part in the 20th century—by raising payroll taxes as need be to finance present law benefits. Not surprisingly, these money's worth ratios drop to about 0.7 and falling. Not surprisingly, poll results find Social Security to be a much less attractive proposition for younger workers.

The interaction between these two issues sets up a difficult problem in political economics. Taxes could be raised or replacement ratios cut to keep the system in long-term PAYG balance. But the mere act of doing that worsens the money's worth ratios for younger cohorts and threatens the future popularity of the Social Security system. The question of how to bring the system into financial balance while preserving its political popularity was the central issue faced by the Advisory Council.

2.   New Approaches

The council had three different approaches for dealing with these twin problems. Each approach takes advantage of the macroeconomic proposition that future returns on both stocks and bonds are likely to exceed the implicit PAYG return of the present OASDI system. Two of the approaches take advantage of the additional macroeconomic proposition that the best way to insure a healthy retirement system in the 21st century is to raise retirement, and national, saving now.

One approach, known as the Maintain Benefits (MB) plan, involves minimal changes in benefit schedules, tax rates, and hence underlying rates of national saving. The trust fund finances would be preserved, and the money's worth ratios for younger workers raised (see the MB line in Figure 3), by a huge investment of Social Security funds in equities (combined with the forecasting projection that the returns on common stock would continue to exceed those on bonds). There are a number of institutional and political difficulties with such an approach, and in fact in the end those favoring the MB approach only wanted to "study" central fund equity investment, not actually do it. From a macroeconomic point of view, the most telling criticism of the MB approach is that it requires virtually no new national saving, and hence basically entails an asset swap with the private sector. In the end the OASDI trust funds would hold more stocks and fewer bonds, and private savers would hold fewer stocks and more bonds. But the country would be no richer in the long run because there would have been no new wealth creation.

A second approach, called the Personal Security Accounts (PSA) plan, involves a replacement of the present defined benefit system with large-scale defined contributions held outside the OASDI trust fund, similar to the Chilean system. These accounts would be privately owned and managed, hence increasing their riskiness. The OASDI benefit schedule would revert to a poverty-line flat benefit, again increasing the risk that individuals who did not invest well would not receive many retirement benefits. Since the present day payroll tax would be largely diverted to the personal accounts of individuals, there would also need to be a huge amount of transition financing—new borrowing and new taxes—for such a plan.

From a macroeconomic point of view the problem here is arbitrage. Basically, the government would be doing a huge amount of transition borrowing so that individuals could invest in their higher-yielding PSA accounts. The money's worth ratios turn out to be highest for this plan (see the PSA line in Figure 3), but these can be misleading because of the arbitrage, and because the money's worth ratios are expectations, with a large potential variance because of the investment risk.

3.   The Individual Accounts Plan

I personally do not favor either approach and have come up with an intermediate approach that preserves the important social protections of the present Social Security system, does this in a financially prudent way without relying on OASDI equity investment or arbitrage, and still adds what I consider to be badly needed new saving for retirement. My Individual Accounts (IA) plan does all three.

The first component of the IA plan is what might be called kind and gentle benefit cuts. These cuts would really be cuts in the real growth of benefits over time for high-wage workers, with disabled and low-wage workers being largely protected from any cuts. The IA plan would include some technical changes such as including all state and local new hires in Social Security and applying consistent income tax treatment to Social Security benefits. These changes are also part of the council's other plans, and go some way to eliminating Social Security's actuarial deficit.

Then, beginning in the 21st century, the changes would be supplemented with two other measures. There would be a slight increase in the normal retirement age for all workers. Under present law this normal retirement age is already slated to rise from age 65 to age 67 during the next century: the change would speed up this schedule, and also index it to the overall rise in life expectancy later on in the 21st century. There would also be a slight change in the benefit formula to reduce the growth of real Social Security benefits for high-wage workers. Both of these changes would be phased in very gradually to avoid actual benefit cuts for present retirees and "notches" in the benefit schedule (instances when younger workers with the same earnings records get lower real benefits than older workers). The result of all changes would be a modest reduction in the overall OASDI replacement rate of equation [1] to leave OASDI payroll tax rates stable into the future. When combined with the rising number of retirees, the share of the nation's output devoted to Social Security spending would be approximately the same as at present, eliminating this part of the impending explosion in future U.S. entitlement spending. Of the three plans suggested by our council, this IA plan is clearly the best for achieving short- and long-term balance in the U.S. federal budget.

These benefit cuts alone would mean that high-wage workers would not be experiencing rising real benefits as their real wages grow, so the IA plan would supplement these changes with another measure to raise overall retirement (and national) saving. Workers would be required to contribute an extra 1.6 percent of their pay to their defined contribution individual accounts. These accounts would be owned by workers but centrally managed. Workers would be able to allocate their funds among five to ten broad mutual funds covering stocks and bonds. Central management of the funds would cut down the risk that funds would be invested unwisely, would cut administrative costs, and would mean that Wall Street firms would not find these individual accounts a financial bonanza. The funds would be converted to real annuities on retirement, to protect against inflation and the chance that retirees would overspend in their early retirement years.

All changes together would mean that approximately the presently scheduled level of benefits would be paid to all wage classes of workers, of all ages. The difference between this outcome and present law is that under this IA plan these benefits would be affordable, as they are not under present law. The changes would eliminate Social Security's long-term actuarial deficit while still holding together the important retirement safety net provided by Social Security. They would significantly raise the return on invested contributions for younger workers. They would slow the growth of overall entitlement spending and improve the federal budget outlook, even in the near term. And, since the changes would involve neither asset swaps nor arbitrage, the changes would move beyond the present PAYG financing scheme, by building up the nation's capital stock in advance of the baby boom retirement crunch.

Bibliography

Advisory Council (1997). *Report of the 1994–1996 Advisory Council on Social Security.* Social Security Administration. Washington, D.C.

Trustees of Social Security (1997). *Status of the Social Security and Medicare Programs.* Social Security Administration. Washington, D.C.

Mats Persson

Reforming Social Security in Sweden

1. Introduction

The political development in Sweden in the 1980s included a trend toward more and more generous transfer systems. For example, the replacement rate of the Swedish unemployment insurance became the highest of all rates within the OECD area (see OECD 1996: Chapter 2). A similar example is provided by the sickness insurance; here, too, the replacement rate was raised on several occasions in the 1980s. Around 1990, a person who was absent from work would receive 100 percent of the regular wage during the entire spell of sickness—a figure considerably higher than that of most other countries. At that time, Sweden also had the highest degree of sickness absenteeism from work of all OECD countries, a fact which to a large extent can be attributed to the generous benefit rules (Henrekson et al. 1992).

In recent years, these high unemployment and sickness replacement rates have been somewhat reduced—often at considerable political cost to the incumbent government. As for the Swedish pension system, a major reform—possibly at constant benefit levels—has been on the political agenda for more than a decade. In the rest of this paper, I will discuss the problems connected with the present pension system, with the various reform proposals that have been put forth, and with the political process dealing with these issues.[1]

Remark: I am indebted to John Hassler, Agneta Kruse, Nils-Petter Lagerlöf, and Ann-Charlotte Ståhlberg for helpful comments and discussions on earlier versions of this paper.

[1]   For a general discussion of the Swedish welfare state, and the problems associated with it, see Lindbeck (1997). For a more detailed discussion of the Swedish pension system, see Kruse (1997).

2.   The ATP Pension System

a.   A Background

A basic, compulsory pension was introduced in Sweden in 1913. In the beginning it was at least partly funded and of the defined-contribution type; it has, however, developed over the years into a pay-as-you-go system which gives an equal, and relatively low, amount to everybody regardless of earlier contributions. Today, total payments amount to roughly 4 percent of GDP.

In the 1950s, the basic pension was considered insufficient for some groups who did not have any supplementary pensions. A mandatory supplementary pension, the so-called ATP system, was thus legislated in 1959. It is characterized by the following two main points:

First, the system is of the defined-benefits type: pensions are based on the real income earned during the fifteen best years of one's worklife. To be eligible for a full pension, one has to be working during thirty years. There is, however, a ceiling; although all income is subject to the pension tax, pensions cannot exceed a certain amount. *Second*, the system is mainly pay-as-you-go, although a relatively small fund (with a size of about eight times the yearly amount paid) was built up to compensate for the fall in private saving when the system was introduced.

The system is of approximately the same magnitude as the basic system (today, yearly payments amount to 4.5 percent of GDP), but since it is related to income, it is much more important for the working population than for those outside the labor force.

In recent decades, the supplementary (ATP) system has been criticized on various grounds. Therefore, a government committee was appointed in 1984 to work out a reform proposal. The committee could not, however, agree on any major reform of the system; when its final report was published in 1990, it dealt only with minor technical adjustments (Ministry of Social Affairs 1990). A new committee was thus set up in 1991 and presented a substantive proposal for reform in 1994 (Ministry of Social Affairs 1994). It then seemed as if there was wide political support for a thorough reform, and the parliament decided that the ATP system should be reformed according to the "general principles" of the 1994 proposal. After a while, however, the decision process came to a halt. For almost four years, discussions based on the 1994 committee report went on, and there was a substantial uncertainty associated with the whole issue. A final agreement among the political parties was not reached until January 1998.

b.   Problems of the ATP System

Over the years, several aspects of the ATP system have been criticized in the general political debate, and in the academic discussion. The main arguments have been the following.

1. The population is aging. In the 1950s, when the present system was designed, 10–12 percent of the population was above 65 years of age. Today that figure is around 17–18 percent, and in 2020 it is projected to have reached 20 percent. This is the combined effect of a longer expected lifetime for any given cohort and of variations in the cohort size; the baby boomers of the 1940s will retire in 2005–2015. The effect of all this is that the system is regarded as unsustainable; in fact, most papers and books on the social security problem published in Sweden start with similar diagrams and tables, showing the growing number of persons who are to be supported by the working generation. Worries based on demographic trends are special in the social security debate, since both economists and noneconomists tend to agree. There could, however, be a flaw in their reasoning, since private pension schemes, which are subject to exactly the same demographic changes, are not only being sustained, but are thriving. In fact, a fundamental question for economists to address seems to be the following: Why are state pension schemes so fatally sensitive to demographic changes, while private schemes are not?

2. The system is unfair; since benefits are tied to income, it gives more money to high-income earners than to low-income earners. Also, it gives more money to men than to women, since the latter generally have lower incomes and a lower labor force participation rate. This is the standard argument against systems where there is a connection, however weak, between contributions and benefits. Even if professional economists might dismiss this argument as being irrelevant, it has been very prominent in the popular debate in recent years, and it has created a binding constraint for any future reform: the basic pension system, which gives the same amount to every citizen, regardless of earlier income, should be left virtually untouched.

3. The system is unfair; due to the rather complicated rules for computing benefits (pensions are based on the average real income during the top fifteen years of one's professional career), it favors persons with an uneven lifetime earnings profile—for example, persons with a university education. Since those people tend to be high-income earners, the system has actually been redistributing income from low-income to high-income earners (see Ståhlberg 1990). Since, however, women tend to have a more uneven earnings profile than men, the system also has been redistri-

buting income from men to women, the main losers being low-skilled men and the main winners being women with a university education. While the previous argument has dominated the popular debate in the mass media, this one has mainly catered to the economics profession and illustrates the (unintended) redistributional effects that can arise if a system is not, in the economics jargon, *actuarially fair*. Whatever is meant by this term will be discussed later on in this paper.

4. Since the system is not actuarially fair, it creates a tax wedge in the economy. In practice, this means that the expected present value of an individual's benefits is not equal to the expected present value of his or her contributions. Thus the individual's contribution is not mainly an insurance premium, but rather a tax. The degree to which the contribution should be regarded as a tax depends on the system's deviation from the economic ideal of actuarial fairness.

5. Since the system is of the pay-as-you-go type, it has led to less savings in the economy. This statement is uncontroversial, which is not the case with the following, failing to take into account the openness of the Swedish economy: Since the system has led to a reduction in savings, it has also led to less capital formation. A commonly expressed corollary of this is the following (which was claimed before as well as after the emergence of the endogenous growth theory): Since the system has led to less capital formation in Sweden, it has also reduced growth. Finally, the fact that the real rate of growth in the wage sum has been lower than the real rate of interest implies that the system has imposed an unnecessary cost on the retired, as compared to a fully funded system. This is the argument of Feldstein (1996), and it is valid regardless of the effects of a pay-as-you-go system on capital formation and growth, as long as the real growth rate of the wage sum is lower than the real rate of interest.

Summarizing these five points, we see that they deal with the social security system along two dimensions: actuarially fair versus not actuarially fair, and funded versus pay-as-you-go (PAYG). In fact, I will argue that even point 1 above, which at a first glance seems completely noneconomic, dealing only with demography and the problems of an aging population, is basically a problem of the present system not being actuarially fair. To these two dimensions could be added a third one, which is intimately connected with the issues of actuarial fairness and of funding versus PAYG, but which also has some other aspects, namely that of private versus government-run systems. In the following sections, I will discuss the problems of the present system, and the 1994 reform proposal, along these three dimensions.

3.   Actuarial Fairness

a.   A Definition

A social security system is said to be actuarially fair if the present expected value of each individual's contributions is equal to the present expected value of his or her benefits. There are two terms in this definition that warrant further elaboration: "present" and "expected."

Assume that the system is consistent with a balanced government budget, i.e., that each year's aggregate contributions exactly cover aggregate benefits.[2] Deviations from actuarial fairness are closely connected (but not equivalent to) redistribution; a system that redistributes expected income over individuals cannot be actuarially fair. There are two ways by which the system could redistribute incomes: via the rules connecting benefits to contributions, and via the interest rate. As an example of the former, we could take the rules of the old Swedish ATP system. The pension is equal to the real value of the average income during the individual's fifteen best years, regardless of how much the individual has contributed to the system during other years.[3] As mentioned above, this favors individuals with an uneven lifetime income profile. A person who has been working part-time for fifteen years and full-time for another fifteen will get exactly the same pension as a person who has been working full-time, at the same wage rate, for thirty years. This kind of deviation from actuarial fairness, due to the benefit rules, is neglected within the usual overlapping-generations models of social security, where all individuals are assumed to be identical.

The other kind of redistribution is due to the interest rate in the system being different from the market interest rate. This could be the case for two reasons. Either the system is fully funded, but it is politically constrained to invest its funds in particular, low-yield assets.[4] Or it is PAYG, but the growth rate of the real wage sum is lower than the real market interest rate. Even if the benefit rules are completely actuarial in the sense that all contributions over an individual's

---

2   This is not really crucial; if a system generates, e.g., a deficit, we simply include the tax system into the definition of the social security system. A deficit then means that the present generation of taxpayers, which is essentially equal to the present generation of workers, pays the pensions of the retired; the system thus works at least partly as a PAYG system.

3   Provided that the individual has been working, i.e., that some low threshold level of income has been earned, for at least thirty years.

4   Here I consider only long-term yield. I thus disregard yearly deviations. I also disregard differences in yield due to different risk in the portfolio; when referring to "the market rate," I mean the average yield of a portfolio of assets with the same risk characteristics as the portfolio of the social security system.

lifetime are included in the basis for future benefits, like they are in the case of individual accounts, the system could still redistribute wealth in present-value terms if the interest rate on those accounts is not equal to the market interest rate. If people have different lifetime earnings profiles, an interest rate lower than the market rate (which is usually the case in practice) will be more harmful to those who have made large contributions relatively early in life (for example, people without a university education) as compared to persons who have made their main contributions relatively late in life. This kind of redistribution is difficult to capture in the simplest kind of overlapping-generations models, where everybody is assumed to live for two periods only, working during the first one and being retired during the second.

If the interest rate of the system is different from the market interest rate, there is a third kind of redistribution in funded systems: from the funds of the system to the state (or to future generations of taxpayers). As pointed out above, it is not so meaningful to distinguish between the social security system and the rest of the public sector, but if the (consolidated) public sector engages in inter-cohort redistribution via the pension system, this will of course affect the tax wedges confronting any given cohort.

Finally, if the "interest rate" in a PAYG system deviates from the market rate (i.e., if the growth rate in the real wage sum is lower than the real market rate of interest) there is definitely a loss for each generation, although that loss is not redistributed to anybody.[5] Still, however, this should be regarded as a deviation from actuarial fairness, since each cohort will receive benefits with a present value that is lower than the present value (discounted at the market rate) of its contributions.

I should also say a few words about the term "expected." The main source of uncertainty in pension schemes is connected with the life expectancy of the insured. Strictly speaking, a system can never be fully actuarially fair, because of asymmetric information. In some cases, the individual knows more about the risks that he or she is subjected to; in other cases, the insurance company knows more. The probability distribution of the expectations operator is thus different for the individual and for the insurance company (or state pension authority). From an individualistic welfare theory point of view, it should be the individual's probability distribution that matters, and thus the individual will tend to consider most pension schemes as somewhat unfair—being either too generous or too austere, from that individual's point of view. In this paper, I will disregard

---

[5]   One could of course say that at the introduction of a PAYG system, there is a redistribution to the transitional generation from some future generation(s), possibly infinitely far into the future. This redistribution is, however, not due to the system's rate of return being different from the market rate.

that complication and narrow the concept of actuarial fairness to deal with the interest rate only.

b.   The Old ATP System

The rules connecting benefits to contributions in the old ATP system are characterized by a considerable amount of intracohort redistribution, at any discount rate. It is thus not actuarially fair in the first sense of Section 3.a above. A simple computation shows that roughly 25 percent of the contribution of a typical income earner can be regarded as an (actuarial) insurance premium, in the sense of affecting the basis for the individual's future benefits (see Persson 1991). The remaining 75 percent is a pure tax (i.e., the individual's future benefits are completely unrelated to the 75 percent of the contribution). Since the contribution is around 13 percent of the wage sum, this means that a 9.75 percent *de facto* income tax is added to the regular income tax.

On top of that, the yield of the old system has been lower than the market yield, for the two reasons mentioned above. Although the system is basically PAYG, it has had a relatively small fund which has traditionally been constrained to invest in low-yield assets (government and municipal bonds, and mortgage instruments).

In this perspective, it is instructive to discuss the question raised in point 1 of Section 2.b above: Why do public pension schemes become "unsustainable" when confronted with demographic changes, while private schemes seem to be robust and well-functioning?

For a private insurance company, and for its customers, a longer expected lifetime causes no problems. The actuaries, knowing that the average life expectancy has increased, recalculate the insurance premia; competition between insurance companies will force them to be actuarially fair both in terms of benefit rules and in terms of the interest rate, and rational customers will gladly pay these higher premia, since they know that they face, on the average, a longer period of retirement. A government-run scheme which is not actuarially fair will also have to raise fees when people tend to live longer, but here things are different. From an economic point of view, the increase in the fee will be equivalent to a tax increase; thus changes in the demography will be equivalent to changes in the overall tax wedges of the economy. Thus the increases in the premia necessary to accommodate the longer life expectancy might be rather harmful to the economy.

In my view, this is the reason why the old ATP system has been considered "unsustainable." Needless to say, any pension scheme is "sustainable" in the sense that there is no technical problem in raising the fees to accommodate a longer life expectancy. The problem is purely economic; it has to do with tax wedges and microeconomic incentives.

c.   The 1994 Proposal

The dominant feature of the 1994 proposal was that of actuarial fairness. There should be a strong link between contributions and benefits; all contributions should be registered on individual accounts and be the basis for future payments. In fact, although mainly a PAYG system, it would mimic a funded system with a yield equal to the growth rate of the economy. The ceiling, above which no benefits would be paid, was retained—but for the sake of actuarial fairness, incomes above that ceiling would not be subject to any fee.[6] The result was that the system would be limited in size, and that people who wanted more social security could buy a private pension scheme on top of the compulsory one.

In the same spirit, the proposal also allowed for great flexibility with respect to the retirement age. With an earliest retirement age of 61, the individual will be allowed to choose the date of retirement according to his or her preferences, and the pension is adjusted accordingly. One can also choose a part-time retirement for some year and a full-time retirement thereafter; whatever time profile is chosen, the pension is adjusted in an actuarially fair fashion.

The system would thus be actuarially fair in the limited sense of no intracohort redistribution due to the benefit rules. There were, however, two deviations from this general principle. *First*, the notion of a basic pension was retained, with an equal amount for every citizen. That amount will be approximately the same as in the old system, although there are a few small changes (such as a renaming of the basic pension, and a new method of "phasing in" the supplementary pension on top of the basic one). *Second*, a few nonmarket activities (such as doing military service, and having children) would earn pension rights although the individual would not have paid any corresponding contributions.

Then there was a deviation from actuarial fairness in the sense that the interest rate would deviate from the market rate. Although based on individual accounts, the system was still intended to be a PAYG system. The individual pensions would increase over time at a rate which is related to (but not exactly equal to) the growth in real wages. The fees are computed accordingly, and thus the appropriate "interest rate" for the system is the real rate of increase in the wage sum. This has historically been somewhat lower than the real yield on financial assets (see further Section 4.a below). On top of this PAYG system, however,

---

6   This is a matter of definition. Incomes above the ceiling would not be subject to any fee—but on the other hand, there will be a new tax, which incidentally happens to amount to 50 percent of the fee, imposed on such incomes.

the 1994 proposal included a small funded system; two percentage points of the contributions were intended for individual, funded accounts that were to invest in financial assets at the market rate.

When presented in February 1994, the proposal was the unanimous result of negotiations between the largest parties in parliament. It was then considered a splendid example of the well-functioning and cohesion of the Swedish political system. After a few months, however, the rank-and-file of some of the parties (most notably, the Social Democrats) started to protest against the new system, which was considered even more unfair to low-income earners and to women (according to point 2 of Section 2.b above) than the old system. Also, the new idea of making the system partially funded was criticized on various grounds (see further Section 4.b below).

This criticism emerged at a politically sensitive time. The election in the fall of 1994 ran closer, and after that there was the 1995 EU referendum, and the rapidly increasing unemployment figures and the dwindling popularity of the Social Democrat government trying to reduce the budget deficit. Then there was the difficult question of a Swedish EMU membership, and the 1998 election approaching at an alarming speed. The delicate issue of reforming the social security system thus seemed to have been quietly removed from the political agenda. In the spring of 1997, the Social Democrat leader stated that his party still stood behind the "general principles" of the 1994 proposal. After considerable opposition among the rank-and-file Social Democrats, all parties finally agreed in January 1998 to implement the main features of the 1994 proposal.

4.   Funded versus Pay-as-You-Go System

a.   What Is the Problem?

It is true that national saving will be lower under a PAYG system than under a funded one. If the economy is completely open, this will, however, not affect the capital stock; the only difference is then that under the former system, the capital stock will be owned to a larger extent by foreigners. This may be a source of psychological discomfort, but such feelings are hard to evaluate in economic terms.

If, however, capital is not completely mobile, savings will not be identical to investment, and the PAYG system will imply a lower capital stock. There is some evidence that capital is not completely mobile—or, at least, that it was not completely mobile in the past.[7] Whether this will be the case in the future is an open question—especially so for a small economy like the Swedish one, which is scheduled for further integration with the EMU within the next decade.

Assuming that capital is not (yet) perfectly mobile, the question for economic policy in this context is whether a larger capital stock is warranted from a welfare point of view. If we limit ourselves to the traditional, neoclassical growth theory, we have the well-known result that the economy is on a Golden Rule path if the marginal product of capital, r, is equal to the sum of population growth rate, n, the rate of labor-augmenting technological progress, g, and the rate of depreciation, δ, i.e., $r = n + g + \delta$.

The problem is that these variables are hard to observe in real life. One alternative is to identify $(n + g)$ with the rate of growth of the real wage rate in the private sector, which in the case of Sweden was 2.1 percent per year, on the average, for the period 1960–1993. Another alternative would be to identify $(n + g)$ with the rate of growth in the real wage sum according to the national accounts; during the same period, it was 2.7 percent on the average.[8] Identifying the marginal product of capital with the real yield of long-term government bonds (which was 2.4 percent per year during 1960–1993), we see from the equation above that the Swedish capital stock is not obviously too low from a Golden Rule point of view.

Identifying r with the real yield on equity, on the other hand, which was 9.4 percent per year during the same period,[9] and assuming that the unobservable δ is not larger than 7 percent, it seems to be possible to use a Golden Rule argument for advocating a change from a PAYG system to a funded one. This, of course, relies on the closed-economy assumption that an increase in savings will actually affect the capital stock in the future.

One should observe that the above reasoning is based on the traditional, neoclassical growth theory. If we instead rely on the endogenous growth theory, there might be stronger arguments for increased capital formation. Since that theory is still in its formative stage, and since its policy implications are still to a large extent unexplored, I will refrain from pursuing that line of reasoning in this context.

---

7   The classic reference is Feldstein and Horioka (1980). See Leiderman and Razin (1994) for recent references.

8   Depending on what data set one uses, a wide variety of different figures can be obtained. I do not claim that any of them is very accurate, but the numbers 2.1 and 2.7 might nevertheless indicate the order of magnitude involved.

9   Another alternative is to use the yield on total capital (equity and borrowed capital) in the private sector; it was equal to 9.1 percent.

Regardless of growth theory, forcing the citizens to invest in an "asset" with a yield lower than the market rate of interest will lead to a welfare loss to them. This is the argument of Feldstein (1996) and it is identical to the reasoning of actuarial fairness pursued in Sections 3.a and 3.b above, the difference between the market rate and the return of the social security system creating a tax wedge that will distort labor supply decisions in the same way as will nonactuarial rules for connecting contributions to benefits within the same cohort.

Here one could raise the question of the size of that tax wedge. As mentioned above, the growth rate of the wage rate in Sweden has been 2.1 percent, while the real rate of return on government bonds has been 2.4 percent; the difference is small, and thus the tax wedge seems negligible.[10] Feldstein (1996) advocates, however, the yield on corporate equity as the proper basis for comparison. And since that was 9.4 percent in Sweden, the tax wedge seems sizable. Here is a problem that has not been properly solved in the literature.

The simple side of it is the one connected with capital market theory; investments in a more risky asset should result in a higher return on the average, and if corporate equity is a more risky "asset" than the wage sum, there is nothing special about the PAYG system having a lower return than a funded system with more risky assets in its portfolio. If individuals are risk-averse, it is optimal to employ a safe but low-yielding PAYG system (or a funded system investing in low-yield government bonds) rather than a funded system investing in corporate equity. The more difficult side of the problem is the following. If the return on corporate equity is *much* higher than can reasonably be explained by the standard theories of capital markets, forcing the population into a PAYG system definitely implies a welfare loss. And the figure 9.4 percent seems high indeed. In fact, there is ample evidence of an "equity premium puzzle"(see Siegel and Thaler [1997] for references) to raise suspicions that a massive change from the present PAYG to a funded system investing in equity would lead to a considerable increase in real income—and, maybe, in welfare.

Since there are no simple policy conclusions in the social security debate, however, this argument could easily be rephrased. If there is an "equity premium," and if society is long-lived, so that risks could be intertemporally pooled, then one could ask why we should take the complicated detour of reforming the social security system. An easier way to reap the fruits of this state of the world would be for the government to borrow money at the 2.4 percent real interest rate and invest it in corporate capital at the 9.4 percent real yield; such an arrangement would constitute a safe "money machine," and we would

---

10   Or, if one believes in neoclassical growth theory, the Swedish economy is close to the Golden Rule.

become so rich that the malfunctioning of the social security system would be a second-order problem.

b.   The Old System and the 1994 Proposal

The old system is mainly PAYG, although there is also a relatively small fund involved. Since the system is benefit-defined, the fund's yield does not affect the pensions, but helps the government in times of demographic changes; instead of raising the fees, the yield of the fund can be used to cover the deficits. In the 1994 proposal, there was on top of the PAYG system an idea of partial funding. The wage earners were supposed to save two percentage points of their fees in individual funds; although the system as a whole was compulsory, the individuals would be free to choose among a large number of competing funds with different investment policies.

This would not, however, imply any increase in aggregate saving. The old ATP fund, which was projected to be depleted within the next two decades, was of approximately the same size as the sum of the new, individual funds and would in the long run be more or less exactly substituted for by those. The difference is that while the former was a collective monopoly fund, managed by politicians, the new ones would be individual, competitive, and run by professional fund managers. The yield could thus be expected to be higher, and the risk characteristics of the portfolios could be adjusted according to individual preferences.

The actual implementation of this funded part of the system raised a number of practical questions that were addressed in a new committee report published in the spring of 1996 (Ministry of Social Affairs 1996). Although this report was mainly technical, the policy debate that followed dealt with more ideological issues. A prominent question was whether the people's pension funds really should be handed over to private fund managers and speculators in the financial markets, instead of being subject to "democratic control." Another debate that arose in connection with the proposal that individuals should be free to choose the fund they want, was whether it is fair to have different persons receiving different pensions depending on whether their respective fund managers have been successful or unsuccessful with their speculations. One could of course argue that these ideological problems were relatively small since the funded part of the system was so limited, comprising only two percentage points of the fees amounting to 18.5 percent (including the basic, uniform pension) of the wage sum. This did, however, not convince the critics; who could guarantee that some future government would not increase the funded part to three or four percentage points? The prospect of a completely privatized system, run by private interests, was therefore looming.

These were politically delicate issues, and the discussion dragged on. When the final political agreement was reached in January 1998, the basic elements of the 1994 proposal were retained, and the funded part was increased to 2.5 percentage points.

c.   The Transition

There are two kinds of transition problems. The "social insurance paradox"— saying that when a society changes from a funded to a PAYG system, the generation retiring immediately after the transformation will receive double pensions[11]—provides a convincing public-choice explanation of why democratic societies, as soon as their administrative institutions are sufficiently advanced, will vote for the introduction of PAYG systems.

The other side of the coin is that if we move in the other direction, the persons in the transition generation will have to pay double fees: one to cover the pensions of those already retired, and one to build up their own funds. Thus it will never be possible to collect a political majority for a change from a PAYG system to a funded one.[12]

In the 1994 proposal this problem is elegantly circumvented by reducing the old, collective fund. Since this reduction is balanced by the build-up of the new, individual funds, the transition generation will not have to pay any double fees. This can, however, only go on until the old fund is depleted. After that, any further increase in the funded part of the system—for example, an increase in the two percentage points to three or four—will have to be paid for by raising the fees, or by reducing the pensions of the retired generation, accordingly.

The second transition problem is independent of the funded versus PAYG issue and has to do with the benefit rules. The 1994 committee report suggested that everybody who was born in 1934 and earlier would get his or her pension according to the old (nonactuarial) benefit rules, while everybody who was born in 1954 and later would get pensions according to the new rules. For those born between these years, the pension would be a linear combination of the two systems: a person born in, say, 1949 would get 5/20 of the pension according to the old system, and 15/20 according to the new.

---

[11]   Alternatively, it will receive a full PAYG pension without having paid any contributions to the system.

[12]   It is of course possible to borrow money in order to distribute this extra cost of the transfer over a large number of generations. It is, however, not possible to reduce the extra cost to zero without invoking the "equity premium," i.e., the government can borrow at a low cost and invest the money at a high yield.

5.   Government versus Private System

One is inclined to think that a government versus a private system is equivalent to a PAYG versus a funded system; only the government can maintain a PAYG system. This is, however, not entirely true. A system which is formally a private one, with a fund managed by a profit-maximizing manager, could still be PAYG from a macroeconomic point of view. This would be the case if, for instance, the system was first a government-run PAYG system which was then privatized in the following way. The government issues bonds with a value equal to the system's liabilities, i.e., the government makes these liabilities visible. The bonds are then placed in a fund, which is auctioned off, together with the system's liabilities, to the private insurance industry. Formally, this would be a private, funded system, but in a macroeconomic perspective it is still a PAYG system, since total savings have not increased in the economy, and since the pensions are paid from the yield of the bonds, that is, from the taxes paid by the active generation.

Also, one would be inclined to think that actuarial fairness is equal to a private system. This is probably the case if competition is encouraged by allowing the individuals to choose freely between several funds; then competition would probably drive out at least major deviations from the ideal of actuarial fairness. With a monopoly fund—whether private or government-managed—we would not have such a development, neither with respect to the benefit rules nor with respect to the interest rate.[13]

There is, however, another issue which is more intimately connected with a government-run system as opposed to a privately managed one, namely that of political risk. Let us take the old ATP system as an illustration. Within that system, pensions are supposed to be fixed in real terms. When computing that real value, a large number of issues have to be dealt with, for instance the choice and computation of an appropriate price index. These problems are usually of a technical nature and of minor importance to the pensions. In fact, slight changes in the rules are continuously being made without causing any political debate.

However, those minor, technical changes accumulate over time. Computing the real value (in CPI terms) of the ATP pensions while strictly adhering to the 1975 rules, and then comparing that hypothetical value to the actual value in 1995, we find that the ATP pensions have been reduced by between 12 and 17 percent over these 20 years (see Persson 1996). This tacit reduction has never been subject to any open political discussion, although it is rather sizable. The point is that if a private insurance company had changed the rules in a stepwise

---

13   A recent study indicates that the return on government-managed pension funds is considerably lower than the return on privately managed funds; see World Bank (1994:93–96).

fashion so as to reduce pension benefits by 17 percent, such an action would almost certainly have caused a lawsuit. Changes in a government-run system, however, are decided by society's democratic institutions or their agents, and can never be brought before the court. In fact, it seems as if the private contract between the insurance company and the customer is more reliable than the political contract between the state and the citizen.

Government-run systems thus have a nonnegligible political risk, as has also been pointed out by Diamond (1996:80). To the particular risk of small manipulations should be added the uncertainty involved in the political sector's current inability to make any decisions regarding a major reform. The first ATP reform committee was appointed in 1984, the second in 1991. This means that for at least thirteen years, we knew that the rules of the game might change, but we did not know what the new rules would look like. When the 1991 committee presented its report in 1994, it suggested that those born in 1934 or earlier would receive their pensions according to the old system; thus this group is admittedly subject to less uncertainty than those born in 1954 and later—provided, of course, that the transition scheme outlined in the 1994 report will eventually be implemented.

Based mainly on the welfare loss due to the inherent uncertainty of government-run social security systems, a blueprint for the privatization of the Swedish ATP system was published by Persson (1996). Needless to say, such a thorough reform is not on the political agenda today—and will hardly be, in any foreseeable future.

6.   Summary and Conclusions

Since the late 1970s, the Swedish social security system has been regarded as ripe for reform. The reasons have varied. Some people have demanded a system with more (less) redistribution, that is, a lower (higher) degree of actuarial fairness, while others have emphasized the role of savings and claimed that a shift towards a funded system will boost economic growth.

The reform proposal launched in 1994, and finally decided on in 1998, is characterized by a higher degree of actuarial fairness than the older system. It is also designed to be partially funded. Both these features have caused considerable opposition in the political sphere, the reform has been delayed, and the uncertainty regarding the design of our future social security system has only recently been removed.

In my view, the failure of the old system is not due to changes in demography, but to the lack of actuarial fairness in the sense that the benefit rules redistribute wealth in a rather arbitrary fashion. As for the issue of savings and capital formation, this is an unresolved issue in a small open economy like Sweden. It is, however, clear that a shift from a pay-as-you-go to a funded system, however desirable it may be on other grounds, cannot be justified by the Pareto criterion, since the transitional generation can never be fully compensated for the extra contribution it has to pay.

The main conclusion to be drawn from the Swedish experience is perhaps that any reform proposal—however desirable according to some social welfare function—will meet strong political resistance. Even if it could be shown to be justified according to the Pareto criterion, there would probably be some opposition because information is costly. Thus there is a high probability that even an old system which is hard to justify by *any* social welfare function will persist for a long time. This raises the question of whether the political sector is really suited to be in charge of such an important sector of the economy as the pension system. If all pension schemes were managed by private companies (but were still mandatory and regulated, in order to avoid free riders and moral hazard), competition would force the system towards actuarial fairness; the system would then be more robust than a government-run system, and uncertainty would be reduced.

Bibliography

Diamond, P.A. (1996). Proposals to Restructure Social Security. *Journal of Economic Perspectives* 10(3):67–88.

Feldstein, M. (1996). The Missing Piece in Policy Analysis: Social Security Reform. *American Economic Review* 86(2):1–14.

Feldstein, M., and C. Horioka (1980). Domestic Saving and International Capital Flows. *Economic Journal* 90(2):314–329.

Henrekson, M., K. Lantto, and M. Persson (1990). *Bruk och missbruk av sjukförsäkringen* (Use and Abuse of the Sickness Insurance). Stockholm: SNS Förlag.

Kruse, A. (1997). Pension Systems and Reforms—The Case of Sweden. In *Pension Systems and Reforms—Britain, Hungary, Italy, Poland, Sweden. Final Report, European Commission's Phare ACE Programme 1995*. Brussels: European Commission, February.

Leiderman, L., and A. Razin (eds.) (1994). *Capital Mobility: The Impact on Consumption, Investment and Growth*. Cambridge: Cambridge University Press.

Lindbeck, A. (1997). The Swedish Experiment. *Journal of Economic Literature* 35(3): 1273–1319.

Ministry of Social Affairs (1990). *Allmän pension: Betänkande från Pensionsberednin- gen, SOU 1990:76* (General Pension: A Report of the Pension Committee). Stockholm: Fritzes.

—— (1994). *Reformerat pensionssystem: Betänkande från Pensionsarbetsgruppen, SOU 1994:20* (A Reformed Pension System: A Report of the Pension Group). Stockholm: Fritzes.

—— (1996). *Allmänt pensionssparande: Betänkande av premiereservafredningen, SOU 1996:83* (Pension Savings Report of the Savings Committee). Stockholm: Fritzes.

OECD (1996). *Employment Outlook.* July. Paris.

Persson, M. (1991). Vad är det för fel på ATP-systemet? (What's Wrong with the ATP System?). *Ekonomisk Debatt* 19(3):205–218.

—— (1996). Privatisering av ATP-systemet (A Blueprint for Privatization of the ATP System). *Ekonomisk Debatt* 24(7):555–564.

Siegel, J.J., and R.H. Thaler (1997). Anomalies: The Equity Premium Puzzle. *Journal of Economic Perspectives* 11(1):191–200.

Ståhlberg, A.-C. (1990). Life Cycle Income Redistribution of the Public Sector: Inter- and Intragenerational Effects. In I. Persson (ed.), *Generating Inequality in the Welfare State: The Swedish Experience.* Oslo: Norwegian University Press.

World Bank (1994). *Adverting the Old Age Crisis: Policies to Protect the Old and Pro- mote Growth. A World Bank Research Report.* Oxford: Oxford University Press.

Comment on the Papers by Axel Börsch-Supan, Edward M. Gramlich, and Mats Persson

Winfried Schmähl

1. Introduction

My comment is structured as follows: I will start with some general remarks on the main topic of this conference—pay-as-you-go (PAYG) versus funding. Then I will point out some similarities and differences in the structure of the pension schemes as well as in the reform debate of the three countries under discussion, the United States, Sweden, and Germany. Finally, some remarks will be made focusing on the German situation.

2. Some General Remarks on Comparing Financing Methods

One of the most discussed topics in pension reform since the introduction of social insurance in the late 19th century is how to finance pensions. For a long time the academic discussion focused on comparisons of the two financing methods PAYG and funding. However, the fact was often neglected that in reality we always have to deal with problems of transition from one financing method to another. Not taking this into account can give rather biased information, especially to those who have to make decisions either in private households or as politicians.

There is an explicit or at least implicit assumption in many statements: funding of pensions and/or privatization increases household and national saving, stimulates higher capital formation, and economic growth. Along this line, for example, Siebert argues in his introductory paper to this conference: "In contrast to a pay-as-you-go system, the contributions to a funded system represent savings that are invested in the capital market. Capital accumulation is enhanced" (p. 14). "As a result of lower savings and a lower capital stock, the level of GDP per head and the growth rate are both lower compared to an economy with a funded system" (p. 16). However, the theoretical and empirical bases for such statements are rather weak.[1] A lot of question marks exist concerning the ele-

---

[1] Such comparisons should also not be biased by the approach applied: comparing, for example, a funded scheme with complete equivalence and a PAYG scheme with incomplete equivalence (Siebert, pp. 13, 14, 17) mixes up the effects of the financing

ments of the "chain" (based on neoclassical theory) linking pension fund accumulation to additional private household saving, additional private household saving to additional national saving, additional national saving to additional investment, and additional investment to higher GDP:

Principally, (a) additional saving in a funded pension scheme or (b) a high degree of funding compared to PAYG does not say anything as to whether this is accompanied by a higher domestic saving rate. This will be illustrated by two examples. (a) The Chilean pension reform, which introduced a mandatory but privately managed pension scheme, is often praised as a "success story" in line with the recommendations of the World Bank (1994). Although $30 billion were accumulated by the 13 AFPs (private pension funds) in March 1997, econometric analysis has not shown an increase in private or domestic saving as a result of the pension reform (Holzmann 1996, 1997).[2] Wealth accumulation by pension funds can be offset by the activities of other actors, for example, substitution processes have to be taken into account, at least because there are different reasons for saving. This becomes especially important in the process of transition from one scheme to another, if, as is often the case, a higher "burden" for private households results from financing pension claims acquired in the "old" system, while, on the other hand, additional saving is required to build up a "capital stock" for the household members' own old age.[3]

(b) If the degree of funding (for example, as a percentage of GDP) in various countries is compared, there is also no positive correlation with the domestic saving rate. This becomes obvious in comparing Germany with the United States, the United Kingdom, or the Netherlands, countries with much higher accumulation of pension funds, as can be seen from Table 1.

Although pension assets are much higher in the United Kingdom and the Netherlands, saving rates are rather similar to those in Germany. The U.S. saving rate is "traditionally" much lower, "the lowest saving rate in the OECD" (Feldstein 1995:416), although in the United States even Social Security accumulates huge funds resulting from a surplus of roughly $30 billion each year. Feldstein (1995:411) states: "The surprising thing to me is that Europeans con-

---

method with the design of the pension scheme, concerning the degree of equivalence implemented.

2   Pension reform seems to have stimulated financial markets. But whether this has priority in pension reform may be questioned. Pension schemes should primarily be an instrument for old-age protection, not for improving financial markets or for being an instrument of labor market policy, although the effects on capital and labor markets have to be taken into account when designing the volume and structure of the pension schemes.

3   In many countries, pensioners still have a positive saving rate. Their reaction to changing conditions also has to be taken into account.

Table 1 —   Accumulated Assets in Supplementary Pension Schemes as Percentage of GDP (at the beginning of the 1990s)

Country	Percent (rounded off)
United Kingdom	79
Netherlands	89
United States	59
Germany	
including book reserves	13
book reserves excluded	6

Source: Europäische Kommission (1997: Table II).

tinue to save despite the generosity of social security retirement programs in Europe." He tries to explain this puzzling fact by saying that "members of the European public have less confidence than their American counterparts in the long-term financial promises of governments" (1995:411). This explanation does not seem very convincing to me, at least with regard to Germany. In the currency reforms in Germany after World War II, for example, and in the process of German unification, public pension claims were revalued higher than other types of financial assets.

Even if funding of pensions were to increase national saving, there is no automatic process of increasing capital formation and productivity. "Capitalist economies do not behave like well-oiled equilibrium machines," Solow (1996: 301) remarked.[4]

There seems to be a shift in the arguments by those proposing additional funding and a reduction or elimination of PAYG: Not so much these questioned effects on national saving and capital formation are now put at the center of the arguments, but the different rates of return of funded and PAYG schemes, pointing especially at the high rates of return of equities during the last years. However, higher rates of return are often a result of higher (expected) risk. Higher administrative costs, especially in private funds, have to be taken into account, too. In the mandatory private pension scheme in Chile the high costs are a much-debated topic.[5]

---

[4]   Financial capital has to be transformed into real capital. How this money is invested is decisive for productivity. Accumulated reserves are often in treasury bonds. This, for example, is the case with the U.S. Social Security surplus as well as with the Central-Provident-Fund in Singapore (Burger 1997). How does the government spend this money and how is debt financing influenced?

[5]   Mesa-Lago and Arenas de Mesa (1997) and Valdés-Prieto (1994) give an overview. Mirrlees (1995:384) concludes: "It . . . seems that in many areas of insurance, the administrative costs of public provision are substantially lower than those of private

Two general conclusions can be drawn: (a) The explanatory power of economics to explain reality and thus its applicability in the real world (for example, in preparing political decisions on pension reforms) is obviously limited, because "the view that the function of economics was to explain economic behavior on the basis of some postulates of rational maximizing behavior...has become the religion of economics. The broader perspective, that the function is to explain human economic behavior, and that this behavior may not be consistent with rational maximizing behavior, or even with an as if version of rationality, is regarded as heresy," as Joseph Stiglitz (1983:999) remarked. Especially when major reforms are planned or take place, excluding the possibility of changing objectives (preferences) of economic actors from economic analysis can be an important reason for neglecting influencing factors in explaining developments in the real world.[6] Integrating findings from political science and from sociological and psychological research may provide an opportunity to better explain behavioral reactions of the economic actors to reform measures and may improve the preparation of such measures.

(b) Dealing with reforms of pension schemes in Germany, Sweden, and the United States reminds us of the fact that transition is always an important aspect from an economic as well as political point of view. Transition needs time, and this is why the duration of the transition process is of great importance in the process of political decision-making.

The problems and effects of these transitions depend on the specific conditions of a country: the economic conditions and especially the existing pension scheme and its volume and structure, whether tax-financed and flat-rate or means-tested or having a close contribution-benefit link with pension claims based on former contributions. The structure of the pension scheme—being also the outflow of political objectives—can influence expectations and behavior of economic actors.

The country-specific conditions are therefore a necessary element in analyzing the real world. Taking this into account, there is obviously no blueprint for restructuring, reforming, or developing a pension scheme that is adequate for all countries, whether industrialized, former socialist, developing countries, or countries with emerging markets.

---

provision (largely because of marketing costs). This last consideration may be a good reason for the State to provide a pension system."

6   In this sense, for example, Richard Easterlin states: "I think it is unfortunate that there are economists who arbitrarily define the study of preference change as not 'economics' and hence exclude the study of preferences from the field. This has the unfortunate effect of limiting the potential scope of economic analysis, and erecting a barrier between economics, on the one hand, and sociology and psychology, on the other" Macunovich (1997:125).

This is the reason why a look at some similarities and differences especially in the structure of pension schemes in the United States, Sweden, and Germany seems to be useful.

3.   Some Structural Elements of Pension Schemes in the United States, Sweden, and Germany and Some Tendencies of Proposals for Reform

All three countries have a mix of pension schemes, but the difference in its structure between the United States and Germany is less pronounced compared to the structure of the Swedish pension scheme: The basic "pillar" in Germany is a defined benefit PAYG scheme such as in the United States, but for some years it has been supplemented by some funding in the United States. The German social insurance scheme (statutory pension insurance) is, however, less redistributive than U.S. Social Security. Both countries have *voluntary* funded supplementary (firm-based) pension schemes. In contrast to this, Sweden's first pillar is flat rate, highly redistributive, and the supplementary pension scheme (ATP) of the defined benefit type is *mandatory*.

Concerning the reform proposals in all three countries, reform measures within the PAYG schemes have been discussed, decided upon, or already implemented. In Germany, there is a clear tendency to make the scheme less redistributive by using *finance* measures, i.e. by financing interpersonal redistributive elements of pensions mainly from tax revenue, and by using *expenditure* measures, by i.e., deducting from the full pension in the case of "early" retirement in order to increase the average retirement age (Schmähl et al. 1996), and by reducing pension claims not based on former contribution payments, as in the case of schooling. Measures like these were implemented in 1992 and 1996. In the Pension Reform Bill 1999, presented by the government in June 1997, several additional changes are proposed, pointing in the same direction (Schmähl 1997). Partial funding of social insurance or reducing the present level of PAYG social insurance combined with a shift to funded pensions, as proposed and discussed in the paper of Börsch-Supan, have little political support. This is different in Sweden, as Persson explained with respect to partial funding. In the United States, there exist many proposals for additional funding or even privatizing social security (Gramlich, this volume; Advisory Council 1997), but these proposals have not yet resulted in political decisions.

In the United States, Sweden, and Germany most of the reform measures are changes within the PAYG scheme and not towards funding. At least the proposals of Gramlich (pp. 166–168) seem to make the public social security scheme in the United States more redistributive. In contrast to this, in Sweden and Germany a clear tendency toward a closer contribution-benefit link exists. The reform measures in the Swedish additional ATP system move it principally closer to the German approach in pension insurance and away from the pronounced redistributive approach that has dominated social security in Sweden for a long time.

Sweden goes even further in the direction of "actuarial fairness," since a shift from a defined benefit to a defined contribution scheme is aimed at, but has not yet been implemented.[7] For Sweden a close look at the experience in Latvia may be interesting, because Latvia has already introduced a public pension scheme along the lines of the Swedish reform proposals, introduced with support of the World Bank and an expert from Sweden as the head of the decisive World Bank mission.

4.   Pension Reform in Germany: Some Remarks concerning Börsch-Supan's Analysis and the Present Discussion

Concerning Germany, one has to discuss reforms within the present PAYG scheme and possibilities of increasing funding elements for old-age security, which already exist in a great variety, but take place outside the public sector.[8] Börsch-Supan proposes reducing PAYG financing and at least supplementing it by funding, because, as he argues, "Germany cannot provide the flexibility that is necessary to master the demographic changes to come" (p. 129). However, he points out that there are many different possibilities of adapting the PAYG statutory pension scheme to changing conditions in demography, the economy, and society. Whether "Germany" is flexible enough, in my view depends mainly on whether adequate and convincing decisions are made in the political process.

It is necessary to compare the costs for different groups of the population, for cohorts etc. of changes within the system on the one hand and funding on the other. This is always based on expectations concerning the effects. And these expectations are based on the model that is (explicitly or implicitly) used as well as on the assumptions made concerning behavior.

In his budget equation, Börsch-Supan neglects an often-discussed element: The contribution rate for balancing the budget of the PAYG pension scheme de-

---

[7]   This tendency is also to be seen in occupational pension schemes in the United States and Germany. This is linked to a shift in risk-bearing, as well.

[8]   Recently, proposals have been made for funding in the public pension scheme for civil servants, and some minor funds have been implemented already, however, with rather limited success so far.

pends not only on the (average gross) pension level and the pensioner (dependency) ratio, but also on the ratio of pension expenditure financed from general public revenue (from the federal budget). This is about 20 percent in Germany and is especially an instrument to finance redistributive elements in the pension scheme, so that the contribution-benefit link becomes stronger.[9] Beside its effect on income distribution and employment, this can have a positive effect concerning the acceptance of the pension scheme and in reducing resistance to financing.

Börsch-Supan concedes that a combination of measures may "solve the pension crisis" (p. 145), but doubts whether "the labor market is sufficiently flexible." He sees many more chances when relying on the flexibility of the capital market.

The expectations concerning the development of the labor market and the capital market in the future seem to guide to a high degree the different proposals for reforming pension schemes. Adequately taking into account the risks involved in the different approaches is a topic which has to be elaborated very carefully and in a balanced manner.

Börsch-Supan's main argument for funding is the difference in the rates of return in PAYG and funded schemes realized during recent years and expected for the future. He therefore proposes a shift to mandatory funding and discusses effects during the transition period,[10] arguing that there is less than a " 'double burden,' " but an additional burden. This is, according to Börsch-Supan, "relatively small" (p. 152). For the "average earner" it is 4.2 percent from gross earnings and 6.6 percent from net earnings and would require an increase in savings of about 33 percent—in a period of a still-increasing contribution rate. It seems to be quite realistic that substitution effects cannot be neglected.

In his Figure 18, Börsch-Supan shows that—compared to the present scheme (without changes)—the additional burden will only become effective for a limited time and a limited number of cohorts.[11] But according to Börsch-Supan's assumptions, this additional burden will last until around 2025. This means that the "baby boom" generation, who had less favorable conditions in kindergarten, school, and on the labor market will be burdened additionally for old-age provi-

---

9   This is discussed in detail in Schmähl (1998).

10 For a discussion of transition problems in a simple overlapping generation model when fundamentally changing the pension system in Germany, namely from an earnings-related to a flat-rate scheme, supplemented by additional saving and thereby reducing PAYG and increasing funding, see Schmähl (1974).

11 It is also necessary to take macroeconomic conditions into account when an increase of wealth accumulation is aimed at by changing the financing method. Is there unemployment because of a lack of demand? Starting a transformation of the pension scheme "at the wrong time" can make economic conditions even more difficult.

sion. This does not seem to be considered in the public debate in Germany, where a shift towards funding has been proposed for young people by banks, insurance companies, and some academics.[12]

Börsch-Supan does not deny the risks associated with more funding. He mentions country-specific inflation, and financial and residual demographic risks and sees the solution especially in broad diversification. But there are more risks: exchange rate changes, political risks (such as increases in taxation), and restrictions concerning capital mobility (see Mitchell and Zeldes 1996).

Another important risk element is speculation on the financial markets. The development in Mexico in 1994 or in Thailand in 1997 gives recent examples of risks in "emerging markets."

An additional factor should not be neglected: If pensions are based more and more on funding, the decisions of fund managers become more and more important in financial markets. Even if funds are diversified, uniform decisions of many managers going into a specific market or out of the market may provoke tremendous volatility on such a market, especially in smaller countries.

If funding becomes an approach that dominates worldwide, there will be an intensified effort to transform huge amounts of financial capital into real capital. Even today the developments at the stock exchange may be fueled by pension fund money. It is an open question, however, whether price increases are based on improved economic conditions for firms or on speculative demand for specific equities.

If pension funds worldwide become the dominating factor in capital markets, and in some parts of the world there is more supply than demand for financial capital as a result of a rapidly aging population, then it will become much more obvious than today that funded schemes are not immune to aging either. This applies even more if retirement income in a country is based mainly on funded schemes. This is also an argument in favor of a mix of financing methods.

In my view, a more balanced approach in the discussion on funded versus PAYG pension schemes is necessary, rather than the present mainstream economic arguing in favor of funding. In Germany, above all, reform measures within the existing PAYG pension scheme are necessary, making the contribution-benefit link closer than today (although compared to other countries, Germany already has a low degree of interpersonal redistribution within the pension scheme); some of these measures are mentioned by Börsch-Supan. Disentan-

---

12   There is also the question whether the "efficiency gain" Börsch-Supan mentions for the new scheme will start in about 2025 or whether the amount of "transition burden" has to be taken into consideration, thereby shifting the starting point of the superiority of the new scheme to a future. This leads, among other things, into the discussion of discount rates, time preferences, and evaluation of differences in the burden for different cohorts.

gling insurance and redistributive elements will, among other things, reduce the negative incentive effects of the pension scheme on the labor market. A general rule could be to grant pension claims only if adequate contributions are paid; such contribution payments can also come from general public budgets or other social insurance institutions. This would, among other things, reduce the political risk of overburdening the pension scheme.

However, in my view, there is very little scope in Germany to reduce the standard pension level. Otherwise, this would mean that pensions would hardly exceed the poverty line for an increasing number of contributors, even after many years of insurance. In Germany the poverty line is defined by the means-tested social assistance level, which is about 40 percent of net average earnings (Schmähl 1997a).[13] Instead of reducing the standard pension level by introducing an additional factor into the pension adjustment formula to account for increasing life expectancy (as proposed in a bill of the German government in 1997), I would prefer a link of the (reference) retirement age (for a full pension without deductions) to life expectancy, as it is also proposed by Gramlich (p. 167) and also by a majority of the Advisory Council (1997) in the United States.[14] Taking all aspects together, I do not share the view that the German pension scheme is "on the verge of collapse." However, political decisions based on a clear concept are needed.

Bibliography

Advisory Council (1997). Report of the 1994–1996 Advisory Council on Social Security, Volume I: Findings and Recommendations. Washington, D.C.

Burger, A. (1997). Rentenversicherung in Singapur: kapitalgedeckte gesetzliche Rentenversicherung in staatlicher Hand. *Deutsche Rentenversicherung* (5/6):335–344.

Europäische Kommission (1997). *Zusätzliche Altersversorgung im Binnenmarkt: Grünbuch* (*Additional Old-Age Provision in the Common Market: Greenbook*). Brussels.

---

13   Today, an average earner needs about 26 years of insurance to receive a pension that is just as high as the entitlement for social assistance. However, it has to be taken into account that in most countries that have a low PAYG public pension scheme, a second supplementary scheme exists that is mostly mandatory.

14   Such a link could be decided upon now but become effective around the years 2010/2015, when, according to labor market projections, much better labor market conditions are expected. This shows very clearly that the effects of a PAYG pension scheme on labor markets are important, but also that the development of labor markets is important for the development of the pension scheme. See Schmähl (1989, 1990) for analyses of demographics, labor market, and social security.

Feldstein, M. (1995). Fiscal Policies, Capital Formation, and Capitalism. *European Economic Review* 39:399–420.

Holzmann, R. (1996). Pension Reform, Financial Market Development, and Economic Growth: Preliminary Evidence from Chile. Working Paper 96/94. International Monetary Fund, Washington, D.C.

—— (1997). Pension Reform and National Saving: The Chilean Experience. Forschungsbericht 9703. Ludwig Boltzmann Institut zur Analyse wirtschaftspolitischer Aktivitäten, Vienna.

Macunovich, D.J. (1997). A Conversation with Richard Easterlin. *Journal of Population Economics* 10:119–136.

Mesa-Lago, C., and A. Arenas de Mesa (1997). Fünfzehn Jahre nach der Privatisierung des Rentensystems in Chile: Evaluation, Lehre und zukünftige Aufgaben. *Deutsche Rentenversicherung* (7):405–426. An English version (Fifteen Years after the Privatization of the Chilean Pension System: Evaluation, Lessons and Challenges) will appear in M.A. Cruz-Saco and C. Mesa-Lago (eds.), *Reforming Pension and Health Care Systems in Latin America*.

Mirrlees, J.A. (1995). Private Risk and Public Action: The Economics of the Welfare State. *European Economic Review* 39:383–397.

Mitchell, O.S., and S.P. Zeldes (1996). Social Security Privatization: A Structure for Analysis. *American Economic Review, Papers and Proceedings* 86:363–367.

Schmähl, W. (1974). *Systemänderung in der Altersvorsorge (Changing the Old-Age Security System)*. Opladen: Westdeutscher Verlag.

—— (1989). Labour Force Participation and Social Pension Systems. In P. Johnson, C. Conrad, and D. Thomson (eds.), *Workers Versus Pensioners: Intergenerational Justice in an Ageing World*. Manchester: Manchester University Press.

—— (1990). Demographic Change and Social Security: Some Elements of a Complex Relationship. *Journal of Population Economics* 3:159–177.

—— (1997). Alterssicherung—Quo vadis? *Jahrbücher für Nationalökonomie und Statistik* 216:413-435.

—— (1998). Financing Social Security in Germany: Proposals for Changing Its Structure and Some Possible Effects. In S. Black (ed.), *Globalization, Technological Change and the Welfare State*. (in print).

Schmähl, W., R. George, and C. Oswald (1996). Gradual Retirement in Germany. In L. Delsen and G. Reday-Mulvey (eds.), *Gradual Retirement in the OECD Countries*. Aldershot: Dartmouth.

Solow, R. (1996). The Role of Macroeconomic Policy. In J.C. Fuhrer and J.S. Little (eds.), *Technology and Growth*. Federal Reserve Bank of Boston.

Stiglitz, J.E. (1983). Book Review on George R. Feiwel (ed.), Samuelson and Neoclassical Economics. *Journal of Economic Literature* 21(3):997–999.

Valdés-Prieto, S. (1994). Administrative Charges in Pensions in Chile, Malaysia, Zambia, and the United States. World Bank Policy Research Working Paper 1372. Washington, D.C.

World Bank (1994). *Averting the Old Age Crisis: Policies to Protect the Old and Promote Growth*. Oxford: Oxford University Press.

A General Comment on the Old Age Pension Problem: A Funded System for Those Who Caused the Crisis

Hans-Werner Sinn

1. General Remarks

This is prima facie a comment on the papers by Börsch-Supan, Persson, and Gramlich, but implicitly it is also a comment on other papers of this conference. In most Western countries the general problems of the old-age pension systems are similar, and transition to a funded system is often advocated as a means of removing the distortions thought to be brought about by the pay-as-you-go system. In this comment, I will argue that the nature of the distortions is different from what is commonly thought, and that the proper policy solution to the old-age pension crisis lies in a partial transition to a funded system for those families which have caused this crisis.

Börsch-Supan, Gramlich, and Persson have given useful accounts of the problems facing their national pension schemes, and all three authors have pointed to the demographic problem of an increasing dependency ratio. In qualitative terms, the problems are the same everywhere, but quantitatively they are much more severe in Germany than in Sweden or the United States. Germany was the first country to introduce a state pension system, and it now has the lowest birth rate in the world after Italy. Only 0.6 girls per woman are born. Its dependency ratio is climbing faster than that of nearly all other countries, and will approximate 50 percent in 2030. For Germany, a catastrophe is in sight, and it is small wonder that Axel Börsch-Supan comes up with the most radical reform proposals of the three authors. While Ed Gramlich recommends that the United States use 1.6 percent of the pension contributions for a funded system and Mats Persson advocates a rate of 2 percent for Sweden, Axel Börsch-Supan suggests freezing the absolute contributions to the pay-as-you-go (PAYG) system immediately or, alternatively, phasing them out completely from 2005 through 2045. I find this proposal too radical, but I sympathize with a variant of it.

Given that the situation is less severe in Sweden and the United States, I do understand that Ed Gramlich and Mats Persson favor repairing the existing system rather than a full transition to a funded system. Ed Gramlich suggests cutting the benefit level and increasing the retirement age. Mats Persson advocates the introduction of registered individual accounts within the PAYG system.

The latter is an important proposal, which avoids much of the labor-leisure distortion that has been discussed by so many authors at this conference. With registered accounts and individual proportionality between contributions and pensions, there will be a labor-leisure distortion only to the extent that the present value of the pensions falls short of the present value of contributions, which in turn depends on the difference between the discount rate and the growth rate of the contribution value. Interestingly enough, the proposal coincides more or less with the system which has existed in Germany since 1957. I believe that the German system could also serve as a useful guideline for the United States, if one does not want to go the full way towards a funded system.

2.   No Way to Escape the Labor-Leisure Distortion

Indeed, apart from the fertility considerations that will follow below, registered accounts make the PAYG system Pareto-optimal, because they reduce the labor-leisure distortion to an unavoidable minimum, given that current and future working generations have to pay for the net benefits which earlier generations obtained from the system. I advise the foreign participants of this conference to take notice of the illuminating controversy between Breyer (1989, 1990) and Homburg (1988, 1990) which has recently been resolved by an important article by Fenge (1995) in *Finanzarchiv*. Fenge proved very elegantly that no Pareto-improving transition from a PAYG system to a funded system is possible if, as in Germany, individual benefits are proportional to individual contributions. The essence of the proof is that that part of the contributions which is lost because it pays for the net benefits received by previous generations, and which creates a labor supply distortion, will have to be maintained after the transition to a funded system in order to pay for the elderly. Thus a funded system will not be able to avoid the labor-leisure distortion of the PAYG system. It can be used to change the distribution of resources over the generations but will not be able to improve any generation's well-being without making another generation worse off.

I guess that some of the papers of this conference will have to be rewritten if their authors take proper notice of Fenge's pathbreaking proof. This remark applies in particular to the papers by Kotlikoff et al., Feldstein, Siebert, and Börsch-Supan. All these authors claim that the transition to a funded system will generate welfare gains in the sense of Kaldor-type Pareto improvements, but none of these gains are really dependent on the transition to a funded system. It is true that the capital collected in a funded system could be invested tax-free in the domestic or international capital market (Feldstein and Börsch-Supan), but the resulting welfare gain would also be available if the capital income tax system were overhauled, say by a transition to a cash-flow tax system. It is true that the distortion in the labor-leisure choice that remains even in the German system can be removed by financing the current old generation with a consumption tax (Kotlikoff), but this effect could also have been achieved by coupling a consumption tax with a wage subsidy. If we assume that the transition to a funded system is not accompanied by the invention of better tax systems, but that the set of feasible and Pareto-improving tax reforms has already been exhausted, there is no Pareto improvement from the introduction of a funded system.

3. A Three-Dynasty Model

Fenge's article convinced me that, in a PAYG system of the German type, the transition to a funded system is an issue of justice and fairness rather than one of efficiency and Paretian welfare considerations. Let me therefore have a look at the distributional consequences of alternative reform proposals. I prefer to see the distributional problem under the aspect of family dynasties rather than generations. As illustrated in Figure 1, we should distinguish three types of dynasty.

Figure 1— A Three-Dynasty Model for the Years 2000 and 2030

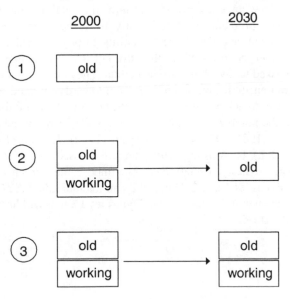

Dynasty 1 is currently dying out. It is characterized by old people who are currently pensioners and have no children.

Dynasty 2 lives a little longer. Its last generation will be retirees around the year 2030, when the financial difficulties of the PAYG system are greatest.

Dynasty 3 lives permanently. It has pensioners now and around 2030, but it always has people of working age.

If we leave the pension formula intact and solve the financial problems by increasing the contribution rate, only dynasty 3 will be hurt. Its working generation in 2030 will have to bear the full burden of the financial mismatch caused by population decline.

If, by way of contrast, we leave the contribution rate constant and reduce the replacement rate instead, dynasties 2 and 3 will be hurt, since their retirees will receive less than the pension formula promised.

In Germany, mixtures of these two policy solutions are currently being discussed. To me, they seem implausible because dynasty 1 never bears any of the financial burden. Indeed, they even seem unfair in the light of the fact that dynasties 2 and 3 would have to bear the burden of adjustment, while only dynasties 1 and 2 caused the problem.

They caused the problem by not having children. In order for the PAYG system to function, each working generation has to do two duties, not just one. It has to pay for the old *and* it has to pay for its children. Carrying out one of these duties is not enough for the survival of the system. Dynasties 1 and 2 have not raised children. They have not invested in human capital and have thus caused the old-age pension problem. It would be only just if they were made to bear the burden of adjustment, and they have the ability to pay given that they did not have to pay for their children. Since they did not invest in human capital, they should now be asked to invest in material capital. They are the natural candidates to bear the extra transitional burden of transition towards a funded system.

An elegant way to achieve this goal would be to make the old-age pensions proportional to the number of children—a proposal which a number of authors including Dinkel (1981), Albers (1990), Sinn (1990), Lüdeke (1995), Lüdeke and Werding (1996), or Werding (1998) have discussed. A reform along these lines would leave dynasty 3 unaffected, but impose the burden of adjustment exclusively on dynasties 1 and 2. Dynasty 3 can maintain the PAYG system, because it invests enough in human capital. Dynasties 1 and 2 will have to invest in material capital instead.

4.   The Fertility Problem

There is one important counterargument to such a solution, and this is the true efficiency problem connected with the PAYG system: the PAYG system is an insurance against being unable to have children. Children are socialized among all three dynasties. Those among the old who had no children are allowed to draw on the working capacity of other people's children to have their pensions financed. To the extent that the state of being without children is bad luck rather than voluntary choice, the PAYG system can be defended as a welfare-increasing insurance device. Seen from this perspective, it would not be a good idea to introduce a child component into the pension formula.

However, like any insurance, the insurance against not having children has a *moral hazard effect*. It reduces the incentive to raise children and to invest in their human capital. Given that one can rely on other people's children, life is more pleasant in a "dink" family than in a traditional family with one wage earner and many kids that need to be nourished.

I mentioned initially that Germany invented the PAYG system a hundred years ago and now has the lowest birth rate in the world after Italy. Small wonder that this is so. Over the generations, Germans have learned that life during old age can be pleasant and have a sound economic base even without their having had any children, unlike in the many centuries before, where childless people had to starve when they became old. Gradually, German fertility choices have changed under the influence of the PAYG system, and now we have the problems which many of the authors of this conference have described so vividly. The crisis of the PAYG system is the implication of a moral hazard effect which, unlike the distortion in the labor-leisure choice, is the true efficiency problem connected with this type of state insurance.

5.   The Fiscal Externality of a Child

In a PAYG system children create a huge positive externality for the rest of society. Suppose a family gives birth to an additional child. This child grows up, works, has children, pays pension contributions and, when old, receives pensions from his or her own children. When the fertility of this child equals the average fertility of the other participants of the system, the marginal positive externality which the child creates is equal to his or her gross contributions to the system. (It has little to do with the difference between the growth rate and the rate of interest.) Suppose the annual income is 50,000 DM, the contribution rate is 20 percent, and the child works for 40 years. Then the total sum of contributions is 400,000 DM or, after discounting with the difference between the discount and growth rates, about 300,000 DM. Imagine, how many children would be born if this sum were paid out to the family which decides to give birth to a child!

6. The Optimal Pension System

The insurance literature has told us how an optimal insurance contract should be designed when there is moral hazard: it should have a deductible element so that less than the full risk is covered. Applied to the PAYG system this wisdom suggests that the proper reaction to the current crisis would be the *partial* introduction of a child component into the pension formula. Some, but not all, of the pensions should be made proportional to the number of children raised. All people should be covered to some extent by the PAYG system, but the smaller the number of children, the smaller the pension should be and the larger the required contribution to a funded system.

I know that changing fertility now will be too late to solve the financial crisis around the year 2030. However, the distortion in the fertility decision is always present, and it always creates welfare losses. Moreover, even without a fertility reaction, justice and the ability to pay consideration require imposing the burden of the crisis predominantly on those who have caused it. Thus, there is every reason to introduce the child-based benefit system now and to supplement it with a funded system for those who do not raise children.

Bibliography

Albers, W. (1990). Die Anpassung des Systems der gesetzlichen Rentenversicherung an demographische Änderungen. In W. Albers, J. Hackmann, and K. Mackscheidt (eds.), *Finanzierungsprobleme der sozialen Sicherung I*. Berlin: Duncker & Humblot.

Breyer, F. (1989). On the Intergenerational Pareto Efficiency of Pay-as-You-Go Financed Pension Schemes. *Journal of Institutional and Theoretical Economics* 145:643–658.

—— (1990). *Ökonomische Theorie der Alterssicherung*. München: Vahlen.

Dinkel, R. (1981). Kinder- und Alterslastenausgleich bei wachsender Bevölkerung: ein Diskussionsbeitrag. *Finanzarchiv* 39:134–147.

Feldstein, M. (1998). Transition to a Fully Funded Pension System: Five Economic Issues. This volume.

Fenge, R. (1995). Pareto-Efficiency of the Pay-as-You-Go Pension System with Intergenerational Fairness. *Finanzarchiv* 52:357–363.

Homburg, S. (1988). *Theorie der Alterssicherung*. Berlin: Springer.

Homburg, S. (1990). The Efficiency of Unfunded Pension Schemes. *Journal of Institutional and Theoretical Economics* 146:640–647.

Kotlikoff, L., K. Smetters, and J. Walliser (1998). The Economic Impact of Privatizing Social Security. This volume.

Lüdeke, R. (1995). Kinderkosten, umlagefinanzierte Rentenversicherung, Staatsverschuldung und intergenerative Einkommensverteilung: Kinderbezogene Alternativen zum heutigen gesetzlichen Alterssicherungssystem. In G. Kleinhenz (ed.), „*Soziale Ausgestaltung der Marktwirtschaft: Die Vervollkommnung der "Sozialen Marktwirtschaft" als Daueraufgabe der Ordnungs- und Sozialpolitik* (Festschrift zum 65. Geburtstag von Heinz Lampert). Berlin: Duncker & Humblot.

Lüdeke, R., and M. Werding (1996). Die Reform des Dualen Familienlasten- bzw. Familienleistungsausgleichs 1996: Wirkungen und Ziele einkommensteuerlicher Kinderfreibeträge und des Kindergeldes nach altem und neuem Recht. *Jahrbücher für Nationalökonomie und Statistik* 215:419–433.

Siebert, H. (1998). Pay-as-You-Go versus Capital-Funded Pension Systems: The Issues. This volume.

Sinn, H.-W. (1990). Korreferat zu K. Jaeger. In B. Gahlen, H. Hesse, and H.-J. Ramser (eds.), *Theorie und Politik der Sozialversicherung*. Tübingen: Mohr Siebeck.

Werding, M. (1998). *Zur Rekonstruktion des Generationenvertrags. Ökonomische Zusammenhänge zwischen Kindererziehung, soziale Alterssicherung und Familienlastenausgleich*. Tübingen: Mohr Siebeck.

Change of the System:

The United Kingdom

and Chile

Richard Disney and Paul Johnson

The United Kingdom: A Working System of Minimum Pensions?

1. Introduction

The United Kingdom (U.K.) scheme of pension provision offers a "halfway house" between traditional comprehensive social security and the radical "privatization" of pensions associated in particular with Chile in the early 1980s. In the United Kingdom, a scheme of basic pension provision through publicly provided "social insurance" has coexisted with extensive private pension provision for many years, with a growing role for the latter as the population has aged. Indeed, as the next section describes, private provision predated public intervention at both the basic level and for the main, secondary, tier of the pension scheme.

Nevertheless, the transformation of the U.K. pension system towards a largely private scheme underwritten by a public minimum has been far from smooth. Between 1978 and 1995 there was a major experiment in comprehensive social security provision, whilst since the mid-1960s there have been constant radical amendments to pension legislation.[1] This volatility of pension arrangements has hardly facilitated individual planning for retirement and has led to problems of design and implementation which have, at different periods, induced substantial foregone tax revenues, excessive public expenditures, and suboptimal pension choices by individuals. The main lesson of the U.K. experience in the last 25 years is that consideration of the macroeconomic consequences of the form of pension provision should not divert attention from the equally important questions of getting the microeconomic incentives right and ensuring that distributional and efficiency goals are achieved.

The structure of the rest of the paper is as follows. The next section provides an overview of the development of the U.K. pension system. This is followed in Section 3 by a brief overview of "where we are now" and prospects for the future. Section 4 contains a discussion of proposals for reform of the basic, or primary, tier of pension provision through social security which in the United

---

1   Reforms proposed in 1968, 1972, and 1997 were abandoned after electoral defeats; major legislative changes were enacted in 1975, 1986, and 1993.

Kingdom is provided by a combination of "social insurance" and income-tested benefits. Reform proposals for simplifying the scheme, by integration or some form of minimum are considered. Section 5 then very briefly considers the future of private provision in the secondary tier, and the interaction of private provision with the residual second-tier social security benefit known as the state earnings-related pension scheme (SERPS). It focuses on the most dynamic part of the U.K. pension scheme, which is the system of largely individual-purchased retirement savings accounts known as Personal Pensions, developed since 1986, and on proposals to extend further coverage by individual or group defined contribution plans. Section 6 briefly summarizes the paper.

2.   Development of Pensions in the United Kingdom

a.   Origins of Beveridge's National Insurance Scheme

The Beveridge scheme of comprehensive "National Insurance," whereby the state provided flat rate benefits against unemployment, sickness, and disability, and an old-age pension, financed by flat rate contributions, arose out of the system of "friendly societies" and other workers' mutual aid associations which developed in Britain in the late nineteenth century. These associations were typically composed of groups of individuals in specific trades, collecting contributions towards mutual insurance, and thereby avoiding the problems of adverse selection and moral hazard through the relatively homogeneous and close-knit natures of the societies respectively. Such associations were unable to withstand the three-pronged attack of the private insurance industry, mass unemployment in the interwar period, and a slow aging of the population derived from increased longevity. Nevertheless, it is interesting that the main element of Beveridge's scheme of "social insurance" which has been retained to the present day, the basic state pension, has its origin in private initiatives among groups of workers.[2]

The Beveridge scheme of "social insurance" reached its apotheosis in 1946, with the passing of the National Insurance Act, which introduced a comprehensive scheme of social protection, financed by flat rate (lump-sum) contributions, notionally levied on employees and employers. These benefits included the basic state retirement pension, the value of which was set to remain constant in real (i.e., price-deflated) terms at a slightly augmented "subsistence level." Those

---

2   For a discussion of this fascinating period, see Gilbert (1966), Gosden (1973), and Harris (1972). A discussion of the evolution of the U.K.'s social security system in an economic context is contained in Creedy and Disney (1985: Chapter 2).

who wished to obtain a higher replacement ratio of pension benefits to earnings were left to buy additional private insurance, although it is not entirely clear whether Beveridge believed that this would come about through a rediscovery of mutual insurance among workers or through the activities of commercial insurance companies, since in his famous report (1942) he had been extremely hostile to the "excess" management charges and misleading sales techniques utilized by life insurance companies to sell life and pension insurance in the interwar years. Such a debate as to pension "mis-selling" raised its head again in the period after 1986 concerning the selling of individual Personal Pensions.

b.   Decline of Beveridge's National Insurance Scheme

In any event, the Beveridge scheme of comprehensive flat rate "floor" benefits financed out of flat rate contributions foundered almost immediately. In the first place, workers reaching pensionable age after 1946 were paid the basic state pension immediately, even though many of them had not paid any contributions. This "transition burden" was to have been financed by a supplement to the National Insurance Fund from the Treasury, but the Treasury resisted any attempts to raise the supplement as successive, larger, generations reached pensionable age. To further cap costs, the basic state pension (BSP) was actually set below the official poverty line which was determined by the rate at which National Assistance, the income-tested benefit introduced in 1948 for families with no other means of support, was to be set. And while there was initially some effort to pre-fund the social security scheme in the 1950s, by the late 1950s the actuality that the National Insurance Fund was in fact being run as a "pay-as-you-go" (PAYG) scheme had been officially confirmed.

Second, the rising real incomes of the 1950s and early 1960s led to pressure to raise the BSP in line with earnings, not prices. Indeed, had the pension remained at its 1946 level, a single person's BSP would currently be worth only around £30 per week ($44) today. As Figure 1 shows, real rises in the BSP took place sporadically until the 1975 legislation (see below), when regular annual indexation was linked to the faster of prices and earnings growth. In 1981, reversion to price indexation took place and the value of the pension relative to earnings has fallen sharply since that time. Indeed a single person's pension BSP is currently worth approximately 15 percent of average earnings (Dilnot et al. 1994) and is projected to fall, as a proportion of earnings, by around 36 percent by the year 2025 (Disney 1996). Nevertheless, the damage had been done in the period up to 1975, when rising real pensions continued to be funded largely by flat rate (lump-sum) contributions.

Figure 1 — Value of Basic State Pension (married couple, 1950 = 100)

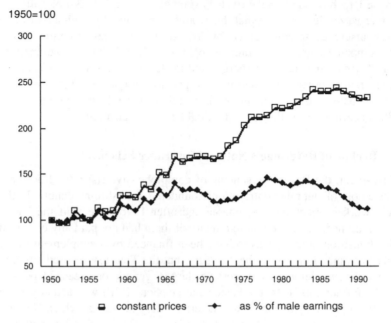

Source: Disney (1996).

The rising real level of the pension throughout the 25 years after 1945, the re-fusal of the Treasury to subsidize adequately pensions for those with insufficient contributions, and, finally, the demographic transition to an aged society which began as early as the 1950s in the United Kingdom all combined to generate a rising National Insurance contribution rate. The flat rate National Insurance contribution was perceived as highly regressive (prospective pension benefits were ignored in such arguments) and there was pressure to raise more revenue by imposing a contribution schedule in which contributions were proportional to earnings. At the same time it was felt that, politically, earnings-related contribu-tions could only be justified by adding an earnings-related component to pen-sions, although doing so would only raise the prospective revenue requirements still further. Thus, pressure for the reform of the Beveridge system mounted.

c.   Company-Provided (Occupational) Pensions and the Development of the Contracting-Out Principle

A protracted period of unsuccessful proposals for pension reform began in the late 1960s. The nature of these proposals needs not detain us, except to note another important facet of the U.K. system of pension provision which has been central to subsequent developments. As we argued previously, basic "social insurance" arose out of private arrangements developed in the late nineteenth century. Although these arrangements did not survive the introduction of National Insurance, a second tier of private provision, company pension schemes (known as "occupational pensions" in the United Kingdom), had developed since the 1930s and covered approximately half the work force by the late 1960s (Hannah 1986). Such schemes were typically salary-related (defined benefit) in the public sector and a mixture of defined benefit and group defined contribution (known as "money purchase") in the private sector. Except for central government employees, they were funded schemes, with funds kept in separate accounts from general company assets and covered by trust law. They provided benefits considerably more generous than those provided by National Insurance, especially in defined benefit plans, although typically early leavers have been penalized.

The necessity to raise revenue by introducing an earnings-related component to National Insurance was therefore coupled with a more explicitly ideological battle concerning the optimal extent and nature of private provision which carried on well into the 1970s. Some in the Labour Party wanted the state to introduce unfunded earnings-related social security benefits which were at least as generous as those provided by private companies, if necessary driving private pension plans out of business. Others, notably the private insurance industry and the Conservative Party, wanted to encourage the expansion of a private pension sector with some form of supplementary earnings-related social security pension for those not covered by private plans. Looking back, even as close to the present as the 1992 Labour Party election manifesto, this battle seems extraordinarily antiquated given the sea change in attitudes to private pension provision that has taken place in the last decade. But there were real problems underlying this debate: first, how to broaden private sector coverage and to provide a viable social security alternative when the private insurance industry had already "creamed off" the best risks into private schemes (i.e., men with stable job histories) and, second, how to levy higher National Insurance contributions to pay for supplementary social security provision for a subset of the work force without company pensions, which would not be popular with the remainder of the work force who were already in company schemes.

The 1975 Social Security Act was the consequence of this protracted debate. Without going into all its complexities (of which there were many), the key elements of the reform, the main components of which were introduced in 1978, were as follows:

— The introduction of a new state earnings-related pension scheme (SERPS) for those who did not have an approved company pension to supplement the basis state pension, which was retained. SERPS and the BSP were to be financed by an earnings-related contribution schedule, up to a ceiling (currently around mean manual earnings). SERPS was more generous in certain respects than existing company schemes, in particular in the treatment of spouses and in choice of the subset of years on which pension benefits would be calculated.
— Approved company pension plans had to be defined benefit (salary-related) and have at least minimum provision compatible with SERPS (for example, in the treatment of spouses).
— Approved company pension schemes could "contract out" of SERPS, guaranteeing to pay a certain pension (known as the Guaranteed Minimum Pension [GMP], now abolished) in exchange for paying a lower rate of National Insurance contribution by employer and employee. This difference between the full ("contracted-in") National Insurance contribution and the contracted-out rate was termed the "Contracted-Out Rebate" (COR). Note that it was not actually paid to companies, but merely that their contribution liabilities were reduced by this amount if their pension plan was approved. The level of the COR was set by the government such that private pension schemes could pay the GMP under conservative projections of real returns and such that the vast majority of schemes would indeed opt to contract out.[3]
— The social security scheme continued to be PAYG-financed, although company pension plans (except for central government employees) continued to be advance or prefunded. All contributors would continue to get the basic state pension, whether contracted in or out.

The 1975 act was an ingenious and complex compromise between interest groups. Like most compromises, it was essentially a backward-looking resolution of past conflicts rather than a forward-looking attempt to develop a program

---

3   Schemes differ in their pensioner-contributor ratios. Thus the optimal COR needed to finance schemes will also differ. Or, to put it a different way, schemes with low pensioner-contributor ratios are given an intramarginal subsidy if there is a single COR for all schemes. This point becomes central when we consider individual "contracting-out" through Personal Pensions later.

of pension provision which answered future questions: for example, how to cope with the continued demographic transition which would see the support ratio of contributors to pensioners projected to decline from 2.1 in 1995 to 1.4 (as originally projected) in the year 2030 (Disney 1996: Table 4.4). It also ignored the question of funding. It was therefore soon shown by our predecessors at the Institute for Fiscal Studies that future payroll tax rates based on the 1975 legislation were likely to be unsustainable after 2010 (Hemming and Kay 1982). Furthermore, the scheme proved overgenerous to contracted-out employees (Disney and Whitehouse 1993), and arbitrarily redistributive among those who remained contracted-in (Creedy and Disney 1985; Creedy et al. 1993). And it took little account of the booming capital market after the mid-1970s, which offered the prospect of considerably higher returns by prefunding a much larger component of pension provision.

d. The Rise of Personal Pensions

In 1985, the Conservative government proposed in a Green Paper that SERPS should be abolished and that all employees who did not belong to a company pension plan should be provided with a fixed proportion of their earnings to invest in a funded retirement savings account. This proposal was opposed in several quarters: the insurance industry and labor pressure groups argued that the statutory supplementary contribution would not generate returns anywhere near as generous as those provided by SERPS and by existing company pensions for those who remained contracted-in to the social security program. Crucially, too, the Treasury argued that it would create an immediate reduction in contribution revenue and potentially, tax revenue, if individuals were allowed tax relief on additional discretionary contributions into such accounts in exchange for the promise of lower expenditure on pensions in the future. But in the mid-1980s, the emphasis was on balancing the budget over the current cycle and any radical measure which reduced tax revenue in the near future was opposed by the Treasury.

The 1986 reform was more tentative, therefore, relying on a combination of sticks and carrots to encourage greater private provision. Again, a complex set of legislation can be summarized in a few points:

— SERPS benefits were downgraded considerably, so that the prospective cost of the scheme at maturity (i.e., around 2030 on) was halved.
— The range of group (company) pension plans which were entitled to obtain approved contracted-out status was expanded to include defined contribution (DC) as well as defined benefit (DB) plans. It was felt that many smaller companies were reluctant to offer defined benefit plans but

might be prepared to offer DC plans instead. Of course DC plans could not offer a Guaranteed Minimum Pension given the absence of any salary-defined component to pension benefits and, instead, it was required that such schemes invest a guaranteed minimum contribution which, it was hoped, would generate something equivalent to a GMP. In any event, indexation of pension benefits post-retirement was shared by the government in both DB and DC plans, providing some degree of coinsurance. However, this flexibility of approved status has not yet led to a substantial reduction in DB coverage relative to DC coverage, in contrast to the United States (Disney and Stears 1996).

— Individuals could establish individual retirement savings accounts, known as Personal Pensions, with a variety of approved insurance companies, now totaling well over 100. If an individual chose this route, opting out of SERPS (or indeed a company pension), the individual would have the contracted-out rebate, plus the net tax refund on the unpaid contribution plus, initially, a 2 percent bonus contribution, paid into their Personal Pension account by the Department of Social Security (DSS). Initially, this sum totaled 8.46 percent of earnings up to the ceiling on National Insurance contributions. In addition, the individual would typically enter into a contract with the insurance company to pay additional, discretionary, contributions into the account. These contributions obtained the same tax regime as company pension plans: contributions obtained tax relief and any tax liability accrued by the accumulated fund would be returned to the fund at the basic rate of tax. Personal Pensions would, however, be liable for tax after the accumulated fund was annuitized, although part could be taken as a tax-free lump sum.[4] There were age-related ceilings on tax-relieved contributions as proportions of earnings, rising from 17.5 percent to 40 percent for older workers (Disney and Whitehouse 1992).

— As a further form of insurance, individuals could revert to SERPS costlessly if they no longer wanted their COR paid into a Personal Pension account, just as company pension schemes could, in principle, choose to relinquish approved status for contracting-out, so that their employees would, in effect, become members of SERPS again.

The government seems to have felt that Personal Pensions were something of a "niche" product for young people who were highly mobile between high-paying jobs. Thus, it was believed that increased contracting-out might arise through the greater opportunity for flexibility among company plans gaining approved status, rather than from the opportunity for purchasing individual pen-

---

4   So this is known as "EET" tax treatment (where E = exempt, T = taxed).

Figure 2 — Increments of Pension Value: Personal Pension and SERPS (sensitivity to alternative net real rates of return)

Increment to pension wealth,
£ per annum

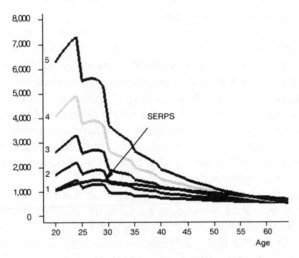

Note: Calculation for professional man aged 20 intending to retire at 65. Real earnings assumed to grow at 2 percent per annum; lifetime earnings profile calculated as described in Disney and Whitehouse (1992). The five different bands for the PP refer to net rates of return between 1 and 5 percent.

sions. But in fact, Personal Pensions proved extremely popular. Instead of the projected 500,000 to a million optants, by 1992 around 6 million people (well over 20 percent of the work force) had opted to buy Personal Pensions; the majority choosing to opt out of SERPS and at least 600,000, rather more problematically, opting to leave a company pension scheme.

The reason why the Personal Pension option became so attractive can be seen from Figure 2. This compares the returns from opting to invest the contracted-out rebate in a Personal Pension (PP) as against choosing to remain in SERPS. Each age interval represents the year-on-year increment to the final value of pension rights from choosing either option. The total pension value is therefore the cumulated area under the PP or SERPS curve, bearing in mind that individuals could opt to switch costlessly out of PP into SERPS at any point in their life.[5] The different bands for the PP refer to different net rates of return, and it is

---

5   The example illustrated here derives from the simulated life cycle earnings of a professional man aged 20; the profiles would look different for individuals starting at

apparent that at typical rates of return in the 1980s (4 percent per annum plus in excess of earnings growth), the accrual from a Personal Pension, especially for younger age groups, far exceeds that from SERPS given the level of the contracted-out rebate. Add in the generous tax reliefs, and the coincident abolition of tax relief on conventional life insurance policies in 1984 and Personal Pensions looked an extremely attractive instrument for tax-free saving.

The problem for the government was that the up-front costs of reductions in contribution revenues from increased contracting-out and of tax reliefs far outweighed the gains in prospective reduction in SERPS expenditure in the future, at least over a restricted time horizon, as was pointed out by the official government expenditure "watchdog," in a heavily critical report (National Audit Office 1991). Indeed, National Insurance contribution rates have been raised in increments, perhaps to be some 2 percentage points higher than they would otherwise have been (a corollary is that they are also lower in the future than otherwise); this is an illustration of implementing the "double burden" for a transition from PAYG to prefunding "by the backdoor."

Given the age-relative return profile illustrated in Figure 2, it is not surprising to find that, unlike, say, Individual Retirement Accounts in the United States, optants for Personal Pensions are predominantly young (see Figure 3). There is a long-term question of whether the young will engage in the long-term planning required to maintain an individual retirement savings account of this kind and, indeed, given the relative instability of the work histories of young workers, whether they will have the income from employment to continue to contribute. We return to this question in Section 5. However, the general point that many young people have opted to invest in a retirement saving asset with a high expected rate of return as opposed to SERPS, with an uncertain future and a prospective low rate of return, is unassailable.[6]

---

any other age, or in another occupation or, of course, for women. The steep decline in PP accruals with age arises as a simple consequence of compounding returns, but also because the government projects that the contracted-out rebate will decline over time. A further complication is that accruals to SERPS, and contributions into the PP, hit the ceiling on National Insurance contributions, which is declining relative to earnings over time, being linked to the basic state pension.

[6]   For evidence that returns on the BSP+SERPS for male workers retiring after 2020 are in fact negative, see Disney and Whitehouse (1993b). Given the frequent changes to SERPS, the oft-quoted assertion in the United Kingdom that investment risk in Personal Pensions is far greater than that associated with social security is absurd (see also Bodie 1990). On the more contentious issue of the relative riskiness of DB and DC plan choice, see Bodie et al. (1988) and, for the United Kingdom, Brugiavini and Disney (1995).

Figure 3 —   Personal Pension Take-Up by Age

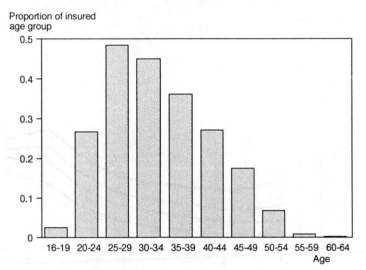

The final key piece of legislation concerning social security reform was enacted in the 1995 Social Security Act. This act was primarily designed to tighten up the regulation of occupational pension plans in the light of the Maxwell fraud but contained several other components which are pertinent to the current discussion. These included:

— Raising the state pensionable age of women to equality with that of men at 65, in stages between 2010 and 2020.
— A technical reform to the calculation of SERPS benefits and the abolition of the GMP in the SERPS scheme which produced a large saving of future government expenditure, indeed again almost halving expenditure on supplementary tier social security benefits by the year 2030 (for details, see Disney [1996]).
— An attempt was made to address the intramarginal subsidies to Personal Pension optants which had in any event been somewhat reduced by the reduction in the COR to 4.8 percent and the reduction of the 2 percent "start up" bonus to only 1 percent for only those aged 30 and above. Given the time profile of increments in Figure 2, it is apparent that the marginal subsidy (here the COR) required to make an individual just forgo their SERPS benefits and contract out into a Personal Pension rises with age. Figure 4 illustrates, for men and women, the COR needed at each age, for different assumed rates of return on the Personal Pension, to

Figure 4 — Median Contracted-Out Rebate by Sex and Age

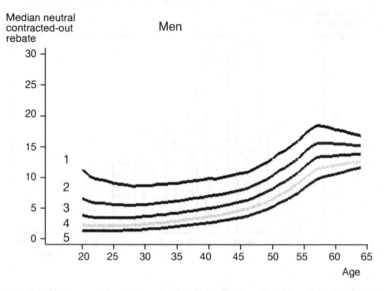

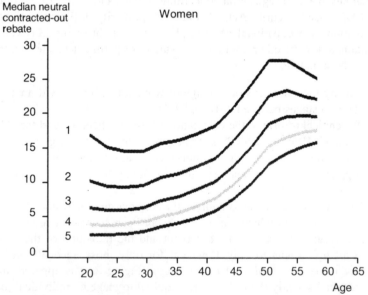

persuade exactly half of the work force to contract out at each age into a
Personal Pension (again there are various nonlinearities, which are to do

with the nonlinear accruals within SERPS). There are obviously large differences in these median CORs by the age group, and in consequence, the 1995 Act introduces age-related contracted-out rebates from 1997/98, for Personal Pensions and other defined contribution schemes.

3.   Overview

a.   Future Prospects for the National Insurance Fund

Table 1 considers the financial consequences of the steady retrenchment of social security provision in the United Kingdom in the 1980s and early 1990s. The costs of the basic state pension are linked primarily to demographic trends and to the adjustment of state pensionable age for women between 2010 and 2020, with minor amendments due to eligibility. To this sum should be added about £11 billion in expenditure on Income Support and help with housing costs for pensioners, although it is hoped that, in real terms, this sum should slowly decline as

Table 1 —   Future Trends in U.K. Social Security Expenditure, Contribution Rates and Support Ratio

	1994/95	2000/01	2010/11	2030/31	2050/51
Basic Pension (£ billion)	26.9	29.8	33.6	41.9	42.3
SERPS (£ billion)	1.8	4.2	8.4	12.0	9.9
Incapacity benefits (£ billion)	6.3	5.7	6.3	6.9	6.5
Other benefits (£ billion)	2.5	2.6	2.4	3.0	2.9
Total (£ billion)	39.9	42.2	50.8	63.8	61.7
N.I. contribution rate (%)	18.3	17.9	17.5	17.4	14.1
No. of pensioners	10.6	11.0	12.4	14.7	14.9
No. of contributors	22.0	22.7	24.0	23.9	22.9
Support Ratio	2.06	2.06	1.94	1.63	1.54

Notes: All expenditures in 1994 prices. "Other benefits" include widows' benefits. The contribution rate is the average joint contribution rate for contracted-in employees. Number of pensioners and contributors in millions. The assumed contracted-out rebate 1997/98 to 2000/01 is 4.95 percent. In fact, it has been subsequently set at 4.6 percent and will be age-related for defined contribution schemes including Personal Pensions.

Source: HMSO (1994: Tables 1 and 3 and Appendix D).

SERPS (or other contracted-out pension arrangements) mature[7]. It will be seen from the support ratio that the change in demographic structure occurs with the retirement of the baby-boom generation in the period between 2010/11 and 2030/31.

Expenditure on SERPS is projected to rise slowly to a peak around 2030/31 and thereafter to decline slowly. Accruals on SERPS are now governed by two regimes: those in the original 1978 act and those since 1986, and there are year-of-reaching pensionable age-specific accrual rates. The peak returns (relative to contributions) are obtained by those retiring at 2000/01 or shortly thereafter, who receive the original more generous treatment and also accelerated accruals, but total expenditure peaks somewhat later. Peak expenditure is now around a quarter of that envisaged in the original 1975 legislation, with a halving of benefits in the 1986 act and the retrospective recalculation of the indexation procedure in the 1995 legislation further downgrading benefits.

The consequences of these changes can be seen in the figure for the combined contribution rate, which is projected to decline slowly from the current figure despite the aging of the population, and to fall sharply after the peak of baby-boom retirement is passed in the middle of the next century. This is, needless to say, in sharp contrast to many other countries. It has been achieved through several factors described in the previous section:

— the core benefit in the social security program, the basic state pension, being flat rate (lump sum) and indexed to prices rather than earnings in a period when real earnings have steadily grown and are forecast to continue to do so;
— the equalization of state pensionable age for men and women between 2010/11 and 2020/21;
— cutbacks in the generosity of SERPS;
— increased contracting-out, especially into Personal Pensions, which has served both to reduce future National Insurance revenue requirements but also to raise current contribution rates;
— the gradual aging of the U.K. population over a much longer period, in contrast to the rather dramatic demographic transitions which are observed in other countries such as Italy and Japan.

---

7   Income Support is the principal means-tested benefit received by those without other sources of income. It was previously termed National Assistance and renamed Supplementary Benefit in 1966. It took on its current nomenclature in 1986.

b.   The Transition from PAYG to Prefunding

The other salient point of the U.K. "experiment" has been the (in effect) "back door" switch from pay-as-you-go funding to funded pensions for a large proportion of younger workers. The so-called "double burden" of the transition has been one of the most analyzed questions of pension reform, with the general assumption that such a transition requires either the possibility of subsidy from a surplus elsewhere in the government budget or such a discrepancy between the attainable rate of return on a funded scheme and that on the existing PAYG scheme that the transition costs to specific generations are small.

However, the United Kingdom starts from two favorable features in considering this issue. First, private provision has been extensive and effectively predates the development of social security at both the basic and supplementary levels. The one postwar experiment in comprehensive earnings-related social security between 1975 and 1995 never caught the public imagination, not least because of the complexity of SERPS, but also because many people already anticipated that the bulk of their retirement income would derive from private sources. In contrast, surveys regularly suggest that people are committed to the maintenance of the basic state pension, even though there is recognition that its future value is likely to be "nugatory," in the words of ex-Cabinet Minister (and currently ex-Member of Parliament) Michael Portillo. Thus, maintenance, and perhaps reform, of the basic state pension remains on the political agenda, while the destruction of SERPS has gained little public attention outside of a particular cohort of left-leaning pension experts.

Secondly, increases in the National Insurance contribution rate can be achieved with very little fuss or realization that the incidence of such payroll taxes is not dissimilar to other direct taxes such as income tax, where political considerations are paramount in setting rates. Two illustrations of this process are:

— In the early 1980s, with growing unemployment and expenditure on other related National Insurance benefits, contribution rates rose sharply at the same time as the government was officially committed to cutting rates of direct tax. Yet there was little public awareness that the two processes had almost entirely offsetting impacts on disposable income.

— The unexpectedly high take-up of Personal Pensions in the late 1980s and early 1990s put the National Insurance Fund into deficit, which was remedied by successive incremental increases in the contribution rate. However, there was again little awareness of this, not least because any increase in the National Insurance contribution below a full percentage point is not formally debated in Parliament. It will be interesting to see whether the quite substantial changes in automatic contributions to Personal Pensions through the DSS as a result of age-relating the contracted-out rebate will be publicly perceived.

So, in summary, the long tradition of private provision and the capacity of the administrative system of social security to introduce contribution rate changes without any degree of public perception have probably played a part in the relatively seamless transition to a pension scheme of minimum flat rate social security supplemented largely by private, funded, provision. In the remainder of this article, we focus on the future prospects and reform agenda for these pension benefits.

4. Reforms to the Social Security "Floor" of Benefits

Although we have argued that the decline of SERPS has been largely unnoticed by current and prospective pensioners, the future of the basic state pension (BSP) has warranted much more attention. For example, even in the 1992 election, the Labour Party fought on a platform of a one-off increase in the BSP coupled with a return to linking the pension after retirement to the growth of earnings not prices. Such a proposal is highly expensive in the long run and, distributionally, is not, in fact, the most sensible way of targeting social security expenditures on the elderly.[8]

There are, however, problems with the operation of the social security scheme in terms of the basic state pension, revolving around the interrelated questions of adequacy, administrative complexity, and distribution. We consider these briefly here, and look at reforms which are designed to alleviate these problems.

The basic state pension in 1996/97 was £61.15 per week for a single person (just under $100) with £36.60 for an adult dependent and an extra £0.25 per week for a person aged 80 or over. Of a total of around 10.5 million pensioners, 8.7 million received these basic rates for a single person or a couple because they had a largely complete pension history and, crucially, had other sources of private income. A person over state pensionable age with no other sources of income and no BSP could, however, obtain the following levels of Income Support:

---

8 See Disney and Whitehouse (1991), Dilnot and Johnson (1992), Disney (1996:80–83), and Johnson (1996).

Income Support Levels

Basic Income Support (£)	Total income (£)	Excess over BSP (%)
Single person: 47.95		
Plus "pensioner premium" of:		
Age 60–74: 19.15	67.10	8
Age 75–79: 21.30	69.25	12
Age 80+: 25.20	73.45	16
Couple: 75.20		
Plus "pensioner premium" of:		
Age 60–74: 28.20	104.10	6
Age 75–79: 31.90	107.10	9
Age 80+: 37.03	112.23	12

In all cases, a person is better off on Income Support than only the Basic State Pension. This generates three objections:

— If Income Support really is regarded as the "poverty line" should not the BSP at least be set at the same level?
— To the objection that most BSP recipients have other sources of income, it should be pointed out that take-up of Income Support (IS) is not 100 percent. IS is not awarded automatically (as in a negative income tax system) and has to be applied for; it is estimated that at least 20 percent of pensioners who are entitled to (some) IS do not claim it. Some 0.17 million pensioners (2 percent of the total) receive *only* Income Support.
— A far greater proportion, around 1.4 million or 13 percent of the total, receive the BSP *and* Income Support. This clearly involves administrative duplication, as the two schemes are administered by separate parts of the DSS.

The situation can be addressed either by administrative reforms or by more radical reforms. The former, the less radical approach, involves establishing a framework by which a pensioner will be guaranteed some level of pension, whether Income Support or something less. Various inquiries into pension reform have adopted such a proposal, typically termed the "Minimum Pension Guarantee" (Commission on Social Justice 1994) or the "Assured Pension" (Retirement Income Inquiry 1996). The simplest, but most expensive version of this is to set the BSP equal to the relevant level of Income Support and to find administrative means of guaranteeing that everyone obtains at least this level of benefit.

There are two obvious drawbacks to this proposal: first it gives significant intramarginal transfers to individuals who do not "need" the extra money because they have other sources of income. Secondly, without greater specificity it does not resolve the administrative problem of people who slip through the net at present. The obvious way to operate a comprehensive system is through the tax system, such as a negative income tax, and we return to this below. Alternatively, the former problem can be resolved by setting the "guaranteed" income anywhere between the BSP and the current level of IS, without resolving the latter problem. However, any system within which there is some form of guaranteed income and a continued "wedge" between the guaranteed income and the level of the income-tested benefit and/or the basic state pension has to resolve how to handle individuals whose circumstances change after assessment: such as a windfall capital gain.

There are, however, more radical proposals and we consider these in turn briefly.

a.   A Negative Income Tax (NIT)?

One more radical approach, which has tended to receive support in the Institute for Fiscal Studies in various guises, is to integrate National Insurance into the tax system and then provide a level of state pension which is determined by the total resources of the individual or couple (such as in the proposal by Dilnot et al. 1984). The problem of targeting is resolved and the administrative duplication of the current system is eliminated by operating the scheme through the Inland Revenue. There are three well-known objections to such a reform:

— The National Insurance scheme appears to be popular with the public, and is certainly popular with administrators as a less transparent way of collecting direct taxes.[9]
— A scheme operated through the tax system must inevitably overcome the problem of lags in assessment and in the payment of tax refunds.
— Depending on the parameterization of the "floor" level and the taper (withdrawal rate), the scheme may be less well targeted than the present system; however, a transparent targeted NIT-type scheme with high tapers (to maximize targeting) may have serious disincentive effects if there are "conventional" labor supply responses.

These objections, and responses to them, are well known and we do not discuss them further here. However, it is interesting that a NIT-type reform has not really attracted any real degree of support in recent debates.

---

9   However, the interesting question arises of whether a scheme of tax reliefs rather than benefit expenditures would have implications for the visible budget deficit (surplus), which is a common means of macroeconomic targeting.

b.   "Basic Pension Plus"

Just before the General Election of 1997, the then Conservative government produced a major pension reform out of the blue, in which it was proposed to introduce gradually a scheme by which the basic state pension was to be replaced by funded individual savings accounts, and SERPS was to be replaced by a proportionate levy on earnings, which would again be invested in an individual savings account. These proposals, therefore, bore a good deal of similarity to the Chilean reform and to the recent proposals of Martin Feldstein for the U.S. social security system. The new scheme was to be termed "Basic Pension Plus."

It is worth focusing on this proposal in a little more detail despite the fact that the Conservative government lost the General Election heavily. This is because among the new Labour ministerial team for social security is Frank Field, who is known to be a supporter of funding the whole pension program.[10] Essentially, Basic Pension Plus proposed that each new cohort entering the labor market would get a rebate from National Insurance contributions (akin to the COR) to finance a replacement for the basic state pension of £9 per week. In addition, if they did not opt to belong to another private scheme (such as a Personal Pension or an occupational pension scheme), they would receive a rebate of 5 percent of their earnings liable to National Insurance contributions to fund a second earnings-related scheme. Thus the model for such a person is that £9 per week plus 5 percent of salary would have been paid into an individual retirement savings account throughout the person's working life. As with Personal Pensions, the rebate would be paid into a private approved account of the individual's choice. Assuming a real rate of return of 4¼ percent, this would be expected to yield (in current prices) a fund of some £130,000 at the time of retirement. The component which was to replace the BSP would be guaranteed by the government.

To reduce the transition cost, it was proposed that each new cohort entering the labor market would enter the new scheme but that existing participants could not join it, although they could of course already opt out of SERPS. In addition, it was proposed to change the tax treatment of pensions, reversing the exemption from contributions to pensions in payment. There are a number of technical difficulties with the proposal, including this change in tax treatment and the treatment of those who contract out by other means, for example, into Personal Pen-

---

10   However, Labour at present appears to be hostile to individual capitalization accounts, preferring to move in the direction of group defined contribution plans, without really addressing the problem of transferability inherent in such plans, and of encouraging employers to provide such plans. Interestingly, neither political party has really focused on developing an instrument akin to 401k plans in the United States, although one of us has advocated further investigation of such a model (Disney 1995). There is no doubt that Labour's views will, however, continue to shift rapidly on this issue.

sions, which would have had to be resolved had the proposal been implemented. Nevertheless, the broad outline of the proposal is clear.

In some respects, this was a strange proposal. It cast uncertainty on the whole future of the BSP at the beginning of an election campaign when previous government policy appeared to have been to allow the basic state pension to wither away by stealth. The replacement of SERPS by a contracted-out scheme of this type has constantly been mooted since 1978, as described in Section 2, but still does not resolve the point that the mere 17 percent or so of the working population who now remain in SERPS are typically the group with low wages, interrupted career histories, etc., for whom it is hard to find an adequate alternative private pension insurance vehicle. In addition, the proposal required some 50 years to attain maturity and, as we have suggested, no pension scheme in the United Kingdom has survived for more than 10 years intact since the 1960s.

Figure 5 — Generalized "Basic Pension Plus" Reform (contribution rates by age)

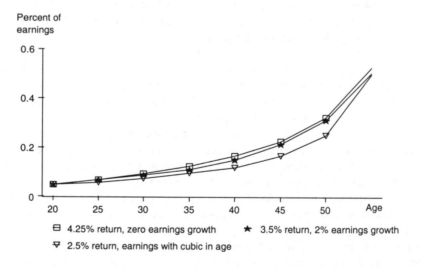

Why not then go for the more radical alternative of a "Basic Pension Plus" for the whole population? Assume that the target is to obtain a real fund value of £130,000 on retirement, as in the 1997 proposal, what contribution rate is needed for each age group to achieve this, starting from a zero fund? It is easy to work this out and, in doing so, to check the calculations in the 1997 proposal. Figure 5 therefore presents the age-contribution rates needed to obtain this fund value under three sets of assumptions (either of the first two may have been those used by the government; their technical discussion does not make it clear) when it is assumed that the £9 per week is a constant additional contribution to the fund (in real terms):

— a 4¼ percent real return per annum coupled with zero real earnings growth, based on male median earnings at age 20;
— a 3½ percent real return per annum (perhaps net of commission charges) with 2 percent per annum real earnings growth, on the same base earnings;
— a 2½ percent real return per annum with earnings growth derived from a wage equation with a cubic in age from the same base earnings.[11]

As Figure 5 shows, not surprisingly, contribution rates rise sharply with age if a "Basic Pension Plus" proposal is implemented across all age groups, although it is of course true that individuals would retain some claims on the previous social security program and therefore the contribution rates required to raise them to the assumed present value of the pension fund would be somewhat less. At the same time, there are quite sharp differences in required contribution rates according to the process assumed for underlying earnings growth; indeed the third option, which we might consider the most realistic, would suggest that at a level of real return close to that assumed by the DSS, the required contribution rate is considerably lower. This illustrates how funded pensions are highly attractive for individuals with regular, cumulative, lifetime employment histories given the differential between the funded return and the PAYG return. But, to reiterate, in the United Kingdom most of these individuals are already in the funded private sector and the "difficult" cases are those largely remaining in SERPS. There remains a case for maintaining a residual SERPS and perhaps a minimum income guarantee to cover such cases (particularly given the apparent absence of a financing problem in the demographic transition, as evidenced in Table 1) while focusing on ensuring that the existing private sector delivers adequate and secure pensions for the majority of the work force. We turn to this issue next.

5.   Reforms to the Supplementary Tier of Private Provision

Since this paper has focused primarily on the social security program, it will not consider existing private pensions at length. It will assume, too, that the com-

---

11   The coefficients of the cubic in age being an average of those derived by Disney and Whitehouse (1996) in their calculations of individual occupational pension entitlements. The formula was: $w = 10,400 + 0.15 \text{ age} - 0.002 \text{ age}^2 + 0.00002 \text{ age}^3$, where 10,400 is base earnings at age 20 (pounds per annum).

pany pension sector is broadly viable in its present form, notwithstanding problems associated with transferability, interrupted career histories, and regulation.[12]

The dramatic shift of young workers out of SERPS and into Personal Pensions is the most graphic example of the transition to a largely funded scheme of pension provision in the United Kingdom. Nevertheless, there have been several criticisms of the Personal Pension "revolution."

— The excess cost to the Treasury of payment of contracted-out rebates and the extra 2 percent "incentive" into Personal Pension accounts, plus the additional costs of tax reliefs on discretionary contributions, seems unwarranted when the excess return on Personal Pensions over SERPS is so large. For example, in 1995/96, according to Inland Revenue statistics, of just over £7 billion paid into Personal Pension accounts, only £2.4 billion was "free" saving; the rest was composed of CORs (£2.4 billion) and tax reliefs (£2.1 billion). The £4.5 million extra cost of these tax expenditures may have generated savings offsets elsewhere in the economy.

— Given the largely youthful nature of optants for Personal Pensions, it is not surprising to find that absolute amounts invested in these accounts are typically rather low. The median annual sum invested via the COR is around £500 ($800) for a man, and significantly less for a woman. For at least half of those with Personal Pensions, no additional contributions are made. From British Household Panel Study (BHPS) data for 1994/95, for those who do make an additional discretionary contribution, the average invested sum is some £800 per annum ($1,280), but this distribution too is heavily skewed. For most people, the contribution is not more than 5 to 6 percent of earnings, which may generate an inadequate pension on retirement. Very few companies match Personal Pension contributions by their employees. It is true that as the COR is now age-related, the proportion of earnings invested will rise, but the average COR is itself expected to fall over time, so average compulsory contributions are unlikely to rise.

— Given the relatively low income of Personal Pension purchasers (typically, many high-income earners are in company pension schemes), and a typical charging structure by insurance companies which involves a lump-sum element and a substantial up-front commission for the broker, little is left from contributions in the early years which is actually invested in the plan. And while returns on Personal Pensions are expected to dominate those from SERPS, there is no clear superiority over com-

---

12   For a discussion of these issues, see, inter alia, Davis (1995), Dilnot et al. (1994), Disney (1995), and Disney and Whitehouse (1996).

pany pension plans. Indeed, since salary-related pension schemes typically provide employer's contributions, and disproportionately benefit long-tenured employers, it is only for high-earning young highly mobile workers that a Personal Pension will dominate a typical company plan. Yet it appears that possibly over a million optants for Personal Pensions chose to leave company pension plans in order to set up a Personal Pension. In November 1994, a report by the Securities and Investment Board, the regulator, identified up to 560,000 individuals who had been "missold" Personal Pensions, of which there were 350,000 "priority" cases; that is, cases where the prospective pension from the Personal Pension was much lower than that from the pension scheme which the individual had left. A compensation package has been agreed upon but, by the end of 1996, only some 10,000 individuals' compensation had been assessed. The total bill for compensation has been estimated at £4 billion and, as a consequence, many insurance companies are dragging their heels in organizing reassessments.

— There is concern over the lack of persistence of contributions to Personal Pensions over time. Looking at BHPS data, only 60 percent of Personal Pension holders over a three-year period made regular annual contributions. Although funds may be started with lump sums, and "topped up" irregularly, many contributors nevertheless enter into contracts with insurance companies which require regular (e.g., monthly) contributions to their Personal Pension account. But young people typically have irregular job histories and there is now evidence of relatively high lapse rates among Personal Pension optants: of 25 percent over the first two years of a contract and a continued lapse rate of 6 percent thereafter. Given that commission and lump-sum charges are levied at the start of the contract, some 30–40 percent of policyholders never make enough contributions to recover the principal net of charges. Since such accounts do, however, automatically attract the COR and tax reliefs, some analysts have argued that, in effect, the tax expenditures are subsidizing charging structures rather than enhancing pension values. Over time, new entrants to the market, using direct selling techniques, are bringing down costs of Personal Pensions, but it is possible that such selling methods may in fact increase lapse rates in the short run.

These criticisms: excessive budgetary cost, low net savings rates, inappropriate transfers, and high lapse rates, can, in principle, be resolved by tougher regulation coupled with a reduction in tax incentives. But these criticisms have led some, such as the Labour Party, to question whether the correct road to a funded privatized pension scheme is through individual savings accounts. Unless employers or groups of employers can be persuaded to offer low-cost pooled retirement saving plans, however, the maintenance of the Personal Pension market will rely on the implementation of much tougher regulation and transparency of charging structures and prospective pension valuations.

6.   A Summing Up

The United Kingdom has made a transition to largely privately funded pension provision, underpinned by a floor of pay-as-you-go social security. The experiment in comprehensive social security initiated in the 1970s has been abandoned. As a result, there are no prospective large-scale financial crises looming in the social security program; indeed, future contribution rates to the National Insurance Fund are projected to stabilize throughout the period during which the baby-boom generation retires and decline thereafter.

It should not be thought, however, that progress to funded pensions has arisen as a result of a "clean break" reform such as occurred in Chile. The U.K.'s program of funded pensions has been built on existing private arrangements coupled with unanticipated changes, such as the unexpected popularity of Personal Pensions. As a result, the U.K. pension scheme requires continued modification concerning, for example, the optimal form of the social security "floor" and the optimal extent of subsidization of, and regulation of, private pensions. It is apparent that excessively large tax expenditures have been devoted to subsidizing already profitable private pensions.

There is another potential long-run problem, concerning the coexistence of different supplementary pension arrangements. There seems to be a case to retain SERPS, for example, in some form, for those who have interrupted career histories. But public choice theory simply suggests that it will be hard to sustain the tax revenues required to finance social security benefits provided for a minority. Likewise, within the private sector, the coexistence of traditional final salary-related schemes and Personal Pensions is open to question. If benefits in salary-related schemes are back-loaded (see Bodie et al. 1988), then younger workers will incur marginal contributions rates higher than marginal accrual rates and it may be optimal for them in some cases to opt to leave the pension plan and join a Personal Pension. But this decision to exit the salary-related plan may render that plan insolvent in the long run. In other words, if individuals have the choice to move between very different types of pension arrangement, the long-run stability of the pension scheme may be in question. Some efforts have been made to analyze these choices (as in Brugiavini and Disney 1995), but the incentive structures intrinsic to the U.K. pension scheme are quite complex and are a continued topic of debate. For this reason, we do not believe that the U.K.'s pension scheme has yet reached a "steady state," and an end to the reform process is not yet in sight.

Bibliography

Beveridge, W.H. (1942). *Social Insurance and Allied Services*. Cmd. 5404. London: HMSO.

Bodie, Z. (1990). Pensions as Retirement Income Insurance. *Journal of Economic Literature* 28(March):28–49.

Bodie, Z., A.J. Marcus, and R.C. Merton (1988). Defined Benefit versus Defined Contribution Plans: What Are the Real Trade-Offs? In Z. Bodie et al., *Pensions in the US Economy*. Chicago: University of Chicago Press for NBER.

Brugiavini, A., and R. Disney (1995). The Choice of Private Pension Plan under Uncertainty. Working Paper 95/5. Institute for Fiscal Studies, London.

Commission on Social Justice (1994). *Social Justice: Strategies for National Renewal*. London: Institute for Public Policy Research.

Creedy, J., and R. Disney (1985). *Social Insurance in Transition: An Economic Analysis*. Oxford: Clarendon Press.

Creedy, J,. R. Disney, and E. Whitehouse (1993). The Earnings-Related State Pension, Indexation and Lifetime Redistribution in the UK. *Review of Income and Wealth* 40 (September):257–278.

Davis, E.P. (1995). *Pension Funds: Retirement-Income Security and Capital Markets: An International Perspective*. Oxford: Oxford University Press.

Department of Social Security (1993). *Social Security Statistics, 1993*. London: HMSO.

Dilnot, A.W., and P. Johnson (1992). What Pension Should the State Provide? *Fiscal Studies* 13(November):1–20.

Dilnot, A.W., J.A. Kay, and C.N. Morris (1984). *The Reform of Social Security*. Oxford: Oxford University Press for Institute for Fiscal Studies.

Dilnot, A.W., R. Disney, P. Johnson, and E. Whitehouse (1994). *Pensions Policy in the UK: An Economic Analysis*. London: Institute for Fiscal Studies.

Disney, R. (1995). Occupational Pension Schemes: Prospects and Reforms in the UK. *Fiscal Studies* 16(August):19–39.

—— (1996). *Can We Afford to Grow Older: A Perspective on the Economics of Aging*. Cambridge: MIT Press.

Disney, R., and G. Stears (1996). Why Is There a Decline in Defined Benefit Plan Membership in the UK? Working Paper W96/4. Institute for Fiscal Studies, London.

Disney, R., and E. Whitehouse (1991). How Should the Basic State Pension Be Indexed? *Fiscal Studies* 12: (August):47–61.

—— (1992). *The Personal Pension Stampede*. Report Series. London: Institute for Fiscal Studies.

—— (1993a). Contracting-out and Lifetime Redistribution in the UK Pension System. *Oxford Bulletin of Economics and Statistics* 55(February):25–41.

—— (1993b). Will Younger Cohorts Obtain a Worse Deal from the UK State Pension Scheme? In M.Casson and J. Creedy (eds.), *Industrial Concentration and Economic Inequality*. Aldershot: Edward Elgar.

—— (1996). What Are Occupational Pension Plan Entitlements Worth in Britain? *Economica* 63(May):213–238.

Gilbert, B.B. (1966). *The Evolution of National Insurance in Great Britain*. London: Michael Joseph.

Gosden, P.H.J.H. (1973). *Self-Help: Voluntary Associations in Nineteenth Century Britain*. London: Batsford.

Hannah, L. (1986). *Inventing Retirement: The Development of Occupational Pensions in Britain*. Cambridge: Cambridge University Press.

Harris, J. (1972). *Unemployment and Politics: A Study in English Social Policy*. Oxford: Clarendon Press.

Hemming, R., and J.A. Kay (1982). The Costs of the State Earnings Related Pension Scheme. *Economic Journal* 92(June):300-319.

HMSO (1994). *Pensions Bill 1994: Report by the Government Actuary on the Financial Provisions of the Bill on the National Insurance Fund*. Cm 2714. London.

Johnson, P. (1996). The Reform of Pensions in the UK. Mimeo. Institute for Fiscal Studies, London.

National Audit Office (1991). *The Elderly: Information Requirements for Supporting the Elderly and the Implications of Personal Pensions for the National Insurance Fund*. London: HMSO.

Retirement Income Inquiry (1996). *Pensions 2000 and Beyond: Volume I*. London: Retirement Income Inquiry.

Sebastian Edwards

Chile: Radical Change towards a Funded Pension System

1. Introduction

Policy-makers throughout the world have become increasingly concerned about the future of social security. This preoccupation is mostly based on mounting evidence suggesting that in a large number of countries—including most of the OECD nations—government-run social security systems are about to become insolvent. Existing projections indicate that in some countries the magnitude of unfunded social security liabilities even exceed GDP. This generalized concern about social security is perhaps best illustrated by the title of a recent World Bank publication on the subject: *Averting the Old Age Crisis*.

Some countries have reacted to these crisis prospects by replacing—either totally or partially—the old government-run systems by privately managed regimes based on individual retirement accounts. The Latin American countries have been particularly active in this front. At the time of this writing, seven countries in Latin America had implemented pension reforms aimed at privatizing at least part of their social security system. This reform effort has been led by Chile, which in 1981 introduced radical changes to its retirement system. An inefficient, distributively unfair and fiscally insolvent system was replaced by an individual capitalization, fully funded, privately managed system. The boldness of the Chilean reforms attracted immediate attention from international specialists in the early 1980s. More recently, and as a result of its perceived success, the Chilean reform attracted the interest of the media. In the last year or so a number of articles analyzing the Chilean experience and discussing its potential applicability to other countries have appeared throughout the world. For example, on April 19, 1997, a long editorial article in the *Financial Times* pointed out that Chile's "[s]ystem of privately managed pension funds. . . is being copied all over Latin America. Furthermore, a growing body of opinion views it as the solution

Remark: I am indebted to Francisca Castro for helpful discussions and for helping me clarify a number of issues related to the Chilean social security system. I have benefited from discussions with Klaus Schmidt-Hebbel.

to the social security crisis awaiting the aging populations of the industrialized world" (page 31). However, a number of observers have recently argued that, in spite of its visionary concept, the Chilean system has important shortcomings and that, in order for it to truly serve the country in an efficient way, it will be necessary to introduce some important reforms.

The purpose of this paper is to evaluate Chile's admired social security reform program. After the introduction, Section 2 provides a brief analysis of Chile's traditional pay-as-you go pension system in effect from 1922 through 1981. In Section 3, I deal with the reforms initiated in 1981. This section is divided into two distinctive parts: the first one focuses on the reforms proper; the second, on the other hand, concentrates on some of the most important results achieved by the reforms up to date. In Section 4, I deal in greater detail with the effects of the Chilean reform on the functioning of the country's labor market, an aspect often neglected in the literature. Section 5 has the conclusions. In it I briefly discuss possible reforms to the privately managed system.

2.   Chile's Traditional Social Security System: An Overview

Like most Latin American countries, Chile adopted a social security system in the 1920s. During its early years, when contributions made by active workers exceeded pension payments, it was based on the collective capitalization of funds. As the system became more mature, it was expected that increasing obligations would be met both by drawing on these funds and by increasing active worker's contributions. Accumulated funds, however, were poorly managed and benefits—especially for the better-to-do—escalated quickly. As a result, the system ran into serious financial difficulties and, increasingly, relied on the government to meet its obligations. For all practical purposes, and in spite of the original intentions of its founders, by the 1970s the system had become an insolvent pay-as-you-go regime.

Two of the most important characteristics of the old system were its lack of uniformity, and its regressiveness from a distributive point of view. There were more than 100 different retirement regimes. While some workers—usually the most affluent—could retire with a very high pension at 42 years of age, blue-collar workers could only retire once they turned 65. Some pensions were not subject to automatic cost of living adjustment. Senior bureaucrats, however, got 100 percent-plus inflation adjustment, as they maintained, through life, a pension equal to the salary paid to an active worker in a position similar to the last one they held—this type of pension was highly sought and was named a "*chaser pension.*" After 50 years of operation, and contrary to its architects' intentions, the system had become increasingly unfair. As a consequence of inflation and mismanagement, between 1962 and 1980 the average pension paid to a blue-collar worker had declined by 41 percent.

The traditional pay-as-you-go retirement system was also characterized by very high contribution rates. In 1973, for example, total contributions—by employers and employees—varied between 16 and 26 percent of wages, depending on the type of job the individual held. If contributions to the national health system were added, total contributions exceeded, for some workers, 50 percent of wages. By 1980 total pension-related contributions had been reduced but still amounted, on average, to 19 percent of (taxable) wages.[1] What made things worse was that there was almost no connection between retirement contributions and (perceived) benefits. These contributions were largely seen as taxes on labor, and contributed significantly to the poor performance of the country's labor market during the 1960s and 1970s; on the other hand, the benefits received from the social security system were seen as entitlements (Cox-Edwards 1992).

Demographic trends affected the Chilean traditional retirement system in a negative way. While in 1955 there were 12 active contributors per retiree, by 1979 there were only 2.5. As a result of this, and of a highly inefficient management, the Chilean system became increasingly unfunded. By the early 1970s the system as a whole was already running a dramatic deficit. The gap between revenues and outlays—administrative costs plus pensions—was made up by the public sector. By 1971 the central government's contributions to the retirement system amounted to almost 3 percent of GDP; the present value of the system's contingent liabilities exceeded 100 percent of GDP.[2]

In 1981, and after significant internal debate, the military government decided to introduce a sweeping reform to the retirement system. The decision to undertake the reform responded to four considerations: (a) the explosive fiscal consequences of the old regime, (b) the high degree of inequality of the old system, (c) its implied efficiency distortions, and, perhaps more importantly at the time, (d) an ideological desire to reduce drastically the role of the public sector in economic affairs. Interestingly enough, in explaining the reform, the Chilean autho-

---

[1]   Parts of this section draw on Edwards (1996). There has been some confusion on the actual level of contributions in the old system. The reason for this is that these rates have traditionally been quoted as a social security aggregate, covering pensions, health, and disability. Total contributions were 54.4 percent in 1973, and were reduced to 37.6 percent in 1980 (Larraín 1991). The rates quoted above refer to pensions only.

[2]   See Meyers (1988) and Cheyre (1988) for an analysis of the flow deficit of the system. I have used data reported by them and Larraín (1991) to make a calculation of the magnitude of the present value of the system's unfunded liabilities.

rities barely referred to the (potential) effects of the new system on domestic savings or on the functioning of labor markets.[3]

3. The Reform

Decrees 3,500 and 3,501, which drastically reformed the country's social security system, were approved by Chile's military government on November 4, 1980.[4] In a speech delivered on November 6, 1980, Minister of Labor, and architect of the reforms, José Piñera expressed that the goal of the reform was to create a retirement system based on "freedom, and solidarity; a fair and yet efficient retirement system; a retirement system for everyone" (Piñera 1988:318).

From a political point of view, the launching of the reforms faced some difficulties. First, many interest groups—including public sector workers, teachers, and workers in the health sector—firmly opposed any changes. Representatives of these groups realized early on that their best option was to line up the support of high-ranking military officers. They were partially successful, as for many months some key members of the (ruling) armed forces opposed the project. Second, the notion of a collectively funded, "solidarity-based" retirement system was deeply ingrained among intellectuals and the public. Piñera, the father of the reforms, has pointed out that because of stiff opposition the implementation of the reform had to be postponed for almost a full year. It was only in 1980 that Piñera and his team were able to persuade a reluctant General Pinochet on the merits of the project. The general himself, however, was not fully successful in convincing his military colleagues. The armed forces did not join the new system—an option not available to any other group in the country—generating criticism, suspicion, and even resentment during the early years of the new system.

In an effort to increase the attractiveness of the new system, and reduce political opposition, the authorities set the new contribution rates at a level that resulted in an increase of net take-home pay for those that joined the new system. On average, those that transferred to the new system experienced an 11 percent increase in after-tax pay (Iglesias and Vittas 1992). It was expected that, given

---

3   The father of the reform, then Minister of Labor José Piñera, has provided a fascinating account of the political economy of the reform. See Piñera (1991).

4   Paradoxically, November 4, 1980, was the tenth anniversary of President Salvador Allende's inauguration. President Allende had also promised to reform the country's social security system. His program, of course, was radically different from that of the military and called for an even greater role for the public sector.

the anticipated higher rates of return on the accumulated funds, the lower contributions would be enough to finance higher rates of replacement for pensions.

a.   Basic Features of the Chilean Social Security Reform

The reform of Chile's social security system replaced a basically insolvent pay-as-you-go regime with a capitalization system, based on individual retirement accounts managed by private companies known as *administradoras de fondos de pensiones* (AFPs). Each AFP can manage only one retirement fund, and there is a strict separation between the retirement fund and the management firm's assets. Largely as a result of this one-fund-per-AFP rule, and of a regulation that establishes a minimum rate of return on the funds (see the discussion below for details), there has been a very low degree of actual portfolio diversification across AFPs.

The system is mandatory for individuals working for a formal employee. Individuals, however, can freely decide which AFP will manage their retirement funds. Moreover, individuals are free to transfer their funds freely between the different management firms. When individuals retire they can choose to buy an annuity, or to withdraw their funds according to a predetermined (actuarially fair) plan.[5] The system also has a survivor's term life insurance component, and a disability program funded with an additional insurance premium. In the reformed system, the state continues to play an important role. It regulates and monitors the operation of the management companies, and guarantees "solidarity in the base" through a minimum pension.

Every worker (non-self-employed) is, thus, required to make contributions equal to 10 percent of her disposable income. A detailed and modern regulatory framework—enforced by an institution especially created for this purpose, the Superintendency of AFPs—regulates investment portfolios and ensures free determination of fees and commissions and free entry into the industry. The Superintendency of AFPs established from the first day very precise norms to secure the diversification and transparency of AFP investments—see Edwards (1996) for a list of requirements to operate an AFP.

Since its inception, the new Chilean retirement system has gone through a number of changes. Between November 1980 and August 1995, for example, the original legal texts were modified more than 30 times. Of the 97 permanent articles of Decree 3,500, 85 had been modified during the first 15 years of the

---

5   At this time there are not enough (available) data to analyze the efficiency of the annuities market. There have been some claims, however, that these still have a very high price, a price that exceeds the actuarially fair price. See Vittas (1995).

reforms (Serqueira 1995). In this subsection I describe with some detail the evolution of the system during its first 15 years.

Coverage and Contribution Rates

As pointed out above, individuals employed in the formal sector are required, by law, to participate in the retirement system. They have to contribute, to the AFP of their choice, 10 percent of their wages. These are invested by the AFP and are accumulated in an individual retirement account. Participants can switch management funds up to four times a year. There is an additional contribution of (approximately) 3 percent of wages as a premium for term life and disability insurance. Both of these contributions are subject to a maximum wage base, which is currently equivalent to approximately US$2,000 per month.[6] Self-employed workers are not required to participate in the system. They have the choice, however, of setting up retirement accounts which are (basically) subject to the same regulations as those of formal sector employees.

There is an important distinction between those individuals that are *affiliated* to the system—that is, people that have, at one time or another, enrolled in an AFP—and those that are active *contributors* to the system. While the percentage of individuals affiliated to the system is very high—almost 99 percent of the labor force—the percentage of active contributors is significantly smaller, and in 1995 stood at 58 percent of those employed. In 1997, those still affected by the old system represented 4 percent of total employment. In 1995 the total coverage of the Chilean retirement system amounted, then, to 62 of the labor force, approximately the same percentage as in the prior traditional system.

The lack of universal coverage represents a serious weakness of the system, and is explained by two basic factors: first, the self-employed are not required to participate in the system and, for a variety of reasons, including tax considerations, have no incentives to make voluntary contributions.[7] Second, the existence of a government-guaranteed (universal) minimum pension creates a moral hazard situation among low-income workers, many of which are self-employed. For these individuals it pays to contribute only sporadically, and only enough as to obtain the minimum pension once they retire.

In addition to the required contributions, employees can make voluntary contributions to the same AFP as the one where they have their retirement account.[8]

---

6   The amount of the maximum "pensionable" salary is set in Unidades de Fomento (UF), Chile's indexed unit of account. The limit is 60 UFs per month. In June 1997 this was approximately equal to US$2,000.

7   Although, as explained below, voluntary contributions are (up to a limit) tax deductible, by contributing to an AFP a self-employed worker is revealing information to tax authorities.

8   There is no special treatment for married couples.

Voluntary contributions have a limit of US$2,000 per month. Required contributions are tax-deductible, as is the income accrued to the accumulated fund during the contributor's active life. Voluntary contributions, on the other hand, are not tax-deductible. Income accrued to voluntarily contributed funds are, however, free of taxes. Once the workers retire, however, their pensions become subject to income tax, as any other source of income.

In spite of tax incentives and of the relatively high average returns obtained by the AFPs during their first fifteen years of operation (see below for details), the volume of voluntary funds has remained very small. Although by December 1995 there were more than 960,000 voluntary accounts, the total voluntary funds accumulated in the system amounted to only 1.9 percent of total funds (Superintendencia 1996).

Accumulated Funds, Investment Rules, and Rates of Return

The volume of pension funds privately managed by the AFPs has increased dramatically since 1981. As can be seen in Figure 1, between 1985 and 1995 they increased from 10 percent of GDP to almost 43 percent of GDP. Furthermore, recent simulations suggest that by year 2010 the accumulated funds will represent 110 percent of GDP, and that by 2020 they will have reached 134 percent of GDP (Fuentes 1995).

Figure 1 — Evolution of Pension Funds as Percentage of GDP, 1981–1995

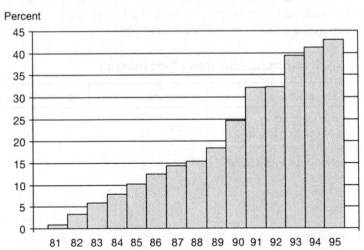

Source: Edwards (1996).

The Superintendencia has tightly regulated the type of assets the funds could invest in. This regulation has taken the form of maximum limits on holdings of a particular type of financial instrument. The rationale for these limits has been safety. Initially, and especially given the opposition to the reform by influential members of the armed forces, the economic authorities decided that it was essential that the funds were mostly invested in high-grade securities. During the early years, funds were largely restricted to government securities—with a limit of 100 percent of the fund—bank deposits, investment grade corporate bonds, and mortgage bonds. In 1985, AFPs were allowed to invest in equities. Although the limit on equities was theoretically set at 5 percent of the funds, strict restrictions on the type of issuing firm seriously limited the AFPs ability to invest in equities. In fact, during the second half of the 1980s most funds invested exclusively in equities of firms that were being privatized. As a result of these restrictions, by the end of 1986 the AFPs had invested in only six stocks, representing less than 4 percent of the total fund.

By 1989, some of these restrictions were lifted, and most AFPs increased their equities positions significantly. At that time equities from 23 firms were being held by the AFPs, adding up to 11 percent of the aggregate funds. However, more that 90 percent of the AFPs equities portfolio was made up of only eight recently privatized firms. In 1989 AFPs were also allowed to invest in real estate, and in 1992 they were permitted to invest up to 9 percent of the fund in foreign securities. Surprisingly, perhaps, there has been a very limited interest in investing in foreign instruments. By December 1995 less than 1 percent of the accumulated funds had been invested abroad. Table 1 contains information on the investment limits in effect as of December of 1996.

Table 1 —   AFP Investment Allocations, 1996 (percent)

Financial instrument	Minimum allocation	Maximum allocation
1. Public sector securities	35	50
2. Securities issued by financial institutions	30	50
3. Credit letters issued by financial institutions	35	50
4. Corporate bonds	0	50
5. Convertible corporate bonds	10	30
6. Stocks	10	20
7. Shares in real estate funds	5	10
8. Short-term commercial paper	10	20
9. Foreign securities	6	12

Source: Superintendencia (1996).

Figure 2 —   Annual Real Rates of Return of the Pension Fund System

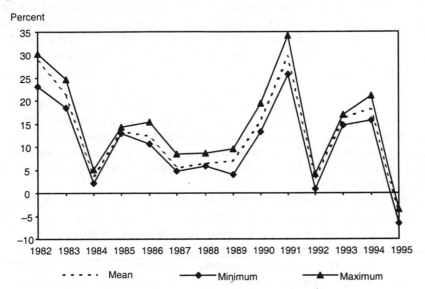

Percent

As can be seen in Figure 2, rates of return on the accumulated funds have, in general, been extremely high, 1995–1996 being an exception. This has been largely the result of Chile's economic circumstances during this period. Between 1985 and 1996, Chile has experienced a tremendous growth period in which the value of assets, and in particular firms, increased at a very fast rate. Additionally, between 1985 and 1991, real interest rates were very high, allowing funds that invested in fixed income securities to experience very healthy returns. Recent studies on the sources of AFP's rates of return show that the return on the stock of two electric utilities (Enersis and Endesa) explains almost 40 percent of the total return of the funds (Valck and Walker 1995; Superintendencia 1996).

In 1995 and 1996, however, and largely as a result of the poor performance of Chile's stock market, the average return obtained by the AFPs was negative in real terms. There is little doubt that in the years to come the average return obtained by the AFPs will be lower than in the first 15 years. This is because both interest rates and stock market returns will move closer in line with international levels, affecting the rate of return of pension funds. In fact, during 1995 and 1996 the AFPs have experienced, on average, a negative real return.

The Chilean system assures a minimum return to those affiliated to an AFP. This minimum is either 50 percent of the average return across AFPs, or 2 percentage points below the average—whichever is higher. Those AFPs that do not obtain this minimum return from their portfolio have to make up the difference from funds withdrawn from an "investment reserve" especially set up for this purpose. This "reserve" has to amount to, at least, 1 percent of the total value of the fund and is invested in a portfolio that exactly mimics that of the fund. If an AFP cannot meet a profitability shortfall out of its reserves, it is liquidated. The state makes up the difference between the actual and minimum guaranteed return, and contributors transfer their funds to another AFP. The existing legislation also contemplates a maximum allowable return, determined as 50 percent or 2 percentage points over the average across AFPs. Those companies that exceed the maximum have to deposit the excess funds on a "profitability reserve," which is part of the fund's (and not the management company's) assets. If in a subsequent year the AFP's portfolio underperforms, this reserve can be used to make up the difference between the actual and minimum return (see Superintendencia 1996:64–67).

The combination of the "one fund per AFP" and the minimum/maximum profitability rules has resulted in AFPs having extremely similar portfolios. In fact, the dispersion in returns has been very small. As will be discussed in greater detail below, the rules limiting the number of funds generate some serious distortions. They increase the administrative costs of running funds and do not allow people with different tolerances for risk to have different portfolios.

Administration and Costs

Some analysts have argued that a privately run system based on free choice is exceedingly costly. It has been argued that by allowing frequent transfers of funds across AFPs, the system as a whole will tend to overspend in advertising and in sales. It has been proposed that a better solution would be to have a public sector institution manage the retirement funds and/or to restrict the participants' ability to transfer their funds across AFPs (Diamond 1994; Mesa Lago 1996).

Fees and commissions are determined freely by the AFPs. Currently they are allowed to charge the following fees: (1) A proportional fee on contributions, (2) a fee for opening a new account, (3) a fee for managing programmed pension withdrawals, (4) a fee for managing voluntary contributions, (5) a flat fee per period when contributions are made. In recent years, however, most AFPs have waived the flat fee (Vittas 1995). In addition to these fees, AFPs were allowed, until 1987, to charge a management fee on every account, including those of inactive workers. On the other hand, and in order to encourage competition, AFPs are not allowed to charge an exit fee. Table 2 contains a schematic presentation of the structure of commissions that AFPs are allowed to charge. Notice, however, that as pointed out above, many AFPs do not charge some of these fees.

Table 2 —   Structure of Commissions and Fees Allowed by the Law

Type of account	Type of commission and/or fee	Structure of commission or fee
A. Individual retirement account for active worker	Contributions to retirement account	Lump sum and/or a percentage of contribution
	Transfer of account	Lump sum and/or a percentage of contribution
B. Individual retirement account of retired worker	Pension payments	Lump sum and/or percentage over each pension payment
C. Voluntary retirement account	Withdrawal or transfer to different AFP	Lump sum

Source: Superintendencia (1996).

During the early years of the system, administrative costs were extremely high. In 1984, for example, they amounted to 9 percent of wages, or 90 percent of contributions to the retirement system. By 1994, however, costs had declined significantly, amounting to 1 percent of wages or 10 percent of contributions. In spite of these high costs, the new capitalization system is significantly more efficient than the old pay-as-you-go regime. For example, Bustos (1995) has calculated that total costs of the new regime are 42 percent lower than average costs of the old system. When measured in relation to accumulated assets, administrative costs have declined from almost 15 percent in 1983 to 1.8 percent in 1993, including sales costs.[9] It has been argued by Vittas (1995) that although Chilean administrative costs as a percentage of assets are not very different from those of U.S. and U.K. insurance companies, they are significantly higher than the costs incurred by government-run provident funds in Singapore and Malaysia—0.1 to 0.2 percent of accumulated assets. Valdés-Prieto (1994b), for example, has estimated that in 1991 marketing and sales costs exceeded one-third of total costs. Margozzini (1995), on the other hand, has calculated that sales costs averaged 20 percent of total costs with marketing costs representing an additional 3 percent. Moreover, there is evidence that in the last few years these costs have increased significantly. The total sales force for the system, for example, increased from 3,500 in 1990 to almost 15,000 in early 1995. All in all, sales costs as percentage of total costs more than doubled between 1988 and 1995.

---

[9]   On the cost structure of AFPs see, for example, Margozzini (1995).

Some critics of the Chilean reform have argued that limiting the frequency with which participants can switch funds provides an efficient way of reducing administrative costs, and thus increasing the net return that accrues to contributors. However, since the costs of opening a new account represents a high percentage of the cost of transferring funds, a more effective solution—and one that would maintain individual's choice—would be to allow AFPs to manage more than one retirement fund. In this way individuals could transfer their retirement savings to different funds, within the same AFP, at a reduced cost. Moreover, the elimination—or, at least, modification—of the minimum return requirement would increase the degree of competition between AFPs, and would allow individuals with different attitudes towards risk to choose the type of fund that better suits their preferences.

In 1981 there were 12 pension management firms. By 1995 the total number had increased to 16 AFPs. In spite of relatively free entry, the industry has a nontrivial degree of concentration. In 1990–1994, for example, 68 percent of all workers were affiliated to the three largest AFPs. The degree of concentration has declined considerably, however. According to a study by the Superintendencia (1996), the Herfindahl concentration index fell from 2200 in 1981 to 1310 in 1995.

During the first fifteen years of operation of the new system, AFPs have been, on average, highly profitable. Their average (real) return on equity has averaged 16.6 percent over a decade and a half, and peaked in 1989–1991 when it exceeded 35 percent per year. This high return, however, hides significant differences across AFPs. For example, in 1994, 11 out of 21 AFPs incurred losses, which in some cases bordered on 50 percent of equity (see Margozzini 1995 and Vittas 1995).

The Role of the Government

Although the Chilean system is based on individually capitalized accounts managed by private firms, the government retains an important role that goes well beyond regulating and supervising the system. First, the government guarantees a minimum pension to poorer participants in the system. Those individuals that have contributed to the system for at least 20 years, and whose accumulated funds cannot cover a minimum pension, receive from the state a transfer that raises their pension to that minimum.

The value of the minimum pension is adjusted by inflation every time the accumulated change in the CPI reaches 15 percent. This means that at the current level of inflation, minimum pensions get adjusted once every two years. Minimum pensions are currently equal to 25 percent of average wages, and 75 percent of the minimum wage. In the past they have been as low as 61 percent of minimum wages (in 1982) and as high as 91 percent of minimum wages (in

1987). The government also guarantees the minimum pension to those individuals that, having opted for a pension based on programmed withdrawals, outlive the program and exhaust their accumulated funds.

Second, and as explained in the preceding subsection, the government guarantees a minimum return on accumulated funds. If an AFP underperforms significantly, and the funds in its reserves accounts—both the investment and profitability reserves—are insufficient to bring the actual return to the minimum level, the government covers the difference. As pointed out, in this case the AFP is liquidated and the participants transfer their funds to another institution. And third, the government also guarantees pension payments (up to a limit) in case an insurance company goes bankrupt.

In addition to its involvement in these areas, the Chilean government also makes pension payments to those individuals that, either by choice or because of their age, did not transfer to the new system. As is discussed in detail below, the cost of paying these pensions has been significant exceeding, in some years, 4 percent of GDP.

From a policy point of view, the involvement of the government in providing and guaranteeing pensions means that, contrary to what has often been argued, the Chilean system relies on the "three pillars" recommended by the World Bank in its report *Averting the Old Age Crisis* (1994). There are, however, two main differences between the Chilean system and those in operation (or contemplated) in other countries. First, in Chile, the "public pillar" plays the role of a provider of last resort; and second, in Chile, the obligatory capitalization pillar is privately managed.

The government guarantees described above introduce a minimum sense of "solidarity" into the system. The cost of this, however, is that the system has important elements of moral hazard. In particular, there is an incentive for (lower-income) individuals to minimize their contributions and to obtain the minimum pension. An easy way to reduce this problem would be to establish some relationship between the guaranteed pension level and the years of contributions. This means that instead of a single guaranteed minimum pension, there would be a guaranteed pension "band," where those with, say, 20 years of contributions would be at the bottom of the band, while those with 30 or more years of contributions would be at a higher level in the band.

b.   Results Obtained by the Reforms

Pensions under the New System: One of the objectives of the Chilean pension reform was to increase the real value of pensions, especially for the poorer groups in the country (see Piñera 1988). Under the new system the value of pensions depends on the amount of funds accumulated. The new system established a retirement age of 65 years for men and of 60 years for women. As I discuss below, there is, however, the possibility of early retirement. When an individual retires he can choose between two systems: (A) he can use the accumulated funds to buy an annuity from an insurance company; or, (B) he can choose to enroll in a "programmed withdrawal" scheme, where the accumulated funds are drawn according to an actuarially determined schedule.

Both of these options have advantages and disadvantages. Under the programmed withdrawal alternative, any balance left when the contributor dies is inherited by his heirs. Also, under this program retirees can continue to transfer their balance across AFPs, thus taking advantage of perceived (and expected) differentials in rates of return. Additionally, if the individual outlives the program and the fund is used up, the retiree gets the minimum pension for the rest of his life. Annuities, on the other hand, assure the retiree a steady and known income stream for the rest of his life. In the case of annuities, however, there are no inheritance provisions, and fees have tended to be somewhat high.

Using a sample of 4,064 individuals that have retired under the new system Baeza and Burger (1995) estimated that the average replacement rate has amounted to 78 percent.[10] The highest (relative) pensions have been obtained by those individuals that have opted for early retirement, with a replacement rate of 82 percent under programmed retirement. Baeza and Burger (1995) attribute this result to the fact that only those that have had rapid accumulation of funds— mostly by making voluntary contributions—can in reality opt for early retirement. Disability pensions—which, as explained earlier, are financed with a 3 percent of wages insurance premium—have also had high replacement rates, reaching 67 percent. Finally, survivor's benefits have reached a 71 percent replacement rate. These replacement rates are significantly higher than the average for the old system—only 50 percent in 1980.

Early retirement is allowed under this new system. Individuals can opt for early retirement once their fund is high enough as to produce a pension that covers at least 70 percent of their current salary. Those opting for early retirement can also choose between programmed withdrawals and annuities. By 1994 there were already 200,000 retirees receiving pensions under the new system. Of these, approximately one-half had opted for annuities, and one-half for programmed withdrawal.

There is also the possibility of lump-sum withdrawals. To qualify for this option two requirements have to be met: (a) The pension has to have a replacement rate of at least 70 percent; and (b) the pension has to be at least equal to 120 percent of the minimum pension. Although there are no exact figures on the per-

---

[10]   These authors calculated the replacement rate on the basis of average real salary in the 120 months preceding retirement.

centage of individuals that have opted for lump-sum payments, Baeza and Burger (1995) found out that 24 percent of the contributors in their sample had taken advantage of this option. They calculated that when these payments are taken into account the effective rate of replacement of the new system increases to 84 percent.

In December 1994, average old age pensions under the capitalization system were 42 percent higher than those under the pay-as-you-go regime. In the case of disability, pensions under the new system were 61 percent higher than under the old one. This extraordinary performance, however, has declined somewhat during the last two years as a result of the negative real return obtained by the system as a whole.

Because the new system is based on defined contributions, it is not possible to know exactly how future pensions will compare with those currently being paid. One can expect, however, two forces that will operate in opposite directions in the future. On the one hand, a lower rate of return on the funds will reduce pension payments. On the other hand, if the steady-state rate of return is higher than 4 percent—the return of the recognition bond, which represented a large percentage of the current retirees fund—we could expect a positive effect on pensions paid in the future.

The actual rate of replacement has differed slightly between annuities and programmed withdrawals. Baeza and Burger (1995) found out that for early retirement the annuities scheme resulted in a replacement rate of 78 percent, while programmed withdrawal resulted in a replacement rate of 83 percent. For standard old-age pensions, however, annuities yielded a replacement rate of 74 percent, while programmed withdrawal resulted in a replacement rate of 83 percent.

An important (indirect) effect of the reform is that it has encouraged the development of an active annuities market. Largely as a result of the pension reform, insurance companies' assets as percentage of GDP have increased by more than four times between 1985 and 1995. Annuities, however, are currently very expensive, costing almost 4 percent of the value of the contract. This aspect of the system has generated important criticisms, including calls for allowing for group purchases of annuities and for a greater regulation of the industry, as a way of reducing their cost.

The Transition

Dealing with the transition is one of the key policy questions in designing a pension reform program that replaces a pay-as-you go system with a capitalization one. The transition poses three basic problems: (A) Determining the transfer rule for workers: Which workers will join the new system, and which ones will stay with the old one? Will workers have a choice? (B) Devising a method for crediting funds to those workers that transfer to the new system, but have already made contributions to the old system. (C) Financing pension payments to old-system retirees. Once contributions from active workers are pulled out of the old system and channeled to the individual capitalization accounts the old system becomes completely unfunded.

The new Chilean pension law established (Title XV, article 1) that workers that joined the labor force before December 31, 1982, had five years to decide whether to join the new system. Those joining the labor force after that date could not participate in the old system, and had to become affiliated with an AFP of their choice. Since those that joined an AFP experienced an immediate increase in net take-home pay of 11 percent, the number of people transferring to the new regime was very high. By the end of 1982 more than a million workers, representing 36 percent of total employment, had already transferred to the new system.

The government dealt with past contributions of transferees by issuing bonds that were deposited in their individual AFP accounts. The rationale for this was to "recognize" past contributions—therefore the bonds became known as *recognition bonds*—and to provide the bases for the new retirement fund. These bonds yielded a 4 percent return in real terms, significantly below the ex post market return, and until 1995 could not be traded in the secondary market.

In order to be eligible for receiving a recognition bond, the individual must have made at least 12 monthly contributions into the old system during the previous 5 years. The actual value of the recognition bond was calculated by using a rather complicated formula, consisting of the following steps:

— The average annual base wage used to determine contributions made to the old system prior to June 30, 1979, was multiplied by 0.8.
— This number was then multiplied by the ratio of total years of contributions to 35 (35 years being the assumed number of working years for obtaining a "normal" pension).
— The resulting number was multiplied by 10.35 for males and by 11.36 for females.
— The number resulting from this calculation was then multiplied by a factor that varied according to the individual's age and gender. For the case of males the factor varied between 1 and 1.11, and for the case of females it varied between 1 and 1.31.

The following examples illustrate the actual implications of the new system. Assume first the case of a 35-year-old male whose average pensionable salary was US$6,000 per year, and who had been contributing to the old system for 15 years. In this case the value of the recognition bond to be deposited in his new

AFP account would be US$20,292.[11] Consider now the case of a 45-year-old female, with an average pensionable salary of US$6,000 and 25 years of contributions. Her recognition bond would amount to US$40,896. Recognition bonds yield 4 percent in real terms and can be redeemed when the individual retires, dies, or becomes disabled. In the case of our hypothetical male worker, at age 65 the value of the recognition bond would be US$70,000; for our female participant the recognition bond would have a value at retirement—recall that women retire at 60 years old—of almost US$74,000. An interesting calculation refers to the hypothetical value of the recognition bond for a 65-year-old individual who has contributed for 35 years to the old system. In a way, this number would reflect the authorities' implicit valuation of a lifetime of contributions to the system. In the case of a male worker this lifetime hypothetical recognition bond would be 9.198 times his average annual base salary. In the case of a woman the hypothetical value of the lifetime recognition bond would be 11.905 times the base salary if she had worked 35 years, and 10.205 times if she had worked for 30 years—recall, once again, that women retire at age 60.

Figure 3 — Fiscal Impact of the Transition as Percentage of GDP, 1989–2015

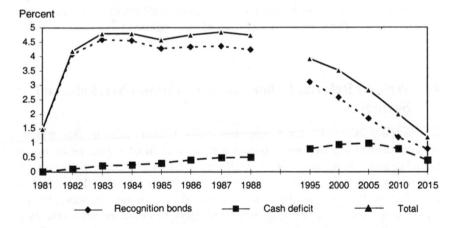

From a fiscal point of view the reform generated two major sources of public expenditures: (a) the servicing and payment of the recognition bonds; and (b) the payment of retirees in the old system. Figure 3 contains data on the fiscal costs of the transition. The "Cash deficit" series contains information on the deficit (as percentage of GDP) stemming from the government's obligations towards "old"

---

11 Strictly speaking, this is only an approximation, since the recognition bond was expressed in UFs, the Chilean indexed unit of account.

retirees. These include both those already retired when the reform was enacted, as well as those that had decided not to switch to the new system. Since most of the "cash" costs are related to pensions due to people that had already retired in 1981, these costs peaked rather early on (in 1983) when they represented 4.58 percent of GDP. In fact, given life expectancy in Chile, these costs start declining rather rapidly after 1995. The "Recognition bonds" series in Figure 3 presents data on the cost of servicing and paying the recognition bonds which were deposited on active workers' retirement accounts. The time path of the recognition bonds' costs are explained by the country's demographics. The pattern of projected retirements is such that the value of maturing bonds peaks in 2005.

Chile has opted to directly finance these costs out of general government revenues. In fact, one of the most attractive features of the Chilean reform is that it made the costs of old-age security very transparent. The government had to recognize sizable unfunded liabilities, and provide for their payment. Some authors have argued that, since these costs are, indeed, quite large, Chilean style reforms are not replicable in other countries (Mesa-Lago 1996). This, however, is not clear a priori and will depend on a number of economic, financial, and especially political factors. At the end of the road, the question is one of cost and benefits. Is it worthwhile maintaining a compulsory, and in most cases largely inefficient, government-run pay-as-you-go system alongside a privately managed one, in order to avoid the fiscal costs of the transition?[12]

4.   Pension Reform, Labor Markets, Capital Markets, and Savings

By changing incentives, taxes, and other rules, pension reforms that replace a government-run pay-as-you-go system with an individual capitalization one are bound to generate important indirect effects. Most analysts have focused on the way this type of reform will impact on national savings. One could argue, however, that even though savings will be affected in an important way, the main impact of a social security reform will be on labor markets. Indeed, to the extent that contributions to the old system have a tax component, the adoption of a new system based on individual accounts will reduce (if not eliminate) the implicit tax on labor, having a tremendous effect on wages and the level of employment. In this section, I use two simple models to analyze the way in which a social security reform of the Chilean type will affect labor market conditions. I then use actual Chilean data to compute the likely effect of the reforms on wages, em-

---

[12]   This is the avenue chosen by some Latin American countries, such as Argentina.

ployment, and unemployment in Chile. I conclude the section with a brief discussion of the likely effects of the Chilean reform on the country's capital market and savings rate.

a.   Social Security Reform and the Labor Market

Most analyses of social security reforms have tended to neglect the effects of the reforms on labor markets (Siebert [1998], Lorz [1998], and Schmidt-Hebbel [1997] are some exceptions). These, however, are potentially very important. This would be especially so if, as is mostly the case (and certainly as was the case in Chile), contributions to the pay-as-you-go system have a pure tax component. In this section, some of the simple analytics of the effects of social security reform, within the Chilean context, are presented.

It can be argued that, in principle, the pension reform has had an important effect on the functioning of the labor market. First, by reducing the total rate of payroll taxes it has reduced the cost of labor and, thus, has encouraged employment creation. Second, by relying on a capitalization system, it has reduced greatly—if not eliminated—the labor tax component of the retirement system. Currently (most) workers see their contributions as a deferred compensation, rather than as a tax. A key question, however, is whether there is still an element of taxation involved in the system. This will depend on a number of factors, including the rate of return on the funds, the perceived future pension income, the magnitude of management fees, the degree of risk aversion, and the rate of discount of workers. Diamond and Valdés-Prieto (1994) have argued that, although it is likely that the new system still retains some implicit tax, this is substantially lower than in the old system.[13] Cox-Edwards (1992) has also argued that the Chilean pension reform system has resulted in a significant reduction in effective taxes on labor. She has argued that this has contributed to the surge in employment creation in Chile, as well as to the rapid increase in (average) real wages since 1985.

In order to organize the discussion, consider the case where, as in Chile and most of Latin America, only a fraction of the labor force is covered by the social security system. Assume that the reform reduces the pure labor tax component from T_0 to T_1 (Figure 4). The effect of this measure on wages and employment will depend on the assumptions made regarding factor mobility, elasticity of the labor supply, and the initial existence of unemployment. The simplest case is characterized by an inelastic labor supply, sector-specific capital (and mobile la-

---

13   A modern and well-functioning labor market has been an important element of Chile's economic success. It has allowed for rapid job creation, and has resulted in the reduction of a rate of unemployment that bordered on 25 percent to one below 6 percent of the labor force.

bor), and full employment. This case is depicted in Figure 4, where $L(C)$ is the demand for labor in the covered sector and $L(N)$ is the demand for labor in the noncovered sector. (It is also assumed that this is an open economy with a larger number of factors of production than traded goods).

Figure 4 — Unified Labor Markets and Social Security Taxes

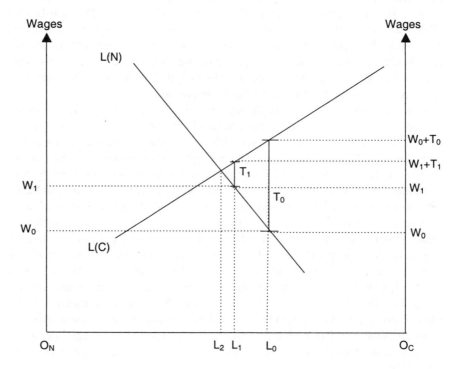

Initially, with a labor tax equal to T_0, the net wage rate is W_0. Since there is perfect labor mobility, there is wage-rate equalization. $O_C L_0$ people are employed in the covered sector and $O_N L_0$ are employed in the noncovered sector. It is assumed that the reform reduces the pure tax component to T_1. Under the above assumptions, this will result in an increase in the net wage to W_1 and an increase in the number of people employed in the covered sector equal to $L_0 L_1$. Naturally, in this case the reform results in an increase in social welfare. Things change somewhat if we relax the assumption of sector-specific capital and inelastic labor supply. In this case, after the reforms there will be an increase in total labor availability and capital will be reallocated from the uncovered to the covered sectors. Naturally, the final effect of this factor reallocation on wages and employment will depend on relative factor intensities.

Consider now the more realistic case where the economy is not always under full employment. Possibly, the simplest way of modeling this case is by assuming a Harris–Todaro type of structure, with equilibrium unemployment. In this case there is no wage-rate equalization across sectors: workers employed in the formal sector of the economy are covered by social security contributions and are paid a minimum wage, W_{min}, that exceeds the equilibrium wage rate. In fact, many authors define the formal sector of the economy as that where workers are subject to social security and other labor laws. Wages in the uncovered sector are set competitively. In this setting, workers prefer to be employed in the high-paying covered sector. In equilibrium the expected wage rate in the covered sector, $E(W_C)$, is equal to the wage rate in the uncovered sector, W_N:

[1] $W_N = E(W_C)$.

Assuming, for simplicity, that the unemployed obtain earnings equal to zero and that the probability of being employed in the private sector is equal to the ratio of openings to applicants, it is possible to write

[2] $W_N = [L_C / (L_C + U)] W_{min}$,

where L_C is employment in the covered sector and U is the number of unemployed. The rest of the model is given by the following three equations:

[3] $L_C + L_N + U = F$,

[4] $L_C = f(W_C, \ldots)$,

[5] $L_N = g(W_N, \ldots)$.

Equation [3] is the labor market equilibrium condition and states that the sum of those employed in the covered and in the noncovered sectors plus the unemployed has to equal the total labor force, F. Equations [4] and [5] are the demand for labor equations in the covered and noncovered sectors. The initial equilibrium is depicted in Figure 5 where curve yy is a rectangular hyperbola that satisfies the Harris–Todaro principle in [2]. Initially, $O_C L_0^C$ people are employed in the protected sector, $O_N L_0^N$ are employed in the nonprotected sector, and $L_0^N L_0^C$ are unemployed. W_{min} is the minimum wage, which is assumed to be set on a net, take-home basis. T_0 is the social security contribution (or, as before, its pure tax component) and W_0 is the equilibrium wage rate in the noncovered sector. (This wage rate is obtained from the intersection of the rectangular hyperbola yy and the demand schedule for the noncovered sector, $L(N)$.) It is clear from this figure that the expected wage rate of those employed in the protected sector and for the unemployed—that is, for the pool of applicants for protected sector jobs—is equal to W_0.

As in the full employment case, the nature of the exercise is a reduction in the social security tax. This case is depicted in Figure 5, under the maintained assumption that the nonlabor factors of production are fixed in their sector of origin and that the supply for labor is inelastic. As in the previous case, the new tax is T_1. As can be seen, employment in the covered sector increases, as does the wage rate in the noncovered sector. The new wage rate in this sector is equal to W_1. It is not possible, however, to establish a priori, and in an unequivocal way, what happens to unemployment. This will basically depend on the elasticities of demand for labor in both sectors.

Figure 5 — Social Security Taxes and Segmented Labor Market

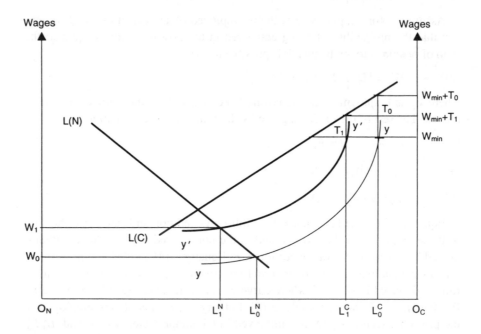

Formally, the effect of the reduction of the tax component on the noncovered sector wages rate will be

[6] $d \log W_N =$ $(1/\Delta) [(U/(L_C + U)) \eta_C (U/F)$

$+ (L_N/F) \eta_C (U/(L_C + U))] (T/(1+T)) d \log T,$

where η_C is the demand elasticity of labor in the covered sector, η_N is the demand elasticity of labor in the noncovered sector, and

[7] $\Delta = \{(U/F) - (L_N/F) \eta_C (U/(L_C + U))\} > 0.$

Equation [6], then, is negative, indicating that increases (declines) in the tax on labor in the covered sector will always result in a decline (increase) in the wage rate in the noncovered sector.

On the other hand, the effect of the social security reform on the number of unemployed will be

[8] $dU =$ $- \{(U/\Delta) \eta_C (L_N/F) [1 + (U/(L_C + U)) \eta_N]\} (T/(1+T)) d \log T.$

As Figure 5 indicated, it is not possible to sign this expression a priori. This means that, in principle, in this setting a social security reform that reduces the tax on labor in the covered sector could generate either an increase or a decrease in the number of unemployed in the economy. Equation [8] clearly shows, however, that the sign of dU will depend on the value of the elasticity of demand for labor in the noncovered sector. More specifically, if

$|\eta_N| < (L_C + U)/U,$

then the social security reform will result in a reduction in the number of unemployed. As before, if the assumptions regarding sector specificity of capital and inelastic labor supply are relaxed, the computations become somewhat more complicated and the probability of ambiguous results increases. More specifically, if F increases as a result of the reform, it is possible that W_n will decline, while U is still undetermined. If, on the other hand, capital is reallocated the results will depend on the capital-labor ratio. If, as is likely to be the case in developing countries, the formal (covered) sector is capital-intensive, the probability that the reform will increase the number of unemployed is even higher. With an inelastic F, wages in the noncovered sector will still increase after the reform.

Interestingly enough, even under the assumption of an elastic labor supply, the model developed here can still provide an estimate of the impact of the reforms on employment. This would be, in fact, the way to interpret [8], under this set of assumptions (of course, with a negative sign).

Even though the model developed above is rather simple, it has enough structure to allow us to simulate the effect of the Chilean reforms on its labor market. Table 3 contains the basic parameter values used in the calculations. The basic values of the parameters correspond to 1981, the year the reforms were launched. In order to make the calculations as sharp as possible, it has been assumed that under the old pay-as-you-go system, the complete contribution was perceived as a tax, while under the new capitalization system it is fully seen as a deferred contribution—that is its tax component is reduced to zero. Additionally, as may be seen from Table 3, I have assumed a range of values for the two elasticities of demand for labor. This allows me to simulate ranges for the effects of the reforms on wages in the noncovered sector and on employment creation. The results obtained from the simulations, under the assumptions used to derive [7] and [8], are presented in Table 4. As may be seen, under the parameters constellation considered in this section the Chilean pension reform appears to have generated, with other things given, an increase in noncovered sector wages ranging

Table 3 — Parameter Values for Simulation

Parameter	Parameter value
F (thousands of people)	3,700
L_C (thousands of people)	1,850
L_N (thousands of people)	1,450
U (thousands of people)	400
η_N	−0.5 to −0.7
η_C	−0.4 to −0.6
T_0	0.26
T_1	0
Note: These data correspond to 1981, the year the reform was launched.	

Source: The basic value of the parameters were taken from Edwards and
        Edwards (1991).

Table 4 — Simulation Results

	High-case scenario	Low-case scenario
Employment creation	119 thousand jobs	75 thousand jobs
Change in wages in noncovered sector	7.7 percent	4.6 percent

Source: Computed by author.

from 4.6 to 7.7 percent, and a net increase in employment ranging from 75 to 119 thousand jobs. If it is assumed that labor supply is inelastic with respect to social security contributions, this effect is equivalent to a decline in the rate of unemployment (with all other things given) ranging from 2.2 to 3.6 percentage points.

An important feature of the model developed here is that under certain circumstances (e.g., a very elastic demand for labor in the noncovered sector) a reform of the social security system may result in a loss of jobs and even in an increase in the number of unemployed. This outcome is, however, quite unlikely. For example, for the parameters considered in Table 3, a reduction in the number of jobs would require an elasticity of demand for labor in the noncovered sector in excess (in absolute terms) of 5.62.

b.   Pension Reforms, Savings, and Capital Markets

Another important effect is that it has contributed to the phenomenal increase in the country's savings rate, from less than 10 percent in 1986 to almost 29 percent in 1996. This effect has taken place mostly through an increase in public sector savings—public savings increased from close to 0.1 percent of GDP in 1983 to more than 5 percent of GDP by 1993. A number of researchers have established that increasing public sector savings represents the most effective way of increasing aggregate savings. In general, higher public savings unleash a virtuous circle, where higher savings generate higher growth, and higher growth (in turn) results in higher private savings (Edwards 1996). Whether the Chilean reform has actually increased private savings directly, is still somewhat of an open question. Although cross-country regression analyses suggest that pension reform affects private savings, there still are no definitive studies on the Chilean case.[14] Haindl (1996), however, has recently attempted to estimate econometrically the effects of the reform on private sector savings. Using an approach based on the inclusion of a series of dummy variables in a time-series analysis of the determinants of savings, he concludes that the reform indeed contributed to the increase in savings.[15] In a more ambitious attempt, Morande (1996) uses modern time-series analysis to estimate an error correction model of savings for Chile. He concludes that there is preliminary evidence supporting the notion that the reform of the pension system encouraged private sector savings. Finally, Bosworth and Marfan (1994) have argued that the contribution of the pension reform to the increase in savings bordered on 3 percent of GDP.

---

[14]   On cross-country studies on savings and social security, see, for example, Feldstein (1970) and Edwards (1996).

[15]   Haindl's (1996) analysis, however, is subject to a number of shortcomings, including the presence of a serious simultaneity bias.

Table 5 — Pension Fund Assets per Financial Instruments (percentages, as of December of each year)

Year	Securities	Financial instructions		Corporate bonds	Firms' shares	Invest-ment funds	Foreign instruments[a]
		Time deposits, financial institutions	Credit notes, financial institutions				
1981	38.1	61.9	9.4	0.6	0.0	0.0	0.0
1982	26.0	26.6	46.8	0.6	0.0	0.0	0.0
1983	44.5	2.7	50.7	2.2	0.0	0.0	0.0
1984	42.1	13.3	42.9	1.8	0.0	0.0	0.0
1985	42.4	21.3	25.2	1.1	0.0	0.0	0.0
1986	46.6	23.3	25.5	0.8	3.8	0.0	0.0
1987	41.4	28.5	21.3	2.6	6.2	0.0	0.0
1988	35.4	29.5	20.6	6.4	8.1	0.0	0.0
1989	41.6	21.5	17.7	9.1	10.1	0.0	0.0
1990	44.1	17.5	16.1	11.1	11.3	0.0	0.0
1991	38.3	13.3	13.4	11.1	23.8	0.0	0.0
1992	40.9	11.1	14.2	9.6	24.0	0.2	0.0
1993	39.3	7.6	13.1	7.3	31.8	0.3	0.6
1994	39.7	6.3	13.7	6.3	32.2	0.9	0.9
1995[b]	40.7	6.0	16.0		36.9[c]	0.4[d]	

[a]As of May 1993, AFPs began to invest in foreign instruments — [b]November 1995. — [c]Corporate bonds + firms' share — [d]Investment funds + foreign instruments.

Source: Valck and Walker (1995) and Banco Central de Chile, *Boletín Mensual*, January 1996.

Pension funds are the largest institutional investors in the Chilean capital market, with assets exceeding 40 percent of GDP, as compared to 0.9 percent in 1981. The asset composition of pension funds is described in Table 5. As discussed above, the performance of AFP portfolios has been impressive in terms of real rates of return, and as shown in Table 6, the returns to individual pension accounts have been higher (on average) than for the financial system as a whole. The massive amount of funds that AFP control has helped create a dynamic and modern capital market. What is perhaps more important, however, is that it has allowed private firms to rely on long-term financing for their investment projects. This has been particularly important for the privatized utilities. Moreover, Chile's new and ambitious (privately funded) infrastructure program will only be possible if there is long-term financing available, of the type the AFPs are able to provide.

Table 6 — Annual Real Rates of Return on Liabilities of the Financial System and on Individual Pension Accounts, 1981–1990 (percentages)

Year	Financial system	Returns to pension account[a]
1981	13.2	5.3
1982	12.1	25.5
1983	7.8	19.4
1984	8.4	2.4
1985	8.2	11.6
1986	4.1	10.9
1987	4.3	4.5
1988	4.6	6.1
1989	6.8	6.7
1990	9.4	15.7
Average 1981–1990	7.8	10.4

[a]For the average assessable income. These returns are lower than the average for the AFPs (reported in Table 1) due to the existence of commissions or fees paid by asset holders.

Source: IMF, based on data provided by Chilean authorities.

5. Conclusions

The Chilean pension reform program has been hailed throughout the world. It has successfully replaced an inefficient, unfair, insolvent pay-as-you go system with a (reasonably) well-functioning privately managed system. Up to now the rates of return of the new system, as well as the pensions being paid out have been very high. This trend, however, is likely to change in the years to come as Chile's rates of return begin to converge towards world levels. In fact, during the last 18 months (1995 and the first half of 1996) the system as a whole has experienced negative returns. An interesting issue is how the system will react to this new state of affairs. The most likely scenario, in my opinion, is one where some of the current shortcomings of the system—including the limitation for multiple funds and the distortionary incentives generated by the government—will be addressed by the authorities. It is not unlikely, then, that the Chilean system will continue to evolve, providing us with fresh lessons in the future. At this point the system is ready for changes. In fact, on June 17, 1997, the Chilean government sent to congress a project aimed at modifying the way in which commissions and fees are negotiated. In particular, the proposal would allow AFPs to charge differential commissions based on the length of time the individual maintains his account with that particular AFP. It is expected that this reform will result in a decline in the costs of administration which, as discussed in the paper, have become increasingly out of hand.

Bibliography

Arellano, J.P. (1982a). Elementos para el analisis de la reforma de la previsión social chilena. *El Trimestre Económico* 49(3):563–605.

—— (1982b). Efectos macroeconomicos de la reforma previsional chilena. *Cuadernos de Economía* 56(April):111–122.

Arrau, P. (1991). La reforma previsional chilena y su financiamiento durante la transición. *Colección Estudios CIEPLAN* 32(June):5–44.

Baeza Valdés, S., and R. Burger Torres (1995). Calidad de las pensiones del sistema privado chileno. In S. Baeza and F. Margozzini (eds.), *Quince años despues: Una mirada al sistema privado de pensiones*. Santiago: Centro de Estudios Públicos.

Bosworth, B.P., R. Dornbusch, and R. Labán (eds.) (1994). *The Chilean Economy: Policy Lessons and Challenges*. Washington, D.C: Brookings Institution.

Bustamante Jeraldo, J. (1995). Principales cambios legales al DL 3.500 en el período noviembre 1990–Mayo 1995 y Desafíos Pendientes. In S. Baeza and F. Margozzini (eds.), *Quince años despues: Una mirada al sistema privado de pensiones*. Santiago: Centro de Estudios Públicos.

Bustos, R. (1995). Reforma a los sistemas de pensiones: peligros de los programas opcionales en América Latina. In S. Baeza and F. Margozzini (eds.), *Quince años despues: Una mirada al sistema privado de pensiones*. Santiago: Centro de Estudios Públicos.

Cheyre, H. (1988). Análisis comparativo del antiguo régimen de pensiones y del nuevo sistema previsional. In S. Baeza and R. Manubens (eds.), *Sistema Privado de Pensiones en Chile*. Santiago: Centro de Estudios Públicos.

Cifuentes, R.S. (1995). Reforma de los sistemas previsionales: Aspectos macroeconómicos. *Cuadernos de Economía* 96(August):217–250.

Cox-Edwards, A. (1992). Economic Reform and Labor Market Legislation in Latin America. Mimeo. California State University.

Diamond, P. (1994). Privatization of Social Security: Lessons from Chile. *Revista de Análisis Económico* 9(1) (June):21–34.

Diamond, P., and S. Valdés-Prieto (1994). Social Security Reforms. In B. Bosworth, R. Dornbusch, and R. Labán (eds.), *The Chilean Economy: Policy Lessons and Challenges*. Washington, D.C: Brookings Institution.

Edwards, S. (1995). *Crisis and Reform in Latin America: From Despair to Hope*. New York: Oxford University Press.

—— (1996). The Chilean Pension Reform: A Pioneering Program. NBER Working Paper 5811.

Edwards, S., and A. Edwards (1991). *Monetarism and Liberalization: The Chilean Experiment*. Chicago: University of Chicago Press.

Fontaine, J.A. (1994). Inversiones extranjeras por fondos de pensiones: Efectos sobre la política macroeconómica. *Cuadernos de Economía* 93(August):161–183.

Fuentes Silva, R. (1995). Evolución y resultados del sistema. In S. Baeza and F. Margozzini (eds.), *Quince años despues: Una mirada al sistema privado de pensiones*. Santiago: Centro de Estudios Públicos.

Godoy Arcaya, O., and S. Valdés-Prieto (1994). Democracia y previsión en Chile: Experiencia con dos sistemas. *Cuadernos de Economía* 93(August):135–160.

HABITAT (1991). *10 Años de Historia del Sistema de AFP*. Santiago: AFP HABITAT, S.A.

Haindl, E. (1996). Chilean Pension Fund Reform and Its Impact on Savings. Working Paper. Universidad Gabriela Mistral, Santiago, Chile.

Harberger, A. (1985). Observations on the Chilean Economy, 1973–1983. *Economic Development and Cultural Change* 33(April):451–462.

Hsin, P.-L., and O.S. Mitchell (1994). The Political Economy of Public Pensions: Pension Funding, Governance and Fiscal Stress. *Revista de Análisis Económico* 9(1)(June): 151–168.

Iglesias, A., and D. Vittas (1992). The Rationale and Performance of Personal Pension Plans in Chile. Working Paper 867. The World Bank.

Larraín, L. (1995). El sistema privado de pensiones y el desarrollo económico. In S. Baeza and F. Margozzini (eds.), *Quince años despues: Una mirada al sistema privado de pensiones*. Santiago: Centro de Estudios Públicos.

Lorz, O. (1998). Social Security and Employment. This volume.

Margozzini Cahis, F. (1995). La industria de las AFP. In S. Baeza and F. Margozzini (eds.), *Quince años despues: Una mirada al sistema privado de pensiones*. Santiago: Centro de Estudios Públicos.

McGreevey, W.P. (1990). Social Security in Latin America: Issues and Options for the World Bank. World Bank Discussion Paper 110. Washington, D.C.

Mesa-Lago, C. (1991). *Social Security and Prospects for Equity in Latin America*. World Bank Discussion Paper 140. Washington, D.C.

Mesa-Lago, C. (1996). Las Reformas de las Pensiones en América Latina y la Posición de los Organismos Internacionales: Comentario a la Propuesta de la CEPAL.

Morande, F. (1996). Savings in Chile: What Went Right? Inter-American Development Bank Working Paper 322. Washington, D.C.

Myers, R. (1988). Privatización en Chile del sistema de seguridad social. In S. Baeza and R. Manubens (eds.), *Sistema Privado de Pensiones en Chile*. Santiago: Centro de Estudios Públicos.

Ortdzar, P. (1988). El déficit previsional: Recuento y proyecciones. In S. Baeza and R. Manubens (eds.), *Sistema Privado de Pensiones en Chile*. Santiago: Centro de Estudios Públicos.

Piñera, J. (1988). Discurso del ministro del Trabajo y Previsión Social con Motivo de la Aprobación de la Reforma Previsional. In S. Baeza and R. Manubens (eds.), *Sistema Privado de Pensiones en Chile*. Santiago: Centro de Estudios Públicos.

—— (1991). *El Cascabel al Gato: La Batalla por la Reforma Previsional*. Santiago: Zig-Zag.

Schmidt-Hebbel, K. (1995). *La reforma pensional colombiana: Efectos fiscales y macro-económicos*. Bogotá: Bolsa de Bogotá, ASOFONDOS.

—— (1997) Pension Reform, Informal Markets and Long-Term Income and Welfare. Documento De Trabajo del Banco Central de Chile, March 4. Santiago.

Sequeira, F. (1995). Una visión sobre el desarrollo legal. In S. Baeza and F. Margozzini (eds.), *Quince años despues: Una mirada al sistema privado de pensiones*. Santiago: Centro de Estudios Públicos.

Siebert, H. (1998). Pay-as-You-Go versus Capital Funded Pension Systems: The Issues. This volume.

Superintendencia de Administradoras de Fondos de Pensiones (1996). *El Sistema Chileno de Pensiones*. Tercera Edición. Santiago, Chile.

Uthoff, A. (1994). Some Features of Current Pension System Reform in Latin America. *Revista de Análisis Económico* 9(1)(June):211–236.

Valck V.E., and E.H Walker (1995). La Inversión de los Fondos de Pensiones. Hitoria, Normativa y Resultados. In S. Baeza and F. Margozzini (eds.), *Quince años despues: Una mirada al sistema privado de pensiones,*. Santiago: Centro de Estudios Públicos.

Valdés-Prieto, S. (1994a). Distributive Concerns when Substituting a Pay-as-You-Go by a Fully Funded Pension System. *Revista de Análisis Económico* 9(1)(June):11–104.

—— (1994b). Cargos por administración en los systemas de pensiones de Chile, Los Estados Unidos, Malasia y Zambia. *Cuadernos de Economía* 93(August):185–227.

Valente, J.R. (1989). Diversificación internacional: Una alternativa para las necesidades de inversión de los fondos de pensiones. *Estudios Públicos* 34(Fall):115–146.

Vittas, D. (1995). Strengths and Weaknesses of the Chilean Pension Reform. The World Bank. Washington, D.C.

World Bank (1993). Human Resources in Latin America and the Caribbean: Priorities and Action. Human Resources Division, Latin America and the Caribbean Region, Washington, D.C.

—— (1994). *Averting the Old Age Crisis: Policies to Protect the Old and Promote Growth*. New York: Oxford University Press.

Zurita, S. (1994). Minimum Pension Insurance in the Chilean Pension System. *Revista de Análisis Económico* 9(1)(June):15–26.

Comment on the Papers by Sebastian Edwards, and Richard Disney and Paul Johnson

Estelle James

1. Introduction

Both Chile and the United Kingdom reformed their public pension systems in the 1980s. The papers by Richard Disney and Paul Johnson and by Sebastian Edwards discuss the nature of these reforms and some of their consequences. Although the reforms were similar in fundamental ways, one would not gather that from a quick reading of these papers. Indeed, Chile is seen—generally and in Edward's paper—as a success story, while for the United Kingdom the problems are emphasized. Because the United Kingdom and Chile offer two different variations on the same basic theme, it may be useful to compare the two reforms, their similarities, differences, and problems, so that other countries can assess which approach is most appropriate for them. The fundamental similarity is that they both establish mandatory multipillar systems with a greater emphasis on prefunding and shared responsibility between the public and private sectors. The most important differences concern the degree of choice and regulation of the private pillar and the kind of safety net provided by the public pillar.

2. Fundamental Similarities

First the similarities: Both Chile and the United Kingdom largely got rid of their publicly managed pay-as-you-go defined benefit (PAYG DB) earnings-related pillar in the 1980s, before pension reform was fashionable. They replaced it with a new fully funded (FF) private, competitively managed pillar which was defined contribution in Chile and a mixture of defined benefit (DB) and defined contribution (DC) in the United Kingdom. In both cases the private pillar was buttressed by a publicly managed social safety net designed to keep old people out of poverty—a universal flat pension in the United Kingdom and a minimum pension guarantee in Chile.

Both countries used a basically similar transitional mechanism: pensioners kept their previous pensions and employers or workers were given the right to choose between the new and the old systems, with incentives to switch. Most young workers chose the new system, because of the incentives, their loss of

faith in the old system, and the fact that they could benefit the most from the expected high rates of return under the new DC system. In retrospect, both governments probably paid more than was necessary to get people to switch. Subsequent reforming governments in other countries (and even subsequent U.K. governments) have paid less, thereby saving money while still making transferees
better off. Currently only 17 percent of workers in the United Kingdom remain
in the state-run earnings-related plan (SERPS) and the proportion is even smaller
in Chile where new entrants to the labor market are required to enter the new
private pillar.

Problems have surfaced in both countries, especially concerning the nature of
the public and private pillars and administrative costs. These problems will be
discussed in greater detail below. Nevertheless, the reforms in both countries
must be judged a success, in the sense that neither Chile nor the United Kingdom
faces a large future fiscal deficit from its social security system, unlike most of
the rest of the world, and neither country is considering a reversion to the old
system.

3.   Differences and Problems

a.   The Funded Private Pillar

A major difference between Chile and the United Kingdom concerns the nature
of the private pillar. In the United Kingdom, workers have considerable choice
—they can stay in the state earnings-related PAYG DB plan, opt out to their own
personal retirement savings (PRS) FF DC plans, or the employer can contract
out into a group plan which might be DB or DC. Given all this choice, the
United Kingdom has allowed considerable discretion to the private plans, with
only light regulation. The light regulation has led to scandals, of which the
Maxwell scandal (in which a major employer misused his company pension
funds) is best known. Even more problematic may be the behavior of many insurance company salesmen who took advantage of uninformed workers and persuaded them to opt out to PRS plans, when they clearly would have been better
off staying in their employers' DB plan. As a result, large lawsuits and investigations are now in process and the U.K. system is in some disrepute.

In contrast, Chile offers much less choice and the available choices are much
more heavily regulated. Although current workers can stay in the state PAYG
DB system, all new entrants to the labor market must enter the private FF DC
system, where covered workers have their own personal saving accounts.
Moreover, the accounts are heavily regulated—each worker can have only one

account, each pension fund can offer only one portfolio, and pension funds are penalized if their returns deviate substantially from the average. As a result, the pension funds emulate each others' behavior (herding behavior), leading to still less choice for workers with regard to investment portfolio and strategy. Workers who would prefer a high yield-high risk portfolio are lumped together with those who would prefer low risk-low yield, implying an "average" portfolio that is probably nonoptimal for both. But in return, gross scandals, deception and above-normal losses are avoided.

Based on the experience of these two countries, regulation and choice seem to be substitutes rather than complements in designing the second pillar. Moreover, there appears to be a trade-off between variety and accommodation of individual preferences (which implies more choice, less regulation), versus simplicity, ease of monitoring and avoidance of gross failure and mistakes (which implies less choice, more regulation). The question of how much choice and how much regulation are controversial issues in the design of mandatory pension systems. Some would argue that a mandatory retirement saving scheme must be heavily regulated to avoid major risks and should offer limited choice, since ill-informed workers will not make sophisticated choices wisely. Others would argue that this distorts financial markets and reduces individual welfare. The United Kingdom illustrates the problems that develop with much choice, little regulation, and Chile the opposite.

b.   Public Pillar

The second important difference concerns the nature of the social safety net. While both Chile and the United Kingdom have a publicly run social safety net, the cost and distributional effects of the two differ. The United Kingdom offers a universal flat benefit that is indexed to prices and has therefore fallen relative to rising real wages. It now pays 15 percent of the average wage. In contrast, Chile offers a minimum pension guarantee tied to the funded private pillar: workers with 20 years of contributions whose accumulation does not yield an annual income that is at least 27 percent of the average wage get supplements from the government to bring them to this minimum level.

On the one hand, the Chilean scheme is likely to be both cheaper and better targeted to the poor than the U.K. scheme—cheaper because it will go only to a small proportion of the covered population and even in these cases will simply be supplementary to the worker's own accumulation, better targeted because only low-income groups will receive the benefits. This enables the promised amount (relative to the average wage) to be almost twice as large in Chile as in the United Kingdom; a major criticism of the U.K. social safety net is its low level. (Of course, in the United Kingdom the 15 percent basic benefit is added to the pension from the private pillar, bringing the total much higher, while in Chile the 27 percent guarantee is inclusive of the pension from the private pillar.)

On the other hand, as with any means-tested or income guarantee scheme, Chile's minimum pension may discourage contributions and encourage evasion after the twenty year point, when the worker has established eligibility. At that point, the effective marginal tax rate on low-income workers becomes very high, in some cases 100 percent, because the pension they would get from their own contributions does not exceed the pension they would get from the government's guarantee. While all U.K. workers have a small incentive to evade the payroll tax needed to finance the flat benefit, low-income workers in Chile have a much larger incentive to evade the contribution to the private pillar because of the very high marginal tax rates they face in the vicinity of the minimum guarantee. This has become a major criticism of the Chilean guarantee.

It may be worth giving a small arithmetic example to compare the cost of the U.K. and Chilean schemes, taking evasion into account. Let us suppose that the interest rate and rate of wage growth are such that a worker with 40 years of contributions would get a 54 percent replacement rate of his own salary and a worker with 20 years' contributions would get 27 percent. Then, an average wage worker in Chile would practically never be eligible for the government top-up (even if he only contributed 20 years), while those earning half the average wage would almost always be eligible (even if they contributed 40 years). These low-wage workers would have a big incentive to underreport their earnings for 20 years and to evade altogether thereafter, because additional contributions will have no effect on their ultimate pension. Workers earning between 50 and 100 percent of the average wage will also have some incentive, albeit smaller, to evade and receive the minimum guarantee. The ultimate cost of the Chilean safety net will depend on the wage distribution in the economy, particularly the proportion of very low-income workers, and their ability to evade contributions. If the bottom half of covered workers have an incentive to evade and manage to evade for half their careers, the government would end up paying them about 10 percent of the average wage (equivalent to 5 percent to all workers). This worst-case high-evasion scenario implies a cost that is 1/3 of the cost per worker in the United Kingdom (where all workers get 15 percent of the average wage). But the labor market distortions stemming from escape to the informal sector may be smaller in the United Kingdom.

Costs and distortions in Chile could be reduced by tying the minimum pension guarantee to years of contributions—for example, at the rate of 0.8 percent of the average wage per year of contributions. Then, workers with 20 years of contributions would get a 16 percent guarantee, while those with 40 years would get a 32 percent guarantee. Because the guarantee would rise with contributory

years, low-wage workers would have an incentive to contribute something each
year, thereby probably reducing evasion and the net cost of the system.

c.   Administrative Costs

Both Chile and the United Kingdom face high administrative costs in their private pillars. This is discussed at length in Edwards' paper but not in Disney and
Johnson's paper, probably because of the lack of data.

In Chile, fees for pension fund management are 10–15 percent of total contributions. Retirees who want to purchase an annuity will have to pay still more,
but few have done so yet; the annuities market is just getting started in Chile.
While fees are based on contributions, as a percent of assets (that is, the deduction from gross to net returns) they now average slightly less than 2 percent.
These administrative costs have been the greatest source of criticism of the Chilean system.

In evaluating these criticisms, Edwards points out that the cost of the new
Chilean system is lower than the cost of the old system. Moreover, the new system required the development of a whole new set of financial institutions, with
heavy start-up costs. Economies of scale are large in the pension fund business.
As a result, administrative costs, as a percentage of assets, were very high at first
but have been coming down steadily through time, and will probably continue to
fall, until they approach costs in mutual funds in the United States, which typically charge slightly over 1 percent of assets. In addition, fees in Chile are front-
loaded, which means they are paid when the contribution is first made, rather
than as an on-going annual charge. Workers who have recently entered the
scheme will consequently face high administrative costs relative to their (small)
assets, while those who have been in the scheme for many years will face much
lower charges as a percent of their (large) assets. Since the Chilean scheme is
new, all workers are now in the first category. If the same fee schedule is continued over their lifetime, the administrative charge will fall to about 1 percent of
assets (consistent with the mutual fund costs discussed above).

Part of the high cost in Chile is attributable to high marketing costs, including
sales commissions. Some marketing costs may be an essential component of a
market system—allocation of capital by a central planner may not incur these
marketing costs but also may not allocate capital according to productivity-
maximizing criteria. Nevertheless, if the pension plan is mandatory, it is important to think through ways of keeping marketing costs low, so that workers are
not being forced by the government to pay high fees. Some mechanisms that
might be considered with this in mind are: using a central clearinghouse to
achieve scale economies in collecting contributions; allowing lower fees for
workers who sign with the fund directly (rather than going through an agent) and

for those who stay with their fund for more than one year; permitting commissions to be paid only on new accounts, not on transferred accounts; allowing each fund to offer more than one portfolio, with different benchmarks, so that greater diversity is available and switching can occur within, rather than between, funds; and limiting the number of transfers to 1 or 2 per year. In small low-income countries the contract for the mandatory system might be awarded to 2–3 investment companies based on competitive bidding over costs. In high-income countries with well-developed financial markets, all mutual funds that meet regulatory standards might participate, providing they charge a fee that is less than 1 percent or even less than 0.5 percent, for the mandatory accounts.

While there has been much discussion of administrative costs of the Chilean scheme, we have relatively little data with respect to costs in the United Kingdom. One might expect costs to be somewhat lower in group (employer-run) plans in the United Kingdom because of smaller marketing costs, better bargaining power and scale economies; but the principal-agent problem in DC plans may have the opposite effect. Cursory data seem to indicate that insurance company fees (who run many of the plans in the United Kingdom) are similar to those in Chile, as a percentage of assets.

In comparing costs associated with funded pension plans in Chile or the United Kingdom with the costs in PAYG schemes in other countries, it is important to bear in mind that fund management costs, but it also provides a service, both to the individual and to the broader economy. The allocation of saving among alternative investments has to be done somewhere in the economy—if not by mandatory pension funds then by other institutions. Thus, if we observe that funded pension plans have higher administrative costs than well-run PAYG plans, this may not represent a net added cost to the economy, but rather a shift of financial management costs from mutual funds and banks to pension funds. We must then ask—which set of institutions is best suited to efficiently manage the economy's financial assets? Compared with other financial institutions, pension companies have the advantage that their funds have been committed for the long term, enabling them to make long-term investments without intermediation; but, if mandatory, they may also be subject to substantial regulations that distort their investment choices. Thus, if funded pension plans play a large role in a country's retirement security scheme, it is particularly important to choose a regulatory regime that protects workers from fraud and excessive risk (e.g., by requiring information disclosure and diversification), while allowing a range of choices away from the corners of the risk-yield frontier.

4. Conclusion

Despite the problems listed above, I believe the pension reforms in Chile and the United Kingdom should be counted as successes, both economically and politically. Economically, the reforms have kept public pension spending, the implicit pension debt, and payroll taxes low in both countries. The Chilean scheme has been given credit in econometric studies for increasing national saving, enhancing financial market development, reducing labor market distortions, and therefore augmenting wages, employment, and growth. Interestingly, there has been little research along these lines in the United Kingdom, perhaps because the funded private system there was not completely new but built upon existing employer schemes and because it prevented the development of a large public PAYG scheme rather than replacing one that already existed. This complicates the task of constructing a counterfactual, which would be needed to determine the net economic impact of the reform. Nevertheless, it should be noted that the U.K. economy is booming, with lower employment and higher wage growth than in many other OECD countries, and this may be due in part to its lower pension payroll burden.

Politically, I would judge these reforms a success also. In both cases they were started by strong governments at a point when unions (who often oppose such reforms) were weak and had no ties to the ruling party. Now new governments are in power in both countries, with stronger ties to labor unions. Nevertheless, no consideration is being given to dismantling the reformed system; rather, the systems are being strengthened. The fact that neither the public nor the policy-makers are interested in turning the clock back in the face of a change of political regime is perhaps the greatest testimony to the success of the pension reform.

III.

Reforming Social Security

Friedrich Breyer

The Economics of Minimum Pensions

1. Introduction

Considering the demographic development in all major industrial nations—rising life expectancy and below-replacement fertility—radical reforms of the existing unfunded public pension schemes are now being seriously debated, at least among academic economists, but to some extent even in the political arena. The most consistent reform proposals are (a) the transition to capital-reserve financing (as in Chile) and (b) the transition to a flat-benefit system. Interestingly, these two proposals are not mutually exclusive but can be combined into a two-pillar system.[1] While proposal (a) will be the subject of a series of other contributions to this conference, my contribution will be confined to an economic analysis of proposal (b). In doing this, I will consider efficiency, equity, and public-choice aspects of flat-benefit pension systems.

In Germany, there has been a lively debate on the introduction of a minimum-pension system over the last decade following the publication of four very different proposals.[2] Naturally, the following discussion will take up the most important points of this debate, and I shall present a proposal of my own which borrows heavily from the previous ones.

The argument unfolds as follows. In Section 2, I shall examine market failure as a justification for the existence and the design of compulsory social security systems. In Section 3, I shall give a brief overview over alternative ways to structure minimum-pension schemes. In Section 4, I shall discuss the incentives inherent in different pension formulae. Section 5 will be concerned with the political economy of unfunded public (minimum) pension schemes. While this whole discussion will take place within the framework of a closed economy, Section 6 will be devoted to problems of coordination of flat-benefit pension

Remark: Helpful comments from Martin Kolmar and computational assistance by Volker Reinthaler are gratefully acknowledged.

[1] If private saving is included, this amounts to the three-pillar system proposed by the World Bank (1994).

[2] The authors are Miegel and Wahl (1985), Die Grünen (1985), Engels et al. (1987), and Wagner (1988).

systems within an international community with free mobility of labor such as the European Union, and Section 7 to problems of transition to a minimum-pension scheme. Finally, Section 8 summarizes the conclusions.

Before I proceed, a brief remark on the scope of the paper is in order. Existing social security systems such as the German Gesetzliche Rentenversicherung (GRV) typically provide a whole array of contingent payments each of which covers the financial consequences of a specific risk: ordinary retirement benefits covering the risk of longevity, early retirement benefits covering the risk of disability, and survivors benefits covering the risk of premature death. To keep the analysis manageable, it will be confined exclusively to the first type of benefits.

2.   Market Failure and Compulsory Public Pension Systems

In a society which is committed to the principle of individual liberty, government intervention is generally thought to be justified if it is capable of bringing about an allocation that is either Pareto-superior to the market solution which would otherwise be reached or more equitable than the latter.[3] Of these two, the equity criterion can be reduced to the Pareto criterion applied to the hypothetical situation behind the veil of ignorance. These considerations will be used in the following to sketch out an "ideal" pension system, seen from a welfare economics viewpoint, against which actual institutions can be assessed.

a.   Types of Market Failure in Annuity Markets

Insurance markets in general and the market for private annuities in particular can be subject to the following types of market failure:

  a. *Adverse selection*: If the insuree is better informed about his particular risk distribution than the insurance company, "good risks," i.e., persons with a lower life expectancy, will be unable to get the desired coverage at fair premiums. In this case, a compulsory *partial* insurance can, under certain conditions, make members of all risk groups better off.[4]

  b. *Externalities and public-good nature of charity*: If some members of society choose not to adequately provide for their old-age consumption (or are unable to do so), they might impose a negative externality on other persons who care for their well-being. Moreover, this externality cannot

---

3   As this is not an essay in political philosophy, I feel safe to refer to the "mainstream" and ignore more radical positions, such as Nozick's (1974).

4   See Eckstein et al. (1985) for a model with two risk groups.

be removed by private charity because of the public-good nature of the latter. Thus, public provision of a subsistence level of consumption—to the old and to the young—is probably a Pareto-improving measure. The negative incentive effects of such a welfare payment on individual provision for old-age consumption justifies compulsion to contribute to such a financing mechanism according to ability.

c. *Absence of markets with infinitely many traders*: As is well known, the Pareto efficiency of perfectly competitive markets holds only in finite-horizon models. With an infinite horizon and thus infinitely many traders, the market equilibrium may be dynamically inefficient, and a publicly organized scheme of transfers from the young to the old is Pareto-improving if the cumulative growth rate of GNP at least equals the cumulative interest rate (Spremann 1984).[5] As in this case every generation can be made better off if the government, with its power to coerce individuals, runs an unfunded pension system (henceforth UPPS),[6] the size of such a transfer scheme should be as big as possible.

d. *Absence of markets for real annuities*: One specific risk which is systemic and thus cannot be eliminated by pooling even in large insurance companies is the risk of inflation.[7] Hence, it is often argued that a UPPS is the only one which can perfectly insure workers against this risk.

e. *Strategic aspects of international policy-making:* If the country is large enough to have an impact on the world capital market and is, moreover, a net lender, a UPPS can be used strategically to depress saving and thus raise the world interest rate (Persson 1985). This can make residents of the home country better off even when the interest rate (slightly) exceeds the world growth rate.

If these five alleged types of market failure are looked at more closely, it becomes obvious that not all of them are perfectly compelling or apply equally well to annuity markets: while type *b* is certainly convincing, the information asymmetry underlying type *a* seems to be less typical for the longevity risk than for other risk types.

---

[5] This condition applies both to a small open and to a closed economy (Samuelson 1975). For a large open economy the condition is somewhat more complicated (Breyer and Wildasin 1993).

[6] I refrain from using the more popular short-cut PAYG for "pay-as-you-go" system because this term does not do justice to the real-world public pension systems in which every member has to pay his contribution when he *enters* the system (as a worker) and, if he is lucky, gets something back when he *leaves* (as a pensioner).

[7] Strictly speaking, inflation can be attributed to inadequate monetary policy and therefore can be classified as a government failure rather than a market failure.

The empirical content of type *c* market failure would have been judged quite favorably forty years ago, when most UPPSs were introduced or expanded, but is extremely doubtful today given the rapidly shrinking population size forecast for the next century. Thus the introduction of a new UPPS, e.g., in one of the reform countries of Eastern Europe, can certainly not be advocated on these grounds. To be sure, this does not mean that the abolition of an existing UPPS would be Pareto-improving, but instead that an intergenerational conflict seems inevitable.[8] An additional problem connected with this justification of government intervention is that in a democracy the infinite maintenance of a UPPS is hard to guarantee. A similar objection can be raised against type *e* considerations because being a net lender is not a very stable characteristic of a country.

More generally, if the future development of rates of return to the different types of pension systems, i.e., growth and interest rates, is uncertain, the individual participant benefits from a diversification of his pension claims (Merton 1983). But this means that the size of a UPPS should be limited to leave room for additional old-age provisions on the capital market, at least for middle and higher income segments.

Type *d* market failure, finally, is not perfectly convincing either. For one thing, life insurance companies with carefully diversified portfolios containing a high percentage of real assets such as stocks and real estate do provide some hedge against the inflation risk (i.e., their nominal returns are positively related to the rate of inflation). On the other hand, given the usual positive correlation between expected return and risk, a completely risk-free (real) annuity would not maximize the expected utility of the typical pensioner unless he is infinitely risk-averse.

b.   Implications for the Design of Public Pension Systems

In the more policy-oriented literature on public pension systems, two major goals of these systems are typically stressed:

1.   preventing poverty among the aged,
2.   helping them to maintain their previous standard of living.

Now what is the relation of these goals to the types of market failure identified above, and which institutions are most suitable for reaching these goals provided they are defensible on welfare-economic grounds?

---

[8]   I do not elaborate on this point to which another contribution to this conference is directed. Surveys of the recent literature on this subject are given in Breyer (1997a) and Homburg (1997).

The first goal is clearly related to type *b* market failure and thus has a sound welfare-economic foundation. To some extent, it is also related to type *a* if "good risks" choose not to buy "unfair" annuities in the absence of compulsion, and to type *d* because in the absence of government intervention, unanticipated hyperinflation may incur poverty for retirees with only nominal annuities.

The second goal is closely connected to types *c* and *d* of market failure: someone who wants to smooth consumption over the life cycle would benefit from a financing system which allows income to be shifted from working to retirement age at a high rate of return and low risk. The empirical facts cited above, however, do not lend support to government intervention, in particular running a UPPS to reach this goal. Moreover, for someone who is not interested in an even consumption path but wants to consume at a faster rate as long as he is young (and perhaps more capable of enjoying certain expensive goods), the smoothing of the income stream provided by a compulsory membership in a UPPS may even decrease lifetime utility. This effect originates from a particular capital market imperfection, viz., the inability to borrow against future retirement benefits. Thus private markets provide better means against underannuitization than against overannuitization through a public system.[9]

In summarizing the arguments put forward so far, it seems safe to say that government intervention directed at goal 1 is justified on efficiency grounds while goal 2 has a rather dubious welfare foundation.[10] This preliminary result, however, refers only to goals and not to specific instruments applied by governments in the pursuit of these goals—a topic to which I turn now. Specifically, I shall examine two idealized instruments:

A. a flat retirement benefit provided to every person above a certain age,
B. a system where the (monthly) retirement benefits are positively related or even proportional to the stream of contributions paid by the retiree during his working life.[11]

To avoid complications, I shall at this point not go into the details of the methods used to finance the costs of these programs or to calculate individual

---

9   That overannuitization is a real phenomenon is shown by the fact that savings rates of the very old are typically positive. Börsch-Supan and Stahl (1991) explain this evidence with the existence of health-related consumption constraints. Note that a bequest motive alone cannot account for a rising amount of wealth in old age.

10 For a similar view, see, e.g., Vaubel (1983, 1996).

11 Note that this does not secure (relative) equivalence of total contributions and total benefits as long as life expectancy varies, e.g., between different occupational groups (see Breyer 1997b).

claims. For the flat-benefit system, this will be the topic of the following sections.

System A is clearly not suitable for reaching goal 2 (nor does it attempt to do so). However, it is equally clear that it is quite well suited to reaching goal 1, provided the benefit schedule is truly flat, i.e., there is no other requirement for collecting the full benefit than being a citizen (or, alternatively, a resident) of the country in which system A is operated, and the benefit level does not fall short of the subsistence level. There remains the question why a separate institution is needed at all to prevent poverty among the aged given that a universal welfare-payment system exists. What is the advantage of having two (or even more) institutions with the purpose of fighting poverty? A separate institution for the aged seems to make sense only if it plays by different rules than the general social-assistance system, in particular if the benefits it provides are not means-tested (see Section 3) and if one of its goals is to avoid stigmatization of its beneficiaries, which may even be a desirable feature of the general system of assistance payments to provide incentives to work.

In contrast, system B is not designed to pursue goal 1 and therefore misses it in all cases in which the working history of the individual is not complete and his income not large enough to compensate this failure. Empirical evidence is provided by the large number of retirees in Germany who collect subsidiary social-assistance payments because of insufficient claims to retirement benefits. What is perhaps more surprising, however, is that system B is not even certain of reaching goal 2. There is a very simple theoretical reason for this failure: there would be a clear-cut connection between instrument B and goal 2 if everybody worked the same number of years and there was no borrowing and lending, i.e., in each period consumption equaled income for everybody so that the retirement benefit would be exactly proportional to the (average) level of consumption during the working life. Accordingly, this relationship fails to hold in all other cases.

We can thus conclude that government intervention in the market for old-age security by running a UPPS with compulsory membership can be justified on the basis of Paretian welfare economics if its goal is the prevention of poverty and the instrument used is a flat retirement benefit. There is no compelling reason why the government should force individuals to maintain their previous standard of living throughout their retirement age, much less to use an "income-related" benefit system as an instrument.

3.   Types of Minimum-Pension Systems

The term "minimum-pension system" is by no means unambiguous because there is a wide variety of ways to design such a system, which can be classified according to the following six criteria.[12] Although not all combinations of these six criteria make sense,[13] examples for most of the alternatives of any single criterion can be found in other countries, many even in EU member states (Schulte 1993) (examples are given in parentheses).

1. Position within a compulsory social security system:
    a. a flat-benefit pension can be the *only* type of service provided by the UPPS (Netherlands),
    b. a flat-benefit pension can be *one of several* services provided by the UPPS (Norway, Sweden, United Kingdom),
    c. a minimum-pension provision can be *integrated* into an otherwise income-related UPPS (Austria, France, Switzerland).

2. The minimum pension can be granted:
    a. conditionally on a *means test* (Austria, Belgium, France),
    b. unconditionally (all other countries mentioned above).

3. Recipients of the minimum pension can be all persons over a certain age threshold:
    a. who *reside* in the respective country (all of the above-mentioned countries),
    b. who have the *nationality* of the country.

4. Other requirements for a claim to the minimum pension:
    a. can be *absent* (France),
    b. can refer to the *duration of residence* (Nordic countries, Netherlands),
    c. can refer to the *duration and/or size of contributions to the plan.*

5. The plan can be financed:
    a. out of *general taxes* (Belgium, Denmark),
    b. through an *earmarked tax* (related to income) (Norway, Sweden, Netherlands),
    c. through a (flat) *contribution* (United Kingdom).

---

[12] For similar classifications, see Hauser (1993) or Schmähl (1993b).

[13] For example, a means-tested minimum pension below the general social assistance level (2a, 6c) would entail unnecessary administration costs.

6. The size of the minimum pension can be:
    a. *at the poverty line used for social assistance to the nonaged* (France),
    b. *above* this level (Netherlands),
    c. *below* this level (United Kingdom).

With respect to the fourth and fifth criteria, the term "contribution" is typically used to characterize systems in which the benefits must be "earned" through previous payments into the plan or other activities (such as child-rearing) while "tax" means that no such connection exists.

Sometimes, the debate centers around a few "prototypes," i.e., specific combinations of the six criteria, which are related either to an actual system or a prominent proposal. Of these, it is worthwhile to mention three:

A. The integration of a minimum-contribution provision in a pension system built upon the principle of intracohort fairness ("minimum-contribution system").[14]
B. A uniform retirement benefit (means-tested or not), financed out of general taxes ("tax-financed flat benefit").
C. A uniform retirement benefit (not means-tested) financed through a uniform lump-sum contribution ("Beveridge plan").

4.   Incentive Effects of Minimum-Pension Systems

The provision of a minimum pension can distort working and saving incentives in a variety of ways, depending upon the design of the system. To structure the following discussion, I shall first concentrate on the benefit side before I turn to the financing side.

a.   Incentives Related to the Benefit Side

The most severe distortion of incentives is implied in a means-tested minimum-pension benefit. First, it becomes financially unattractive to work beyond the threshold age for the claim of benefits, but this effect is probably of lesser relevance because few people in this age group are able and willing to work a significant amount of time. Second, and more importantly, saving for retirement age in any form (including life insurance contracts) is discouraged because the

---

[14]   In Germany, this proposed system is known as the *Voll eigenständiges System* (Wagner 1988).

return is taxed away at a 100 percent rate as long as it does not exceed the minimum-pension level.

In addition, it is sometimes argued (e.g., by Schmähl [1993b:222]) that a guaranteed retirement income would reduce working incentives already in earlier phases of life because the provision for one's old age was one important motive for working. I do not discuss this point here because to the extent that it asserts more than just an income effect (which, on its own, is not Pareto-relevant), it has to do with the way in which the system is financed and this will be taken up in a moment.

b.   Incentives Related to the Financing Side

The problems related to the financing side can be discussed by looking at the following equation for the lifetime income, I, of a person who works ℓ hours at a gross hourly wage rate, w, and is subject to contributions ("taxes"), $T(\ell)$, and retirement benefits ("pensions"), $P(\ell)$ where r denotes the interest rate:

[1] $$I = w \cdot \ell - T(\ell) - \frac{1}{1+r} \cdot P(\ell).$$

Utility-maximizing choice of labor supply implies that the net income of an additional hour of work is equated to the individual's marginal rate of substitution between consumption and leisure (MRS), whereas profit-maximizing employers hire labor at a quantity where the gross wage, w, equals the marginal productivity of labor (MPL). Assuming that there are no other taxes, Pareto optimality requires the equality of MRS and MPL, and thus

[2] $$\frac{dI}{d\ell} = w - \frac{dT(\ell)}{d\ell} + \frac{1}{1+r} \cdot \frac{dP(\ell)}{d\ell} = w \quad \Leftrightarrow$$

[3] $$\frac{dT(\ell)}{d\ell} = \frac{1}{1+r} \cdot \frac{dP(\ell)}{d\ell}.$$

In a minimum-pension system of type B, retirement benefits, P, are a flat amount, independent of labor supply, ℓ, so the right-hand side of [3] vanishes. Furthermore, financing out of general taxes means that the left-hand side of [3] is strictly positive. Hence, such a system necessarily violates Pareto optimality.

In an ideal type C system, the contribution, T, is levied as a lump-sum amount as well, so that the left-hand side of [3] is zero, too, and Pareto optimality is restored. However, enforcement of a positive tax is virtually impossible with people with very low incomes. In the extreme case of welfare recipients, the tax would have to be financed through an additional transfer to the individual, so that a new distortion would result.

One alleged solution to this problem has been proposed by Engels et al. (1987): the lump-sum tax is collected only in periods in which the income exceeds a certain threshold, and the level of the retirement benefit is proportionally reduced for these periods. The disadvantage of this "solution" is that the retirement benefit is no longer flat but to some extent income-dependent, so that it begs the question of how to secure the minimum subsistence pension for the respective group of pensioners.

c.   An Alternative Financing Mode

Is there any escape at all from this impasse? Apparently there is no "first-best solution" to this problem, i.e., a system that combines the three features (a) flat benefits, (b) a nondistortionary tax, and (c) no problems in collecting the tax from every adult. Given that (a) is the defining criterion of every minimum-pension system and hence cannot be given up, the choice has to be made between (b) and (c). But instead of sacrificing one of these completely as in the systems discussed above, a second-best solution may very well consist in a compromise in which each feature is retained for part of the population.

More specifically, the system could be financed by an earmarked tax on all incomes with the following characteristics ("quasi-uniform contribution"):

— an exemption, E, at or near the amount of exemption of the general income tax,
— a proportional schedule up to some (low) income ceiling, F,
— a flat tax for all incomes above F,

formally:

$$[4] \qquad T(y) = \begin{cases} 0, & y \leq E \\ t \cdot (y - E), & E \leq y \leq F \\ t \cdot (F - E), & y > F. \end{cases}$$

Clearly, the exemption helps to circumvent the levying problems and the ceiling removes labor supply distortions for the income groups above this ceiling. But there remains a sizable distortion in the lower-middle income class. How important this distortion would be, of course, depends upon the parameters t, E, and F as well as upon the income distribution and the age limit for the collection of the minimum pension.

A very rough calculation made for West Germany in 1989 shows that for a minimum pension equal to the social-assistance level paid to every person over age 65 and an exemption of E = DM 15,000, a ceiling of F = DM 30,000 (F = DM 40,000) would require a tax rate of t = 0.4 (t = 0.269).[15] Although these tax rates may appear high, it has to be borne in mind that 82 (66) percent of the working-age population would fall either in the first or in the third segment of the schedule in (4) and thus would face a zero marginal tax rate.[16]

A judgment of the described labor supply distortions should not be made without considering and evaluating the alternatives. One of the main arguments against flat pensions and in favor of the existing system of income-related benefits is that a contribution which corresponds to a well-defined future benefit would meet less resistance and lead to less avoidance than a tax whose proceeds are used for purely redistributive purposes (Schmähl 1993b:317). This point of view is disputable because it is based on a very peculiar notion of individual rationality. For someone who is myopic and looks exclusively at present benefits and losses (perhaps because future payments are uncertain for political reasons), the contribution to a UPPS is *always* a tax, which is used to redistribute income to the aged. In contrast, with full rationality combined with the strong belief that the present pension system will remain valid for the next 50–60 years, the individual would have to take into account that his future benefits, discounted back to his working life, will fall short of his contributions, so that equation [3] is violated. The difference between these two terms thus has the same effect as a wage tax and distorts the labor supply decision.

In the same vein, the present system is defended with the argument that through the principle of equivalence between contributions and benefits, it would correspond to the general principles governing a free market economy (Schmähl 1993b:324). This argument is not very convincing either because, first of all, for the present and future working generations the principle of equivalence will not hold in absolute terms, but at most in relative terms within each generation. Secondly, the present system lacks a crucial feature of market processes, namely voluntary participation, and more generally it does not seem to be an advantage of a government program to lead to market-like results because if this were so, the question would arise whether government intervention was necessary to begin with.

---

15   For a more detailed presentation of the results, see Breyer (1996).

16   The Council of Advisors to the German Minister of Finance favors a gradual reduction of the ceiling for contributions to the present income-related UPPS, which would be a step towards the system described here. See Bundesministerium der Finanzen (1994:65).

5.   The Political Economy of Minimum Pensions

One of the main dangers to the existing income-related pension system lies in the willingness and ability of the next generation of workers to honor the obligations inherent in the "intergenerational contract" and to keep the level of retirement benefits stable even when this implies substantially rising contribution rates. The current debate on the reform of the German pension system demonstrates that a (proportional) reduction of the benefit level must be considered a real possibility. On the other hand, such a strategy would save future taxpayers less money than it appears at first because at the low end of the income scale, retirement benefits would become so small that recipients would have an additional claim to social assistance.

A minimum pension at the subsistence level, in contrast, seems to have the advantage that it asks from the following generation only something which the latter can't deny. There is one problem with this argument, though. In times of financial problems, the transfer to the older generation could be reduced by changing the *guaranteed* minimum pension to a *means-tested* one. Rational expectations would then imply that today's workers anticipate this switch, in which case the negative incentive effects on present savings reappear.

Again, the political stability of a pension system should not be judged on its own but in comparison with the relevant alternatives. In this respect, the existing income-related system in Germany is in general considered to be very stable because present workers' future benefits are protected by Article 14 of the Grundgesetz. However, as can be already inferred from previous decisions of the German Supreme Court, the real rate of return on contributions which is guaranteed this way can lie substantially below the corresponding long-term interest rate and even the judges at the Supreme Court can be expected to weigh rate-of-return considerations against problems of financing the benefits in times of a shrinking workforce.

Looking at the theoretical literature on the political economy of UPPS one finds a variety of aspects which contribute to the stability of such a system:[17]

— the belief that the system, if it is not abolished right away, will last for a long time (Browning 1975),
— a veto power of the older generation (Hansson and Stuart 1989), and
— the inherent income redistribution from the rich to the poor (Tabellini 1990).

The last two points demonstrate that, contrary to some authors' intuition, an openly redistributive system may get even more political support than one where

---

[17]   For a survey, see Breyer (1994).

relatively poor young taxpayers are asked to finance old-age pensions whose size is far in excess of the subsistence level and certainly in excess of their own claim to retirement benefits.

6. Minimum Pensions and Migration

Up to this point I have implicitly assumed a closed economy. However, we live in a community of countries which subscribes to the principle of free movement of people and commodities, and thus any set of minimum-pension schemes of the member countries has to address the issue of who provides for those who move from one country to another, and how much? There are two possible answers to this question and they are distinguished as to which of the following principles is guiding the system of benefits: (a) the principle of nationality, and (b) the principle of residence.

System *b* has the advantage that it corresponds closely to the justification of a mandatory pension system, viz., the altruism of the young generation, which is probably the stronger, the closer and the more visible the poor (and old) are to the rich (and young). Furthermore, it was argued above that the size of benefits should be tailored towards the minimum subsistence level, but this latter figure clearly varies from one place of residence to another.

The theoretical literature (see, e.g., Epple and Romer 1991) suggests, however, that under a pure residence principle an international coordination of the levels and the conditions for the collection of a minimum pension is indispensable. To see this point assume for a moment that one country (A) introduces such a system in isolation and grants the minimum pension without any preconditions. This would induce a massive migration of pensioners or older workers who in their native countries have either only small or exportable claims to retirement benefits. This could easily bankrupt country A's minimum-pension scheme. Not surprisingly, the Nordic countries as well as the Netherlands grant their minimum pensions only conditional on residence in the country for 40 or 50 years, respectively (Schulte 1993:38; Pieters 1993:153). This, however, begs the question how to treat those foreigners who do not meet this condition. As restrictions on mobility (e.g., a limitation of the right to stay) are not possible under EU law, coordination of benefit levels, combined with transfer payments between member states, seems to be called for.

To avoid such a coordination and make room for individual countries' distributional preferences, Sinn (1990) has made a proposal which corresponds to system *a*: in this, every person entering working age would choose a country of residence which would remain his basis of redistributional taxes and benefits, later changes of residence notwithstanding. Although such a system has the theoretical advantages described above, its practical difficulties would be enormous because, in moving, a person would not only take his claims with him but also his liabilities. Thus, its functioning would require international enforcement of tax payments, at least within a union such as the European Union.

7.   The Transition to a Minimum-Pension System

Even if it is acknowledged that the government should not force its citizens to be members in a UPPS that provides more than a uniform minimum pension for all, there still remains the question of what the effects of a transition from an income-related to a flat-benefit system are. Compared to the problems of transition from an unfunded to a funded pension system, which are dealt with in detail in other contributions to this conference, this particular switch has two specific features: first, since the unfunded system is not abolished altogether, the welfare losses (if there are any) to the transitional generations must be smaller, and, second, they might be unevenly distributed because the reduction of contributions and benefits for different income groups is not proportional.

According to proponents of the present UPPS (e.g., Ruland 1987:357), the transition to a flat-benefit system would have two adverse consequences: first, the expropriation of present pensioners of their claims to income-related benefits, and, second, a double burden on future taxpayers who have to finance the fulfillment of the old generation's claims and at the same time form savings for their own retirement consumption. Now, while it is obvious that both negative effects cannot be present at the same time because present pensioners either keep their claims or lose them, it must still be asked how the transitional burden can be distributed in an equitable way.

A criterion for intergenerational equity introduced by Schulenburg (1990: 210) looks at the highest net burden (social security taxes minus benefits) placed on any single generational cohort and proposes minimizing this maximum burden ("minmax criterion"). So, even if through a transition to flat benefits a burden is placed either on present pensioners or on present tax payers, the crucial question is whether the highest of these burdens exceeds the loss for one of the future generations if the current UPPS is retained.

The answer to this question, of course, depends upon the way in which the transition is performed and what particular type of minimum-pension system is introduced. The design of a transitional scenario is also restricted by the legal protection of existing claims to retirement benefits. Taking both considerations into account, the following scenario of a system of uniform benefits, as it is described in Section 4.a, seems to make sense, where time 0 denotes the starting point of the transition (e.g., January 1, 2000).

1. All persons who are already pensioners at time 0 receive income-related pensions for the rest of their lives as if there were no change in the existing UPPS.
2. All workers at 0 receive a weighted average of income-related and flat pensions, where the weight of the latter (α) equals the fraction of their working life still ahead at time 0.
3. All persons starting their working life at 0 or later only have a claim to the flat benefit.
4. For all persons in the second group, the basis on which their contributions are levied is a weighted average of their actual income and the (low) income ceiling in a mature flat-benefit system, where the weight of the latter is again α.
5. As soon as the last of these persons has left the labor force (i.e., at most, 50 years after point 0), the transition is finished and the flat-benefit system with quasi-uniform contributions is in full force.

Through the last two provisions it is assured that those generational cohorts which receive reduced benefits also pay reduced contributions.

In the Appendix, I present calculations for an idealized example which is not intended to give a "realistic" approximation to the true situation in Germany (or any other country, for that matter). Its sole purpose is to examine the general possibility of using the transition to flat benefits to distribute the demographical burden "more evenly" among present and future generations. The example abstracts from many real-world problems such as:

— taxpayers with incomes below the income ceiling,
— the cost of social-assistance payments to pensioners whose income-related pensions are below the poverty line,
— disability pensions and pensions for surviving dependents.

The calculations show that a transition to a uniform-benefit system can indeed improve the distribution of net burdens if the minmax criterion is applied to birth cohorts as groups. The maximum net burden in that case occurs several generations earlier but is smaller than under the existing UPPS. However, if it is applied to individuals and the burden is considered in relation to lifetime income, then it can be seen that in the lowest income group there is an increase in the maximum net burden by about 50 percent. In terms of different criteria of justice, it thus might be concluded that a gradual transition to uniform benefits improves intergenerational equity at the expense of intragenerational equity. The latter effect, however, may be judged less problematic because the adverse intragenerational effects can be corrected through the tax-transfer system, e.g., by lowering the tax rate in the lowest tax bracket and raising it in the upper brackets.

8.   Conclusions

In summarizing the results of the economic reasoning presented in this paper, the following conclusions can be drawn concerning the economics of minimum-pension systems.

First, given the present demographic circumstances, mandatory contributions to an unfunded public pension system can be justified by the usual welfare criteria if and only if they are used to finance subsistence level retirement benefits.

Second, there is an unavoidable trade-off between securing a minimum-pension level irrespective of past earnings and leaving labor supply decisions undistorted. If this conflict is resolved in favor of the former goal, it is nevertheless important to keep the labor supply distortions to a minimum.

Third, minimum-pension systems are subject to the discretion of future generations to honor their obligations, much the same as income-related systems are, but they have the advantage that the burden placed on future generations is smaller.

Fourth, the gradual transition to a minimum-pension system shifts part of the demographical burden created by the unfunded financing mode towards earlier generations but—contrary to a widespread conviction—it does *not* increase the maximum burden placed on any of the present or future generations. In order to have a beneficial effect on the intergenerational distribution, however, it is necessary that the transition is begun before the demographic change is fully completed.

Appendix: A Numerical Example of a Transition to Flat Benefits

The following calculations are based on a stylized reproduction of the German population in 1997:

— Every person works for 45 years and lives for 15 years as a pensioner.
— Each cohort of workers consists of three income groups of equal size. The yearly gross income levels are normalized to 1, 2, and 3 units of

money. (The lowest figure represents the income level at which the income-related pension just equals the social-assistance level, and the highest figure denotes the present income ceiling for contributions.) There is no growth in per capita incomes over time.

— Up to time 0, all cohorts of workers and pensioners are of equal size. From period 1 onwards, cohorts entering the labor force shrink by 1 percent per year.

— In the income-related system, the retirement benefit is 60 percent of previous yearly wage income. In the flat-benefit system, it is 0.6 units of money for every pensioner.

— If a flat-benefit system is introduced, the transition starts either in year 0 or in year 5 and is performed according to the rules 1 through 5 explained in Section 7.

— In the calculation of net burdens (lifetime contributions minus lifetime benefits), the interest rate is assumed to be zero.

The results of the calculations are presented in Figures 1 and 2. Figure 1 (upper panel) shows the time path of the contribution rate if the present system remains valid forever. In this case, the contribution rate rises from 20 percent in period 0 to 26.83 in the new steady state which is reached in period 60. Figure 1 (lower panel) shows the sequence of net burdens on the generation entering the labor force in the respective period. The net burden is positive for all generations, t, with $t \geq -43$ because they are still working when the first smaller generation enters the labor force. Of the total burden on each cohort, one-half is borne by the highest, one-third by the middle, and one-sixth by the lowest income group. The maximum per capita burden is reached for cohorts entering the labor force in the new steady state (period 59 onwards), and its size is 6.15 units of money or a little over 9 yearly average gross incomes. The maximum burdens on each member of the respective income groups are 3.08, 6.15, and 9.23, respectively.

Figure 2 (upper panel) shows the sequence of net burdens for the case in which the transition to flat benefits is started in period 0. It shows that the maximum per capita net burden is now 6.05 and it falls on the cohort appearing in $t = -13$. Thus, if the minmax criterion is applied to birth cohorts as a whole, this type of transition is just preferable to the continuation of the income-related system. If, instead, one looks at members of each income group separately, it can be seen from this figure that in the lowest income group the maximum net burden is now increased to 4.67, on cohort +5, which compares to 3.08 in the existing UPPS.

Figure 2 (middle panel) gives the same results for the case in which the new contribution formula is already applied 5 years in advance of the reduction of benefit levels. This measure helps to shift part of the burden to earlier cohorts and reduces the maximum per capita burden to 5.70 units of money, which now falls on cohort –15. Shifting the start of the new contribution formula still further backwards to period –10 (not shown) would reduce the maximum burden further to 5.35, on cohort –17.

Figure 1 —   Existing Income-Related Pension System

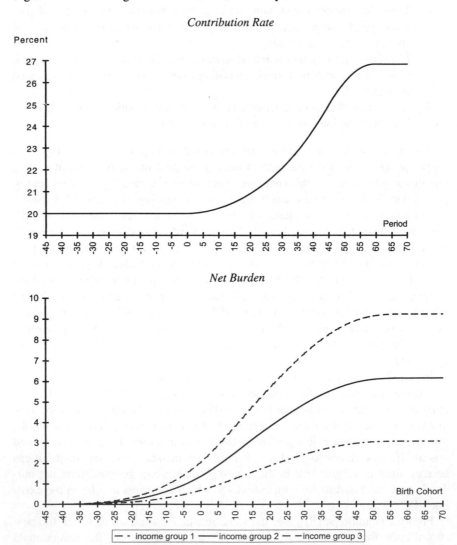

Figure 2 —   Switch to Flat Benefits

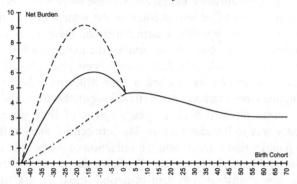

Switch to Flat Benefits in Period 0

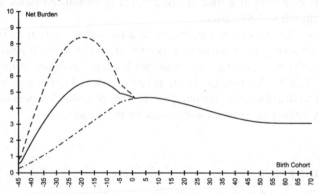

Switch to Flat Benefits in Period 0 and to New Contribution Scheme in Period –5

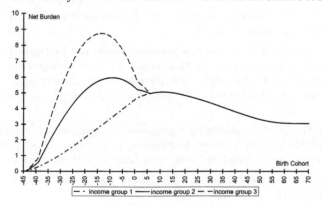

Switch to Flat Benefits in Period 5 and to New Contribution Scheme in Period 0

The calculations presented so far show that a transition to a uniform-benefit system distributes the burden imposed by the pay-as-you-go financing system more evenly among generational cohorts, and this the more so the earlier the reduced pension benefits are taken into account in the system of levying the contributions of workers. One possible interpretation of these findings is that a transition to uniform benefits could have reduced the maximum loss due to participation in the UPPS considerably had it only been planned sufficiently far ahead. Now that we have already reached the point in time where smaller cohorts are entering the labor market, a theoretical insight of what could have been achieved by a reform initiated 5 or 10 years ago is of little practical value. Therefore the only way to introduce a time lag between the start of the application of the new contribution formula and the reduction of the benefit claims is to postpone the latter. Figure 2 (lower panel) shows the result for the scenario which starts the new contribution system in period 0 and the transition on the benefit side in period 5. Again, it can be seen that the maximum net burden falls to 5.97 units of money if a time lag of 5 years is introduced (with a lag of 10 years it would fall to 5.88 units).

This shows that the earlier a transition to a flat-benefit system is started and, moreover, the sooner the contribution system takes the reduced pension claims into account, the smaller is the maximum net burden. Therefore, it might be justified to say that if a flat-benefit system is not introduced in the very near future, its potential to distribute the demographic burden of unfunded pension schemes more evenly among generations will evaporate more and more.

Bibliography

Börsch-Supan, A., and K. Stahl (1991). Life-Cycle Savings and Consumption Constraints. *Journal of Population Economics* 4:233–255.

Breyer, F. (1994). The Political Economy of Intergenerational Transfers. *European Journal of Political Economy* 10:61–84.

Breyer, F. (1996). Zur Kombination von Kapitaldeckungs- und Umlageverfahren in der deutschen Rentenversicherung. In Gesellschaft für Versicherungswissenschaft und -gestaltung, e.V. (ed.), *Die Alterssicherungssysteme vor der demographischen Herausforderung—Das Säulenmodell der Weltbank als Lösungsansatz.* Bonn: Irmgard Vollmer.

—— (1997a). On the Pareto-Improving Abolition of Unfunded Public Pension Systems: An Application of Growth Theory. Forthcoming in K. Jaeger and K.-J. Koch (eds.), *Trade, Growth, and Economic Policy in Open Economies.* Berlin: Springer.

—— (1997b). Sind äquivalente Renten "fair"? In R. Hauser (ed.), *Reform des Sozialstaats I.* Berlin: Duncker & Humblot.

Breyer, F., and D.E. Wildasin (1993). Steady-State Welfare Effects of Social Security in a Large Open Economy. In B. Felderer (ed.), *Public Pension Economics*. Supplementum 7 of the Journal of Economics. Vienna: Springer.

Browning, E.K. (1975). Why the Social Insurance Budget is Too Large in a Democracy. *Economic Inquiry* 13:373–388.

Bundesministerium der Finanzen (ed.) (1994). *Perspektiven staatlicher Ausgabenpolitik.* Gutachten erstattet vom Wissenschaftlichen Beirat beim BMF. Bonn.

Eckstein, Z., M. Eichenbaum, and D. Peled (1985). Uncertain Lifetimes and the Welfare Enhancing Properties of Annuity Markets and Social Security. *Journal of Public Economics* 26:303–326.

Engels, W., et al. (Kronberger Kreis) (1987). *Reform der Alterssicherung*. Frankfurt/Main.

Epple, D., and T. Romer (1991). Mobility and Redistribution. *Journal of Political Economy* 99:828–858.

Die Grünen (1985). Antrag des Abgeordneten Bueb und der Fraktion DIE GRÜNEN, *Grundrente statt Altersarmut*. Bundestags-Drucksache 10/3496.

Hansson, I., and C. Stuart (1989). Social Security as a Trade among Living Generations. *American Economic Review* 79:1182–1195.

Hauser, R. (1993). Mindestsicherung im Alter—ausgewählte ökonomische Aspekte unter Berücksichtigung von Wanderungen. In W. Schmähl (ed.), *Mindestsicherung im Alter. Erfahrungen, Herausforderungen, Strategien*. Frankfurt/Main: Campus.

Homburg, S. (1997). Old-Age Pension Systems: A Theoretical Evaluation. In H. Giersch (ed.), *Reforming the Welfare State*. Berlin: Springer.

Homburg, S., and W.F. Richter (1993). Harmonizing Public Debt and Public Pension Schemes in the European Community. In B. Felderer (ed.), *Public Pension Economics*. Supplementum 7 of the Journal of Economics. Vienna: Springer.

Merton, R. (1983). On the Role of Social Security as a Means for Efficient Risk Sharing in an Economy where Human Capital is Not Tradable. In Z. Bodie and J. Shoven (eds.), *Financial Aspects of the United States Pension System*. Chicago: University of Chicago Press.

Miegel, M., and S. Wahl (1985). *Gesetzliche Grundsicherung. Private Vorsorge—der Weg aus der Rentenkrise*. Stuttgart: Verlag Bonn Aktuell.

Nozick, R. (1974). *Anarchy, State, and Utopia*. New York: Basic Books.

Persson, T. (1985). Deficits and Intergenerational Welfare in Open Economies. *Journal of International Economics* 19:67–84.

Pieters, D. (1993). Regelungen zur Mindestsicherung im Alter in den Niederlanden und in Belgien. In W. Schmähl (ed.), *Mindestsicherung im Alter. Erfahrungen, Herausforderungen, Strategien*. Frankfurt/Main: Campus.

PROGNOS (1995). *Perspektiven der gesetzlichen Rentenversicherung für Gesamtdeutschland vor dem Hintergrund veränderter politischer und ökonomischer Rahmenbedingungen.* DRV-Schriften, Band 4.

Ruland, F. (1987). Sozial- und rechtspolitische Bedenken gegen eine Grundrente. *Zeitschrift für Rechtspolitik* 20:354–359.

Samuelson, P.A. (1975). Optimum Social Security in a Life-Cycle Growth Model. *International Economic Review* 16:539–544.

Schmähl, W. (1988). Übergang zu Staatsbürger-Grundrenten: Ein Beitrag zur Deregulierung in der Alterssicherung? In T. Thiemeyer (ed.), *Regulierung und Deregulierung im Bereich der Sozialpolitik.* Berlin: Duncker & Humblot.

—— (ed.) (1993a). *Mindestsicherung im Alter. Erfahrungen, Herausforderungen, Strategien.* Frankfurt/Main: Campus.

—— (1993b). Alternative Strategien für die Mindestsicherung im Alter in Deutschland. In W. Schmähl (ed.), *Mindestsicherung im Alter. Erfahrungen, Herausforderungen, Strategien.* Frankfurt/Main: Campus.

Schulenburg, J.-M. Graf von (1990). Von der Marktwirtschaft zur "sozialen" Marktwirtschaft —eine Operationalisierung des Begriffs "sozial." In W. Fischer (ed.), *Währungsreform und Soziale Marktwirtschaft. Erfahrungen und Perspektiven nach 40 Jahren.* Berlin: Duncker & Humblot.

Schulte, B. (1993). Praktizierte Formen der Mindestsicherung im Alter—ein rechtsvergleichender Überblick. In W. Schmähl (ed.), *Mindestsicherung im Alter. Erfahrungen, Herausforderungen, Strategien.* Frankfurt/Main: Campus.

Sinn, H.-W. (1990). Tax Harmonization and Tax Competition in Europe. *European Economic Review* 34:489–504.

Spremann, K. (1984). Intergenerational Contracts and their Decomposition. *Journal of Economics* 44:237–253.

Tabellini, G. (1990). A Positive Theory of Social Security. NBER Working Paper 3272. Cambridge, Mass.

Vaubel, R. (1983). Reforming Social Security for Old Age. In H. Giersch (ed.), *Reassessing the Role of Government in the Mixed Economy.* Tübingen: Mohr Siebeck.

—— (1996). Reforming the Welfare State in Western Europe. In H. Giersch (ed.), *Fighting Europe's Unemployment in the 1990's.* Berlin: Springer.

Wagner, G. (1988). Bedarfs- oder beitragsorientierte Grundsicherung in der Rentenversicherung?—Ein politiknaher Vorschlag: Voll eigenständige Sicherung. In F. Klanberg and A. Prinz (eds.), *Perspektiven sozialer Mindestsicherung.* Berlin: Duncker & Humblot.

World Bank (1994). *Averting the Old Age Crisis. Policies to Protect the Old and Promote Growth, Summary.* World Bank: Washington, D.C.

Comment on Friedrich Breyer

Roland Vaubel

The organizers of this conference should be congratulated for commissioning a paper on this subject. They have discovered a gap in the literature, and Friedrich Breyer's way of addressing the subject is both original and to the point.

The most obvious flaw in his argument is that his proposal for financing social security does not follow from his argument. He rightly points out that, in the case of a lump-sum benefit and contribution, some individuals would probably be unable to pay the contribution. He writes: "In the extreme case of welfare recipients, the tax would have to be financed through an additional transfer to the individual, so that *a new distortion* would result" (pp. 281–282, emphasis mine). Since the contribution or tax cannot be collected from every adult, he suggests that the whole pension system ought to be financed by a proportional payroll tax (with an exemption and a ceiling on the amount of tax). This is a non sequitur. What is needed is merely a tax to finance the contributions for those who cannot pay them out of their own income. Since these transfers are a substitute for welfare payments later, they do not constitute "a new distortion" either. The distortion is not due to the minimum pension system but to the separate and prior decision to guarantee a certain standard of living to those who are unable to provide it for themselves.

Second, Breyer believes that the transition from the pay-as-you-go system to a funded system cannot be Pareto-improving, and he claims that, consequently, "an intergenerational conflict seems inevitable" (p. 276). This is not correct. Breyer ignores that the transition to an actuarially fair funded system can yield considerable efficiency gains because it would permit free choice and competition (at least potential competition) between providers of insurance. The pay-as-you-go system, by contrast, cannot survive except as a state insurance monopoly (or some equivalent).[1] If, in the funded system, the burden of financing the existing unfunded liabilities which have accumulated under the pay-as-you-go system were distributed over the current and all future generations in the same way in

---

[1]   The transition to an actuarially fair insurance system would also remove some other distortions (notably of labor supply decisions), but these could also be removed in the unfunded system.

which it would have been distributed under the pay-as-you-go system, the transition would be Pareto-improving.

To avoid intergenerational conflict, the burden of financing the accumulated liabilities of the old unfunded system ought to be spread over all future generations. Indeed, this is important regardless of whether a fully funded system or a mere reduction and equalization of unfunded pensions is the aim. The obvious solution is Buchanan's proposal (1968) of transforming the old liabilities into consols ("recognition bonds") or other nonrepayable debt of an infinite maturity which would have to be serviced by all future generations.[2] Breyer, by contrast, wants to impose the burden of financing the old liabilities on one or two generations. Politically, this is simply a nonstarter. To paraphrase Abraham Lincoln: you can fool all people some of the time, and you can fool some people all of the time, but you cannot fool a majority of the people for one or two generations.

There are two standard objections to Buchanan's proposal, one economic and one political. The economic objection is that there would be a dramatic increase in public debt with all its adverse consequences. This objection is mistaken. The debt is already there (the unfunded liabilities of the public pension system), it would merely be rendered explicit and transferable. The political objection is that the proposal is too radical because it would suddenly stop the old system to which people are used. That need not be so. The transition could proceed through voluntary contracting-out. Those who preferred to stay with the public insurance could do so. The bonds would only be issued to pensioners who retire under the old system and to those members of the working generation who wished to switch from the public to a private insurance. This latter could be asked to write off part of their claims because the book value exceeds the expected value and because they would exchange a very risky for a safer asset. To permit contracting-out is politically attractive. The British example shows that it is feasible (see Disney and Johnson in this volume).

Third, if the burden of financing the old unfunded liabilities is spread over all future generations, the result is more likely to be consistent with existing notions of intergenerational equity. Historically, the pay-as-you-go system has benefited two or three generations who happened to live at a relatively unfortunate time. It has benefited the first generations who lived under the system: the workers who retired after 1891 and all those who retired while the system was expanding. These are at the same time the generations who—as workers—had suffered from the early stages of the industrial revolution or who lived through World War I, the Great Depression, and World War II and its aftermath. To compensate these unfortunate generations, Adenauer finally adopted the pay-as-you-go system in 1957. We now live in more comfortable circumstances. There is no distribu-

---

2   For a more detailed discussion, see Vaubel (1983).

tional reason to prolong the pay-as-you-go episode. It is time to pick up the bill and to make sure that everybody pays a fair share. Breyer wants to minimize the maximum net burden during the next two generations. Why not minimize it over all future generations?

Fourth, Breyer compares net burdens in terms of income, not in terms of utility. In his calculations, this does not affect the preferred solution because he assumes that there is no growth. But that is probably not a relevant scenario. Later generations are likely to enjoy higher incomes. They can shoulder larger burdens in terms of income.

My fifth comment concerns the section on "Minimum Pensions and Migration." Breyer writes: "As restrictions on mobility (e.g., a limitation of the right to stay) are not possible under EU law, coordination of benefit levels, combined with transfer payments between member states, seems to be called for" (p. 285). The premise is not correct, and I doubt the conclusion. As for the premise, the member states may and do in fact exclude those citizens of other member states who would have to rely on welfare payments of the host country. As for the conclusion, coordination of insurance benefit levels and transfer payments between the member states do not seem to be called for in the Europe of today and for the foreseeable future because international migration in response to differences between the rates of return of the national pay-as-you-go systems seems to be virtually nonexistent. If such migration ever became a problem, it would be another reason for moving to an actuarially fair funded system where each citizen of the Union would have the right to obtain his mandatory minimum pension from any of the national insurances or from private insurance companies.

Finally, I should like to question Breyer's list of market failures (pp. 274–275). The strategic (ab)use of unfunded social security by governments (e) and—as he admits in footnote 7—the problems generated by inflation (d) are not market failures but government failures. I also do not agree (Vaubel 1990) that Samuelson's case for pay-as-you-go systems "would have been judged quite favorably forty years ago" (p. 276). If the time horizon were infinite (which is highly unlikely), Samuelson's argument might have justified public debt but it never justified an unfunded public pension system. This is because, once more, an unfunded system is inconsistent with (at least potential) insurance competition whereas public debt is not.

In conclusion, I thoroughly agree with the direction in which Breyer is moving but the solution he has arrived at is still far from "second best."

Bibliography

Buchanan, J.M. (1968). Social Insurance in a Growing Economy: A Proposal for Radical Reform. *National Tax Journal* 21:386–395.

Disney, R., and P. Johnson (1998). The United Kingdom: A Working System of Minimum Pensions? In this volume.

Vaubel, R. (1983). Reforming Social Security for Old Age. In H. Giersch (ed.), *Reassessing the Role of Government in the Mixed Economy*. Tübingen: J.C.B. Mohr.

—— (1990). *Sozialpolitik für mündige Bürger: Optionen für eine Reform*. Baden-Baden: Nomos.

Martin Feldstein

Transition to a Fully Funded Pension System: Five Economic Issues

Reforming the current pay-as-you-go pension systems is the most important fiscal issue facing governments around the world. The current systems involve high and rising marginal tax rates that reduce real incomes and distort economic incentives. A failure to make significant reforms can lead to a withering of political support for existing programs and therefore a decline in the incomes of retirees. Appropriate reforms can raise real incomes of all employees, protect the incomes of retirees, and enhance overall economic performance.

The current paper discusses the process of replacing the existing pay-as-you-go (PAYGO) pension programs like the U.S. Social Security program of Old Age and Survivors Insurance with a prefunded system based on mandatory individual accounts.[1] My emphasis is not on the details of any particular plan but rather on how a prefunded plan can deal with five important practical issues:

(1) How expensive would the transition be? That is, to what extent do the employees during the transition years have to "pay twice," paying for their own retirement and for the benefits of existing retirees?

(2) How would replacing a PAYGO system with a prefunded system that delivers the same level of benefits affect national saving and capital accumulation?

(3) What rate of return does the nation earn on this additional capital?

(4) How can individuals deal with the risks inherent in a funded system of individual accounts?

(5) What are the distributional effects of replacing a PAYGO system with a prefunded system?

Before looking at these five issues, I will discuss three more basic questions: How would replacing a PAYGO system with a prefunded system affect economic welfare? What are the reasons for preferring a mandatory system to a

---

[1] This paper draws on research with Andrew Samwick that has been reported in Feldstein and Samwick (1996, 1997). That research is part of a larger project on Social Security at the National Bureau of Economic Research.

purely voluntary arrangement and a system based on individual accounts to national investment fund?

1. Why Prefund Old-Age Pensions?

Many popular discussions of replacing the U.S. Social Security system with a system of prefunded benefits have based their case on the idea that the existing system is "bankrupt" and "unsustainable." Neither of these is true and the real reason to prefund lies elsewhere.

Consider the notion that Social Security is bankrupt because the trust fund will be empty by the year 2030. While that would constitute bankruptcy for a private pension, it is not relevant for a government program. Since there are no trust funds for defense spending or education, there is no discussion about the "bankruptcy" of those programs. The ability of the Social Security program to continue to pay benefits depends on political support rather than trust fund balances.

The argument that the current system is unsustainable is partly correct: either benefits must be reduced or taxes raised. It is however possible to sustain the level of future benefits specified in current law by raising taxes. In the United States, the payroll tax devoted to old-age pensions would have to rise from the current 12.4 percent[2] to about 16 percent after the year 2030 if the existing benefit rules are to be maintained and eventually to about 19 percent, an amount equivalent to raising the payroll tax from 5 percent of GDP to 7 percent of GDP.[3] Such a tax increase would be feasible even though it would obviously cause a significant rise in the distortions caused by the existing tax system.

The real reason for shifting from a PAYGO system to a prefunded program is that doing so would raise the economic welfare of the population. The key to this is the fact that the rate of return in a funded system is very much higher than the implicit rate of return that is produced by a PAYGO system. That in turn implies that the funded system can provide any given level of benefits at a much lower cost to working-age people than a PAYGO system can.

Although a PAYGO system does not earn a rate of return on invested funds, the increase of the tax base that results from a growing labor force and increasing average wages implies that retirees in a PAYGO system can get back more in benefits than they paid in taxes during their working years. Looking ahead,

---

2   This includes disability and survivor benefits but excludes health care.

3   The tax rate increase required to maintain existing benefit rules would be substantially greater in Germany and would come on top of existing total taxes that are already a substantially higher share of GDP.

this implicit real rate of return on PAYGO contributions is likely to be 2 percent or less (reflecting labor force growth of about 1 percent and growth in real wages per worker of an additional 1 percent). In contrast, additions to the stock of private capital earns a real rate of return of about 9 percent.[4]

To see the impact of this on the cost of providing a given level of retirement benefits, consider a simple example in which individuals work from age 25 to 65 and retire from age 65 until death at age 85. To make the calculation transparent (albeit an approximation), represent the working years by the midpoint at age 45 and the retirement years by age 75. Thus the individual saves in a prefunded system at age 45 and dissaves 30 years later at age 75. With a 9 percent rate of return, each dollar saved at age 45 grows to $(1.09)^{30} = 13$ dollars at age 75. In contrast, each dollar contributed to a PAYGO system with an implicit 2 percent rate of return grows to $(1.02)^{30} = 1.8$ dollars at age 75. Thus it takes 7 times as many dollars paid at age 45 in a PAYGO system to buy the same benefits at age 75. This calculation implies that the long-run Social Security payroll tax rate of 19 percent could therefore be replaced by a prefunded system with a contribution rate of 2.7 percent.[5]

The lower contribution rate to fund the same benefits has two advantages. First, replacing a 19 percent tax with a 3 percent mandatory contribution reduces the distortions to labor market decisions about labor force participation, the number of hours worked, effort, choice of occupation, and the form of compensation. Second, even if there were no labor force response to lower tax rates, the lower contribution rate would mean more disposable income and therefore a higher level of consumption.

Of course, this comparison refers only to the long-run values associated with the PAYGO and prefunded systems. In the near term, the shift to a prefunded system requires taxes to finance the benefits of existing retirees as well as savings for the self-funded retirement of transition generation employees. The shift to a prefunded system therefore only raises overall economic welfare if the future gains exceed in present value (taking into account the declining marginal utility of consumption as incomes rise) the extra payments made by the transition generations. It can be shown that this is true and the present value of economic welfare is increased if three conditions are satisfied:

---

[4]   See Rippe (1995) and Poterba and Samwick (1996). I return below to some caveats about this rate of return.

[5]   A detailed disaggregated calculation based on demographic projections of the U.S. Bureau of the Census and the actuarial assumptions of the Social Security Administration implies that the 19 percent PAYGO payroll tax could be replaced in the long run by a contribution of only 2 percent to a funded system that provides the same level of benefits. The primary reason for the difference is that the Social Security actuaries project a PAYGO rate of return that is even less than 2 percent.

(1) the marginal product of capital exceeds the rate of growth of the wage base;

(2) the rate at which future consumption is discounted (the social time preference discount rate) exceeds the rate of growth of the wage base;

(3) the economy is growing.

For a discussion of why there are necessary conditions, see Feldstein (1995, 1996a).[6] The first of these conditions has already been discussed and the third condition is obviously true. The reason for the second condition and the explanation of why it is satisfied is presented in Feldstein (1995, 1996b) and will not be discussed here.

In short, substituting a prefunded system for a PAYGO system raises the present value of economic welfare under conditions that are very likely to prevail in modern industrial countries.[7]

2. Why Make Participation Mandatory?

It would in principle be possible simply to abolish the existing system, compensate employees for the present actuarial value of either the taxes that they have already paid or the benefits that they can expect under current law (net of the future taxes that they would pay), and allow them to make whatever arrangements they want to finance their own retirement consumption. As a practical matter, however, there are two objections to this approach.

First, some individuals are too short-sighted to provide for their own retirement. A society that made no provision for helping those who had no resources when they were too old to work would leave them to private charity and a standard of living that many in society would regard as unacceptably low. *Second*, the alternative of a means tested program for the aged might encourage some lower-income individuals to make no provision for their old age deliberately,

---

[6] A revised version of Feldstein (1995) appears as an appendix to my introductory chapter in Feldstein (1996b).

[7] Note that the rise in the present value measure of economic welfare does not imply that the shift from PAYGO to prefunded would be a Pareto improvement that makes all generations better off. Although Feldstein and Samwick (1997) shows how a transition can be designed that does indeed make all generations better off. An examination of Kotlikoff's (1996) Pareto-improving transitions shows that they also are a combination of fiscal reforms (which generate the Pareto improvements) and PAYGO replacement. But a Pareto improvement is too demanding a standard for policy analysis. The case for the transition is that the gains to the gainers are larger in present value (taking into account the decline in marginal utility of consumption) than the losses to the losers.

knowing that they would receive the means tested amount. For individuals with low enough income, that combination might provide higher lifetime utility than saving during their working years. A mandatory system of individual saving would prevent poverty in old age while avoiding the temptation to "game" the system in that way.

The options that I have studied therefore always assume that individuals would be required to save some fraction of their wage and salary income up to some limit.

3.   Why Individual Accounts?

A common feature of "privatized" pension systems is that they permit individuals to contribute their mandatory saving to individual accounts that can be invested in private financial assets, accounts that I have called Personal Retirement Accounts (PRAs). Some advocates of mandatory saving have proposed an alternative of requiring the funds to be held and invested by the government. Although none of the benefits of the higher rate of return would be lost by this alternative type of investment, there are other disadvantages that strengthen the case for the private individual PRA accounts.

Private accounts would reduce the political risk that the government would want to direct the investment funds or to preclude certain kinds of investments (e.g., in certain products like cigarettes or in certain countries with which the United States is currently having disagreements). If the government controlled the accounts, there would be less prospect of innovative products—e.g., minimum guaranteed rates of return, mixtures of defined benefits and defined contribution payouts, etc. Government controlled accounts could also easily be shifted into a defined benefit system, giving politicians the opportunity to redistribute funds toward favored groups just as the current U.S. Social Security system redistributes from the young workers to older workers, from two-earner households to single-earner households, etc.

Although this administrative arrangement is very important, I will not discuss it further in this paper. I turn instead to the first of the five issues listed above.

4.   The Nature of the Transition

Although many proposals for pension reform assume a combination of a universal PAYGO pension and a mandatory prefunded "private" pension, for simplicity and clarity I have analyzed a pure prefunded system without a PAYGO portion. More specifically, I assume that in the long run the existing PAYGO system would be completely replaced by a fully funded one based on individual Personal Retirement Accounts (PRAs). The combination of PAYGO benefits and funded annuities during the transition and the level of the funded annuities after the transition is complete would be set to equal the level of future benefits specified in the current Social Security law.

There are many possible transitions to such a system but there are only two basic alternatives: immediate transition with "recognition bonds" and a gradual substitution from PAYGO to a prefunded system.

The method of recognition bonds that was pursued by Chile substitutes new government bonds for the existing implicit claims of retirees and current employees. Individuals receive these recognition bonds, the Social Security system is eliminated, and employees are required to save in special mandatory saving accounts. Individuals may be required to use these recognition bonds as assets of the mandatory saving accounts or may be allowed to sell them and place the proceeds in the new mandatory accounts. The government could service the recognition bonds or pay them off over some horizon and could do so with different possible taxes. This is essentially the approach studied by Kotlikoff (1996) who studies different tax possibilities but does not explicitly require a mandatory saving account since he assumes that individuals are rational life-cycle savers who make appropriate provision for their old age once the existing PAYGO system is eliminated.

Andrew Samwick and I have calculated the value of the recognition bonds that would be given to these individuals in the United States based on obligations at the end of 1995 (Feldstein and Samwick 1997). If future benefits (net of the taxes that remain to be paid before retirement)are discounted at a real discount rate of 4 percent, the value of the newly created debt would be $7 trillion, about equal to GDP and twice the size of the existing national debt as conventionally measured. If the future obligations were discounted at a real rate of 2 percent (about equal to the historic real yield on U.S. government debt), the present value of the claims would be equivalent to a debt of $12 trillion.

Recognition bonds may be an appealing method of transition in countries where the existing system of PAYGO pensions is seen as a failure. In the United States, however, Social Security pensions are a very popular program. We therefore analyze a gradual transition that keeps the existing structure of the Social Security pensions. Indeed, the transition studied in Feldstein and Samwick (1997) can be thought of as a plan in which the government guarantees the Social Security retirement benefits that are projected under current law but uses a transition to a fully funded system to pay for these benefits.

More specifically, existing retirees would receive benefits that are funded exclusively on a PAYGO basis using the existing payroll tax. During a long transition period, future retirees would receive a mixture of PAYGO benefits and benefits based on the assets accumulated in individual mandatory PRA accounts. In the long run, the PAYGO system would be completely replaced by a fully funded system of individual PRAs.

The key problem of any transition is that the employees during the transition period must pay the PAYGO taxes to support the existing retirees and at the same time accumulate assets for their own retirement. This creates the false impression that existing employees would pay twice as much during the transition years as they would have paid if the PAYGO system were continued unchanged. That is false for two reasons. First, the amount that individuals have to save for their own retirement is far less than the amount that they must pay for the PAYGO taxes that support existing retirees. As the illustrative calculation earlier in this paper indicated, a PAYGO system that requires an 18 percent payroll tax could be replaced in the long run by individual savings equal to less than 3 percent of the same payroll tax base. Thus in the transition the maximum amount that individuals would be require to save in addition to their contribution to the PAYGO system would be that 3 percent. Second, over time the cost of the PAYGO system declines as the initial retirees die and the new retirees substitute an annuity financed by the mandatory accumulated assets for PAYGO benefits.

Feldstein and Samwick (1997) present a transition that begins with a 2.0 percent mandatory saving in addition to the existing 12.4 percent PAYGO tax, a combined mandatory payment of 14.4 percent of the payroll tax base.[8,9] As the initial retirees die and are replaced with individuals who receive annuities based on the mandatory savings in their PRAs, this 14.4 percent declines (in spite of the increasing ratio of retirees to working age population). The combined mandatory payment declines from 14.4 percent in the first year of the transition to 13.8 percent by the 10th year of the transition and to 13.2 percent by the 15th year of the transition. In the 19th year the combined mandatory payment is less than the 12.4 percent that would be required under the existing PAYGO system.[10] The combined mandatory payment then declines rapidly from 10.7 per-

---

8   This simulation, based on the actuarial assumptions of the U.S. Social Security actuaries and the demographic projections of the U.S. Bureau of Census, is designed to maintain the relation of retirement benefits to preretirement income the same as that is given in current Social Security law. The 12.4 percent is the current employer-employee payroll tax for the Old Age, Survivors and Disability programs; it excludes the tax to support the Medicare portion of the Social Security program.

9   Since the payroll tax base is about 40 percent of GDP, this is equivalent to a bit less than 6 percent of GDP.

10   This assumes that nothing would be done under the existing PAYGO system to enhance the trust fund and postpone the date at which the funds are exhausted and the tax rate must jump to the new higher equilibrium, currently projected at about 18 percent in the year 2030.

cent of payroll in the 25th year to 6.9 percent in the 35th year and eventually to 2.02 percent of payroll.

5.   The Effect on National Saving and Capital Accumulation

The ability to reduce the PAYGO taxes and still provide the same retirement benefits reflects the fact that the mandatory savings increase the nation's capital stock and that the rate of return on that capital is much higher than the rate of return implicit in the PAYGO program. This section discusses the nature of the increased capital accumulation while the next section discusses the rate of return that can be earned on that incremental capital.

The transition analyzed in Feldstein and Samwick (1997) keeps the government's budget deficit unchanged. That is, the PAYGO benefits are financed out of current payroll taxes. Similarly, all of the taxes that result from the incremental mandatory saving are contributed to the mandatory PRA saving accounts. Thus, there is no increase or decrease in the national debt relative to the baseline that would prevail with the unchanged PAYGO system.

If the shift to the prefunded system of Private Retirement Accounts does not alter other private saving, the increase in national saving is equal to the net flow into the PRAs. In addition, the return on the investment in the PRAs would also be an addition to national saving. How large would that increase in national saving be?

The PRA contributions start at 2 percent of payroll, the difference between the 12.4 percent existing payroll tax and the 14.4 percent combined payment referred to earlier. In the Feldstein–Samwick (1997) analysis, that mandatory saving rate remains between about 1.5 percent and 2.0 percent of the covered payroll throughout the 75-year simulation period. That mandatory saving represents the gross inflow to the PRA accounts. After the first year the net inflow is smaller because retirees are receiving annuity payments from these accounts. Indeed by the 25th year the annuity payments are more than twice as large as the 1.5 percent payroll tax inflow, implying a net outflow of 1.7 percent of payroll. But the return being earned on the accumulated balances from earlier net contributions causes the total assets of the PRAs to grow. That asset growth represents net national saving and therefore a net increase in the nation's capital stock. The accumulated balances in the PRA accounts increase from 2 percent of covered payroll in the first year of the transition to 25 percent of payroll after 10 years and 82 percent of payroll after 25 years. In the long run, the PRA balance stabilizes at about 2.3 times covered payroll, an amount equal to about the future level of GDP. Stated differently, the PRA balances increase the nation's capital stock by about 6 percent after 15 years, 18 percent after 35 years, and 34 percent in the long run.

What if other private saving responds to the shift from the PAYGO system to the prefunded system? Any such induced change in other private saving would change the net impact on national saving and the capital stock.

To consider the likely change in other private saving, note first that the shift to a mandatory prefunded system does not alter the benefits that individuals would receive in retirement. The transition has been calibrated to keep the combination of PAYGO benefits and PRA benefits equal to the PAYGO benefits specified under current law. The shift to the prefunded PRA system therefore does not induce individuals to reduce private saving because of an expected increase in retirement income. The primary reason for the change in other saving is the effect of the transition on the level of disposable income during preretirement years.

Consider first how private saving would be expected to respond in the long run when the prefunded system has fully replaced the PAYGO system. While the retirement benefits from the PRAs would be the same as the PAYGO benefits would have been, the mandatory contributions to the PRAs during the working years would be far less than the PAYGO taxes would have been. This implies that the disposable income of individuals in their preretirement years would increase while the disposable income during retirement would remain the same. Instead of increasing consumption only during the preretirement years, individuals would spread the higher disposable income during their working years between higher consumption at that time and in retirement, i.e., they would save some of it. The response of private voluntary saving would therefore increase the national saving rate and the resulting rise in the capital stock in addition to the increase that comes directly from the balances of the PRA accounts.

During the early part of the transition, the extra mandatory saving (i.e., the combination of the PRA contributions and the PAYGO tax) would exceed the baseline PAYGO tax, causing a decline in disposable income. In the first year, for example, individuals would experience a decline in disposable income equal to 2 percent of GDP. Individuals who experienced such a decline in disposable income during their working years (while their expected retirement benefits remained unchanged) would presumably want to reduce some of their saving in order to cushion the decline in consumption and spread the consumption decline between their working years and their retirement years. However, this effect is likely to be very small because most individuals have little or no saving that can be reduced in this way. Even at age 60, the median financial wealth of households is less than six months earnings. Even that is generally wanted as a precautionary balance to be available for uncertain events and would therefore not be reduced to spread the income decline.

Thus the rise in saving during the early transition years would be less than the previous discussion implied and the rise in saving in the long run would be greater. There is, however, no doubt that the net effect of the transition from the PAYGO system to the prefunded PRA system would be a rise in national saving and therefore a larger capital stock and a higher level of real national income.

6.   The Rate of Return on the PRA Accounts

The lower cost of providing benefits by a prefunded system reflects the difference between the rate of return on the assets of the PRA accounts and the implicit rate of return of the PAYGO system. The example used to illustrate this advantage in Section 1 of this paper assumed a real rate of return of 9 percent on the PRA assets and that same 9 percent was used in the detailed simulations of Feldstein–Samwick (1997). What is the basis for using such a rate? And why might the appropriate rate be lower?

The relevant rate to use is the real rate of return that the nation earns on the additional capital accumulated in the PRA accounts. That return includes the interest, dividends, and capital gains that accrue on the assets in those accounts plus the additional taxes that the government collects as a result of the rise in the capital stock. In short, the relevant rate of return is the real pretax return on capital.

Several statistical studies have concluded that the real pretax rate of return on additions to the nation's stock of nonfinancial corporate capital has averaged about 9 percent over the past several decades (Poterba and Samwick 1996; Rippe 1995). These calculations do not involve share price performance but compare the sum of interest, profits, and taxes paid to the reproduction value of the corporate capital stock. Although there are year-to-year fluctuations in this rate of return, there appears to be no trend. If anything, the rate of return in recent years appears to be higher than this historic average.

A real 9 percent rate of return is of course higher than most investors experience, even in untaxed pension accounts and Individual Retirement Accounts. A portfolio of stocks and bonds balanced to reflect the debt-equity mix that companies use to finance themselves has earned a real rate of return of about 5.5 percent over both the postwar period and the entire period since 1926. However, while such pension account returns are not subject to personal income taxes, the corporate earnings that finance dividends and that lead to capital gains are earnings after the taxes paid at the corporate level. The Federal, state, and local taxes paid at the corporate level have averaged about 40 percent of the pretax return to capital (Rippe 1995). The net 5.5 percent return therefore corresponds to a return of slightly more than 9 percent before all taxes, confirming the estimate obtained directly.

In using a 9 percent rate of return on the assets in the PRA accounts I have implicitly assumed that the government would use the additional tax revenue that it collects because of the PRA accumulation to supplement the returns in the PRA accounts. That is, the government would provide a matching contribution equal to about 3.6 percent of the value of the assets in each PRA account.

Since this is the amount of the extra tax revenue collected by the government on the profits earned on the incremental capital stock, it would not increase the budget deficit.

Although a 9 percent return is the rate that researchers have inferred from the historic experience, there are several reasons for assuming a lower rate of return:

(1) The increase in the capital stock would reduce the rate of return on capital. For instance, the 34 percent long-run rise in the capital stock referred to above would be expected to reduce the historic 9 percent real rate of return to about 7.2 percent.

(2) Not all of the 3.5 percent return that government collects would be available as a matching contribution to the PRA accounts. This would be particularly true of the taxes collected by state and local governments. Of course, although those funds are not given to the PRA accounts, they are of value to the nation as a way of funding additional state and local spending or reducing the taxes levied by state and local governments.

(3) Administrative costs for operating the PRA accounts and the associated annuities might reduce the available funds by as much as a full percentage point (Mitchell 1996; Poterba et al. 1997).

(4) Not all incremental saving flows into the corporate sector. Some of the increase in the national capital stock would enlarge the stock of owner occupied housing. Because of the particularly favorable tax treatment of such housing, the pretax rate of return on such housing is less than 9 percent.

(5) To the extent that some of the incremental saving goes abroad instead of being invested in the domestic capital stock, the resulting corporate tax revenue is collected by foreign governments rather than by the US treasury. Although this may be important for some of the smaller economies of Europe, the historic experience implies that about 80 percent of sustained increases in saving in the United States tend to remain and be invested in the United States (Feldstein and Horioka 1980; Feldstein and Bachetta 1991; Mussa and Goldstein 1994).

(6) Not all of the tax collected from corporations may reflect a return to incremental capital. To the extent that tax revenue reflects a tax on such

things as profitable ideas or brand images, the 9 percent overstates the total return on capital.

These issues deserve further exploration. But to get a sense of what a very much lower rate of return on capital would imply, consider the implication of substituting for the 9 percent a return of only 5.4 percent, the rate of return that investors earn after the corporate income tax. While substituting 5.4 per cent for 9 percent in the detailed calculations and simulations would change the specific quantitative estimates, there is no change in the general conclusion that a pre-funded PRA system could deliver the same benefits as the PAYGO system with much lower contributions during working years.

To see this, consider again the example of an individual who saves at age 45 and dissaves at age 75. Recall that with a 2 percent PAYGO implicit rate of re-turn a dollar saved at age 45 would grow to 1.8 dollars at age 75. In contrast, with a 5.4 percent real rate of return, a dollar saved at age 45 would grow to 4.8 dollars at age 75. If a PAYGO system requires a payroll tax of 18 percent, a pre-funded system with a 5.4 percent rate of return would require contributions of only 6.8 percent. While that would not be as attractive as the 2.5 percent contri-bution that would be possible with a 9 percent real rate of return, it clearly repre-sents a substantial reduction in cost relative to the PAYGO alternative.

7.   Risk

The analysis of the choice between a PAYGO system and prefunded system should address the issue of the risks born by retirees under the two alternatives. While this is sometimes characterized as a problem of the riskiness of portfolio returns, it is important to bear in mind that the unfunded PAYGO system is itself very risky in a different way.

The unfunded PAYGO system is very risky because the level of future bene-fits depends on the willingness of future voters and future Congresses to support the taxes required to provide such benefits. In the past, the unfunded PAYGO system was a popular one with the relatively low rate of tax and the high implicit rate of return made possible by an expanding system. But in the future the PAYGO system is likely to be much less popular as the payroll tax rate rises and the implicit rate of return declines. The level of benefits that the political system will support in this context is very uncertain.

During the past 15 years, the effective level of U.S. Social Security benefits has been reduced by making benefits taxable (above a certain fixed nominal in-come level) and then reduced again by increasing the fraction of benefits subject to tax. The real value of future benefits was also reduced by postponing the normal retirement age from 65 to 67. More recently, there was much discussion about slowing the growth of benefits by reducing the rate of inflation adjustment relative to the official Consumer Price Index. Other proposals include subjecting benefits to a means test that would further lower the net benefits paid to individuals with higher incomes.

These political risks are likely to increase over time as the financing problems of the Social Security program grow. There is moreover no way that an individual can hedge these political risks.

A prefunded program involves the risks of fluctuating portfolio returns. Individuals can protect themselves against these market fluctuations by saving somewhat more in their PRA accounts than would otherwise be required, thus providing a higher expected accumulation of retirement benefits to act as a cushion against the risk that the actual return would be less than the expected return. The analysis in Feldstein–Samwick (1997) shows that the additional PRA saving required to be virtually certain of receiving an annuity equal to the benefits specified in the current Social Security rules is quite small.

More specifically, detailed simulations indicate that a prefunded system with a 9 percent rate of return can finance an annuity equal to the Social Security benefits in current law with a PRA contribution rate of 2 percent of payroll. If the value of the PRA assets is subject to market fluctuations, there is a 50 percent chance that a 2 percent PRA contribution rate will lead to a retirement annuity that is less than the desired level. However, even with the substantial volatility implied by the historic experience of fluctuating equity prices (an average year-to-year fluctuation of about 18 percent in the average value of share prices), raising the contribution rate enough to provide a cushion that makes it very likely that the individual's annuity will at least equal the Social Security benefits projected in current law still leaves the required contribution far below the tax rate in a PAYGO system.[11]

In short, risk appears to be a quite manageable problem in a prefunded system in which individuals invest in a broad index of stocks and bonds.

8.   Distributional Questions

The shift from a PAYGO system to a funded system involves three kinds of distributional issues: During the transition, which are the age groups that win and

---

[11]   Although "oversaving" in this way can provide a probability greater than 0.95 that the PRA benefits will exceed the Social Security benefits in current law, as a practical matter a conditional pay-as-you-go benefit could provide a guarantee that individuals receive the full amount provided in current law.

which are the age groups that lose? How would replacing the PAYGO system with a prefunded system affect the relative income of typical employees and high-income individuals? How can the poor be protected in a system of individual accounts?

a.   Impact on Different Age Cohorts

Because the existing PAYGO tax rate is not sufficient to finance the benefits specified in the current Social Security law, there must eventually be a change in either the taxes or the benefits or both. The mix and timing of the changes determine the PAYGO baseline to which the transition to a funded system can be compared. One simple but politically unlikely assumption is that no change would be made until the trust fund is exhausted in 2030 and that at that time taxes would be raised from 12.4 percent to the 16 percent level needed to fund the benefits specified under current law. Such a baseline would leave the expected incomes of everyone who would retire by 2030 unchanged, i.e., everyone born before 1965 would be unaffected. In contrast, a transition to a PAYGO system would temporarily raise the combined tax rate and mandatory PRA contribution for those who are not yet retired. The increased combined rate would continue until the reduction in the PAYGO tax exceeds the mandatory saving. In the specific transition studied in Feldstein–Samwick (1997), this occurs after 19 years. Such a transition (in which mandatory PRA contributions begin at age 30) has the following distributional consequences: Those who are retired when the transition begins are completely unaffected. Those who are at least 45 years old will always face a higher combined mix of taxes and PRA contributions. Those who are younger will face a higher mix for 19 years and then a lower mix. The younger they are, the more likely that the present value of the combined payments will be lower in the transition than in the baseline.

Alternative modifications to the current PAYGO system would create different baselines and therefore different relative distributional effects. For example, a combination of benefit reductions and a gradual tax increase under the PAYGO system would cause the transition to a funded system to be relatively favorable to existing retirees and those who would retire in the near future.

b.   Effects on Individuals with Middle and High Incomes

After the transition to a funded system, the average employee would be very much better off than under the existing PAYGO system while high-income individuals would generally be worse off. Consider first the average employee who would pay a 20 percent effective income tax and who under the PAYGO system would face a combined employer-employee Social Security payroll tax rate of 19 percent. Each $100 of gross wage would produce a net take-home wage of approximately $61.[12] The shift to a fully funded system would have two effects. By increasing the capital stock, it would raise the productivity of labor and therefore the wage rate. The 34 percent rise in the capital stock referred to above would imply an increase in real wages of about 7 percent. Each $100 of gross wage would become $107. More important, however, the payroll tax rate of 19 percent would be replaced by a PRA contribution of less than 3 percent. Applying the sum of the 20 percent income tax rate and the 3 percent PRA contribution to the $107 gross wage yields a net take-home wage of $82, an increase of 34 percent from the $61 take-home wage with the PAYGO system. The source of this gain is of course the large increase in the capital stock which is owned by these wage earners and used to finance their retirement. I find it impossible to think of any other government policy that could have such a large and favorable effect on the disposable incomes of average working individuals.

The increase in the total capital stock makes capital less scarce and drives down its return; the calculation referred to in Section 6 above implies that the pretax rate of return on capital would decline from 9 percent to 7.2 percent. This 20 percent decline in the rate of return on capital would cause a decline in the income of high-income individuals for whom capital income is relatively important and for whom the level of taxable wages is only a small part of total compensation.

c.   Protecting the Poor

In a government defined benefit program, whether funded or unfunded, the benefits can be set to achieve any desired degree of income redistribution and income maintenance. In contrast, in a funded system based on individual accounts, each individual's retirement benefits depends on the amount that he or she earned and saved during the working years. It is of course possible, however, to introduce an element of redistribution to protect the poor. During the transition, the PAYGO system continues to operate and provides the same protection of the poor as under the pure PAYGO system. After the transition, the very high rate of return in the funded system relative to the PAYGO system makes it very easy to provide at least this amount of income maintenance for the poor while leaving all others much better off than they would be under the PAYGO system.

As an example of this, Feldstein–Samwick (1996) calculated that the PRA annuities of all retirees could be raised to at least 50 percent of the median annuity

---

12   This is an approximation because it ignores the fact that the employer's portion of the payroll tax is excluded from the individual's taxable income. It also excludes the Medicare portion of the payroll tax which could be very large, increasing the effect described in the text.

(a higher standard of income maintenance than the current Social Security system achieves) by levying a 5 percent tax on all PRA accounts at age 65 and redistributing the funds to those whose PRA pensions would otherwise be less than 50 percent of the median. Since the PRA contributions during working years that would be required to fund a PRA annuity equal to the projected Social Security benefits is only 2.0 percent of covered wages, this redistributive function could be financed by increasing the PRA saving rate from 2.0 percent to 2.1 percent.

9.   Concluding Comments

The transition from unfunded PAYGO pension systems to fully prefunded or partially prefunded systems is now taking place in many countries around the world. The countries that have already begun this process are as different as Chile and Australia, Mexico and England.[13] The specific rules and transition arrangements differ from country to country but they all have the common feature of creating individual accounts in which mandatory saving is accumulated and invested in private financial assets to finance retirement benefits. The increased longevity of the population in every country implies that the alternative to such a prefunded system is a PAYGO system with a much higher rate of tax than currently prevails.[14]

The analysis summarized in this paper shows that such a system can provide a substantial reduction in taxes while maintaining or increasing retirement benefits. The funded system avoids the political risks of an increasingly costly and unfavorable PAYGO program. Although the returns on a funded portfolio are also risky, the potentially adverse consequences of the fluctuations in asset prices can be avoided by a relatively small increase in the mandatory saving rate. The high rate of return on the funded assets means that the retirement income of the poor can be protected at relatively low cost.

While further analysis can indicate options for improving the transition to a prefunded system, the key missing ingredient now is the political will to impose the short-run costs that would produce such large long-run benefits.

---

13   For descriptions of several of these systems, see Feldstein (1996).

14   Note that the cause of the increased cost of PAYGO systems is increased longevity and not a temporary "baby boom" retirement bulge.

Bibliography

Feldstein, M. (1995). Would Privatizing Social Security Raise Economic Welfare? NBER Working Paper 5281. Cambridge, Mass.

—— (1996a). The Missing Piece in Policy Analysis: Social Security Reform. *American Economic Review, Papers and Proceedings* 86(2):1–14.

—— (1996b). Privatizing Social Security. Chicago: University of Chicago Press (forthcoming).

Feldstein, M., and P. Bacchetta (1991). National Saving and International Investment. In D. Bernheim and J. Shoven (eds.), *National Saving and Economic Performance*. Chicago: University of Chicago Press.

Feldstein, M., and C. Horioka (1980). Domestic Saving and International Capital Flows. *Economic Journal* 90(June):314–329.

Feldstein, M., and A. Samwick (1996). The Transition Path in Privatizing Social Security. NBER Working Paper 5761. Cambridge, Mass.

—— (1997). The Economics of Prefunding Social Security and Medicare Benefits. *The 1997 NBER Macro Annual*. Cambridge, Mass.: MIT Press.

Kotlikoff, L. (1997). Privatization of Social Security: How It Works and Why It Matters. In J. Poterba (ed.), *Tax Policy and the Economy*. Cambridge, Mass.: MIT Press.

Mitchell, O. (1996). Administrative Costs in Public and Private Retirement Systems. In M. Feldstein (ed.), *Privatizing Social Security*. Chicago: University of Chicago Press.

Mussa, M., and M. Goldstein (1993). The Integration of World Capital Markets. In Federal Reserve Bank of Kansas City (ed.), *Changing Capital Markets: Implications for Monetary Policy*. Kansas City, Mo.

Poterba, J., and A. Samwick (1996). Stock Ownership Patterns, Stock Market Fluctuations, and Consumption. *Brookings Papers on Economic Activity* (2):295–357.

Poterba, J., O. Mitchell, and M. Warshawsky (1997). New Evidence on the Money's Worth of Individual Annuities. NBER Working Paper 6002. Cambridge, Mass.

Rippe, R. (1995). Further Gains in Corporate Profitability. *Economic Outlook Monthly*, Prudential Securities, August.

Comment on Martin Feldstein

A. Lans Bovenberg

Feldstein's paper nicely summarizes the recent work of Martin Feldstein on social security reform. Indeed, it was Martin Feldstein who put the issue of social security reform on the policy agenda about 25 years ago.

In discussing his paper, I will start by exploring the relative returns on pay-as-you-go (PAYG) and funded systems. Subsequently, the transition of PAYG to funded systems is investigated, including the possibility of a Pareto-welfare-improving reform that protects current generations. I then discuss how substituting individual retirement accounts for PAYG systems would affect the poor by affecting intragenerational distribution. After analyzing the impact on political risks of moving towards funding, I turn to the consequences for labor supply and national saving. The discussion concludes by stressing the benefits of diversifying pensions over various systems in order to contain risks.

1. PAYG versus Funded Systems: The Relative Returns

Feldstein argues that moving from PAYG systems to funded systems yields large long-run gains. The intuition behind these substantial gains is the well-known Aaron condition (see Aaron 1966). This condition compares the before-tax return on capital, which is the return on funding, and the real growth rate of labor income, which is the return on PAYG systems. The more the before-tax return exceeds the growth rate of labor income, the larger the long-run gains from switching from PAYG to funded systems become.[1] Since Feldstein assumes a rather high before-tax return on capital of 9 percent and real growth of labor income of only 2 percent, he arrives at substantial long-run income gains from funding.

Section 6 of Feldstein's paper acknowledges that a return on capital of 9 percent may be on the high side. I share this concern because of a number of reasons. First of all, Feldstein includes the corporate tax in the before-tax rate of return. However, the corporate tax represents largely a tax on rents and entrepre-

---

[1]   In the short run, however, funded systems are always less favorable to the first generation because funding requires an initial period during which premiums are used to build up assets rather than to pay benefits.

neurship. Moreover, in countries in which the top personal tax rate substantially exceeds the corporate tax rate, high-income individuals will have strong incentives to shift their labor income towards the corporate sector. As a result of this income shifting, a substantial part of the corporate tax in these countries is likely to represent a tax on labor income. Accordingly, the recorded *average* return on corporate income substantially overstates the *marginal* return on additional capital. In fact, some industrial countries may not tax capital at all at the margin, due to interest deductibility, various opportunities for tax arbitrage, and tax competition. The effective tax rate on marginal pension saving is likely to be especially low, also, because of tax preferences for the elderly.[2] In this connection, Gordon and Slemrod (1988) found that revenues from capital income taxes in the United States may actually be negative.

Another reason why the paper may overestimate the gap between the return on funding and that on PAYG involves the general equilibrium effects of aging. Aging is generally believed to depress the return on PAYG by inhibiting the growth of the labor force and hence employment. However, by making capital more abundant relative to labor, aging is likely to depress also the return on capital. Moreover, through the same channel, aging boosts the growth of wages and hence the growth of labor income. In this way, aging may exert a much smaller influence on the Aaron condition than is commonly believed. Indeed, in a closed economy that does not have access to the international capital market, not only PAYG but also funded systems are vulnerable to the effects of aging. Funded systems can be shielded from aging only if capital can be easily invested in foreign, younger countries with abundant labor. However, as Feldstein has established himself in his seminal paper with Horioka, capital is in fact quite immobile internationally, especially between, on the one hand, the emerging markets with their substantial labor resources, and, on the other hand, the OECD countries with their aging populations.

Among the mature European countries, however, capital mobility is likely to increase substantially in the near future, especially if EMU proceeds. In individual European countries, therefore, marginal saving is invested mainly abroad. Hence, corporate taxes on marginal savings accrue to the foreign rather than the domestic treasuries. This is another reason why European countries should not include the corporate tax in the marginal national return to saving.

Part of the return to capital, and to equity in particular, compensates for risk. This risk premium should not be included in the return to those who cannot af-

---

2   These preferences imply that the income tax rates at which pension premiums are deducted typically exceed the rates at which pension benefits are taxed under the income tax. This provides incentives to save. For the effects of tax arbitrage, see also Stiglitz (1985).

ford to bear risk and hence are not able to reap the equity premium. This especially applies to older and poorer individuals who have to rely on individual retirement accounts, which are of the defined contribution (DC) type, and hence cannot benefit from intergenerational risk sharing implicit in defined benefit (DB) schemes.

In this connection, I am not convinced that individual accounts (the so-called personal retirement accounts) advocated in Section 3 of the paper yield a higher return than do collective schemes that impose various restrictions on individual choice. In particular, collective schemes are able to take on more risk because they can benefit from intergenerational risk sharing and thus can plan over a longer horizon. Hence, these collective schemes are better able to exploit the equity premium than individual accounts are, especially if these collective schemes can delegate investment policy to competitive investment managers. Europeans tend to favor collective institutions that deal with unexpected shocks on the basis of incomplete contracts through the governance structure of voice (rather than exit). Americans, in contrast, are typically quite concerned about the political risks associated with the governance structure of voice and hence rely on complete contracts and the disciplining device of free entry and exit. Indeed, Feldstein emphasizes the political risks inherent in collective institutions but is silent about the advantages of these institutions in terms of risk sharing.

2.   The Transition: Protecting Current Generations

Feldstein discusses the transition period from PAYG systems to funded systems. In the transition analyzed in the paper, it takes almost two decades before a funded scheme produces a lower mandatory contribution rate than the current PAYG system. This is quite a long time, especially for the political process. Moreover, in terms of lifetime utility, most existing generations experience a loss. The reform may thus not be implementable in a democratic political system, where the present generations decide. Accordingly, future generations may have to share in the costs of paying off the public debt implicit in current PAYG systems in order to prevent a welfare loss for current generations.

Also other reasons would support shifting part of the costs of the transition to future generations. First, future generations benefit most, in terms of lower pension premiums, from the transition to a funded system. It would seem fair to confront these generations with part of the costs of the transition.

Second, as economic growth proceeds, future generations are likely to be substantially better off than present generations. Indeed, current generations transfer large stocks of knowledge to future generations. When implementing a pension reform that benefits future, richer generations at the expense of current, poorer generations, the government may want to transfer resources away from future generations to compensate current generations.

Third, if future spending cuts are expected to reduce tax rates in the future, the present government can smooth tax rates over time by shifting part of the present costs of public spending to the future. This tax-smoothing argument may well apply to Germany; present German generations are already paying off another large public debt, namely the one inherited from the communist regime in East Germany.

Whether the government can implement a Pareto-improving transition that benefits also current generations depends on the size and nature of initial distortions. Without such distortions, the PAYG system is Pareto-efficient: the only way to boost saving is to make current generations poorer. Hence, more information about the size and nature of preexisting distortions is crucial in order to determine whether a Pareto-improving transition towards funding is feasible.

Feldstein focuses on capital-market distortions caused by capital-income taxes, which drive a wedge between the social benefits and social costs of capital accumulation (i.e., between the before-tax return on capital and the discount rate). Moving towards a funded pension system exploits the arbitrage possibilities produced by the capital-income tax. Intuitively, a shift from PAYG to funding produces first-order welfare gains by alleviating the distortions produced by the capital-income tax. However, as noted above when discussing the rate of return on capital, I am not convinced that the marginal tax wedge on capital income is actually substantially positive. In any case, even if the marginal capital tax were large, abolishing capital taxation would be a more direct way to address capital-market distortions than changing the pension system.

Others have focused on labor-market distortions as the source of the potential for Pareto-improving pension reforms. In fact, several recent papers have shown that a Pareto-improving transition to a funded system is feasible if at the same time the link between pension premiums and pension benefits is tightened (see, e.g., Breyer and Straub 1993; Raffelhüschen 1993; and Kotlikoff 1995). Indeed, in Europe, labor-market distortions are more important than capital-market distortions. Whereas Americans are especially concerned about excessively low savings depressing capital accumulation, Europeans are more concerned about various labor-market distortions harming employment.

Another issue that is likely to complicate the transition to a funded system is public debt policy. Shifting the costs of paying off the PAYG debt to future generations will often require a larger fiscal deficit. Another reason why a transition to a funded system raises the recorded fiscal deficit is that contributions to individual retirement accounts are typically deductible from income tax. Accordingly, introducing funded plans erodes the income tax base. In any case, additional private saving would erode consumption tax bases, such as the base for the value-added taxes in the European countries. These effects on the fiscal deficits would be a major complication for the EU countries, which are currently struggling to meet the EMU convergence criteria and the deficit ceilings in the stabilization pact.

3.   Redistribution and the Disadvantaged

Most of the analyses of Pareto-improving pension reforms assume that generations are homogeneous. However, once one allows for intragenerational heterogeneity, Pareto-improving reforms that benefit all individuals within any generation are even more difficult to establish. To illustrate, whereas strengthening the link between pension premiums and pension benefits may boost efficiency by enhancing labor-market incentives, it may hurt the poor. Indeed, the inefficiencies of current PAYG systems originate to a large extent in redistribution, or in other words, in the provision of insurance against human-capital risk.

Individual retirement accounts do not provide human-capital insurance because they do not redistribute resources from the rich to the poor. Feldstein argues that only very limited resources (about 5 percent of the retirement accounts) would be required to compensate the poor for the lack of redistribution in individual accounts.

This estimate for these resources seems to be on the low side for a number of reasons. First, the various reasons cited in Section 6 of the paper for why the return on capital may be lower than 9 percent tend to accumulate for the poor. In particular, information and administrative costs absorb a large part of the gross return in small retirement accounts because these costs rise less than proportionally with the size of the account. Indeed, the rich tend to have better access to information. Moreover, the poor are less able to benefit from high-risk premia on equity because they are less able to bear risk. Finally, the disadvantaged often suffer from liquidity constraints and thus feature high discount rates. Accordingly, a transition that requires temporarily higher pension contributions is especially costly for them.

Feldstein maintains that funding would benefit the poor by raising their wages. This is doubtful because capital tends to be a better substitute for unskilled than for skilled labor (see, e.g., Hamermesh 1993). Accordingly, capital accumulation may well further widen income disparities as capital accumulation replaces unskilled workers, but boosts the demand for skilled laborers (who can operate modern equipment). Indeed, there is ample evidence that the technological progress embodied in new capital and stimulated by investments in intangible capital is biased towards unskilled labor.

The most important reason why the estimate for the resources needed to compensate the disadvantaged is on the low side is that closely targeting the poor generally implies serious disincentives for the poor. Whereas targeting is cheaper in terms of tax revenue, it may well be more costly in terms of efficiency because it implies high marginal tax rates for the poor. Moreover, it may harm social cohesion, as the poor would be discouraged from working. In any case, it would increase the burden on workfare-type programs aimed at raising the labor participation of the poor. Accordingly, some of the efficiency costs of redistribution are shifted away from the pension system to other programs. Hence, the effect of privatizing social security on labor-market distortions is likely to be limited if the incomes of the poor are protected; unavoidable distortions associated with redistribution are shifted from the pension system to other government programs and to implicit taxes in the form of government regulations.

The key question in this connection is whether spreading relatively small disincentives over the entire population is better (as in many current PAYG systems, which provide a flat benefit to the entire population) or whether confining relatively large disincentives to a relatively small group at the bottom end of the income distribution is to be preferred (as targeting redistribution to the poor would do). The literature on optimal income tax may provide insights on this trade-off. It suggests that marginal tax rates at the bottom end should be lower, the more people earn incomes in that range (see, e.g., Mirrlees 1997). Hence, as technological progress makes the income distribution more skewed, it may be optimal to move away from systems that target the poor very closely.

Another reason why individual retirement accounts are likely to harm the work incentives for the disadvantaged is that these saving accounts are mandatory in order to combat myopia and moral hazard (see Section 2 of Feldstein's paper). For the same reasons, the ways in which the funds in these accounts can be invested and withdrawn are subject to various restrictions. All these mandatory provisions and restrictions act as implicit taxes, thereby discouraging labor supply. This is likely to be the case especially in the United States, where, as Feldstein notes, large numbers of individuals are not saving voluntarily at all at the moment. Moreover, especially the poor, who tend to be subject to high discount rates, will perceive the mandatory contribution as a tax. This is even more so because the disadvantaged tend to benefit from means-tested programs during retirement. Accordingly, the poor are likely to find forced saving especially costly. They thus face incentives to drop out of the labor force in order to avoid the taxation implicit in forced saving.

4.   Political Risks

In Section 3 of his paper, Feldstein argues that privatizing social security would alleviate political risks. However, just as individual retirement accounts may shift labor-market disincentives away from the middle class to the poor (see Section 3 on redistribution above), so may they shift political risk away from the middle class to the disadvantaged. Indeed, individual retirement accounts supplemented by transfers targeted at the poor are likely to raise political risks for the poor, who then have to rely on explicit redistributive transfers. Unexpected shocks to the budget must be absorbed by these relatively small benefits. More generally, the political process may not be able to sustain targeted programs that benefit a relatively small group. Hence, targeted benefits for the poor may result in poor benefits.

It should be noted that individual retirement accounts are also subject to substantial political risk. Indeed, various government regulations are needed, for example, regarding the size of the mandatory contributions, restrictions on how to take out contributions, the choice of investment managers, and the tax treatment of pensions. Moreover, the transitional arrangements will engender political conflict. Indeed, regulations will need continuous modifications because of unexpected developments.

5.   Labor Supply

The shift of labor-market disincentives to other programs (see Section 3 on redistribution above) is one reason why Feldstein possibly overstates the positive labor-supply effects. Another reason is that incentives for additional financial saving make it less attractive for individuals to save in the form of human capital. Hence, human capital does not last as long and people retire earlier. This is exactly what can be observed in the Netherlands. Substantial tax incentives for pension saving induce older workers to retire early, thereby reducing labor supply and exacerbating existing distortions on the labor market. Indeed, leisure (i.e., early retirement) and delayed consumption (pension saving) are complements. This is an argument against providing generous tax incentives to pension savings in economies suffering from substantial labor-market distortions that cannot be reduced directly.

In the long run, labor supply will be depressed through another channel, namely the substantial positive income effects for the middle- and higher-income individuals associated with the higher return on their pension saving. Part of these long-run welfare gains will be spent on additional leisure.

6.   National Saving

Feldstein acknowledges that the initial saving response may be limited because of consumption smoothing over the life cycle; households finance their temporarily higher pension contributions by dissaving. Feldstein argues, however, that this dissaving effect will be quite small in practice because households in the United States do not have any saving to reduce. In Europe, however, households do save more and may thus respond to the transition by reducing other saving. In the United States, corporate saving may well fall. Moreover, households could borrow more, for example, against the value of their homes. If households cannot borrow because of liquidity constraints, they are likely to be subject to high discount rates. In that case, the temporarily higher premiums are particularly costly for these constrained households.

A reduction of other saving would be particularly likely if, following Feldstein's suggestion, retirement saving were to be tax-favored, for example, by exempting it from both corporate taxes and personal income taxation. In that case, a substantial part of the funds invested in individual retirement accounts would likely replace other saving subject to higher tax rates. Experience suggests that agents are very creative in taking advantage of arbitrage opportunities created by "marginal" subsidies. Indeed, tax arbitrage is becoming a more important issue, as financial innovation and internationalization allows agents to increasingly exploit differences in tax treatments of different types of saving. This tax arbitrage depresses the impact of individual retirement accounts on national saving through two channels. First, private saving increases less substantially than expected. Second, public saving declines as the tax base is eroded.

7.   Conclusions

A key issue in pension design is hedging against fundamental risk and uncertainty over a long time horizon. We are actually quite ignorant about how the economy functions, let alone about how it will develop in the future. To contain risks, countries are well advised to diversify their eggs (of pension premiums) over various baskets (i.e., pension systems).

What does diversification imply for concrete pension policies? European countries should move part of their public PAYG system to a privately funded basis. Indeed, European pensions need a dose of flexibility, incentives, and experimentation. However, a wholesale shift away from PAYG to funded schemes is costlier and riskier than Feldstein's analysis suggests. Accordingly, I would favor a three-pillar system as recommended by the World Bank (see World Bank 1994; Bovenberg and van der Linden 1997). Such a three-pillar system would provide the individual with a well-diversified portfolio of income protection in old age.

The first pillar would insure against lifetime human-capital risk. It would be mandatory and redistributive. To avoid excessive moral hazard and work disincentives for lower-income individuals, this system should provide a flat benefit financed out of general tax revenues. Such a PAYG scheme would give the elderly a claim on the human capital of the young, thereby reducing the vulnerability of the elderly to a low return on capital. Indeed, in addressing aging, industrial countries should rely not only on financial saving but also on saving in the form of human capital. This may help also to raise the effective retirement age.

Also, the second pillar would be mandatory in order to combat myopia and facilitate intergenerational risk sharing for the lower-middle-income individuals. In contrast to the first pillar, the second pillar would be funded and would involve a strong actuarial link between premiums and benefits. This second pillar could be integrated with mandatory unemployment insurance. In particular, individuals would be allowed to withdraw funds not only at retirement but also during periods of unemployment and for the purpose of maintaining human capital. This would facilitate a more flexible allocation of learning, leisure, and work over the life cycle.

The third pillar would be voluntary and would be tailored to the needs of middle- and higher-income individuals. To encourage the development of the third pillar, European governments could freeze, or gradually reduce, PAYG benefits to middle- and higher-income individuals.

Within the second and third pillars, the government can facilitate intergenerational risk sharing, for example, through the tax system, by issuing indexed bonds, or by guaranteeing a minimum return. Indeed, the political process remains a valuable risk sharing device in the face of fundamental uncertainties, some of which we cannot even imagine in advance.

In pension insurance, the search is on for new mixes of competitive and control mechanisms (and the associated governance structures of exit and voice) which each feature their own comparative advantages in reducing risk in a world with many uncertainties. The work of Martin Feldstein is an invaluable contribution to this exciting process of institutional innovation.

Bibliography

Aaron, H.J. (1966). The Social Insurance Paradox. *Canadian Journal of Economic and Political Science* 32.

Bovenberg, A.L., and A.S.M. van der Linden (1997). Can We Afford to Grow Old? Research Memorandum 134. CPB Netherlands Bureau for Economic Policy Analysis, The Hague.

Breyer, F., and M. Straub (1993). Welfare Effects of Unfunded Pension Systems when Labor Supply is Endogenous. *Journal of Public Economics* 50:77–91.

Gordon R.H., and J. Slemrod (1988). Do We Collect Any Revenue from Taxing Capital Income? In L.H. Summers (ed.), *Tax Policy and the Economy* 2. Cambridge, Mass.: MIT Press.

Hamermesh, D. (1993). *Labor Demand.* Princeton: Princeton University Press.

Kotlikoff, L.J. (1995). Privatization of Social Security: How It Works and Why It Matters. Working Paper 5330. National Bureau of Economic Research, Cambridge, Mass.

Mirrlees, J.A. (1997). Information and Incentives: the Economics of Carrots and Sticks. *Economic Journal* 107:1311–1329.

Raffelhüschen, R. (1993). Funding Social Security through Pareto-Optimal Conversion Policies. *Journal of Economics*, Suppl. 7:105–131.

Stiglitz, J.E. (1985). The General Theory of Tax Avoidance. *National Tax Journal* 38:325–337.

World Bank (1994). *Averting the Old Age Crisis: Policies to Protect the Old and Promote Growth.* Oxford: Oxford University Press.

Laurence J. Kotlikoff, Kent A. Smetters, and Jan Walliser

The Economic Impact of Privatizing Social Security

1. Introduction

Privatizing social security is a growth industry. Chile, which privatized in the early 1980s, was a lone pioneer for a while. But in recent years, the United Kingdom, Argentina, Peru, Colombia, Mexico, Bolivia, and several other countries have followed suit. Today a host of other countries, from the Ukraine to the United States to China, is seriously exploring the privatization option.

The lure of privatizing social security is an enhanced rate of economic growth and a higher standard of living. Chile's remarkable economic performance in the years since it privatized has done more than anything to equate social security's privatization with economic progress. But Chile's economic success has many fathers, including the privatization of state-owned enterprises, the limitation of government spending, the opening of the economy to international trade, and the improvement of commercial regulations. Parceling out exactly the right amount of credit to Chile's social security reform is a task that will entertain economic historians for years to come.

This paper tries to understand the economic contribution of privatizing social security, not by looking at actual economic outcomes in a real economy, but by simulating economic outcomes in a stylized model, albeit one closely parameterized to U.S. economic conditions and fiscal policies. The model is the Auerbach–Kotlikoff dynamic life cycle model, which has recently been enhanced to include intragenerational heterogeneity, kinked budget constraints, and a more realistic formulation of income taxation.

Simulating the economic impact of privatizing social security is also a growth industry. Indeed, the present study is the fourth of our own recent simulation exercises (see Kotlikoff 1996, 1997; Kotlikoff et al. 1997). But unlike its immediate predecessors, the current paper benefits from a more realistic formulation of U.S. wage and capital income taxation and adjustments in these forms of taxation along the transition path. It also includes, for the first time, income tax exemptions and intragenerational heterogeneity in longitudinal age-wage profiles.

Remark: The views expressed in this paper are those of the authors and not necessarily those of the Congressional Budget Office.

Other studies in this literature include Seidman (1986) and Feldstein (1995), who use partial equilibrium frameworks, and Arrau (1990), Arrau and Schmidt-Hebbel (1993), Raffelhüschen (1993), and Huang et al. (1997), who use general equilibrium frameworks (although not as detailed a framework as that embodied in the current version of the model).

We model the privatization of U.S. Social Security as involving three elements: (a) forcing workers to contribute to private retirement accounts, (b) giving retirees and workers (in retirement) only those Social Security benefits which they accrued as of the time of the reform, and (c) financing Social Security benefits during a transition period using either wage taxation, income taxation, consumption taxation, or a combination of income taxation and deficit finance. To preview our findings, in the absence of deficit finance, all methods of financing the transition leave the economy in the same long-run position—one with a 40 percent higher capital stock, a 7 percent larger supply of labor, a 14 percent higher level of per capita income, a 7 percent higher real wage, and a 19 percent lower real interest rate. Notwithstanding the elimination of Social Security's highly progressive benefit schedule, all members of future generations—poor and rich alike—gain substantially from privatization. These long-run gains come at the cost of moderate welfare losses experienced by those generations who are elderly or middle-aged at the time of the reform. Although the long-run positions of the economy end up the same under the three financing alternatives, the short-run positions are quite different. Consumption tax finance produces much more rapid economic gains than does either wage or income tax finance. Indeed, income tax finance actually reduces output per person in the first decade of the transition.

This paper proceeds in the next section by describing the model, calibration, and our strategy for modeling Social Security's privatization. Section 3 presents results, and Section 4 summarizes and concludes the paper.

2.   The Model

The Auerbach–Kotlikoff model is a general equilibrium model with 55 overlapping generations that solves the perfect foresight path of the economy over a 150 year period.[1] The model has three sectors: households, firms, and the government. Households allocate their full lifetime resources (the present value of their time endowment plus the present value of their inheritance) to consumption and leisure over their 55-year life span (ages 21 to 75). Their decisions concerning

---

1   The current model can be run with more than 55 years of adulthood and with more than 150 years within which the economy reaches its new steady state.

how much to consume and work in each period are based on the time-path of after-tax wages and interest rates they experience over their lifetimes. A household's retirement decisions are endogenous; since there is a nonnegativity constraint on labor supply, retirement occurs when households seek to supply negative amounts of labor. Labor and consumption choices are derived from a time-separable CES utility function. The principal preference parameters of this utility function are its intertemporal and intratemporal elasticities of substitution, which we set at 0.25 and 0.8, respectively. Those values accord with empirical findings (see Auerbach and Kotlikoff 1987). We choose a 1.5 percent pure rate of time preference to achieve realistic growth of consumption over the life cycle.

The model captures intragenerational as well as intergenerational heterogeneity. Following Fullerton and Rogers (1993), each cohort is divided into 12 lifetime-earnings classes with distinct age-productivity profiles. Productivity increases with age until approximately age 30 (real age 50) and declines thereafter. Allowing for intragenerational heterogeneity significantly improves the model's calibration to the current tax system.

Firms are perfectly competitive and maximize profits subject to a CES production function. Thus, wage rates and interest rates always correspond to the marginal products of labor and capital, respectively. For the purpose of the simulations presented below, the CES function is restricted to be of the Cobb–Douglas form with a capital share of 25 percent.[2]

The government collects taxes to finance government consumption and government transfers. In particular, the model can accommodate consumption taxes, wage taxes, income taxes, and capital income taxes. Tax schedules can be proportional or progressive. The model also captures the payroll taxes that finance Old-Age and Survivors Insurance, Disability Insurance, and payroll-taxed Medicare benefits. And it incorporates the finance of debt service and the possibility of deficit finance.

One important new feature of the model is its inclusion of kinked budget constraints. The U.S. income tax schedule includes an exemption and a standard deduction, which reduce the income tax base significantly. The tax-free amount of income causes a kink in the marginal tax-rate function, since marginal tax rates are zero below the deduction level and positive above the deduction level. The model deals with this problem by assigning shadow (virtual) marginal tax rates to agents who decide to stay at the kink. Households at the kink face a zero average tax rate and a positive marginal tax rate that is consistent with their being at the kink. Note that the model solves the forward-looking optimization problem of the household and thus simultaneously solves the kinked budget constraint problem for all periods of life. The model also includes the payroll tax

---

2   Note that the 25 percent figure is net of depreciation.

ceiling, which also creates a nonconvexity in the budget constraint. This problem is solved by invoking a search procedure over the relevant range.

a.   Calibration

Demographic Structure, Exogenous Growth, and Intergenerational Heterogeneity

We assume that the population grows at a rate of 1 percent, the average growth rate of the labor force over the last decade. Implicitly, each cohort has 1.22 children at age 1 (real age 21). In addition, we assume an annual 1 percent rate of technological growth, leading to exogenous wage growth of 1 percent per year. We adopt the same strategy as Auerbach et al. (1989) to achieve balanced growth by assuming a growth rate of the time endowment that matches that of technological change.

Following Fullerton and Rogers (1993), we divide each cohort into 12 distinct earnings classes. The highest and lowest class, classes 12 and 1, account for the 2 percent of the population with the highest and lowest lifetime earnings, respectively. Classes 11 and 2 comprise the remaining 8 percent of the top and bottom lifetime-earnings deciles, with classes 3 through 10 reflecting the other 8 lifetime-earnings decile. Each class has its own lifetime-earnings profile, estimated from the Panel Study of Income Dynamics.[3] In order to reproduce a realistic number of work hours, leisure in the CES utility function receives the same weight as consumption. As a result of the exogenous efficiency profiles, endogenously derived labor income ranges from $7,660 to $58,000 at age 5 (real age 25) and from $9,660 to $140,000 at age 25 (real age 45).

Social Security Benefits

U.S. Social Security benefits are based on a measure of average indexed monthly earnings (AIME) over a 35-year work history. The AIME is converted into a primary insurance amount (PIA) in accordance with a progressive formula. In particular, the 1997 benefit formula has two bend points. The PIA is calculated as 90 percent of the first $455 of AIME, 32 percent of the next $2,286 of AIME, and 15 percent of AIME above $2,741. We approximate the benefit formula with a sixth-order polynomial which is applied to the dollar-scaled AIME generated by the model. We achieve replacement values between 25 and 75 percent for the lifetime richest and lifetime poorest, respectively. Since ap-

---

3   See Altig et al. (1997) for a detailed description of our estimation strategy that differs from Fullerton and Rogers (1993) by grouping individuals, not households.

proximately 50 percent of Social Security benefits are paid to survivors and spouses, we multiply benefits by a factor of 1.95.

The model also takes into account Social Security's maximum taxable earnings of currently $65,400. Those with earnings above the maximum taxable earnings pay only the tax for the first $65,400 of their labor income. Thus, the lifetime rich do not face a positive marginal payroll tax, and their labor supply choice is not distorted by Social Security.

Although the U.S. Social Security System does provide a marginal return in benefits in exchange for marginal contributions, understanding the degree of benefit tax linkage at the margin is extremely complex. Furthermore, for many working women Social Security's spousal benefit results in a zero marginal benefit tax link, since expected benefits based on their own work history fall short of 50 percent of their husband's benefit. In four of our five simulations we assume therefore zero perceived benefit tax linkage. The residual simulation assumes 25 percent benefit tax linkage; i.e., it assumes that workers perceive that, at the margin, every dollar contributed to Social Security yields 25 cents in benefits measured as a present value.

Finally, the model incorporates the CPI indexation of benefits. This feature is important if the transition to a privatized system is financed by consumption taxes. Since the model's numeraire is the producer's price of single output, the consumer price rises by the amount of the tax when direct consumption taxes are imposed. Indexation of benefits thus simply amounts to raising benefits by the percentage change in consumption taxes. The indexation of benefits insulates the real income of those poor initial elderly in our model who are subsisting almost entirely on Social Security.

Disability and Medicare Benefits

Americans can qualify for Disability Insurance if they are unable to work and do not qualify for retirement benefits. Disability Insurance (DI) is financed on a pay-as-you-go basis. The payroll tax is subject to the Social Security earnings ceiling. To incorporate DI, a flat benefit is paid to all agents under the age of 45 (real age 65). Payroll-tax-financed Medicare (HI) benefits are implemented in a similar fashion by providing a flat benefit to all agents over the age of 45 (real age 65). However, the HI payroll tax is not subject to the earnings ceiling. Both DI and HI benefits are indexed to real wage growth and the price index.

Financing Other Government Spending

Government purchases of goods and services, government interest payments, and non-social-security transfer payments are financed with consumption taxes and income taxes. Government purchases take up a share of 21.7 percent of output (national income), government interest payments are 1.5 percent of income, and non-social-security transfers—a flat benefit for all agents—comprise 1.6 percent of output. In total, government revenues thus represent 24.8 percent of output.

Initial Tax Structure

The U.S. progressive federal income tax is captured by a progressive wage tax with a deduction against wage income and a proportional capital income tax. The progressive wage tax is approximated by a second-order polynomial. The tax rates accord with the current statutory tax rates after correcting for the fact that higher-income earners generally itemize their deductions and, thereby, lower their taxes. To be precise, the model makes the first $9,660 of labor income tax-free, reflecting the personal exemption and a standard deduction for the 1.22 children. This assumption lowers the tax base by a percentage that is in line with empirical values.

As a result of the specification, the average marginal tax rate on wages in the steady state (excluding the payroll taxes) is 20.7 percent. The top income class faces an average wage tax rate of 22 percent and an average marginal tax rate of 30.7 percent, with top rates reaching 36 percent over the life cycle. Median earners face average and average marginal wage tax rates of 10.5 and 18.3 percent, respectively, with top marginal rates reaching more than 19 percent. The lifetime poorest are below the exemption and deduction level and pay no taxes.

Capital income is subject to a flat 20 percent tax rate. However, the effective marginal tax rate on capital income is only 16 percent, since we allow for 20 percent expensing. The expensing rate approximates the preferential tax treatment of new investment. The effective marginal tax rate on capital then reflects the average effective marginal taxation of the U.S. capital stock, including housing capital (see Auerbach [1996] for more details).

The initial steady-state tax structure also includes a 11.3 percent tax on consumption. The consumption tax rate reflects the 0.088 ratio of U.S. sales and excise taxes and duties to aggregate consumption. The additional 2.5 percent consumption tax approximates the consumption tax treatment of employee benefits, especially tax-deferred defined contribution accounts.

The model generates state and local income tax revenues via a 3.7 percent proportional income tax. We subtract property taxes from tax revenues, following the Tiebout view of local taxes. The proportional income tax rate is adjusted downwards to account for tax evasion on all levels of government.

Given our specification of Social Security benefits, the model generates payroll tax rates for Old-Age and Survivors Insurance (OASI), DI, and HI. The OASI payroll tax rate is 9.9 percent of wages, the DI tax rate is 1.9 percent of wages, and the HI tax rate collects 2.9 percent of wage income. Thus, the total

Social Security payroll tax rate is 14.7 percent. This rate falls short of the statutory rate by 0.6 percentage points, which reflect the trust fund contributions that are not explicitly included in the model.[4]

Bequests

The model incorporates a joy-of-giving bequest motive. The weight of bequest for each of the 12 earnings classes is derived endogenously for the initial steady state such that the ratio of the bequest to economy-wide mean income corresponds to the ratio originally estimated by Menchik and David (1982) and updated by Fullerton and Rogers (1993). Bequests range from $4,800 to $450,000 for the lowest and highest lifetime-earnings classes, respectively. Bequests are made at the very end of life to the generation that is 20 years younger and to the same income class to which one belongs. Hence, inheritances are received at age 35 (real age 55) and are not equalizing.

Initial Steady State

The macroeconomic variables in the model's initial steady state correspond closely to those observed in the U.S. economy. For example, personal consumption expenditure and government purchases represent 73.1 percent and 21.7 percent of output, which are the same values observed for the United States when output is measured as net national product. Since we are running the model here as a closed economy, the remaining 5.2 percent of output represents domestic investment as well as national saving; i.e., the initial steady state exhibits a saving rate of 5.2 percent. The initial steady state also features a capital-output ratio of 2.6. The pretax rate of return is 9.7 percent, which is close to the postwar U.S. marginal product of capital (see Feldstein and Samwick 1997).

b.   Modeling Social Security's Privatization

Privatizing Social Security generally involves (a) forcing workers to contribute to private accounts, (b) giving retirees and workers Social Security benefits equal to only those they have accrued as of the time of the reform, and (c) financing Social Security benefits during a transition period.

In our model, privatizing Social Security contributions just requires setting the model's Social Security payroll tax rate to zero; i.e., there is no need to add a formal private pension system to the model. Since the agents in our model are not liquidity constrained, forcing them to contribute to private accounts will not

---

4   Within the boundaries of the model, the Social Security Trust Fund is irrelevant if agents see through the veil. Prefunded social security benefits are then equivalent to private savings.

affect their net saving or labor supply decisions because they are free to borrow against their mandated retirement accounts. This said, it is worth pointing out that in the particular economies simulated here, only the poorest 10 percent of agents actually seek to borrow against Social Security. So were we to add a liquidity constraint (specifically, a constraint against negative net wealth), it would not materially alter our findings.

To capture the second feature of privatization, namely giving retirees and workers their full accrued Social Security benefits, we phase out Social Security benefits starting 10 years after the privatization reform occurs. The 10-year delay reflects the need to give current retirees the same benefits they would otherwise have received. In the model, Social Security benefits are received for 10 years from 45 to 55 (real age 55 to real age 65). Starting in the 11th year of the reform, we phase out Social Security benefits by 2.2 percent (of the baseline benefits) per year for 45 years.

We use three alternative taxes to pay for Social Security benefits during the privatization transition: wage taxation, income taxation, and consumption taxation. We also consider a five-year delay in the use of income taxes, with the government issuing debt during the five-year period to finance Social Security benefits. The goal here is to partially insulate the initial elderly from a higher fiscal burden. After the five-year period, the per capita level of debt accumulated during the five-year period is held constant. Payment of interest on this debt (in excess of the amount of additional debt that can be floated while still maintaining the same level of debt per capita) is financed through an increase in income tax rates.

The transition to a privatized Social Security system alters the income tax base. Since we maintain a constant level of government purchases per effective worker in each transition, we need to adjust income tax rates along the transition path even in those simulations in which income taxes are not used to pay the Social Security benefits accrued under the old system. The shares of (endogenous) revenues to be made up by the two components of the income tax, the progressive wage tax and the proportional capital income tax, are determined by the amount of revenues generated by each tax in the original steady state. For example, if the wage tax generates twice as much revenues as the capital income tax in the initial steady state, then two-thirds of requisite revenue are assumed to be collected by the wage tax. Consequently, a faster growth of the capital income tax base compared to the wage tax base will result in a larger relative reduction in capital income tax rates.

c.   Other Aspects of Privatization

The model described above incorporates many complex details of reality. However, as any model, our model also abstracts in important ways from reality and the exact numerical results should therefore be interpreted cautiously. In particular, while the model captures the fact that Social Security provides retirement income and redistributes from rich to poor, it does not capture other insurance aspects of Social Security; the model incorporates neither individual earnings risk nor aggregate rate of return risk. It also abstracts from longevity risk.

Indeed, one of the questions surfacing regularly in the privatization debate is whether a private annuities market will provide reasonably priced real annuities that could replace Social Security's real annuity. One element of a real annuity is the protection against inflation risk. The latter has been facilitated this year by the U.S. Treasury's decision to issue indexed bonds. By investing its portfolio into indexed bond an annuity insurer can readily provide indexed annuities. Nevertheless, a remaining problem for the existence of fairly priced annuities is the possibility of adverse selection in the annuities market. By putting a larger segment of the population into the annuities market, privatization could reduce adverse selection. Even larger welfare gains may, however, be obtained by simply mandating the annuitization of private retirement accounts (Walliser 1997).

One should also bear in mind that current Social Security benefits are anything but risk-free. The defined benefit nature of the public Social Security system means that benefits are tied to the growth rate of aggregate wages which depends on the rate of population growth and the rate of technological progress. Social Security is also subject to the risk of political interference. Privatization would instead shift some risk to the rate of return on capital.

To sum up, privatization involves more than just changing the way retirement income is financed. Moving to a privatized Social Security system would alter the allocation of risk in the economy.[5] The model abstracts from this change and its effect on the macro economy and welfare.

---

[5]   Similar arguments apply also to investment strategies in a partly funded public system (Smetters 1997).

3.   Findings

a.   Macroeconomic Effects

Table 1 presents the macroeconomic effects of five alternative privatization reforms. The top panels of Figures 1–5 graph this information. Consider first

Table 1 — Percentage Change in Capital Stock, Labor Supply, Output, Wages, and Interest Rates Relative to Steady State

Run	Finance of Social Security benefits	B-T-L	Years of deficit finance	Year of transition			
				5	10	25	150
			Capital stock (K)				
1	W	0.0	0	0.72	1.40	6.39	40.10
2	W	0.25	0	0.70	1.65	6.73	37.47
3	Y	0.0	0	−1.71	−3.28	−0.53	40.10
4	Y	0.0	5	3.03	0.00	−8.01	27.12
5	C	0.0	0	2.39	5.29	14.80	40.10
			Labor supply (L)				
1	W	0.0	0	0.66	0.58	4.17	6.82
2	W	0.25	0	0.67	0.64	2.86	4.93
3	Y	0.0	0	−0.88	−0.79	3.28	6.82
4	Y	0.0	5	7.00	−5.62	−1.42	4.88
5	C	0.0	0	2.67	2.69	4.57	6.82
			Output (Y)				
1	W	0.0	0	0.65	0.79	4.45	14.28
2	W	0.25	0	0.60	0.89	3.81	12.23
3	Y	0.0	0	−1.06	−1.38	2.35	14.28
4	Y	0.0	5	6.10	−4.07	−2.89	10.12
5	C	0.0	0	2.60	3.33	7.03	14.28
			Wages (W)				
1	W	0.0	0	−0.02	0.20	0.62	7.02
2	W	0.25	0	0.00	0.25	0.93	7.00
3	Y	0.0	0	−0.21	−0.64	−0.93	7.02
4	Y	0.0	5	−0.94	1.46	−1.72	4.93
5	C	0.0	0	−0.07	0.63	2.36	7.02

B-T-L: marginal benefit tax linkage; C: consumption tax; W: payroll tax; Y: income tax.

Table 1 — Continued

Run	Finance of Social Security benefits	B-T-L	Years of deficit finance	Year of transition			
				5	10	25	150
	Interest rates (r)						
1	W	0.0	0	0.20	−0.44	−1.69	−19.00
2	W	0.25	0	0.14	−0.60	−2.59	−18.63
3	Y	0.0	0	2.62	4.05	5.27	−19.00
4	Y	0.0	5	2.87	−2.60	7.98	−13.71
5	C	0.0	0	0.40	−1.73	−6.75	−19.00

B-T-L: marginal benefit tax linkage; C: consumption tax; W: payroll tax; Y: income tax.

Runs 1, 3, and 5, which use wage taxation, consumption taxation, and income taxation, respectively, to privatize Social Security. A quick glance at the tables and figures shows that each of these three runs produces the same quite striking long-run results. The capital stock rises by 40 percent, labor supply rises by 7 percent, output, as well as output per person, rises by 14 percent, the real wage rises by 7 percent, and the real interest rate falls by 19 percent.

Although the long-run position of the economy is the same in each of these runs, the time it takes to get close to the economy's long-run position and the size of the short-run economic response depends critically on the choice of the tax used to finance transitional Social Security benefits. Take wage tax finance. After 25 years, the capital stock is only 6 percent larger, which is only 15 percent of its ultimate increase. In the case of income tax finance, the capital stock is actually 1 percent smaller 25 years after the transition, notwithstanding the fact that it ultimately ends up 40 percent larger. With consumption tax finance the transition is much faster, but it is still rather slow. After 25 years the capital stock is 15 percent larger which is less than two-fifths of its long-run increase.

One reason why the transitions take time is that Social Security benefits are reduced gradually over a 55-year period. A second reason the transitions are slow is that the capital stock is a stock and even substantial changes in annual saving rates take quite a while to materially alter it. This feature of neoclassical economics—that policy-induced economic transitions are very slow—was one of the main messages of Auerbach and Kotlikoff (1987). The third reason the transitions are slow applies in the case of wage and income tax finance. Using those tax instruments means that in the short run, there will be quite high marginal tax rates on labor supply and capital income. This gives households an incentive to substitute current leisure and consumption for future leisure and consumption. Indeed, in the case of income tax finance, the short-term disincentive to work leads to a 1 percent decline in aggregate labor supply.

With consumption tax finance, the short-run saving incentives are quite different. The additional consumption tax starts out at a 10 percent rate and then declines over time to zero. The temporarily high price of consumption gives agents an incentive to delay their consumption expenditures and, consequently, save more. Moreover, using the consumption tax rather than an income or wage tax to finance transitional Social Security benefits places a larger fiscal burden on the initial elderly and a lower one on those who are young and middle-aged. Since the elderly, who are closer to the end of their lives, have higher propensities to consume than do the young and middle-aged, redistributing from them to younger cohort leads to less overall consumption and more national saving. Furthermore, most of this redistribution to the young occurs through a efficient one-time tax on existing non-social-security wealth.

Benefit-Tax Linkage

Run 2 repeats the wage tax finance transition, but assumes that workers perceive a 25 cent on the dollar linkage between marginal Social Security tax payments and marginal Social Security benefits. Having positive perceived benefit-tax linkage reduces the payroll tax's distortion of labor supply and lessens the efficiency gains from privatizing Social Security. This translates into growth in capital, labor supply, and output that is 2 to 3 percentage points smaller than with zero benefit tax linkage. This simulation suggests therefore that the degree of benefit-tax linkage can play an important role in determining the gains from privatization.

Debt Finance

Run 4 indicates that financing transitional benefits with debt alters privatization's macroeconomic impact in both the short and long run. In this run, the first five years of transitional benefits are financed with deficits. After year 5, debt per effective worker is held constant, and revenue from income taxes is used to pay Social Security benefits during the remainder of the transition as well as to pay interest on the additional debt accumulated during the preceding 5 years. Since the economy ends up with more debt in the final steady state, the long-run increase in the capital stock is smaller—only 27 percent compared with 40 percent in the no-debt finance case.

Figure 1 —   Payroll Tax Finance of Benefits

Macro Effects

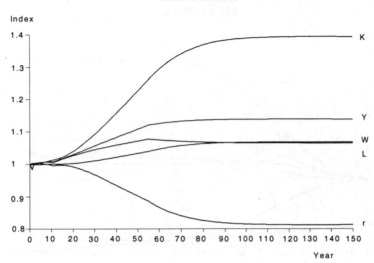

Remaining Lifetime Utility

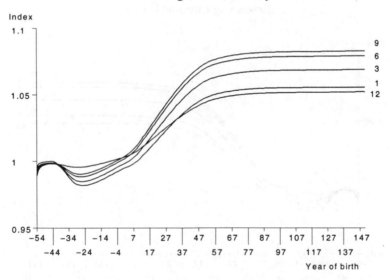

Figure 2 — Payroll Tax Finance of Benefits with 25 Percent Benefit–Tax Linkage

Macro Effects

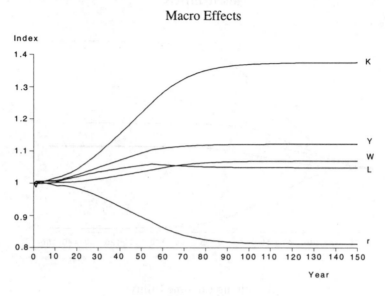

Remaining Lifetime Utility

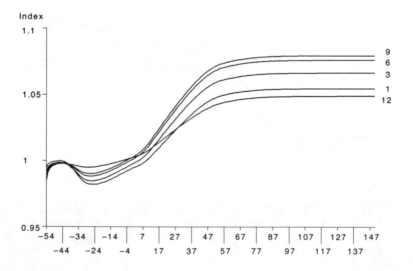

Figure 3 —   Income Tax Finance of Benefits

Macro Effects

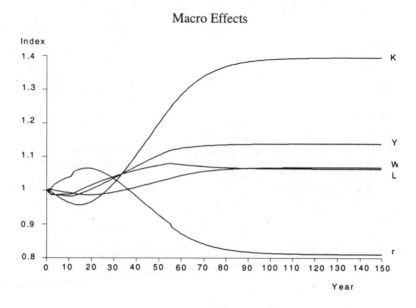

Remaining Lifetime Utility

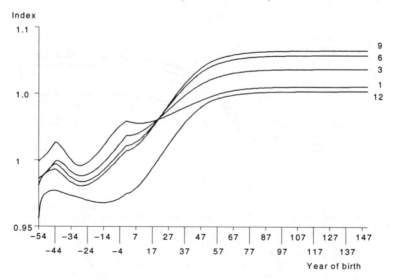

Figure 4 —   Income Tax Finance of Benefits with 5 Years of Debt Finance

Macro Effects

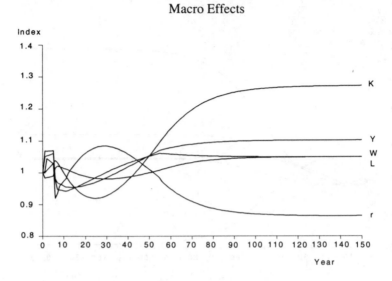

Remaining Lifetime Utility

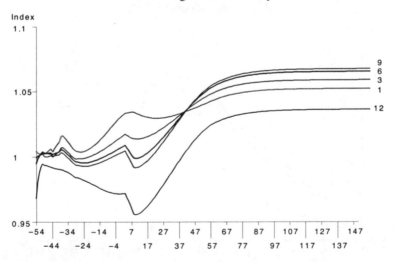

Figure 5 — Consumption Tax Finance of Benefits

Macro Effects

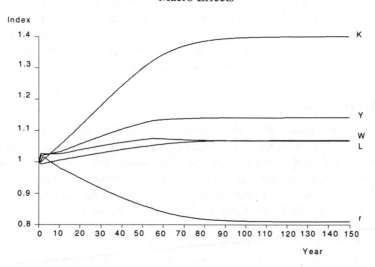

Remaining Lifetime Utility

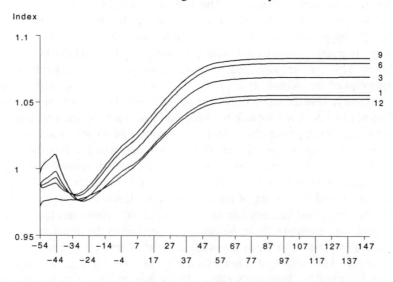

Although deficit finance depresses long-run capital formation, it stimulates capital formation in the short run. Recall that the temporary issuance of debt delays the increase in income tax rates. This leads to additional short-term saving as agents take advantage of the temporarily low income tax rates by working harder, so that in year 5 of the transition the capital stock is 3 percent higher than in the initial steady state and 5 percent higher than in the same transition (Run 3) but without short-term deficit finance. However, the debt issuance simply delays the short-run crowding out of capital arising from income tax finance of the transition. Indeed, the capital stock in the 25th year after Social Security privatization begins is 8 percent smaller than its initial value.

b.   Welfare Effects

Table 2 and Figures 1–5 show the welfare effects of the different privatization policies. The welfare effects are measured here as the percentage increase in both consumption and leisure in each year of remaining life (entire life for newborns) in the preprivatization economy needed to generate the same level of utility the agent enjoys as a result of the privatization reform. The first thing to note is that all households, poor and rich alike, who are born in the long run gain from privatizing Social Security. For each of the income classes, the welfare gain exceeds 5 percent. The gains are larger for middle income classes. Class 9, for example, enjoys an 8 percent welfare gain. The welfare gain for the top income class is 5 percent; for the bottom income class it is 6 percent.

What explains these differences? The answer is that different features of the privatization policy affect different income groups differently. First, we are eliminating the progressive Social Security benefit schedule. Second, we are eliminating the regressive (due to the ceiling on taxable earnings) Social Security payroll tax. Third, we are adjusting downward long-run income tax rates due to the expansion of the income tax base associated with the long-run improvement of the economy. This reduction in income tax rates benefits income tax payers, a set of agents that does not include the very poor, who pay no income taxes because of the tax exemptions and deductions. Fourth, this reform, which replaces Social Security's payroll tax with another distortionary tax that hits the rich as well as the poor at the margin, has a bigger impact on households with higher earnings, since they already face a higher marginal income tax rate. Since the distortion rises with the square of the tax rate, those households face a multiple of the labor supply distortion of low-income households. However, those households which have earnings above the payroll tax ceiling in the initial steady state (represented by class 12 in Table 2 and Figures 1–5) benefit less from privatization, since their labor supply was not affected by the payroll tax at the margin.

In considering these long-run welfare effects, it is important to bear in mind that the privatization reforms being simulated do not include redistributive features. But the privatization of Social Security could be made more progressive. One could, for example, privatize Social Security by having the government match workers' contributions to their individual retirement accounts on a progressive basis. Obviously, this would produce relatively higher gains for low income classes.

Table 2 — Percentage Change in Remaining Lifetime Utility for Selected Income Classes

Run	Class	Year of birth						
		−54	−25	−10	0	10	25	150
1	1	−0.42	−1.80	−1.18	−0.51	0.10	2.04	5.57
	3	−1.10	−1.48	−0.75	−0.16	0.66	2.94	6.91
	6	−0.73	−1.11	−0.39	0.20	1.14	3.67	7.96
	9	−0.57	−0.91	−0.21	0.37	1.37	3.97	8.33
	12	−0.87	−0.39	−0.02	0.34	0.88	2.36	5.27
2	1	−0.53	−1.81	−1.16	−0.52	0.10	2.02	5.44
	3	−1.42	−1.52	−0.86	−0.21	0.59	2.91	6.62
	6	−1.06	−1.26	−0.51	0.13	1.05	3.48	7.59
	9	−0.85	−0.97	−0.34	0.30	1.26	3.75	7.92
	12	−1.23	−0.48	−0.10	0.26	0.76	2.14	4.87
3	1	−0.11	−0.25	1.92	2.95	2.79	3.32	5.57
	3	−1.36	−1.03	0.55	1.88	2.20	3.64	6.91
	6	−1.87	−1.50	−0.04	1.15	1.72	3.85	7.96
	9	−1.84	−1.79	−0.45	0.79	1.48	3.91	8.33
	12	−4.29	−2.96	−3.03	−2.43	−1.63	0.95	5.27
4	1	0.21	0.19	1.76	3.02	2.89	2.69	4.83
	3	−0.29	−0.31	0.59	1.47	1.13	2.01	5.48
	6	−0.72	−0.64	−0.03	0.65	−0.25	1.35	6.10
	9	−0.72	−0.89	−0.34	0.23	−0.90	1.04	6.31
	12	−3.30	−1.95	−2.82	−2.92	−4.35	−2.12	3.28
5	1	−0.31	−2.32	−0.83	0.09	0.91	2.85	5.57
	3	−1.18	−2.11	−0.10	1.01	1.95	4.03	6.91
	6	−1.16	−1.63	0.52	1.74	2.77	4.95	7.96
	9	−1.19	−1.39	0.84	2.09	3.15	5.33	8.33
	12	−2.80	−2.06	−1.09	−0.20	0.76	2.67	5.27

The tables and figures show not only the long-run winners from privatization, but also the short-run losers. In Run 1, which continues to finance Social Security benefits with a proportional wage tax, benefits accrue to richer income classes earlier during the transition. The reason for this finding is straightforward: Social Security replaces a larger fraction of income for the poor than for the rich, a factor that is enhanced by the progressive benefit schedule. Reducing benefits and removing the redistribution implied by Social Security thus requires a larger growth in wages for the poor than for the rich to improve their welfare relative to the status quo.

In contrast, financing the transition with an income tax in Run 3 puts a higher burden on the middle class and especially the very high income classes. This result follows from the specifics of the income tax code, which exempts low-income households from taxation. Thus, class 1 does not contribute at all to financing the transition when income tax finance is employed. Class 12, however, gets hit especially hard, since the nondistortionary payroll tax (class 12's income exceeds the payroll tax ceiling) is replaced by a fully distortionary income tax. Run 3 also raises the tax rate on capital income, which affects high earners the most.

Finally, take Run 5, which uses consumption tax finance. All generations over age 25 (real age 45) at the time of the reform are made worse off by the reform, although their welfare losses are moderate. In the case of initial 54-year-olds, there is a 0.3 percent loss for the poorest income class, a 1 percent loss for middle-income classes, and a 2.8 percent loss for the highest income class. For 25-year-olds, the welfare losses are more uniform across income classes, ranging from 1 to 2 percent. For this cohort, the poorest income class fares the worst.

4.   Summary and Conclusion

Our simulation study shows that Social Security's privatization can have a significant and beneficial long-run impact on the economy and individual welfare. Although the long-run gains are substantial, they do not come overnight. Even if one uses consumption taxation, which produces the most rapid transition, to finance the reform, the half-life of the transition exceeds 25 years. The long-term gains are also not costless. Although privatizing Social Security reduces economic distortions, the lion's share of the large welfare gains enjoyed by future generations from Social Security's privatization comes at a price of welfare losses suffered by initial generations.

Bibliography

Altig, D., A.J. Auerbach, L.J. Kotlikoff, K.A. Smetters, and J. Walliser (1997). Fundamental Tax Reform and Macroeconomic Performance. Mimeo. Congressional Budget Office, Washington, D.C.

Arrau, P. (1990). Social Security Reform: The Capital Accumulation and Intergenerational Distribution Effect. Working Paper 512. World Bank, Washington, D.C.

Arrau, P., and K. Schmidt-Hebbel (1993). Macroeconomic and Intergenerational Welfare Effects of a Transition from Pay-as-You-Go to Fully Funded Pensions. Mimeo. World Bank, Washington, D.C.

Auerbach, A.J. (1996). Tax Reform, Capital Allocation, Efficiency, and Growth. In H. Aaron and W.B. Gale (eds.), *Economic Effects of Fundamental Tax Reform*. Washington, D.C.: Brookings Institution.

Auerbach, A.J., and L.J. Kotlikoff (1987). *Dynamic Fiscal Policy*. Cambridge, England: Cambridge University Press.

Auerbach, A.J., L.J. Kotlikoff, R. Hagemann, and G. Nicoletti (1989). The Economics of the Demographic Transition. *OECD Staff Papers*.

Feldstein, M. (1995). Would Privatizing Social Security Raise Economic Welfare? Mimeo. Harvard University.

Feldstein, M.S., and A.A. Samwick (1997). The Transition Path in Privatizing Social Security. Forthcoming in M.S. Feldstein (ed.), *Privatizing Social Security*. University of Chicago Press.

Fullerton, D., and D.L. Rogers (1993). *Who Bears the Lifetime Tax Burden?* Washington, D.C.: Brookings Institution.

Huang, H., S. Imrohoroglu, and T.J. Sargent (1997). Two Computational Experiments to Privatize Social Security. Forthcoming in *Macroeconomic Dynamics*.

Kotlikoff, L.J. (1996). Privatizing Social Security: How It Works and Why It Matters. In J.M. Poterba (ed.), *Tax Policy and the Economy* 10. Cambridge, Mass.: MIT Press.

—— (1997). Simulating the Privatization of Social Security in General Equilibrium. Forthcoming in M.S. Feldstein (ed.), *Privatizing Social Security*. University of Chicago Press.

Kotlikoff, L.J., K. Smetters, and J. Walliser (1997). Privatizing U.S. Social Security—A Simulation Study. Forthcoming in K. Schmidt Hebbel (ed.), *Pension Systems: From Crisis to Reform*. Washington, D.C.: The World Bank.

Menchik, P.L., and M. David (1982). The Incidence of a Lifetime Consumption Tax. *National Tax Journal* XXXV:189–203.

Raffelhüschen, B. (1993). Funding Social Security Through Pareto-Optimal Conversion Policies. In Bernhard Felderer (ed.), *Public Pension Economics. Journal of Economics/Zeitschrift fur Nationalökonomie* 7:105–131.

Seidman, L.S. (1986). A Phase-Down of Social Security: The Transition in a Life Cycle Growth Model. *National Tax Journal* XXXIX:97–107.

Smetters, K.A. (1997). Investing the Trust Fund into Equities: Unmasking the Large Hidden Liability for Future Generations. Mimeo. Congressional Budget Office, Washington, D.C.

Steuerle, C.E., and J.M. Bakija (1994). *Retooling Social Security for the 21st Century.* Washington, D.C.: The Urban Institute Press.

Walliser, J. (1997). *Essays on Annuity Pricing and Social Security Privatization.* Ph.D. dissertation. Boston University.

Comment on Laurence J. Kotlikoff, Kent Smetters, and Jan Walliser

Andrew A. Samwick

1. Introduction

The goal of this paper by Kotlikoff, Smetters, and Walliser (KSW) is to characterize a particular set of transition paths that phase out the existing pay-as-you-go (PAYG) system of old-age insurance in the United States. Their analytical framework is a substantially enhanced version of the Auerbach–Kotlikoff (1987) overlapping generations model that has been used for a decade to conduct dynamic fiscal policy simulations. The simulation results for the long-term impact of the reforms are broadly similar to those obtained by Feldstein and Samwick (1996, 1997), even though the methodologies have many differences. As is essential in this type of analysis, KSW are up front and explicit about the welfare losses to the transition generations. In fact, the principal improvement in the methodology in this paper is to allow for intragenerational heterogeneity and thereby conduct another dimension of welfare analysis.

My remarks will focus on three main aspects of the KSW research. Since the details of a model as rich as the one in this paper are often difficult to synthesize, I first discuss the key elements of the transition. What makes the privatization work in this model? I then discuss the major shortcoming with the model in its current form; namely, that it fails to incorporate any type of income uncertainty. Given that Social Security is designed to provide insurance, this is an important omission. It is simply not clear that even the qualitative results would hold up if various forms of uncertainty were introduced into the model. KSW do not emphasize this point enough in their exposition. Lastly, the KSW model is similar to many reform proposals that switch from a defined benefit to a defined contribution system. I conclude my remarks by commenting on the way the KSW model handles the pitfalls that might arise in such a switch.

2. Elements of the Transition

Much is made in this paper of the increase in economic efficiency that is obtained in the KSW plan through greater tax-benefit linkages. The tax-benefit linkage corresponds to the extent to which an additional dollar of contributions generates a benefit stream with an actuarial present value of a dollar. The higher the tax-benefit linkage, the lower the effective tax rate on labor supply and the consequent distortions. In the current PAYG system, the tax-benefit linkage differs from (and is typically less than) 100 percent due to both explicit and implicit redistribution. The explicit redistribution is intergenerational—the startup generations reaped windfall gains, and the current generations must service that obligation. As the authors have argued forcefully in other contexts (see, e.g., Kotlikoff and Sachs 1997), there is also substantial intragenerational redistribution. While some of this redistribution is simply to provide higher replacement rates to workers with lower lifetime earnings, there is also redistribution that is less straightforward; for example, redistribution to one-earner couples relative to two-earner couples.

There are several problems with the way these improvements are obtained by KSW. The first is that although they acknowledge the scope for reintroducing redistribution in the privatized system, none of their simulations do so. It is simply misleading to compare a privatized system without redistribution to a PAYG system with redistribution, given the importance of the tax-benefit linkage in generating the efficiency gains.

The second is that the actual amount of tax-benefit linkage in the current system is vastly understated. The baseline is taken to be zero, and the only other value used is 25 percent. There is simply no good reason for not using the actual tax-benefit linkages, which have been calculated in Feldstein and Samwick (1992), among other places. The folly is compounded when it is undertaken by the same authors who rail against the redistribution from two- to one-earner couples, which can generate linkages in excess of 100 percent for the worker in a one-earner couple! The reader should bear in mind that a linkage of zero literally means that a worker believes that her retirement benefits would be completely unaffected if she paid $100 less in contributions. Given that the perception that Social Security is a "tax" is more common among economists than the public at large, in the absence of direct evidence, 100 percent is as (un)reasonable a benchmark as zero.

The third problem is that the analysis assumes that households are not liquidity constrained in their consumption decisions. In other words, they are assumed to be indifferent to the particular timing of cash flows over their life cycle, caring only about the present value of their taxes, net of transfers. In short, they are the standard life-cycle consumers that are saving actively for their retirement at all ages. While the assumption that households behave this way makes the model more tractable, it may give misleading results. Liquidity-constrained households will view forced saving—even at an actuarially fair rate—much like a tax. If a household is liquidity-constrained, its marginal utility of consumption is too high in the current period and too low in future periods (compared to its optimal path in the absence of the constraint). For such a household, a policy that had a zero present value but took resources today and returned them in the future would lower welfare. This will also lessen the extent to which a higher tax-benefit linkage generates an efficiency improvement.

Another source of efficiency gains in the model is the switch from payroll to consumption tax finance of the unfunded liability of the current system (in some scenarios). At first glance, such a proposal would appear politically unacceptable, as the consumption tax is similar to a lump-sum tax on existing wealth, which is held disproportionately by the elderly in a life-cycle model of consumption. The subtlety in the KSW analysis is that because Social Security benefits are indexed to the consumer price index, the poorest elderly households who live entirely off Social Security will not be affected. Their income and expenditures will rise proportionately under a national consumption tax. The simulation results presented in the paper clearly show that the consumption tax finance of the transition is not the worst case for the lowest-income elderly. Given the automatic protection of the poor elderly, policy options that include consumption tax finance deserve more consideration than they typically receive. In practice, the middle-class elderly may fare worse than the rich elderly may, largely because they consume more of their accumulated wealth while alive than do the rich, who leave sizable bequests.

My last point about the transition itself is simply to acknowledge the contributions of the latest round of methodological improvements. The model allows for intragenerational heterogeneity in lifetime earnings profiles, a feature that may be unique among general equilibrium models used for policy analysis. Allowing for this heterogeneity also enables KSW to incorporate a more realistic income tax schedule, including the standard deductions and personal exemptions of the U.S. tax system, as well as the maximum taxable earnings level of the Social Security system. Although some elements of the tax code like the earned income tax credit and estate tax are still absent, incorporating kinked budget constraints is an important advance.

3.   Consumption under Imperfect Capital Markets

Even with heterogeneity in lifetime earnings profiles, the life-cycle model under certainty that is used in this paper will not match the cross-sectional moments of the wealth distribution. In this model, there are simply too many people doing too much saving before retirement, and there is likely to be far more dissaving after retirement than what is observed in practice. The model must therefore be omitting some important element of household consumption decisions.

The most significant such omission is income uncertainty and the precautionary saving motive it generates. A recent literature has demonstrated that income uncertainty is essential to the theoretical explanations of empirical regularities in consumption at both the macroeconomic (Caballero 1990) and microeconomic (Carroll 1997) levels. "Saving for emergencies" is routinely cited as the most important reason for saving in survey data, and precautionary saving has been estimated to be responsible for up to one-half of the wealth of the typical household during its working years (Carroll and Samwick 1995). In the absence of income uncertainty, the KSW model is missing the "insurance" in social insurance.

Considering the effects of income uncertainty on this analysis requires more than noting that if households *also* have a precautionary motive for saving, then saving will be higher than what the model currently predicts. It raises the possibility that the wealth data that are being matched by the current model using a certainty model were actually generated by a substantially different consumption process. There is a growing body of evidence, discussed in Carroll (1997), that the appropriate way to model the typical household during its working years is as a "buffer-stock" saver rather than a life-cycle saver. In a buffer-stock model, households are impatient enough to want to borrow against their future income in the absence of uncertainty, but they are prudent enough to realize that they need at least a small stock of wealth in order to buffer their consumption against near-term fluctuations in income. Buffer-stock savers do not begin accumulating resources for retirement until very late in their working years.

It is important to note that the omission of income uncertainty in the KSW model is not one of carelessness but one of tractability. Adding in a reasonable parameterization of income uncertainty and allowing for the heterogeneity in preferences across households that is required in that model would make the model too difficult to solve. It is a modeling choice to simplify the income process in favor of the completeness of a general equilibrium model. Nonetheless, KSW do need to explain how the simulation results may be affected by this simplification. Some progress can be made in this regard by realizing that buffer-stock savers behave much like the liquidity-constrained households discussed above. Relative to the life-cycle savers modeled by KSW, they find tax increases more difficult to bear and tax reductions more valuable. It is therefore not the case that considering income uncertainty would lead the authors to make substantially different predictions, since the main benefit of privatization is that it reduces the payroll tax in the long run. What it does suggest is that transition options that are more gradual, like the deficit finance transition, are better than they appear in this analysis. It might also be worth considering options that incorporate the heterogeneity across households explicitly through multiple reform options (see, e.g., Samwick 1997).

4.   Switching from Defined Benefit to Defined Contribution Systems

Like most reform proposals, the KSW model establishes a defined contribution system for all prospective benefits and a particular combination of taxes to finance the remnants of the PAYG defined benefit system. Depending on how the transition is managed, switching to a defined contribution system may change features of the system other than the average level of benefits in retirement. These features include income redistribution, exposure of the participants to risk, and the provision of annuities.

The typical PAYG system redistributes income from high lifetime earners to low lifetime earners through a progressive benefit formula. It is important to note that in the United States, Social Security is really the only program that uses a permanent rather than an annual measure of income as the basis for redistribution. Since the KSW model is designed to take advantage of explicit tax-benefit linkages in a defined contribution system, it does not have a redistributive element built in. It is common for skeptics of privatization to suggest that if the progressive benefit formula were eliminated, the redistribution that is now implicit would not be done explicitly. A normative response to this objection is that in a democracy, such consent is to be valued for its own sake. But the positive response is to simulate a privatization that keeps the amount of redistribution constant. KSW outline how this could be done through a progressive schedule of government matching contributions, but until they incorporate it formally, their analysis will not be convincing. In Feldstein and Samwick (1996), we calculated the cost of restoring a reasonable amount of redistribution to the privatized system. Our results showed that it would not be expensive to maintain a minimum benefit level, primarily because the redistribution, like the prefunding of benefits, could be achieved at the rate of return on capital, which exceeds the implied rates of return on the unfunded system. Additionally, future generations of low-income workers will benefit substantially from the changes in factor prices— higher wages and lower interest rates—that result from the increase in the national capital stock.

In the typical discussion of privatization, it is often assumed that workers and retirees, as investors in risky securities such as the stock market, bear all of that risk under the new system. It is the price they pay for achieving the higher rates of return on their contributions, and it raises a difficult issue of what would retirees with defined contribution accounts have done, for example, had they experienced the asset market returns of the 1930s? There is probably some truth to the conjecture that only the government can provide insurance of this type, but it should also be noted that during the 1930s, a PAYG system would also have experienced extreme financial difficulties as well. In either system, a substantial amount of redistribution from future generations would likely be enacted. One advantage of the PAYG system is that such a transfer mechanism is already in place, whereas it would take more explicit action to create it in the new system.

A third feature of the defined benefit system that is not automatically replicated in the defined contribution system is the access to group annuity markets. Under the PAYG system, the government implicitly purchases group annuities at an actuarially fair rate. Administrative costs are on the order of 0.80 percent of annual benefit payments. As is well known, administrative costs on individual-based insurance contracts are substantially higher than those on group-based contracts. Unless the role of marketing by private insurance providers and selection by the better risks in the population can be restricted, the gains of privatization could be wasted on higher administrative costs. KSW have been careful to restrict these possibilities—investment choices are restricted to passively managed accounts and annuitization is mandatory for all participants.

In summary, the KSW analysis of Social Security reform remains at the forefront of the debate. KSW provide clear answers to policy questions in which clarity is essential. There are only two important caveats in the way their model has been implemented. The first is the treatment of the tax-benefit linkages, a problem that could be corrected without much difficulty. The second is that modeling consumption behavior in the absence of income uncertainty is going to lead to potentially misleading results. If not in the formal model, then critically in the exposition, KSW must acknowledge this shortcoming and discuss the impact of the omission on their predictions.

Bibliography

Auerbach, A.J., and L.J. Kotlikoff (1987). *Dynamic Fiscal Policy*. Cambridge: Cambridge University Press.

Caballero, R.J. (1990). Consumption Puzzles and Precautionary Savings. *Journal of Monetary Economics* 25:113–136.

Carroll, C.D. (1997). Buffer Stock Saving and the Life Cycle/Permanent Income Hypothesis. *Quarterly Journal of Economics* 112:1–56.

Carroll, C.D., and A.A. Samwick (1995). How Important Is Precautionary Saving? Working Paper 5194. National Bureau of Economic Research, Cambridge, Mass.

Feldstein, M.S., and A.A. Samwick (1992). Social Security Rules and Marginal Tax Rates. *National Tax Journal* 45:1–22.

Feldstein, M.S., and A.A. Samwick (1996). The Transition Path in Privatizing Social Security. Working Paper 5761. National Bureau of Economic Research, Cambridge, Mass. Forthcoming in M.S. Feldstein (ed.), *Privatizing Social Security*. Chicago: University of Chicago Press.

—— (1997). The Economics of Prefunding Social Security and Medicare Benefits. In J. Rotemberg and B. Bernanke (eds.), *Macroeconomics Annual 1997*. Cambridge: MIT Press.

Kotlikoff, L.J., and J. Sachs (1997). It's High Time To Privatize. *Brookings Review* Summer: 16–22.

Samwick, A.A. (1997). Discount Rate Heterogeneity and Social Security Reform. Working Paper 6219. National Bureau of Economic Research. Cambridge, Mass.

Harrie A.A. Verbon, Theo Leers, and Lex C. Meijdam

Transition towards a Funded System: The Political Economy

1. Introduction

One of the great achievements of the welfare state after World War II is the reduction of old-age poverty. This success is mainly due to the existence and development of public pension systems which, as is well known, are predominantly financed by a pay-as-you-go (PAYG) system. So, the success of the welfare state has been partly the result of a redistribution of resources from the young to the old. However, most probably, the first generation of retirees under the PAYG system is for the time being the only generation that gains from the public pension system in the sense that this generation sees its lifetime income increased. Given that dynamic efficiency prevails, all other generations that are currently alive can expect to experience a reduction in lifetime income relative to the situation where no PAYG-financed public pension system existed. These unequal gains of the PAYG system are of course due to well-known demographic developments, such as the increase in average life expectancy and the decrease in the fertility rate. Given the above stated fact that continuing the current system would imply a loss in lifetime income for young workers, it is of interest to analyze whether the PAYG systems will be converted somewhere in the future into funded systems. If this can be expected, how will this affect current decisions? To answer such questions, insight into the effects of demographic, economic, and political developments on the decision-making process is needed.

In this paper we want to discuss the above issue in the context of the public choice literature. This literature studies the mechanisms that direct a government in deciding on issues regarding public pension schemes.[1] Two models are commonly distinguished. The first one takes the model of a direct democracy as a starting point; the second one considers decisions on public pension systems in a representative democracy. It will appear that in a direct democracy, it is not very likely that a conversion to a capital-reserve (CR) system will be voted upon.

---

[1] This paper is not meant to be a survey paper. For a survey, see Breyer (1994) and Verbon (1993).

Whether a transition will occur in a representative democracy depends to a large extent on the existing size of the system and, probably, on the extent to which individual political power is endogenous or not. In particular, if in a closed economy, the PAYG system is relatively extensive, a gradual diminishing of the PAYG system can be expected. However, if individuals incur costs in order to gain political influence, this counteracts a possible shrinking of the PAYG system.

2.   The Median-Voter Model

In a democracy most government decisions are determined somehow by the preferences of the citizens currently alive. So one has to make assumptions about the way these preferences are translated into the actual decisions taken by the government. Regarding public pensions, the model of direct democracy was initially analyzed as the relevant institutional framework in deciding on the structure of public pension schemes. In a direct democracy, every voter casts a vote on the relevant characteristics of the public pension scheme and has the same weight in the decision-making process. There are no politicians in this model or, if they do exist, they should actually be considered loyal executives who passively put the decisions of the voters into operation.[2]

The birth of the public choice approach to public pension schemes can be traced back to 1975, when Edgar Browning published a now classic paper on decision-making. He considered a three-overlapping-generations model in which the two younger generations produce consumption goods which cannot be transferred over time, while the old generation is retired and does not have means of its own. Thus an economy is considered in which lending or saving is not possible: the capital market is assumed to be completely absent. Let us assume that the generations currently alive decide on a transfer system in which every worker contributes the same fraction, τ, of his produced consumption goods. Suppose, moreover, that every generation forms its preferences by assuming that the size of the transfer decided upon will be maintained indefinitely. For simplicity, every worker is assumed to produce consumption goods with value w and there is no population growth.

Before deriving the choice of τ, let us first consider the rate of return, $t-1$ say, on the contributions for the three generations if the transfer system is to be intro-

---

[2]   As is well known, if individuals decide independently of each other, for every individual an incentive exists to let the other members contribute to the system without contributing oneself. The political process can be assumed to "solve" this free-rider problem by forcing all members of the decisive generation to cooperate.

duced for the first time. For the old generation (of age 3) the rate of return is infinite, of course, because it receives a transfer without having contributed to the system. For a middle-aged individual (of age 2), ι follows from $\tau w \iota = \eta$, where η is the transfer to be received in the next period. As the budget restriction of the transfer system implies that $\eta = 2\tau w$, it follows that $\iota = 2$. A young individual (of age 1) will contribute to the system in the first and second period of her life, so that the rate of return follows from $\tau w \iota^2 + \tau w \iota = \eta = 2\tau w$, which implies $\iota = 1$. So, the rate of return on the contributions increases with age.

It can then be expected that the preferred contribution rate will increase with age as well. This is, in fact, easily demonstrated. Introduce the following additive separable utility function for an individual of age i $(i = 1, 2, 3)$:[3]

$$[1] \qquad U_i = \sum_{j=i}^{3} u(c_j),$$

where $c_j = (1-\tau)w$ with $(j = 1, 2)$, and $c_3 = \eta$. The felicity functions $u(c_j)$ are assumed to obey the conventional Inada conditions. Inserting the budget restriction, i.e., $\tau w = \frac{1}{2}\eta$, in U_2 and differentiating with respect to η shows that the optimal transfer for an individual of age 2, η_2 say, is implicitly given by

$$[2] \qquad u'(\eta_2) = \frac{1}{2}u'(w - \frac{1}{2}\eta_2),$$

where u' is marginal utility of consumption per period. For the optimal transfer of the youngest generation, η_1 say, the following has to hold:

$$[3] \qquad u'(\eta_1) = u'(w - \frac{1}{2}\eta_1).$$

If, however, the preferences of the individuals of age 2 determine the transfer, and we replace η_1 in [3] by η_2 from [2], we derive that the total marginal utility of the benefit η_2 equals $-\frac{1}{2}u'(w - \frac{1}{2}\eta_2)$ which is obviously negative. In other words, the transfer preferred by the individual of median age is higher than the one preferred by the youngest individuals.

As the oldest individuals prefer a benefit as high as possible, under majority voting the benefit η_2 will be chosen. Moreover, assuming that this benefit will be maintained, every young generation is confronted with a benefit that is too high to generate maximum lifetime utility. Future median voters will not be willing to

---

3   In the sequel, preferences of individuals in isolation are considered. Intergenerational transfers are between individuals via the public pension system. As an alternative to these transfers, however, intergenerational transfers within one's own family are possible. The preferences for a public pension system can then be seen to be dependent on the family size of the individuals concerned, as demonstrated by Breyer and Schulenburg (1990).

decrease the transfer to the level that is optimal for all future generations, because for these individuals equation [2] determines the optimal transfer again.

The above gives the basic argument of Browning's paper. Note once again that completely imperfect capital markets were assumed. If capital markets are perfect, on the other hand, the political choice is between the PAYG system or no public system at all, where individuals provide for their own old-age consumption by investing their savings in a CR system. Under majority rule the age of the distinguished individuals is the determining factor again for the preferences as we will now demonstrate. Suppose that in the three-overlapping-generations model a pension benefit, η, has to be financed. The old will of course prefer the PAYG system. The individuals of age 2 are able to generate a pension benefit, η, by saving τw which, including the accrued interest, will give η in the next period if $\tau = \eta/(wR)$, where R is equal to one plus the interest rate. Under the PAYG system the contribution would equal $\tau = \frac{1}{2}\eta/w$. These individuals will thus prefer the PAYG system if $R < 2$.

The individuals of age 1 pay a contribution rate under the PAYG system that is equal to $\frac{1}{2}\eta/w$ during the first two periods of their lives. Had they invested these contributions, the accumulated value at the start of their last period would equal $\frac{1}{2}\eta (R^2+R)$. They would thus prefer the PAYG system if and only if $\frac{1}{2}\eta (R^2+R) < \eta$ or if $R < 1$. Obviously, in our simple model with no income or population growth, it would be inefficient to save if $R < 1$. So the young prefer an efficient financing system. A PAYG system will be chosen by the majority nevertheless if $R < 2$.

Let us now return to the issue of conversion from the PAYG system to the CR system. Such a conversion might be deemed worthwhile because of the increasing costs of the PAYG system due to the aging of the population. From the above analysis we conclude, however, that under the median-voter model two opposing forces are at work. First, under aging of the population the age of the decisive voter tends to increase, which decreases the likelihood that the decisive voter will prefer a conversion. Second, if aging occurs, this decreases the internal rate of return of maintaining the PAYG system. It stands to reason that, unless the PAYG system becomes unrealistically inefficient for the median voter, the first effect will dominate, so that a conversion from a PAYG system to a CR system is not very likely.

In the Browning model, public pensions arise because the median voters assume that the current decisions regarding the public pension scheme will remain unaltered forever. However, if one looks at the actual operation of public pension schemes, then it is striking that these systems are changed so often. So, it appears that the expectations of the median voter regarding the future political decision-making process are nonrational;[4] she incorrectly assumes that revoting will not take place when she is no longer the decisive voter. By simply looking at the past, however, individuals can learn about changes that are enacted in the decision-making process regarding public pension plans. At the extreme individuals can have rational expectations about the current and future mechanisms driving the decisions about public pension schemes. Then, the question arises whether the information currently living individuals have can be used to shape the future evolution of the scheme. In the next section a model with rational individuals will be sketched.

The median-voter model is restricted because in many Western democracies decisions are actually taken by representatives elected from the voting population. In these representative democracies many decisions are taken without consultation of the voters. But (if only to get reelected) the politicians will take decisions which reflect the interests of the voters somehow. So, it can be expected that not merely the interests of the median voters count. In the next section we turn to modeling decision-making under a representative democracy.

3. Representative Democracy

a. Exogenous Political Power

Under the assumption of a representative democracy the government consists of a sequence of drafts of elected politicians. Each draft of politicians is under the influence only of current generations. We assume that at each period two generations are around, say the old and the young. The relative political power of these generations depends upon the support they can provide for the government's survival. So, politicians do not take account of future generations' interests if the support from current generations does not depend upon their offspring's utility. Indeed, the common assumption to make is that intergenerational altruism is absent.

In a representative democracy one of the determining factors for the outcome of a political decision-making process will be the wealth accumulated by the old, and the welfare position of the young. Intuitively, one would expect that in a representative democracy it will hold that the more the old have saved in the past, and thus the richer they are during retirement, the less they will be able in the political decision-making process to capture all the potential gains of a trans-

---

4   After Browning's seminal paper, several direct-democracy models allowing for changes in the public pension system have been analyzed. For a survey of these models, see Verbon (1993).

fer system. By the same token, the richer the young are, the less political support they will receive for their wish to restrict the development of the public pension system.[5] Moreover, the number of individuals in a generation can be assumed to be of importance for the reelection chances of the government. In an overlapping-generations model the above gives some support to a decision-making function of the following form:

[4] $W_t = \rho(n_t)U_{t-1} + (1 + n_t)\gamma(n_t)U_t,$

where U_t and U_{t-1} are the utility functions of the young, born at time t, and the old, born at time $t-1$, respectively. The parameters $\rho(n)$ and $\gamma(n)$ can be interpreted as measures for the political power of an old and a young individual, respectively. The parameter n_t is the rate of population growth at time t, which is determined exogenously. It is possible that population aging decreases the relative political influence of an old individual. This is, for example, the case if the increased scarcity of labor due to a drop in population growth gives the young more economic power, which in turn leads to their having increased political influence. A decrease in the relative political influence of an old individual may also be caused by the fact that the relatively small number of young can organize themselves more easily into a pressure group. This is of course due to the free-rider problem of organizing pressure groups (see Olson 1965). In the results to be presented below, it will be assumed, however, that the political power of an old (young) individual is a negative (positive) function of n. So population aging, i.e., a decrease in n, implies an increase in the relative political influence of old individuals.

The utility of the current young is a function of their future consumption which, in turn, is determined by the future state of the public pension system. So, the future of the system or, at any case, the currently held expectations of the future of the system have a major impact on the current functioning of the system. The question now is the following: suppose individuals have correct beliefs about the future development of the system and suppose that a demographic change occurs or is expected to occur. Under which conditions will this lead to a (possibly gradual) diminishing of the PAYG system in favor of the CR system? In answering this question we discuss some of our own research on this issue (Meijdam and Verbon 1996, 1997).

---

5   The majority-voting models, however, mostly lead to another conclusion: the more the median voter has saved, the higher the tax rate will be (see, in particular, Boadway and Wildasin 1989). This is due to the fact that in majority-voting models the influence of the respective generations is distributed in an extremely asymmetric way. Only the median generation, whose members are of median age, has any influence. If this generation has accumulated wealth, it will pay to invest this wealth in a PAYG system.

We start from the obvious assumption that decisions on public pension schemes are taken by politicians while decisions on savings are taken by individuals.[6] Savings can be done for many purposes, of course, but one of the most important purposes for savings in the Western world is to provide for retirement income.[7] So, actually, we have two pension systems operating beside each other: a pension system formed by private savings operating on a funding basis and a pension system based on transfers between generations. So, conversion can be handled in this framework by considering it as a shift from the collective (PAYG) system to the private (CR) system.

If the political decision and the savings decision are separated, then we have to make some assumption about the interaction between these two pension systems. Let us assume that the groups relevant for the decision-making process, the politicians and the savers, i.e., adopt Nash behavior. So, they take the actions of the other group as given, being unable to exploit knowledge about possible behavior of other groups, including groups acting in the future. Since the young's savings decisions are assumed to be decentralized and uncoordinated, the young take aggregate savings and tax rates as given when deciding on their savings. It is assumed that every individual born at time t works a fixed amount of time at wage w during the first period of his life. A part of this wage is taxed away by the government by a lump-sum tax, τ, to be transferred to the old. The remainder is used for savings for old age, s_t, and for consumption, $c_t^y = w_t - \tau_t - s_t$. When old, the individual consumes the return on his savings and the transfer payment, η, from the government. So, the consumption at time $t+1$ of an old individual born at time t is equal to $c_t^r = (1 + r_{t+1})\, s_t + \eta_{t+1}$. It is assumed that lifetime utility of a nonaltruistic individual born at time t can be represented by the following separable utility function:

[5] $U_t = u(c_t^y) + u(c_t^r),$

where, for simplicity, the rate of time preference has been taken equal to zero. The first-order condition for maximization of lifetime utility reads as

[6] $u'(c_t^y) = (1 + r_{t+1})\, u'(c_t^r),$

where $u'(c)$ represents marginal utility. This condition states that the young use savings to equate the marginal rate of substitution of consumption in the first and the second part of their lives to the rate of return on savings.

---

6   Note that median-voter models may imply that, one day or another, both decisions are in one and the same hand, namely in the hand of the median voter.

7   In the Netherlands, for example, over 75 percent of savings are old-age savings.

The government runs the public pension system as a PAYG scheme. Abstracting from administrative costs the budget restriction of this scheme reads as

[7] $\eta_t = (1+n_t)\tau_t$.

As the link between the current and the future tax rate goes via current savings, this immediately implies that politicians take future tax rates as given. In that case the first-order condition for the tax rate at a given time, t, that maximizes target function [4] is

[8] $\dfrac{1}{\gamma(n_t)}u'(c^r_{t-1}) = \dfrac{1}{\rho(n_t)}u'(c^y_t)$.

The above model can be put in the framework of an open or a closed economy. In both cases the two first-order conditions, equation [6] and equation [8], determine the dynamics of the system. Assuming, as we do, that politicians are forward-looking, they use the system to write the current endogenous variables as a function of all expected values of the endogenous variables and the rate of population growth. The short-run consequences of once-and-for-all changes in n can then be derived analytically. The idea is to write a linearized version of the model equations in a dynamic form that can be solved recursively forward in time.[8] For the above model the linearized model can be condensed to a system describing the changes in the endogenous variables τ_t and s_t:

[9] $\begin{bmatrix} \Delta\tau_{t+1} \\ \Delta s_t \end{bmatrix} = J \begin{bmatrix} \Delta\tau_t \\ \Delta s_{t-1} \end{bmatrix} + M \begin{bmatrix} \Delta n_t \\ \Delta n_{t+1} \end{bmatrix}, \qquad t = 0,1,...,$

where M is a matrix describing the effects of the current and next-period change in n on the state variables and J is the matrix that describes the temporal relation between the endogenous variables.

From [9] the politicians in the government can calculate the effects of current or future changes in n on the current endogenous variables. So, for example, a government at time zero that receives information on changes in the rate of population growth can calculate by means of [9] the effects on the future tax rate and set the optimal current tax rate. Population aging appears to have political-power effects, reflected by $\rho' = \partial\rho/\partial n < 0$ and $\gamma' = \partial\gamma/\partial n < 0$, and demographic effects, the latter consisting of two elements. First, a decrease in n implies that a certain level of savings per worker, ceteris paribus, leads to a higher capital-labor ratio in the next period, which might be called a capital-thickening effect. This has a depressing effect on savings and so the room for consumption in-

---

8   This is the case if the system in [9] is saddlepoint-stable. This places restrictions on the matrix J, to be defined below. See Blanchard and Kahn (1980).

creases. Second, population aging implies that total consumption per worker in the economy has to be shared with a larger number of pensioners, the dependency-ratio effect. This effect has a depressing effect on consumption and the PAYG tax rate. The interplay of these political-power effects and demographic effects determines the effects on the PAYG system. We will not go into the details of the analysis, but merely present one result that can be derived for the closed-economy case: *An anticipated once-and-for-all decrease in* n *initially increases individual consumption if the tax rate is not "too large." In that case the tax rate will increase. Otherwise the effect is ambiguous.*

This result gives some clue as to the political feasibility of a conversion policy. In particular, the size of the PAYG scheme, measured by the tax rate, appears to be a determining variable for the effects of population aging. So, if the PAYG system is relatively small compared to the CR system, an anticipated decrease in population growth will lead to the initiation of a PAYG scheme. This explains why in an economy where a PAYG scheme previously had not existed, such a scheme might be installed in the face of an aging population. The reason is that in this case, at the time of the actual change in the rate of population growth, the political-power and capital-thickening effects are relatively strong compared to the dependency-ratio effects. So, all young individuals living before the time of the population shock are able to increase their consumption due to the anticipation of the increased consumption possibilities for the elderly which are engendered by the future change in political power. However, an increase in consumption by the young at any time will not be left unchallenged by the old living at that time. So, through the political process, part of the consumption gains of the young has to be shared with the old, leading to an increase in the tax rate. This redistribution will take place at all periods before the actual shock occurs. As a result, the tax rate will gradually increase and savings will gradually decrease, leading to a partial replacement of the CR system by the PAYG system. Therefore, all generations born after the demographic shock may lose, while those born before the shock will gain. In that case, the fruits of the gain in political power are only reaped by those who are old at the time of the shock or before the shock. All future generations, however, are locked in a disadvantageous situation which they cannot alter, even though they have the option to change the system. This is demonstrated by the calculations the results of which are reproduced in Figures 1, 2, and 3. Here, an economy is considered that is in a steady state without an existing PAYG system. Then at time $t=0$ a permanent decrease in n is expected to occur three generations later. The figures appear to confirm the result by Cutler et al. (1990), who suggest that expected decreases in the rate of population growth will lead to short-run gains: clearly, a gain in consumption for the current generations occurs. However, these gains entail losses for future generations. If no PAYG system were present anyhow, i.e., $\tau_t = 0$, future generations would *gain* from the decrease in population growth.

Figure 1 — The Effect of an Expected Permanent Decrease in n on Consumption and Capital

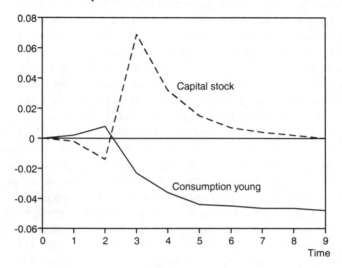

Figure 2 — The Effect of an Expected Permanent Decrease in n on Savings and Taxes

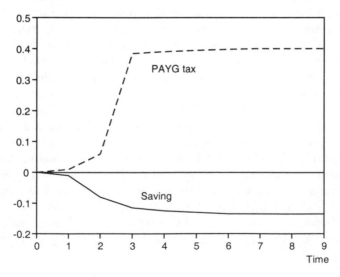

Figure 3 —   The Effect of an Expected Permanent Decrease in n on Utility

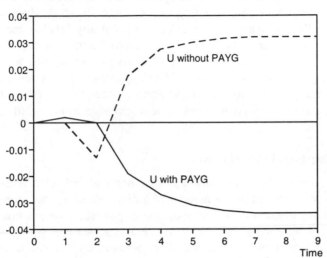

On the other hand, it should be stressed that even though the individual political power of the old increases due to population aging, this does not necessarily
imply that an extension of the PAYG system at the cost of shrinking the CR system is inevitable. From the above-stated result we can also learn that if the political power of the old is already relatively large, then the costs of population
aging, resulting in lower consumption possibilities for the young, can dominate
the political-power effect. This contradicts a result by Hansson and Stuart
(1989). They analyzed the case of an unexpected increase in political power of
the old which, in terms of our model, might be due to the aging of the population. In fact, they consider the initiation of a public pension scheme as arising
from a (permanent) change in the target function in favor of current and future
old individuals under the assumption of dynamic efficiency. According to their
results, such a change would imply a windfall gain for the old individuals at the
time of the initial change. Their model generates a sequence of monotonously increasing tax rates. In a general equilibrium closed-economy framework, however, future tax rates may decrease even if the initial effect on the tax rate is
positive. The point is that the effect of increased political power is counteracted
by the decreasing wage rate and the rising interest rate both resulting from the
decrease in savings. This demonstrates that the "overinsurance" result that is
often found in (public choice) models with exogenous interest rates may be
mitigated if general equilibrium effects are taken into account.

The above-stated result tells us that an increasing role of the PAYG system might result from the political process, confronted with an aging population. The relative size of the PAYG system compared to the CR system is a determining variable in that respect. So, returning to our central question whether a conversion from a PAYG system to a CR system is politically feasible, the conclusion of our analysis appears to be ambiguous. It might be the case that if the PAYG system is already very extensive, as is generally the case in Northern Europe, a partial and gradual conversion from PAYG systems to CR systems will be enacted. In countries such as the United States, where the PAYG system is less extensive, such a conversion might be less probable from a political point of view.

b.   Endogenous Political Power

The drawback of the above model is that political influence is exogenously given and only affected by the number of individuals in a generation. So, if under the above-mentioned case of exogenous political power a conversion of PAYG to CR were to be considered, counteracting measures from the old could be expected to prevent such a result. Such measures might entail more intensive lobbying activities in order to gain more influence on the political decision-making process. To get more insight into what determines the political power of a generation, the individual decision to invest in gaining political influence should be modeled explicitly. This would be in line with a model by Kristov et al. (1992), which endogenizes the relative political power. In that model the relative political power is the result of expenditures by old and young individuals on political activity. The more old individuals spend compared to young ones, the higher their utility is weighted by politicians. In this section a preliminary attempt is made to endogenize political power.

We abstract from savings decisions. This leads us somewhat away from the focal issue in this paper, namely whether a conversion from PAYG under CR can be expected in an aging population. So, we restrict ourselves to a consideration of changes in the tax rate as a result of aging which might then be interpreted as a relative change in the impact of the PAYG system versus the CR system.

Individuals have to incur costs in order to gain political influence. So, consumption when young equals $c_t^y = w - \tau_t - l_t$, where l_t is the costs of gaining influence incurred by the young at time t. Consumption when old equals $c_t^r = s + \eta_{t+1}$, where s is an exogenously given endowment of an old individual. It is assumed that the "investment" in political influence can only be made when young. These investments, however, lead to political gains both when young and when old. This is represented by the following decision-making function:

[10] $W_t = \rho(l_{t-1})U_{t-1} + (1+n_t)\gamma(l_t)U_t,$

where the functions $\rho(l_{t-1})$ and $\gamma(l_t)$ indicate the gain in political influence of the old and young due to their respective investments. Assuming logarithmic felicity functions, the first-order condition (compare with [8]) with respect to τ_t gives

[11] $c_t^y = \dfrac{\gamma(l_t)}{\rho(l_{t-1})} c_{t-1}^r.$

So, consumption is allocated to both generations in accordance with the relative political influence they have obtained by means of their political investments. From [11] the effects of the political investments on current and future political influence can be derived as follows:

[12] $\dfrac{d\tau_t}{dl_t} = -\dfrac{\rho(l_{t-1}) + \gamma'(l_{t-1})c_{t-1}^r}{(1+n)\,\gamma(l_t) + \rho(l_{t-1})},$

[13] $\dfrac{d\tau_t}{dl_{t-1}} = \dfrac{\rho'(l_{t-1})c_t^y}{(1+n)\,\gamma(l_t) + \rho(l_{t-1})}.$

Equation [12] expresses that by investing in political influence the young can depress current tax rates, ceteris paribus. They will be more effective in this if their marginal political influence is relatively high. Equation [13] expresses that the old, as a result of their past investments, have increased their current political influence. The reaction coefficients [12] and [13] are inputs for the young individuals when they decide on the allocation of their lifetime consumption possibilities. Maximizing [5] with respect to l_t gives

[14] $(1 + \dfrac{d\tau_t}{dl_t})c_t^r = (1+n)\dfrac{d\tau_{t+1}}{dl_t}c_t^y.$

So, individuals invest in gaining political influence until the relative net cost in current consumption equals the relative gain in future consumption. Notice that [11] and [14] define again a dynamic system that can be written, as in [8], in the form of forward-looking equations from which current reactions to expected or unexpected shocks can be derived. Here, we will restrict ourselves to a steady-state analysis to find out what the long-run consequences of exogenous changes on political investments and the size of the public pension system will be. Notice in this respect that outside the steady state, individuals can try to increase their lifetime utility by investing in political influence. In the steady state, however, these investments appear to be "wasteful," in the sense that these investments merely diminish the part of total endowments that is available for consumption. This follows from the fact that in the steady state, total consumption per worker equals

[15] $$c^y + \frac{c^r}{1+n} = w + \frac{s}{1+n} - l.$$

Assuming, for simplicity, that $\rho(l) = \gamma(l) = l$, and substituting [12] and [13] into [14], we have as our steady-state equations

[16] $$c^y l = c^r l,$$

[17] $$c^r(1 - \frac{l+c^r}{(1+n)l+l}) = (1+n)c^y \frac{c^y}{(1+n)l+l}.$$

From these equations the endogenous parameters of the system, namely the tax rate and political investments, can be solved quite easily to get

[18] $$\tau = \frac{1}{2(2+n)}w - \frac{3+2n}{2(2+n)(1+n)}s,$$

[19] $$l = 0.5\frac{s}{1+n} + 0.5w.$$

Notice from [19] that the size of the political investments depends on total endowment per worker, $w + (s/(1+n))$. Not surprisingly, from these solutions it follows that an increase in endowments when young, w, or old, s, leads to more investments, l. In the steady state, however, a higher young (old) endowment leads to a higher (lower) tax rate. Aging $(dn < 0)$ leads to more political investments. However, from [18] we infer that the effect of these increased efforts depends on the relative size of the endowments of the young and old. Unless the elderly have much larger endowments than the young, the tax rate will increase. Notice that population aging in itself implies that the total endowment per worker will rise. Half of the increased consumption possibilities, however, is used for additional lobbying activities with no effects on individual consumption. Regarding the prospects of conversion policies, this simple and incomplete model suggests that if individuals invest in gaining political influence, the political support for such a conversion diminishes compared to the case of exogenous political power. The basic point is that population aging will entail more political investments, most probably leading to a higher tax rate and thus a more prominent position of the PAYG system in the economy.

Obviously, the above modeling is but a first attempt to endogenize political power in the area of public pensions in a meaningful way. The dynamics of the above model should be investigated. In particular, it is of interest to consider un-

der which conditions short-run gains can be obtained from more political investments, and whether the direction of the changes is towards more or less
PAYG. Although these types of models are simple, their dynamic nature, including their stability properties, turn out to be very complicated.

4. Concluding Remarks

In this paper we have tried to shed some light on the political feasibility of
(partly) converting PAYG systems into CR systems. Under the "classical" median-voter model as proposed for the first time by Browning (1975), the prospects for such a conversion are rather bleak. As under an aging population the
median voter tends to get older, while the rate of return under the PAYG system
does not decrease too quickly, the median voter will stick to the PAYG system.
Under some form of representative democracy where all living generations have
some influence on the political decision-making process, conversion seems more
likely to occur than under a direct democracy, and depends on political and economic factors. If political influence is merely determined by the size of the old
and young generations then, somewhat ironically, one might infer that a conversion following a process of population aging is more likely to occur if the influence of the old is relatively large. The reason for this counterintuitive result is
that if the old are highly influential, and have thus been able to make the politicians decide in favor of a relatively large PAYG system, the economically adverse consequences of a PAYG-financed public pension system under population aging tend to dominate the political pressures against diminishing the size of
the public pension system.

Bibliography

Blanchard, O.J., and C.M. Kahn (1980). The Solution of Linear Difference Models under
    Rational Expectations. *Econometrica* 48:1305–1311.

Boadway, R.W., and D. Wildasin (1989). A Median Voter Model of Social Security. *In-
    ternational Economic Review* 30:307–328.

Breyer, F. (1994). The Political Economy of Intergenerational Redistribution. *European
    Journal of Political Economy* 10:61–84.

Breyer, F., and J.M. Graf von der Schulenburg (1990). Family Ties and Social Security in
    a Democracy. *Public Choice* 67:155–167.

Browning, E.K. (1975). Why the Social Insurance Budget Is Too Large in a Democracy. *Economic Inquiry* 13:373–388.

Cutler, D.M., J.M. Poterba, L.M. Sheiner, and L.H. Summers (1990). An Aging Society: Opportunity or Challenge? *Brookings Papers on Economic Activity* (1):1–56.

Hansson, I., and C. Stuart (1989). Social Security as Trade among Living Generations. *American Economic Review* 79:1182–1195.

Kristov, L., P. Lindert, and R. McClelland (1992). Pressure Groups and Redistribution. *Journal of Public Economics* 48:135–163.

Meijdam, A.C., and H.A.A. Verbon (1996). Aging and Political Decision Making on Public Pensions. *Journal of Population Economics* 9:141–158.

—— (1997). Aging and Public Pensions in an Overlapping-Generations Model. *Oxford Economic Papers* 49:29–42.

Olson, M., Jr. (1965). *The Logic of Collective Action*. Cambridge: Harvard University Press.

Verbon, H.A.A. (1993). Public Pensions: The Role of Public Choice and Expectations. *Journal of Population Economics* 6:123–135.

Comment on Harrie A.A. Verbon, Theo Leers, and Lex C. Meijdam

Bruno S. Frey

1. The Political Economy Approach

The political economy approach to social security deviates fundamentally in several aspects from the more orthodox approach, which essentially applies welfare theory to the problem. As witnessed by several papers at this conference, this has been done by using a social welfare function in order to derive what is optimal for a society. Some scholars prefer to take a less demanding approach by looking at Pareto optimality. In both cases, society's behavior is evaluated from outside and it is implicitly assumed that the decision-makers in society demand such an evaluation and are willing to carry out the necessary policy consequences.

The political economy approach (see, e.g., Mueller 1989, 1997) starts from the presumption that the individuals living in a society are able to evaluate the social security system for themselves. For this purpose, the citizens use given political and administrative decision-making procedures. In a representative democracy, it is significantly important to vote for a parliament which determines the basic features of social security after deliberation, and reforms them if they are considered to be lacking. The government and public administration are responsible for implementing the general directions given by the representatives of the voters. No "benevolent dictator" (as in the social welfare maximizing approach) is needed, but evaluations *and* decisions are undertaken by the legitimized bodies. In this process, advice by scholars with specialized knowledge of the social security system is sought and taken into account by the political actors. The economic advisors are not disregarded, rather their advice is fed into the political process. In a well-functioning democracy, the politicians have an incentive to follow the voters' wishes in order to be reelected. In the social-welfare-maximizing approach no such incentives exist; as a consequence the conclusions offered by economic advisors often remain unheard and have little or no effect.

The political economy approach seeks first to understand why the social security system is what it is. The preferences and constraints of the major economic and political actors are analyzed in a positive (explanatory) way. The basic idea is that is the (equilibrium) outcome of the struggle between the many different interests exists in a society acting *within* the institutions. Only if this process is well understood does it make sense to move on and consider the (equilibrium) outcomes that emerge when different institutions are chosen. This constitutional choice (see, e.g., Buchanan 1991; Frey and Kirchgässner 1994) is made by the citizens behind the veil of ignorance. In the case of social security, the institutions and rules established determine *how* the decisions about social security are to be made, and *who* will be able to participate. The constitutional stage establishes, for instance, how the interests of the future generations—who are not participants in the current politico-economic process—are to be represented. It may well be that the individuals deliberating behind the veil of ignorance find it sufficient that the citizens are now actively part of the process because many of them have children and therefore care intensively about their future well-being. The basic presumption is again that once the fundamental institutions and rules have been established, the politico-economic process generates a particular outcome (also with respect to the social security system). Accordingly, there is no room for persons outside the system to influence that (equilibrium) outcome.

2.   Verbon, Leer, and Meijdam's Approach

The three authors restrict their analysis to the first stage; they study the politico-economic process producing a particular social security system. Two institutions are considered, direct and representative democracy. They identify the former with the median-voter model. This is, however, correct only if many different alternatives are advanced under competitive conditions, so that this process converges to an alternative situated in the median voter's position.

Representative democracy is modeled by using a "power" approach. As the authors are well aware, the political process is effectively excluded if the power weights are exogenous. It can enter only when the power weights are endogenously determined, especially by the activity (investments) of particular interest groups.

The usefulness of working with a function representing "political power" may be disputed, but this is to some extent a matter of terminology. In any case, I would have wished for a more extensive treatment of the differential political participation of the old and the young, as well as of pressure groups. Most importantly, trade unions, government bureaucracy, and private insurance firms come into mind. They all have high stakes when a transformation of social security from pay-as-you-go to capital funding is considered. For example, the first two groups may be strongly interested in gaining control over the high capital funds accumulated, which after a short period of time make up a sizable part of nonresidential capital (Feldstein [1997:35] estimates it to comprise about 45 percent of the U.S. capital stock, exclusive of owner-occupied housing and unincorporated businesses). For obvious reasons, private insurance firms have opposite interests and would prefer a mandatory pension system with privatized, individual savings accounts.

The authors have succeeded in the difficult task of integrating individuals' economic and political behavior. While they have chosen a rather special model (one could think of other equally reasonable models), they have been able to show that such a political economy model is able to produce new and partly unexpected results. What has been disregarded is the linking of the model to empirical evidence. But this would go much beyond the scope of a conference paper. One possible avenue would be to analyze the popular referenda about old-age pensions as undertaken mainly in Switzerland (see, in general, Frey [1994]). This would, for example, allow us to derive the implicit weights that could be attributed to future generations and would therefore offer us insights that go beyond the often sterile discussion of the social rate of discount in orthodox welfare economics.

3.   Extensions

Many of the papers presented at this conference consider a time period extending 50 and sometimes 100 years into the future. Such a long time horizon is perfectly appropriate because the demographic changes extend far into the future. This also applies to Verbon, Leer, and Meijdam's paper on the political economy of moving from a pay-as-you-go system to a funded system. In view of this long future time horizon it is somewhat surprising that the political system implicitly or explicitly considered is the *nation-state as it presently exists*. While it is certainly true that *current* social security systems are all organized along nations, this need not be so in the future at all. I suggest that a political economy analysis of social security should transgress the borders of the nation-state in at least two respects: European integration and global relationships.

a.   European Integration

Present members of the European Union have varying problems with financing social security in the future. While Germany has to deal with a very serious problem of an aging population, France and the United Kingdom seem to be less affected. It could well be imagined that an effort will be made to ease the problems by involving the European Union. In particular, the trend towards harmonization may even extend to social security payments and pensions. It seems to be most unlikely that within the Union, which is at least partially committed to redistribution (and presently undertaking much effort in this direction), it would be tolerable to have either widely different payments by individuals and firms into the system, or widely different pensions. A more optimistic scenario could envisage competition between various social security systems, with the European Union citizens being able to freely choose which system they want to belong to. In this case, the more efficient social security system will emerge as the dominant form, while the others are doomed to disappear. However, in view of the EU's reluctance to admit institutional (political) competition, such a development is unlikely to happen.

The situation will also be drastically different when 10 or 12 new nations enter the EU. A broader political economy analysis would have to consider their future demographic development, as well as integration of their social security system into the Union. Irrespective of how far the EU is extended in the future, it is necessary to seriously study the decision-making rules under which social security decisions will be made, and especially what flows of redistribution are likely to be caused thereby in the future.

b.   Global Relationships

While several of the papers in this volume consider cross-national movements of capital and labor, political prerequisites and consequences must also be considered. The following politico-economic issues will certainly be relevant: With respect to capital, will a large-scale outflow of domestic capital be tolerated (especially by the trade unions) and, conversely, will the potential host countries erect barriers to their inflow? Depending on how these questions are answered, the rate of return will be affected (mainly due to endogenous political risk). With respect to labor, would a large-scale inflow of foreign workers (to compensate for the aging of the national population) be tolerated or would it lead to strong resentment and political instability?

These are only some of the issues that need to be considered when one looks into the longer-run future of social security.

Bibliography

Buchanan, J.M. (1991). *Constitutional Economics*. Oxford: Blackwell.

Feldstein, M. (1997). The Case for Privatization. *Foreign Affairs* 76(4):24–38.

Frey, B.S. (1994). Direct Democracy: Politico-Economic Lessons from Swiss Experience. *American Economic Review* 84(2):338–348.

Frey, B.S., and G. Kirchgässner (1994). *Demokratische Wirtschaftspolitik*. Munich: Vahlen.

Mueller, D.C. (1989). *Public Choice II*. Cambridge: Cambridge University Press.

—— (ed.) (1997). *Perspectives on Public Choice*. Cambridge: Cambridge University Press.

List of Contributors

AXEL BÖRSCH-SUPAN
Professor, Department of Economics, University of Mannheim; Center for Economic Policy Research, London; National Bureau of Economic Research, Cambridge, Mass.

BARRY BOSWORTH
Senior Fellow, The Brookings Institution, Economic Studies Program, Washington, D.C.

A. LANS BOVENBERG
Deputy Director, CPB Netherlands Bureau for Economic Policy Analysis, The Hague, The Netherlands

FRIEDRICH BREYER
Professor, Fakultät für Wirtschaftswissenschaften und Statistik, Universität Konstanz, Constance

D. PETER BROER
Staff Member, Macroeconomic Modelling Division, CPB Netherlands Bureau of Economic Policy Analysis, The Hague, The Netherlands; Associate Professor, Faculty of Economics, Erasmus University, Rotterdam, The Netherlands

GARY BURTLESS
Senior Fellow, Economic Studies, The Brookings Institution, Washington, D.C.

E. PHILIP DAVIS
Deputy Head of Stage Two Division, Monetary, Economics and Statistics Department, European Monetary Institute, Frankfurt am Main, Germany (secorded from the Bank of England); Associate Member, Financial Markets Group, London School of Economics; Associate Fellow, Royal Institute for International Affairs; Research Fellow, Pensions Institute, Birkbeck College, London

RICHARD DISNEY
Professor of Economics, Queen Mary and Westfield College, University of London; Research Fellow, Institute for Fiscal Studies, London

SEBASTIAN EDWARDS
Professor, Anderson School, University of California, Los Angeles; National Bureau of Economic Research, Cambridge, Mass.

MARTIN FELDSTEIN
Professor of Economics, Harvard University, Cambridge, Mass.; President of the
National Bureau of Economic Research, Cambridge, Mass.

BRUNO S. FREY
Professor, Institute for Empirical Economic Research, University of Zurich

EDWARD M. GRAMLICH
Member of the Board of Governors of the Federal Reserve System, Washington,
D.C.; Professor, School of Public Policy, University of Michigan

KETIL HVIDING
Economist, European Department, International Monetary Fund, Washington,
D.C.; Organization for Economic Cooperation and Development, Paris

ESTELLE JAMES
Lead Economist, Development Economics Research Group, World Bank,
Washington, D.C.

PAUL JOHNSON
Deputy Director, Institute of Fiscal Studies, London

LAURENCE J. KOTLIKOFF
Professor of Economics, Boston University, Boston, Mass.; National Bureau of
Economic Research, Cambridge, Mass.

THEO LEERS
Ph.D. Candidate, Faculteit der Economische Wetenschappen, Katholieke
Universiteit Brabant, Tilburg, The Netherlands

OLIVER LORZ
Assistant, Economics and Social Sciences Department, University of Kiel

LEX C. MEIJDAM
Assistant Professor of Public Finance, Faculteit der Economische Wetenschappen, Katholieke Universiteit Brabant, Tilburg, The Netherlands

MANFRED NEUMANN
Professor, Friedrich-Alexander-Universität Erlangen-Nürnberg, Volkswirt-
schaftliches Institut, Nuremberg

MATS PERSSON
Professor, Stockholm University, Institute for International Economic Studies

Andrew A. Samwick
Assistant Professor, Dartmouth College, Department of Economics, Hanover, New Hampshire; Member of National Bureau of Economic Research, Cambridge, Mass.

Winfried Schmähl
Professor of Economics and Director of Economic Department, Center for Social Policy Research, University of Bremen, Germany

Horst Siebert
President of Kiel Institute of World Economics, Germany; Professor of Theoretical Economics, University of Kiel, Germany; Member of the Council of Economic Experts, Wiesbaden, Germany

Hans-Werner Sinn
Professor and Director of Center for Economic Studies, University of Munich, Germany

Kent A. Smetters
Congressional Budget Office, Washington, D.C.

Roland Vaubel
Professor, Lehrstuhl für Volkswirtschaft III, Universität Mannheim, Mannheim, Germany

Harrie A.A. Verbon
Professor of Public Finance, Katholieke Universiteit Brabant, Tilburg, The Netherlands

Jan Walliser
Congressional Budget Office, Washington, D.C.

Index

Institut für Weltwirtschaft an der Universität Kiel

Symposia and Conference Proceedings

Horst Siebert, Editor

Steuerpolitik und Standortqualität
Expertisen zum Standort Deutschland
Tübingen 1996. 192 pages. Hard cover. DM 98/Sch 715/SFr 89.

Sozialpolitik auf dem Prüfstand
Leitlinien für Reformen
Tübingen 1996. 224 pages. Hard cover. DM 98/Sch 715/SFr 89.

Elemente einer rationalen Umweltpolitik
Expertisen zur umweltpolitischen Neuorientierung
Tübingen 1996. 378 pages. Hard cover. DM 148/Sch 1085/SFr 126.

Monetary Policy in an Integrated World Economy
Tübingen 1996. 280 pages. Hard cover. DM 128/Sch 934/SFr 109.

Towards a New Global Framework for High-Technology Competition
Tübingen 1997. 223 pages. Hard cover. DM 98/Sch 715/SFr 89.

Quo Vadis Europe?
Tübingen 1997. 343 pages. Hard cover. DM 128/Sch 934/SFr 109.

Structural Change and Labor Market Flexibility
Experience in Selected OECD Economies
Tübingen 1997. 292 pages. Hard cover. DM 118/Sch 861/SFr 101.

Redesigning Social Security
Tübingen 1998. 387 pages. Hard cover. DM 148/Sch 1085/SFr 126.

Mohr Siebeck, Tübingen